# Abuse of Power

## *The Acadians*

*Dedicated to Phyllis*

# Abuse of Power

## *The Acadians*

By Bill Smallwood

*Borealis Press*
*Ottawa, Canada*
*2004*

# Canadä

*The Publishers acknowledge the financial support
of the Government of Canada through the Book Publishing
Industry Development Program (BPIDP)
for our publishing activities.*

**National Library of Canada Cataloguing in Publication Data**

Smallwood, Bill, 1932-
    Abuse of power: the Acadians / Bill Smallwood


(Threads; 1)
ISBN 0-88887-198-8


I. Title. II. Series: Smallwood, Bill, 1932- Threads; 1.


PS8587.M354A73 2004          C813'.6          C2003-901516-5
PR9199.4S62A63 2004

Illustrations by Eugene Kral
Cover design and book typesetting
by Chisholm Communications, Ottawa


*Printed and bound in Canada on acid-free paper*

# Contents

# *Prologue*

The well-dressed, heavyset man stepped down from the carriage. Colonel Charles Gray[1] looked up at the boy still seated in the coach and was freshly reminded of his dead brother. The boy had the good looks of the Gray family men. Sadly, most of them were dead now, their lands and fortunes forfeit because they had chosen to fight for Scotland's freedom against the English oppressors. Only two Grays were left—this boy[2], sent south for safety because he was too young to serve with the clans and Charles Gray, a half-pay colonel who, with his English wife, had been living quietly in Nottinghamshire, England, during the Scottish troubles.

As the elder male survivor of the family, Charles had fulfilled his obligations as best he could. He had arranged for his brother's widow a marriage to an English candle maker and, for her son, an appointment to the Royal Navy. Lieutenant Colonel Gray had not been able to obtain the usual navy appointment. No, his sixteen-year-old nephew had been assigned to the personal staff of the new governor of Nova Scotia. Not a grand assignment but it would have to do.

Colonel Gray gave the boy a weary smile and motioned him to descend from the coach. The slight figure in the uniform of a sub-lieutenant of the Royal Navy presented his backside to any dockyard personnel who might be watching as he carefully descended the three steps to the ground, carrying his hat in one hand and holding his sword-scabbard close to his side.

And who, the old colonel thought, might the new governor of Nova Scotia be? None other than Edward Cornwallis, colonel of the regiment that had delivered death and destruction to the Grays, their kin and their homeland. Hopefully, the boy had lived long enough in the English south and was young enough not to realize the depth of his homeland's hatred of everything English.

Entirely unaware of his uncle's ruminations, William Gray pulled on his hat, carefully using three fingers to properly position the awkward thing on his forehead. His black hair resisted the pressure of the hat and curled over the edge of the blue material. William lifted the hat and swept his hand over his unruly hair, quickly forcing the hat back down to hold it in place. He was more successful this time and better satisfied with the result.

"I want to thank you again, Uncle, for purchasing my rank," William studied his boots as he added, "since there was no place in Mother's new Munro household for a male Gray."

"I wanted you for the army, my boy," the colonel said apologetically, "but there wasn't the opportunity. We had to settle for what we got."

"I won't let you down, sir."

"I know I'll be proud of you, William."

Two footmen dragged William's travel chest from the coach's luggage rack and dropped it on the pier by his feet. Colonel Gray squeezed the boy's shoulder and climbed back into the carriage. One of the footmen folded the three steps back up under the body of the coach and then mounted a little perch at the rear. Colonel Gray waved the knob of his cane in a gesture of farewell, and the coach moved away.

William didn't turn to face the ship moored at the end of the pier until his uncle's carriage had gone through the dockyard gate and disappeared from view. A sailor double-timed down the pier, and stopped smartly in front of William. He touched his knuckles to his forehead in salute. "Beggin' yer pardon, sir, ye be for *Sphinx*?"

"Sub-Lieutenant Gray of Governor Cornwallis's suite assigned to HMS *Sphinx*."

The sailor hefted the chest onto one shoulder. "Foller me, then, sir, if ye will."

## *Endnotes*

[1] Family sources told of a Charles Gray who obtained a position for his nephew with the new governor of Nova Scotia. Invention: a colonel living on half-pay in Nottinghamshire.

[2] William Gray was a clerk on the personal staff of Governor Cornwallis. I found a reference in the minutes of the Colonial Council that he had signed some documents during a period of time when the governor was sick with his arthritis. So, Gray was an enterprising fellow but, since a clerk couldn't tell the story of the fall of Beauséjour, the Expulsion, the siege of Louisbourg and the capture of Quebec, I invented Sub-Lieutenant William Gray.

# Chapter One

Captain's Log,
H.M.S. Sphinx,[1]
Sloop of War, 6th rate,
Commissioned 27 February, 1749
Captain William Lloyd, RN

*15 March 1749.*
Sea trials complete. Shortage lists dispatched to admiralty.
Dockyard personnel discharged from ship.
*9 April 1749.*
Warning orders received from admiralty. Area of operations, North Atlantic. Destination, Bay of Fundy, Annapolis Royal.
*11 April.*
Sphinx is ready in all respects for sea. Requested a pilot for the Bay of Fundy.
*27 April.*
Ordered to receive Governor Cornwallis and his retinue and give them passage to Nova Scotia.
*7 May, 1749.*
I should have sailed for Portsmouth had the winds and weather permitted which was at SW and still continuing to blow very strong.
*9 May, Tuesday.*
Governor Cornwallis, whom we saluted, is come on board.
*10 May, Wednesday.*
Came to sail at noon. No Bay of Fundy pilot.
*12 May, Friday.*
Instructions from Governor Cornwallis. I am to brief Sub-Lieutenant William Gray of the governor's suite in such detail and correctness as if I was briefing the governor personally.
*11 June 1749.*
Gave chase to ship that proved to be *Fair Lady*, transport, bound for Annapolis Royal. In company with *Fair Lady*.

*14 June, Wednesday.*
Standing offshore, Nova Scotia. None on board familiar
with these waters. Charts unreliable.
*20 June, Monday.*
Encountered a sloop from Boston carrying two pilots to
the British garrison at Louisbourg, Cape Breton. Got a
pilot out of her to carry us into Chebucto Harbour.
*21 June, Tuesday.*
Anchored on Malagash Roads. 2 A.M.; boat came alongside with fresh beef for the ship's company.
*22 June, Wednesday.*
Anchored in Chebucto Harbour in twelve fathoms.
*23 June, Thursday.*
Moved up harbour.

*29 June 1749*
*On Chebucto Harbour*

"Where's Sub-Lieutenant Gray?"

The three *H.M.S. Sphinx* officers standing at the taffrail,
the rail around the stern, all turned to look at the fourth member of the party who, given his startled expression, was most
obviously Sub-Lieutenant Gray.

"Guard! Locate Lieutenant Gray and have him report to
me immediately." The voice boomed from the captain's cabin
where Governor Cornwallis was quartered.

It was a beautiful spring day; the breeze coming up the
harbour was as light and warm as a lady's caress. Consequently, the gun ports and transoms were open. In older ships,
voices from the captain's cabin might not have been heard on
the deck however, the newfangled ventilators built into this
sloop gave sound the opportunity to travel twice as far as one
thought possible.

Captain Lloyd regarded the slight boyish figure in the
naval uniform and laughingly said, "Lieutenant, I think you
had better respond to the governor."

Holding his dress sword close to his side, Sub-Lieutenant
Gray double-timed across the deck and disappeared down the
companionway toward the captain's cabin.

Lloyd sighed. "After the governor acquires permanent quarters ashore and I return to my cabin, I must remember how well voices can be heard on *Sphinx*."

The officers resumed their study of four vessels slowly coming up harbour. Second Lieutenant Hardy handed the 'bring 'em near,' eyeglass, to the captain. "It's a sloop of war, sir, tending three transports."

Lloyd raised the eyeglass and inspected the approaching ships while, from below, he heard the lieutenant's knock on the governor's door followed by the stern voice of Governor Cornwallis.

"Enter."

"351," Captain Lloyd read aloud the numbers on the pennant flying from the approaching warship.[2] "Please check that number against the secret admiralty list, First Lieutenant Johnson."

The first lieutenant had already taken a small brown book out of the ship's toss bag, and had been scanning the pages. At the captain's command, he fumbled, almost dropping the bag. The canvas bag weighted heavily with iron shot sewn into its bottom and with several vent holes near the top of the clasp contained naval codes, secret admiralty lists, and orders. Captains were meant to defend it with their lives but, if it appeared that all was lost, the bag was to be tossed overboard denying the enemy its contents. All three officers groped for the bag but Johnson maintained his grip on it.

"Sub-Lieutenant Gray reporting, sir. You wanted to see me."

On deck, the officers straightened up, adjusting their uniforms and swords as they heard the governor say in a weary, preoccupied tone of voice, "Yes, but just a moment while I finish this entry."

Still clutching the toss bag, Lieutenant Johnson whispered, "Sorry, sir." He carefully stowed the bag in the signals box as he continued checking the admiralty list. After a moment he said, "She's *Albany*, sir; Captain John Rous commanding."

The governor's voice was heard again. "When the first of our ships enters the harbour, I wish to be informed as quickly as possible."

The lieutenant was heard to reply. "Sir, there are four ships coming up the harbour."

Lloyd turned his head in the direction of the ventilator on the deck and, raising his voice a fraction, said, "It's the sloop of war, *Albany*, Captain John Rous commanding, escorting three transports."

"The *Albany*, a sloop of war..." Lieutenant Gray's voice faltered slightly but he finished up bravely, "commanded by Captain John Rous, is escorting three transports, sir."

There was a moment of quiet followed by a snort or cough; the officers on deck weren't sure which. "Now that you and our fine Captain Lloyd have completed that task, I have another job for you, little Sir Echo." There was definite mirth in the governor's voice. The governor attempted to give a degree of confidentiality to his orders by lowering his voice, but the ventilators were efficient sound carriers. "I've decided that the site for our fort will be on the western side of the harbour. Go ashore as soon as you can and find a source of drinking water along that shore. It's my intention to enclose such a brook or stream within the walls of our settlement. Now that the transports are arriving, I must decide the settlement's exact location without delay."

"Aye, sir."

Captain Lloyd looked at the second lieutenant and nodded his head.

Lieutenant Gray emerged on deck as the captain's orders were barked out: "Boat's crew launch jolly boat! Armourer, issue cutlasses to boat's crew."

The four sailors that made up its crew quickly launched the jolly boat. Dashing below deck again, Gray retrieved a notepad, quill, and ink and even remembered to stow his dress sword. Back on deck, the armourer handed him a pistol that Gray, after a moment's hesitation, jammed into his belt.

"Excuse me, sir." The armourer delicately reached around and affixed the pistol's hook to the lieutenant's belt. "There, sir. She'll ride snugger that way. Remember to undo the hook if you go to use her." The armourer then handed Gray a bag that contained flints, powder, and shot. "In case the first shot don't finish the argument," he said with a smile.

Gray mumbled his thanks.

Lieutenant Johnson handed the young lieutenant a lead 'n line to sound the depths of the water. Moving in closer to Gray he whispered, "Cornwallis will want to know the type of beach, the depth of water on approach, and whether or not there is any sign of hostiles."

Gray nodded and started toward the bulwark, his mind racing as he contemplated the problems of this, his first independent command.

He knew, of course, that it was naval tradition that sailors boarded vessels before officers. Gray's problem was that he hadn't had time to ask if he had enough rank to qualify as an officer but he quickly saw that the problem had been solved for him; the jolly boat crew was already aboard and waiting for him alongside. Well! Then what about leaving the boat? Officers were supposed to disembark first but he wondered, if he were first over the side on a rocky beach, would it be his duty to hold the boat for the others?

He suddenly realized that he had been standing at the bulwark, lost in his own thoughts. He lost no further time going over the side and descending to the boat.

Gray took the seat in the stern decidedly pleased that he had been assigned a jolly boat, a fine little craft. She had oars for four and could carry up to eight armed men. Gray imagined himself with a party of marines ... landing on a hostile shore ... leading his men up a secret path ... catching the enemy asleep ... he glanced around, startled out of his reverie. The sailors were looking at him expectantly.

"Um! Er."

He looked around. The breeze being what it was, they could not use the boat's sail, at least until the way back. They would have to row to the western shore.

"Make for the western shore. We are looking for signs of fresh water. I also want to know the depth of water along the shore, from three hundred yards out. Who's the best man to take the soundings?"

One of the sailors, eyes squinted and bobbing his head up and down, asked, "Beggin' your pardon, sir, but do you want to know who's the best leads'man?

"Er. Yes."

Two of the sailors responded, "Denham."[3]

"Then it will be Denham who swings the lead."

"I always do, sir." was the straight-faced reply from the smallest sailor.

* * *

The ship's officers had watched the lieutenant clamber over the side and lower himself hand-over-hand to the ship's boat. In short order the boat was headed for the western shore.

The first lieutenant cleared his throat. The captain always took that as a sign that Johnson wanted to ask a question or make some sort of comment not usually allowed by naval etiquette. Lloyd thought, it's a beautiful day and we're just standing around waiting upon the governor, so why not. "Yes, Lieutenant?"

Johnson glanced nervously at the ventilator. Lloyd casually strolled to the bulwark from which he had a better view of the approaching ships. "Captain Rous is doing a nice job herding those transports into the roadstead. What's his seniority?"

Lieutenant Johnson checked the admiralty list. "September 24, 1745. He's junior to you by nine months, sir."

"He might have interesting news from England; they left there sometime after we did. Make signal that the commanding officer of 351 is to report to *Sphinx*."

Johnson returned the admiralty list to the toss bag and took out the book *Signal Book for Ships of War*. He handed the book to the second lieutenant. "Make it so, Hardy."

Lieutenant Hardy departed to make the signal and wait for the acknowledgment or reply.

Lloyd smiled. "Yes, Johnson?"

"Why does he use the lowest rank of officer? I mean, why does Governor Cornwallis use Sub-Lieutenant Gray so often for important tasks?" Johnson leaned forward so he could speak without being overheard. "The governor has two aides on his staff, both older men. He should use the men with experience."

"Perhaps so, Johnson, but you should use their army ranks when speaking of them."

"Aye, sir." First Lieutenant Johnson rephrased his question. "Why doesn't the governor use his lieutenants instead of the young lieutenant?"

Lloyd considered his reply. He realized that he must be careful not to be critical of the governor and yet provide some insight for his second-in-command who might, under some circumstance, be called upon as acting captain of *Sphinx* to work directly with the governor.

"Last year Cornwallis was a lieutenant-colonel commanding a regiment in the Highlands fighting Prince Charles," the captain began. "He was successful because he knew his trade of soldiering. This year he's the governor appointed by the Lords of Trade and Plantations to build a fortress. He's no longer a soldier, and he has to rely on others to get his fortress built." Lloyd paused, thinking, where do I go from here without being critical of our commander?

"Our governor is brave, sensible, and good-natured. Just imagine talking through the ventilator to one of our admirals! Governor Cornwallis took my humour with very good grace," Lloyd said carefully. "A senior administrator like a governor must choose his staff wisely."

Captain Lloyd looked out over the water. He took the 'bring em near' from under his arm and sighted at the jolly boat now working along the western shore. "It looks like Gray is going ashore. That wouldn't be a bad spot for a fortress." He tucked the eyeglass back under his arm and continued the earlier conversation. "What do you know about the governor's two aides?"

Lieutenant Johnson said, "Lieutenant Bulkeley, Irish Dragoons, wealthy ..."

"Why do you say that?" interrupted the captain.

"Well, sir," explained Johnson, "you know how much luggage he brought on board *Sphinx*, and he told me himself that he paid passage on a transport for a valet, a groom, a butler ... oh yes ... three blood horses. So I'm pretty sure he's rich." [4]

"How well prepared is he to help build a fortress in the wilderness?"

"I don't think he's given it a thought. All he talks about is his horses."

"What about the other aide?"

"There seem to be only two things that concern Lieutenant Horatio Gates." Johnson gave a small chuckle. "Soldiering and being the Duke of Leeds's son from the wrong side of the blanket."

Lloyd smiled. "Governor Cornwallis might regret his choice of aides, I don't really know. They're good soldiers but, it could probably be said, not well suited for this task." He paused for a moment before adding, "I hope he was a better judge of men when he appointed his other officials," and instantly regretted his indiscretion.

Irritated with himself, Captain Lloyd turned away and studied the western shore of the harbour.

Lieutenant Johnson followed his captain's gaze. The officers could see that the boat party had gone ashore.

By this time, resigned that he must finish the lieutenant's lesson, for the 'good of the service,' he continued. "Meanwhile, he has Sub-Lieutenant William Gray: young, keen, and learning quickly. Our governor may not the best judge of men but he's no fool. He'll use Gray and men like him—if he can find them—to get the job done. We English always muddle through."

\* \* \*

"What depth, Denham?" Gray was looking ahead to the shore. There was a small cove and marsh. A large hardwood tree stood sentinel at the edge of an army of pines marching up the hill as far as the eye could follow.

"No bottom at four fathoms, sir."

"Stop soundings. It's plenty deep here. Take us to shore."

"Y'mean, sir, belay soundings, sir?"

"Yes, I do."

"Aye, sir. Makin' for the cove, sir."

Gray worked at the pistol hook and finally freed the weapon. He continued to watch the shore very carefully. "Bring in the oars."

"Aye, sir. Ship oars, mates!"

The forward momentum of the boat carried the men to the gravel beach almost under the shadow of the hardwood tree. Denham jumped out and steadied the boat so the young officer could step ashore with dry feet.

The cove was a riot of colour—the green marsh grass, the violets along the edge of the brook that emptied into the cove, the small white blossoms crowding the water's edge and, further up the slope, the little delicate pink flowers carpeting the entrance to the pine forest. The sun felt almost tropical; the harbour breeze didn't reach this far into the cove. Gray's dark wool tunic gathered the heat and his silk shirt and neckpiece became pasted to his flesh. He wiped his brow with his handkerchief and shoved it back in his sleeve cuff.

Gray jerked his thumb at three of the sailors. "You three on the other side of the brook. Denham and I will go up this side. Stay alert. We may not be alone here." He watched the three sailors attempt to jump from rock to rock, getting quite wet in the process, but didn't wait for them to reach the other side of the brook. "Move out about thirty feet, Denham. Keep me in sight."

Gray started up the hill, looking for the source of the brook. The climb was steep and getting steeper when he found the spot where the water seeped out of the ground. He knelt to taste the water. The governor will be pleased with this, he thought. He stopped drinking. The hairs on the back of his neck rose. He slowly looked up but could see nothing unusual. He remained crouched down and studied the area. Suddenly, he could see three Indians above him. They were so still they had seemed part of the forest. Two were standing, and what Gray had at first mistaken for a boulder was a third Indian crouched down and watching him. They wore loincloths and carried small axes; their dark eyes were fixed steadily upon him. Before he could take in any more detail, there was a loud curse from one of his men on the other side of the brook.

"Denham, make to the other side of the brook!" Gray leaped the brook and ran down the hill in the direction of the commotion. One of his sailors was hollering and gibbering, "Yiiii! Lookit me 'and!"

Through the trees, Gray could see the sailors. One was bent over and holding himself as if in terrible pain. The others were peering at something under a tree. As Gray got closer he could see it wasn't some*thing* but some*one* in the uniform of a French soldier. Another similarly attired figure lay on the ground, a musket lying a few feet beyond his outstretched hand.

Not a hand, Gray corrected himself, bones. Both soldiers appeared very dead. The injured sailor's cutlass was lying on the grass.

"Pick up your weapon, sailor," Gray ordered.

"They're just bones, uh, sir." The sailor started to cry, hugging his hand to his stomach.

One of the sailors kicked at the other body seated against the side of the hill and supported by the trunk of a tree. It fell over. "Just a pile of bones inside a uniform, sir." He looked at the officer. "Who was they, sir?"

The Englishmen looked up the hill as someone came crashing toward them through the trees. The sailor who had been crying quickly retrieved his cutlass. The sailors grouped themselves on either side of their officer. The intruder was almost upon them; it was Denham.

With a sigh of relief, Gray gave his pistol to Denham and ordered him to maintain a watch. "Shoot anything or anyone coming down that hill." He turned his attention to the others. "Tell me what happened."

"Buster and me come 'round the tree and saw the musket near the sittin' Frenchie," the sailor said. "Buster knockt the musket down with 'is cutlass."

Buster nodded his head and swallowed hard several times. "That's when I fell over t'other one in the grass, sir. When I fell, I stuck my 'and out to save m'self and it went right tru da bastard's back." He shivered. "Nothin' dere but bones."

"Well they've been dead a long time, and we've found the governor's fresh water. Let's get back to the boat." Gray looked up the hill, "Keep a sharp eye, Denham; you're the rear guard. Follow us down the hill, and don't let us out of your sight."

Starting downhill, Gray realized that he was no longer sweating; in fact he was quite cold. I wonder what cooled me the most, he thought, the two dead Frenchmen or the three live Indians. Christ! His neck hairs were rising again. Without looking around he ordered, "Close up, Denham, quickly."

In a group the Englishmen reached the beach and found the ship's boat as they had left it. Gray boarded the craft, and the sailors pushed off. It was not until they were at the entrance to the cove that Gray looked back. He could see no one but he knew the Indians were still there; he could feel their eyes watching them.

Sub-Lieutenant Gray turned away from the shore. The breeze had died. They would have to row back to the ship.

*30 June 1749*
*On board H.M.S. Sphinx*
*Chebucto Harbour*

Dear Mother,

I greet you fair and wish you very well. Good weather and pleasant company graced our passage. We arrived at Chebucto, 21 June. I have been so employed and active since our arrival that this is my first opportunity to put thoughts to writing.

Please inform Uncle John that I am much pleased with my position, realizing that it was because of his approaches to Admiral Pitts that I received my commission and appointment. I will not betray his confidence in me.

When we arrived at H.M.S. Sphinx and found she was a sloop of war, Governor Cornwallis ordered me to discreetly inquire as to why he and his suite were not assigned to a ship of the line or at least a frigate, which was the type of accommodation expected by a captain/general.

At first, Captain Lloyd was loath to discuss such matters with a sub-lieutenant, but he soon came to understand that I was to be accommodated. An affable officer, Captain Lloyd made it clear to me that the sloop of war was more appropriate for the confined waters and currents of the Bay of Fundy. The draught of the Sphinx was considerably less than a frigate so she could carry the same calibre of gun closer to the shore. She was quite long-legged, performed well to windward, and, with row-ports between the guns, could be manoeuvred in and out of tight places.

With that explanation, the governor was more content with the Atlantic passage, although he complained to me and to his aides at every opportunity about the five feet clearance deck-to-the-beams. The governor could stand tall only between the beams.

But we didn't go to the Fundy. The ship's pilot we picked off a passing sloop was familiar with the Atlantic shores, not the Fundy. We entered Chebucto and waited for the transports to arrive.

Mother, I was impressed as the ship's pilot brought us into the strange harbour, obviously not strange to him. He was a Yankee but nevertheless all the men, including Captain Lloyd, were respectful of his pilot's skills. In future, Chebucto will have need of good pilots. Captain Lloyd claims it is one of the most magnificent harbours in the world. I vowed to take every opportunity to learn more about this area.

I was particularly pleased, therefore, when the governor ordered me to take a craft to explore the western shore of the harbour. I had a crew, and we took soundings as we proceeded. On going ashore, we found a fresh-water source that the governor, when told about it, determined would be the centre of the settlement. Work crews, along with the soldiers to protect them, began clearing the trees today. Imagine, where I first walked will be the heart of the fortress! I don't mean to suggest that I was the first white man to pass this way. Certainly not. In fact we found traces of French soldiers who had visited the harbour in '46 or '47. Poor devils! A lot of them died of ship's fever, which we, thanks (we believe) to the new ventilators installed in most of our ships, have avoided.

I had contact with savages while on the western shore. There was nothing to fear—I had my crew with me and they were well armed, as was I—but I took one thing away with me from the experience; they are in their element in the forest and we cannot hope to see them in time for effective action. I tried mentioning this to the governor and he told me to discuss it with his aide, Lieutenant Bulkeley, who scarcely acknowledged my concerns. He said the savages would learn fear of the British redcoat if they hadn't already. Good news! I am just back from the governor. Tomorrow I will take my trusty craft and explore the eastern shore looking for a site for a sawmill. We are going to need much lumber for this city we will build here at Chebucto.

I remain, your affectionate son,

William

*7 July 1749*
*On Chebucto Harbour*

*Sphinx* began firing a seventeen-gun salute welcoming the Indians boarding the transport ship *Beaufort* [5] to parley with Governor Cornwallis. Sub-Lieutenant Gray and Lieutenant Hardy watched the *Sphinx* gun crews handling the guns and charges. Between cannon blasts, Hardy spoke so that only Gray could hear him.

"The governor ordered seventeen guns fired to honour those savages." Hardy checked the deck around them before continuing, "Rear admirals only get thirteen guns, but these bloody savages get seventeen! The captain ordered me to make it so, but told me to call it gunnery practice in the log. Then he went below and took the first lieutenant with him." Hardy smiled ruefully. "Usually he watches the action and provides comment to the gun crews afterward. How many is that?"

"Nine." Gray had been counting the cannons' discharges: one every five seconds.

When Gray didn't comment, Hardy continued, "I looked at them through the 'bring em near,' dressed in rags and beads and stuff. I couldn't see their faces through the glass because they had painted red and black stripes across their foreheads. They don't rate a friendly wave from the pier but your governor gave them a Royal Navy salute of seventeen guns!"

"I guess he thinks gunpowder is cheap," Gray said. "That's seventeen."

In a voice loud enough to be heard by the crew, Lieutenant Hardy ordered, "Stand down from gunnery practice. That was well done!"

The gunnery mate repeated the order, and then looked at Hardy. "Secure from gunnery practice, sir?"

"Negative! A parting salute will be required—er, we'll resume gunnery practice at the end of the parley." Hardy turned to Gray. "We just wait now."

They were gazing over the starboard bulwark. Hardy pointed at a rude structure of sawn planks being built on a hill on the eastern shore. "That's your doing?"

"Well, yes, I guess it is," Gray admitted. "I recommended the site to the governor. The craftsmen are building a shelter for the lumberjacks and guards."

"Where do the guards come from?"

"From those two transports newly arrived in the harbour. Now that we no longer hold Louisbourg, Governor Cornwallis brought the Louisbourg regiments to garrison here."

Lieutenant Hardy shook his head in disgust. "It's a sad thing to win a fortress in battle and then hand it back to the enemy. I wonder if anyone in London has an idea what they're doing?"

Gray gave him a grin. "London has bigger fish to fry than worry about the opinions of naval officers ... of any rank." They stood quietly for several moments. "I asked the governor not to use the Louisbourg regiments as guards at Mill Cove," Gray said.

"The soldiers of English line regiments not good enough for the likes of Sub-Lieutenant Gray?"

"Your pardon, sir, but in my short time here I realized that the savages move through the trees like ghosts. I suggested to the governor that he use Gorham's Rangers rather than the red-coats. The men from Hopson's and Warburton's regiments were garrison troops at Gibraltar and Louisbourg before coming here. All they know is walls and ramparts. If they ever had any skills in the field, they've long since lost them."

"Why Gorham? Why not some troops from Phillips's Regiment at Annapolis?" Lieutenant Hardy indicated that they should walk the deck. The two men left the starboard bulwark and paced the short length of the deck as casually as if they were strolling in a garden. "Phillips's men have experience with Indians."

"They fought from walls, earth and log, but walls nonetheless. We need soldiers who can deal with the savages in their own element, the forest."

The two officers had reached the larboard-port side of the vessel. Hardy inspected the western shore with his glass. "They're not getting much clearing done," he said.

"The governor says they are a lazy, shiftless lot and won't do a lick of work. In fact, when Cornwallis ordered the settlers to help throw up defensive works, they refused,"[6] William snorted. "At the last council the governor ruled that each settler be paid one shilling and six pence per diem for work on a defensive line around the town. That's more than the soldiers get for the same work! But we might see some progress now."

Hardy tucked the eyeglass under his arm, and the officers continued pacing. "All right," he asked, "what's so special about Gorham's Rangers that makes them better than Phillips's Regiment?"

"They know the trails of Nova Scotia," Gray said. "Most of them are full Indian or half French. They can handle themselves in the wild. They would be best able to protect those people at Mill Cove."

"But the governor said no?"

"Lieutenant Bulkeley doesn't like Captain John Gorham to begin with. Bulkeley said the Rangers in their smelly buckskins offend his sensibilities. He suggested the Rangers be stationed at the head of the basin, the direction from which we might expect an Indian attack. He wanted to leave the defence of the settlement to the regular troops of the garrison who make a much better show in their red coats, white breeches, and black gaiters." Gray spread his hands expressively and let them drop to his sides. "And that's where Gorham is now, building a fort twenty miles from where he's needed." He spoke emotionally. "Those Mill Cove people are there because I suggested it. I wanted better protection for them, but Cornwallis agreed with Bulkeley."

They had reached the stern. Gray asked for Hardy's eyeglass. After a moment spent adjusting it, he examined Georges Island. Hardy stood with his hands on his hips. "That's one place where things are going just as planned." He pointed to a large grey area on the side of the island. "Sailors from *Sphinx* helped the crews of the transports to ferry stores and ammunition. See! It's all under cover now, safe and sound."

They resumed walking. "If you want something done right, get the navy to do it," Hardy said. Both officers chuckled.

"I was ordered to lay several navigation buoys in the harbour and approaches." Gray raised the eyeglass to see if he could pick out one of them. "The nearest one is a white can buoy in twenty-two feet of water on the southeast part of Pleasant Point Shoal." He put the glass down. "Can't see it from here. Anyway, the captain of the port ordered me to use redcoats."

"How did it go?" Hardy asked.

"They did well enough in the dog work, but when it came to laying the buoys I got more out of Denham and his lads than …"

"Who's Denham?" Hardy interrupted.

Flustered by the question, Gray hesitated. While the sailors of *Sphinx* had been assigned to him with a petty officer in charge, the real leader of the group had been Able Seaman Denham. The petty officer had let things progress naturally in the working party, which was the navy's way, allowing Denham, with his leadership qualities, to get the work done quickly and effectively. On board *Sphinx*, Denham was just a pair of hands and kept in his place. When ashore on detachment, he quite often became the linchpin of the entire operation. Not sure how to respond to Hardy, Gray changed the subject.

"We got the information about the shoals and rocks from a 1732 chart of the harbour made by Thomas Durell," he said. "Durell had identified another shoal just off the northwest corner of Cornwallis Island and called it Spaniard Shoal. When we had marked it with a can buoy, Denham, er, the shore party thought we should rename it after someone who's here now. It's called Ives Knoll in honour of the officer who sent us out to do the work."

"What's Ives's background?"

"Apparently our governor was impressed with stories of Captain Benjamin Ives during the capture of Louisbourg in '45; Ives served under Pepperall in a Massachusetts regiment. Cornwallis appointed him Captain of the Port of Halifax."

Returning up the starboard side, passing the waiting gun crews, Lieutenant Hardy remarked, "I can see a redcoat at Mill Cove. He just went inside."

Gray quickly added, "And that's where he'll be if the workmen need help against attackers inside looking out."

Lieutenant Hardy made no comment. Instead, he asked questions about the cove. Gray was proud of his knowledge of the area and was very willing to share it. "The water in the cove has a good depth. We could take *Sphinx* and probably a vessel with as much draught as *Beaufort* almost in to the shore. Plenty of fresh water. There's a stream that, even at this time of year, has a vigorous flow. It has a fall of about ten feet within sight of the beach.[7] Fir and spruce come right to the water's edge. It's an ideal spot for a mill. I suggested that I take a party up that stream to see if it could be used as an Indian warpath but the governor had other tasks for me. I was sent to …"

"Lieutenant, sir!" One of the lookouts was pointing at *Beaufort*. "The savages are going over the side and getting into their canoes."

Another voice called out, "Signals, sir!"

Lieutenant Hardy checked the signal flags on *Beaufort* and compared them to the signal book.

"Captain on deck!"

Both officers saluted Captain Lloyd. "What does she read?" asked the captain.

"It's our number, sir. It reads receive visitors," Hardy said.

The only harbour traffic was a half-dozen canoes full of Indians heading straight for *Sphinx*.

"Oh, Lord!" Rubbing the back of his neck, Lloyd ordered, "Beat to quarters! Muster ship's company!"

*9 August 1749*

Gray stood in the shade of "his" hardwood tree near the brook. The areas around it and the brook had been cleared. Streets had been marked off, and half-finished huts, more or less in straight lines, cluttered the side of the hill. All the pines had gone into the making of the palisade that snaked up the hill from the water line. Soldiers raised dust as they dug into the hill at the spot planned for the parade square. They'll have a hard time making the spot flat, Gray thought, watching them. It's mostly rock. Indeed, as far as he could see, the soldiers had made little impression on the shape of the hill despite their strenuous efforts. "Give me the life of a sailor!" he said to himself. "Life for Willie Gray is just wonderful today."

Governor Cornwallis had come ashore to take up quarters in his wood frame house several hundred yards uphill from the tree. After helping with a couple of packing cases and moving a chair or two, Gray had been dismissed with a wave of the governor's hand. He had quickly departed the house, seeking shade under the only tree left in the settlement. Perhaps he should return to *Sphinx*, but for now he relaxed under the old hardwood tree and savoured a few moments of freedom.

"Gray? Gray of the gov'nuh's staff?"

Gray turned to find himself looking into the weather-beaten face of a tall, lean man in the green uniform of His Majesty's Independent Rangers. Noting the captain's rank, Gray saluted.

"Yes, sir," he said. "I'm Sub-Lieutenant Gray."

"Ah'm not much for that salutin'." Returning Gray's salute, the captain said, "I'm John Gorham. Ah've been building a fort up on the Sackville River. My men were in Chebucto for supplies last week. When they got back they tol' me you were asking questions 'bout the Indians." Gorham smiled down on Gray. "Not often a navy man wants t' know 'bout Indians."

"I'm pleased to meet you, sir," Gray said. "Perhaps you haven't heard. This settlement and fort isn't Chebucto any more. It is now called Halifax in honour of the chairman of the Lords of Trade and Plantations, George Dunk. And yes, I'm very curious about two incidents in which I was involved with the natives."

"I thought you said you was callin' this Halifax."

"Yes, sir. George Dunk is a close friend of Governor Cornwallis, and he's also known as Lord Halifax."

"Good thing!"

Gray looked down at his boots and smiled. Without looking up he continued. "The first time I saw Indians they were dressed in loincloths and blended in with the trees like ghosts. The next time their faces were painted red, they had black streaks over their foreheads and noses, and they made a lot of noise."

Captain Gorham became very alert. "Where did you see 'em with painted faces?"

"They were on *Beaufort* having a parley with the governor. We had fired a seventeen-gun salute from *Sphinx* when the Indians came in their canoes. They swarmed over *Beaufort's* decks and ..."

"Parley? What was they parleyin' for?"

"To ensure that we had peace with the Indians. They signed the treaty ..."

Gorham shook his head negatively. "Did they make a ceremony of washin' off the paint?"

"No. Governor Cornwallis said that ..."

"Was they active, dancing like?"

"Yes, sir. They danced on *Beaufort*, and after the parley they came over to *Sphinx*."

Gorham took his hat off and rubbed his thinning hair. "Ah'm surprised the *Sphinx* captain let 'em on his warship."

"Governor Cornwallis ordered *Sphinx* to receive them as visitors," Gray said. "The Indians came and danced around and around. They made little chopping motions at the cannons. One of them kept laughing and shouting, 'thunder ship, thunder ship' in a rhythmic chant. Then they all began to do it."

"How'd you get em to stop?"

"Captain Lloyd had the crew make the space where the Indians were dancing smaller and smaller until they were against the bulwark. The Indians really had no choice but to board their canoes."

Gorham spoke very seriously. "You can tell the gov'nuh that his treaty means nothing to the Micmac. They came with

war paint; they left with war paint. As far as those savages
know," and here Gorham tapped William's shoulder to emphasize each word, "*they made a fool of the English chief.*"

"Good Lord! I must tell the governor. Here I was afraid Captain Lloyd would be in trouble for pushing the Indians off the
ship and then resuming what he called gunnery practice while
they were virtually under the guns. All the while they …"

"What happened?"

"The Indians were barely over the side when the captain
ordered the men to resume gunnery practice. The guns were
fired, one every five seconds. I guess Captain Lloyd meant to
frighten them, but the Indians stood in their canoes and bared
their chests. They hollered and waved their paddles in the air
after the cannon were silent, and paddled away, chanting."

Captain Gorham rubbed and rubbed his hair. He put his
hat back on before speaking again. "You tell the gov'nuh he has
trouble. Those savages came with war paint and weren't forced
to take it off. Then they counted coup on the cannon of *Sphinx*
and stood up to the barrage of the thunder ship. They'll believe
themselves invincible!"

Gorham straightened his hat and uniform. "Ah must
return to my men." He walked away, briskly, but then stopped
and returned to face Gray. "Believe me! We will have serious
trouble with the Micmac." He poked his finger at Gray stress-
ing each word. "*Tell the gov'nuh!*"

Sub-Lieutenant Gray returned to the governor's house.
Lieutenants Bulkeley and Gates and the governor were engaged
in discussing a number of nettlesome problems: the threat from
the Acadians; the need for a proper road through the forest to
Minas Basin; the production problems at the sawmill; and
where the small log-and-earth forts would be located and who
would build them since the soldiers were unskilled.

"What do you want, Gray?"

"Sir, I was speaking with Captain Gorham, who thinks we
have a problem with the Indians."

In a tired, resigned voice the governor replied, "Lieutenant
Gray, we have a treaty with the Indians. If Gorham has problems, talk to me tomorrow about them. Right now, I have

pressing matters I wish to address without delay."

"Aye, sir, but I believe that …"

"Tomorrow, Lieutenant."

It would be too late. An Indian war party was already paddling down the chain of lakes whose waters emptied into Chebucto at the 'place of many trees.'

\* \* \*

Harry Acton[8] was always the first one out of the guard's shelter each morning. It probably wasn't seemly for a corporal to begin the day's work ahead of the troops and lumberjacks, but Acton didn't like the smell of sweaty bodies in the confined space of the guard hut so he rose as soon as he could and washed in the brook. And since he was going that way anyway it seemed logical to pick up some timber and carry it back to the sawmill. "Can't go empty-handed," he said to himself. Acton liked talking to himself, but he didn't want anyone to catch him at it.

Corporal Acton stopped by a pile of timber and turned to look out over the harbour at the main settlement. "The boys will soon have those little forts finished."

There were fewer transports in the harbour now. A lot of the settlers lived in Halifax instead of on the ships. The little warship was there, the one the governor had used as his headquarters for the first couple of months.

The sun had risen behind Acton, and he was able to see such details as the raw slice on the side of the hill intended for a parade square. "Poor blighters!" He was thinking of the countless soldiers who were going to be drilled on the square after it was finished as well as the men who were trying to build it.

A couple of lumberjacks walked toward him, talking to each other. Acton could just make out what they were saying. "… tired of oatmeal." The man who was speaking patted his belly. "It's filling, though."

Three other men were some distance away, and two of them ran to catch up to the others. One of them was a young fellow from New Hampshire. "I don't know him. I'll have to ask his name," Acton said to himself.

Acton had fallen into the habit of leaving his musket at the guard hut each morning when he went to wash. When he saw a flicker of colour out of the corner of his eye he thought, I'm two hundred yards away from my weapon. Aloud he said, "It's probably a bird."

"What did you say, Corporal?" asked the man who had been talking about oatmeal.

Acton coughed to hide his embarrassment, putting his hand to his mouth. "Tell you what, Thomas ..." Acton started to reply and then, seeing the looks of horror on the faces of the two men, hesitated. "What's the matter?"

The two men were frozen in place. Suddenly two explosions sounded right behind Acton and the men's faces disappeared. They fell like slaughtered cattle. A volley of muskets fired from everywhere—in the trees, near the pile of timber, and from the bank of the stream. The young man from New Hampshire went down, legs and arms flapping. So did his friend who had been running with him. The third man turned and fled to the guard hut.

Acton didn't waste any time. He ran for his life. He jumped the two bodies in front of him and raced for the hut. Lean brown bodies with painted heads and faces appeared all around him. There must be thirty or forty of them, he thought. Filthy bastards! He kept running. He noticed the New Hampshire boy was still alive.

Suddenly something struck the side of Acton's face. An Indian, seemingly coming out of nowhere, had hit him with a club. Acton's legs kept moving but he was starting to fall ... falling ....

There was a roaring in Acton's ears. For a moment he thought he was back fighting with bare knuckles for the regiment and losing. "I must have been knocked out for a while." He became aware that someone was screaming, and he was startled to discover he could only see out of one eye. The front of his chest was red. "B-bl-blood," he stammered. He tried to move but found he was trussed up like a pig. Acton squirmed sideways and saw the New Hampshire boy lying nearby with a gaping chest wound.

The corporal watched in horror as an Indian knelt on the boy's chest. The screaming stopped.

"Get off his chest," Acton yelled. "He can't breathe!"

The Indian grasped the boy's hair at the back of his head. With his knife in the other hand, the painted man cut a circle and, with some effort, pulled off the hank of hair and attached flap of skin. When the Indian got up off the New Hampshire boy's chest, the screams started again but quickly faded to whimpers.

With the dripping trophy in his hand, the Indian made his way toward Acton. He dragged the helpless corporal into a sitting position and readied his knife. Several voices called out, "Beau Soleil!" The Indian standing over the corporal responded and moved on, leaving Acton alone. Sitting, Acton had a better view of what was going on.

There were more Indians than he had first thought. They moved about easily and seemed to be in no hurry. Several were talking and pointing at the guard's hut. A small Indian had just finished scalping the boy who had been running with New Hampshire. "That boy's name is Mark," Acton said to himself. "I should have learned New Hampshire's name before this morning."

New Hampshire's body was jerking and he was making horrible gurgling noises. An Indian passed, casually carrying two human heads by the hair, one in each hand, as if he was carrying buckets of water.

Beau Soleil, standing in the group that had been discussing the guard hut, looked back at Acton.

Corporal Acton rolled away and struggled against the leather strips binding his hands and feet. He kept rolling until he came up against an outcropping of bedrock overlooking the beach.

The Indian followed him and said something that made the other Indians laugh. He reached down and grabbed Acton by the hair. "Noooo," Acton moaned. "Not me you don't!"

Acton twisted to one side, kicking at the Indian with both feet. He missed.

Lying there trussed and fully extended, it was easy for Beau Soleil to put his knee on the white man's chest. He pulled hard on Acton's hair, jerking the soldier's head forward and back several times.

"Oh, Christ!" Who would have thought that hair pulling would be so painful! Acton's good eye blurred with tears.

Beau Soleil pulled Acton's head back so that he could look right into the soldier's face.

"I'm not bloody crying," Acton said. He tried to find eyes in the grotesque red and black face of his enemy, but with his eye full of tears he couldn't. He could see the knife, though. The bastard is going to slit my throat, thought Acton.

The Indian waited for the soldier to stop struggling. When Acton was very still, Beau Soleil slowly moved his knife up Acton's face, finally inserting it into the soldier's nostril. Acton tasted blood, but he didn't move.

"You, be no bad," Beau Soleil said.

The knife moved across Acton's sight from right to left and back several times, like a teacher's wagging finger. "No bad." The hand on his hair relaxed slightly, and Beau Soleil took some of his weight off the soldier's chest.

Corporal Action nodded his head; he understood. "No bad."

The Indian cut the leather strips that bound the soldier's feet and motioned for him to stand. With some difficulty, Corporal Acton accommodated him. Then Beau Soleil pushed him toward the stream.

Acton looked at the four bodies strewn around him. At the guard hut, muskets were sticking out of the gun ports, but otherwise there were no signs of life. No one was coming after him.

The Indians moved off. Acton was shoved again, harder this time. He looked across the harbour at the parade square, and stumbled as he was pushed again. With one last look at the guard hut, Corporal Harry Acton turned and trudged up the stream into a life of captivity with the Micmac.

\* \* \*

At the following morning's staff meeting, Governor Cornwallis's anger was evident. "That priest, LeLoutre," he stormed, "induced those savages to attack! We lost twenty Englishmen at

Canso. They almost captured a sloop of war at Minas and," Cornwallis slammed his fist on the table, "they massacred four of my men at Mill Cove!"

The council members and the governor's military advisers were crowded into the front room of the small frame house the settlers called the Governor's Mansion.

Gorham didn't wait for permission to speak. "As soon as we heard about the massacre, I sent my men after 'em. They caught up with two Indians in possession of white men's body parts."[9]

"You mean scalps?"

"No, not scalps." Gorham looked around the room. "Heads."

From the entranceway Gray spoke quietly. "They took one of the guards prisoner at Mill Cove." In a stronger voice, Gray continued, "Any evidence of him?"

"No," Gorham drawled, "but he might be offered for ransom if they think we'll pay."

Governor Cornwallis looked defiant. Gray thought he was going to refuse and held his breath.

"We'll pay," the governor finally said.

The men in the room breathed a collective sigh of relief. Gray hadn't been the only one holding his breath.

"Did you ask the Indians you caught why they broke the treaty?" the governor asked.

"No," Gorham replied. "We killed 'em."

Governor Cornwallis looked surprised.

"And then scalped 'em."

Shocked silence filled the room.

Gorham added, "It's the language they understand."

Lieutenant Bulkeley leaned forward in his seat. "We should declare war on the heathens. Make them regret that they took the lives of Englishmen. Send a regiment to pursue them until there are none of them left."

"No." The governor raised both hands palms up as if to push away Bulkeley's suggestion.

Bulkeley sat back in his chair wearing a sulky expression.

"I want Captain Gorham to handle this." Cornwallis

warmed to the subject. "The Micmac signed a treaty and broke it, and were probably incited to attack us by that French missionary, LeLoutre."

Glancing at Lieutenant Gray, Gorham made as if to speak. The governor ignored him. "The Indians are no better than *banditti* and shall be treated as such. Captain Gorham!"

"Yes, gov'ner."

"I hereby give you the authority to recruit another one hundred men from New England to hunt them down." Cornwallis gestured to his treasurer, Mr. Davidson, "See that sufficient funds are available to the captain."

Davidson, surprised, his eyes almost popping out of his fat little face, asked, "How much, sir?"

Annoyed, the governor replied sharply, "Whatever Gorham's Rangers need, see to it! I want the job done!"

Mr. Davidson bent over his work and scribbled some notes. Gray was sure he saw a sly smile slide onto the treasurer's face. He didn't like the man at all. There was talk throughout the settlement about the treasurer's little business activities. Gray's friends on *Sphinx* believed that Davidson charged an "eighth" on all deliveries of molasses and rum. *Sphinx's* purser denied it, of course, pursers being what they are; he was undoubtedly getting his share of the cut, too.

Gray shook his head. I shouldn't think ill of the man just because I don't like him and he's the subject of rumour, he thought.

The governor motioned to the treasurer. "And make another note! I want it known that I call on all His Majesty's officers, civil and military, and all His Majesty's subjects to destroy the Micmac wherever they're found. Ten guineas for each Indian, living or dead." Remembering something Captain Gorham had said, he added, "Or his scalp, as is the custom in America."

## *Endnotes*

[1] The log of the *H.M.S. Sphinx* had just been made available from the Royal Navy archives when I was researching the story. It is correct. Of course, entries concerning Gray have been invented.

[2] I couldn't find the pennant number in the archives that would have been assigned to *H.M.S. Albany*, so I assigned one.

[3] Names of crew members, other than the captain, are fictitious.

[4] Information on Bulkeley is taken from the book, *Halifax, Warden of the North*, articles by H.W. Hewitt, the *Dictionary of Canadian Biography*, documents and correspondence on microfiche at the N.S. Archives.

[5] From microfiche of Minutes of H.M. Council.

[6] Minutes of H.M. Council.

[7] Taken from the book, *The Story of Dartmouth*, by Dr. John Martin.

[8] Acton is a fictitious character based on an incident described in an article by Hewitt.

[9] Taken from the Minutes of H.M. Council and *The Story of Dartmouth*, by Martin.

# Chapter Two

## 15 February 1750

Dear Uncle Charles;

I trust you are well and enjoying better weather than we are having in Halifax. It is cold. Even the seawater of Bedford Basin is frozen. I am told there is enough fresh water from the Sackville River present in the salt water to cause this effect. The snow is over three feet deep in the woods around the settlement. Fortunately, my duties have not caused me to go in that direction.

Half of the settlers and garrison are now living ashore. Those are the ones with good fortune. The people forced to live on the ships in the harbour are suffering more from the cold than we are.

There is much dissatisfaction among the settlers. They were promised large tracts of land with deep and fertile soil. Certainly that is not the case on this coast, where the land is rocky and sour to the extreme. Such fertile land as was promised can only be found on the Minas side occupied by the French settlers, called Inhabitants.

Instead of the fifty acres of land they were expecting, the settlers received a building lot within the protection of the settlement's defences and another five acres in the wilderness. Few settlers bother to venture forth to inspect their holdings since the Micmac serve up death to any English they find in the forest.

Death is all around us. There is a regular trade in human scalps. The governor will pay ten guineas for any Indian scalp delivered to the Provost Marshal at Halifax. The French pay for English scalps delivered to Louisbourg. Once the scalp is separated from its owner, who is to say the thing is Indian, English, or French?

Fever is killing dozens every day. Cartloads of bodies are taken to the cemetery just south of the palisade. The gravediggers are well served with rum before they go out; they have that inner warmth and the exertion of digging to

29

foil the cold. The soldiers on the other hand, sent to protect the gravediggers and the mourners, suffer badly; their uniforms provide scant protection from the penetrating wind.

I assure you I continue well. Surprisingly, so do all of my friends and superiors. Most of the deaths occur amongst the dregs of the settlement, the shiftless and the lazy. I wonder what is in the military routine we follow that provides a shield against the fever?

The governor is a changed man. Where once I said that he was of good humour and forgiving, I must now have the opposite opinion. He tells me, "Sub-Lieutenant Gray, you are thoughtless and have scant regard for my requirements." He told Lieutenant Bulkeley, "You are totally unskilled for the tasks at hand." (Perhaps it is true about Bulkeley, but the criticism was made with several others present.) He rails against the stupidity of the settlers and, when given the latest mortality figures by Lieutenant Gates, said, "Ship fever will purge Halifax of its worst human element!" At an earlier time, the human suffering caused by the fever would have concerned our governor.

Perhaps the constant threat from the Micmac or the fact that the French Inhabitants are proving to be deadly enemies wears on the governor. I know that he is heartsick about his old friend, George Dunk, Lord Halifax of the Lords of Trade, who is very critical of the costs of the expedition. The Lords of Trade have asked for substantiation of expenditures. Governor Cornwallis is relying on Mr. Davidson to provide the figures. (I do not hold Mr. Davidson in much regard.)

It is further evidence of the governor's ill humour that he had Stephen Adams and Thomas Keys,[1] two men of good repute, punished severely for having doubts about the honesty of Mr. Davidson, in whom Governor Cornwallis places utmost trust. The governor took the comments of these two persons as a personal affront! They were found, in the governor's words, "guilty of having reported false news to the prejudice of the settlement and scandalous lies of His Excellency the governor." Neither man took the twenty lashes very well. Thomas begged for mercy, but the punishment was delivered.

Pass best wishes to Mother. I should have written her at

this time but had little to say that was good news. Just tell her that I am well and have acquired great knowledge of Bedford Basin, Halifax Harbour, and the sea approaches. 1750—a new decade that does not bode well by its beginnings.

Your affectionate nephew,
William

Written at 7 Holles Street,[2] Halifax.

*Spring 1750*
*Halifax*

Gray looked at the man seated at the other side of the table and tried not to let his distaste for him show. "I need twenty guineas, Mr. Davidson."[3]

"Write a letter detailing why you require the funds, and I will obtain approval for you." Davidson smugly added, "If I can. Money doesn't grow on trees, you know. Although I believe Lieutenant Bulkeley thinks it does. He's back from Boston having bought more street lanterns. That's over two hundred of the damn things he's purchased from Apthorpe and Hancock." Peering over the top of his spectacles, he explained, "Apthorpe and Hancock are the chief royal purveyors."

Davidson thought the young pup was dense in the head to be so unimpressed. He continued, "I wouldn't mind an eighth of their business, let me tell you!" The treasurer buried his head in his ledgers again. "They charge the Crown as much as they can get away with." He shook his head again. "But why buy street lanterns? When it gets dark good people should be safely inside for the night. There's no need to light the streets and lanes for the rabble off the ships who ..."

There was no end in sight to the chatter, so Gray interrupted. "I have approval from the governor. He said to issue me a money belt as well."

"Approval! Money belt!" The treasurer picked up a rag and wiped his pen dry. He snapped the top of the inkwell closed and carefully placed the pen alongside the inkwell, aligning both with the edge of the table. It took a while before he was satisfied with the arrangement. Then Davidson turned in his chair and reached into a cabinet for some paper. "It's still necessary for you to write a letter so we have a record of what the money will be used for."

"The governor doesn't want anyone to know what I'm doing. I can sign for the money, but I cannot give you an explanation."

"Just *give* you money?" asked Davidson incredulously. He leaned forward and placed his elbows on the table, folding his hands under his chin. "I have to know what the funds are for."

Neither man spoke for several moments. Davidson sat with his chin in his hands, elbows on the table, and Gray stood almost at attention.

"Didn't the governor give you a note, some form of written authorization?" asked Davidson.

"He said not to tell anyone," said Gray. "I have verbal instructions …"

"No explanation, no coin." Davidson leaned back in his chair. "I cannot give out money without a reason. Besides, you can tell me; I'm the governor's right-hand man."

I have to make a choice, Gray thought. On the one hand, the governor said to tell no one but, on the other, I can't wait for the governor to issue written instructions. He decided. "Ever since Thomas Keys and Stephen Adams were given twenty lashes for accusing the administration of lining its own pockets …"

"Yes! Yes, I know."

"The governor wants to eliminate every breath of scandal."

"I know, I know. Get on with it!"

Gray took a deep breath. "There's a man in Halifax called Mauger who's working with the French at Louisbourg. They have a smuggling ring, bringing in tea and liquor. I've been ordered to track down who's selling the liquor in Halifax and close them down. The governor thinks that if there is no way to sell the smuggled rum, the smuggling will stop."

"And there's someone who will tell you what's going on?" asked Davidson.

"Yes. He'll name names for twenty guineas. I must have the money with me tonight."

"So you shall, my young sir!" Davidson was suddenly all business. He opened the strongbox, counted out the coin and helped the young officer fill the belt. Gray opened his coat and accepted the little man's help to fit the belt under his shirt and around his waist.

"Why, Lieutenant! You're carrying a pistol! Surely that is not needed?"

Gray didn't reply as he made the final adjustments to the money belt and refastened his coat.

"What are you going to do next?" Davidson asked.

"I'll meet a man, Benjamin Storer, on Water Street near the old hardwood tree at dusk."

"It's not long to dusk. You should hurry so you don't miss him." Davidson made some last-minute adjustments to the officer's coat. "The money belt doesn't show."

He opened the door for Gray, who hesitated. "Don't you need a signature for the money?"

"No, no. Hurry along. You're on the king's business." The treasurer stopped still. "But you could be waylaid and lose the money. It would be better if there was a receipt for the twenty guineas."

Davidson scribbled out a receipt and Gray signed it. Then the treasurer hurried the young officer out the door. From outside the closed door, Gray could hear Davidson scurrying around inside, slamming shut the strongbox and rattling the lock, apparently in a big hurry himself.

Checking both directions, up and down the street, Gray placed his officer's hat squarely on his head, tugged on his coat, checked for any lint or hair on the dark blue cloth, and quickly felt for any unsecured buttons. All in order, he stepped out into the late afternoon sun and started downhill toward the harbour.

He enjoyed the soft air as he walked down Prince Street, relishing the fine Nova Scotia spring. Although there were still a number of tree stumps to be dug out, the place was starting to look like a town. Gray glanced up at the lampposts and smiled. The lanterns may have cost a lot but they certainly were attractive.

The top of the hill had been cleared of all trees. With the arrival of more settlers, some from New England, the original stockade had been torn down and the settlement was expanding west to the other side of the peninsula. The governor had asked the Lords of Trade for more suitable immigrants, people willing to work, so boatloads of farmers from the Rhineland were expected during the summer.

Crossing the little brook, Gray confirmed what he had heard; it was almost dry. Halifax would have to rely on wells for drinking water. The governor's plan was to fill in the streambed and call it George Street. He stood for a minute looking at the brook, remembering it the way he had first seen it. It was just above the spring that he had seen his first Indians.

"Colour party! Atten-*shun!*" Soldiers were formed up on the parade square for the sunset ceremony. They looked awkward standing in formation. The rear rank looked out over the heads of the front rank; everyone was uphill of the officer. Gray was reminded of Uncle Charles's sage advice, "When giving orders to your men, always look 'em in the eyes." Good luck, he thought. That'll take a bit of doing.

Gray followed the streambed toward the hardwood tree. When he heard the first notes of the bugle he turned to face the flagstaff. He held a salute while the bugle played "Sunset." He hummed along to the simple tune. "Da de da, da de da, da de da, da de da ... fully aware that whenever he was called upon to salute the Union Jack, *he* knew he was only paying homage to the Scottish part of the flag, the cross of Saint Andrew. The bugle stopped, and in the momentary hush Gray waited until he heard, "Order arms!" Then he dropped his salute and continued down the hill.

Changes had been made in the cove where he had first landed. A pier had been built, and the land levelled to accommodate the new pier. The marsh and flowers were gone. The new pier was called Fisherman's Pier and was used regularly by fishermen who were mostly new settlers from New England.

Looking across the harbour at Mill Cove, Gray saw the

newly finished blockhouse. Major Ezekiel Gilman was in charge of the detachment of soldiers located there, and Governor Cornwallis had given Gilman responsibility for managing the sawmill as well. "Killing two birds with one stone," the governor had said at the time.[4]

"It depends on whether you're killing birds or sawing planks. You shouldn't make an officer run a sawmill," was the unsolicited advice from Lieutenant Bulkeley.

It was the first time Gray had agreed with anything the lieutenant had said, but it made the governor very cross. Gray couldn't imagine how Bulkeley had gotten away with a comment like that, but the lieutenant had recently done some good work that had pleased the governor very much. Bulkeley had brought timber from Boston for Halifax's first church, St. Paul's. The church, a source of great pride for the governor, was almost finished. The pine and oak building stood next to the parade square facing Prince Street, and Cornwallis looked forward to the opening ceremony.

The last light of the sun had disappeared behind the sugarloaf-shaped hill, and shadows were deepening around the church's spire. Lieutenant Gray was becoming uneasy. Where's my man, he wondered. There weren't many passers-by at this time of day. Soon the pimps and their prostitutes would be out, signalling the beginning of the seamy waterfront nightlife. Gray felt under his coat for the money belt, and was reassured by the weight of the pistol against his side. The lamplighter came along and passed a cheery good evening and half-salute to the officer. Gray responded with a nod and an informal wave of his hand.

While Gray waited, he reflected on events of the recent past. There wasn't a more honest man than Governor Cornwallis, so it was not surprising the man had keenly resented the comments of Adams and Keys. The governor had passed laws providing a ten-pound fine and ten lashes for anyone caught selling liquor without a licence. That should have discouraged the smugglers, but there was too much easy money to be made.

Roused from his thoughts by movement near one of the Water Street huts, Gray peered through the gathering gloom.

In the circle of light from one of the lanterns he could see two sailors carrying cudgels and walking directly toward him. They turned at the corner and disappeared from sight. Gray sighed. All of this might be for nothing, he thought.

It wasn't long before another figure loomed out of the darkness. He wasn't carrying a cudgel so Gray assumed he wasn't a sailor. As the man came closer, Gray could see he also wasn't in uniform.

"Lieutenant Gray?" the man asked in a hoarse half-whisper.

"Yes, I'm William Gray. Are you Benjamin Storer?" Gray extended his hand in greeting, but the other man stepped back a pace and cast nervous glances in all directions. "I've got what you want if you have the money," he said.

Opening his coat, Gray started to fish under his shirt for the money belt.

"No! Not here; down by the beach where we won't be seen." Storer abruptly began walking along Water Street where a lane between the huts led to the beach. Gray followed. As they turned the corner, Gray sensed danger from the sudden and almost complete darkness. He ran to catch up with Storer. "This isn't a good idea," Gray said. "We should be ..."

A big man stepped out of the darkness and hit Storer with a cudgel. Storer went down without making a sound. A second smaller figure hissed, "You hit the wrong one! He's not the one with the pistol!"

Gray ran back the way he had come. He reached the end of the lane but was tripped from behind. He fell into the middle of Water Street.

"Get his pistol!"

Gray leaped to his feet. He ran to the other side of the street, tore open his jacket, and jerked at the pistol. It didn't move! In a panic, he struggled to get the weapon out. Then he realized that the pistol was hooked on his belt.

The big man caught up to him and swung the cudgel. Gray caught the blow on his right shoulder. His right arm flopped as if it were broken. Desperately he worked the hook out of the belt with his left hand, and scuttled along the side of the hut trying to keep his back to the wall. Another blow struck him, this time across the top of his shoulders. He pulled on the butt of the pistol. Christ! It was still caught.

Gray jerked hard just as the big man moved in close to finish him off, and the pistol suddenly came free. Gray swung his left arm in an arc and smashed the pistol in the big man's face. By the half-light of the next street lantern, Gray could see the man's nose was broken. The man screamed and fell to his knees, clutching his face.

Gray quickly raised his pistol. His left hand was shaky but at this range he couldn't miss. "Hold!" he ordered the second man, still hidden in the shadows.

"Alarm! Alarm!" Someone up the street had the heard the struggle.

Gray sensed a flood of relief; men from the Provost Marshal's office would soon come to his aid. The sound of running feet made him feel more confident. "Move up here where I can see you."

"Just don't shoot!" cried the little man as he moved slowly into the light. Then he stopped and laughed. "Good night, Lieutenant."

From behind, the big man smashed Gray's head with the cudgel as if he were swatting a pesky fly.

\* \* \*

William Gray was again part of a group of men gathered in the front room of the Governor's Mansion but this time he was seated at a table and was the centre of attention. The governor was also seated and had a thin file open on his lap. "I understand you had nothing broken, William?"

"That's right, sir," said Gray. "Thank you for asking, sir. I came through with some damage, but nothing broken."

"I also understand," continued the governor, "you lost the twenty guineas."

Gray was unhappy with the direction the conversation was going. "Aye, sir. When the patrol found me, my shirt was ripped open, and the belt and pistol were gone."

The governor read the file for several minutes. No one

broke the uneasy silence. Finally Governor Cornwallis resumed his questioning. "Your so-called friendly informer led you into a trap?"

"Aye sir, it looks that way, but I know who he is and he will probably give us ..."

Cornwallis glared at the young man and said, "As I understand it, you did not get the information we required."

Gray sat absolutely still and met the governor's stare evenly. Cornwallis closed the file and placed it on the table. He opened another file and plucked out a sheet of paper. "Fortunately, I have Mr. Davidson to rely upon. Mr. Davidson had his own informer. A man called Amos Skinner gave him a list of names. After some persuasion, Skinner also confessed to being part of the ring. The blackguards are now in custody."

Looking pleased, the governor read from the list: "John Petty, James Follin, Amos Skinner, and Mary Unick have all confessed.[5] After a hearing they'll be punished. The last one, Benjamin Storer, refuses to confess; he claims not to be one of the gang."

"Storer was the man who met me and said he was willing to give me all the names," said Gray.

The governor waved the list in Gray's face and said angrily, "His name is on the list! He's a smuggler! If it hadn't been for Davidson we would have nothing to act on."

Leaning back in his chair Governor Cornwallis spoke more calmly. "As it is, I think Davidson was as foolhardy as you. Skinner is a big man. Confronting him and forcing him to cooperate was risky. Davidson told me that he finally hit Skinner so hard that he ..."

"Broke his nose!" Gray leaped out of his chair. "Skinner is a big man with a broken nose! It was Skinner who knocked out Storer." Gray started to pace. "The second man was small and told Skinner he had hit the wrong man. He said Skinner should have hit me since I had the pistol." He stopped pacing and looked at the governor. "Only Davidson knew that I was carrying a pistol." Gray resumed his seat. "I believe it was Skinner and Davidson who attacked me."

The governor was sceptical. "But Davidson said he broke Skinner's nose to get him to cooperate with us."

"I broke his nose with the pistol. I saw the blood. Davidson made up the story because he knew we would be searching for a man with a broken nose. Skinner gave himself up because he expected to be caught." Gray smiled. "At least this way, Skinner gets the informer's fee for every name he turned in, even his own."

"The broken nose explains why there was so much blood on you. Skinner's nose was bleeding when they stole your money belt. That convinces me about Skinner." Cornwallis picked opened a short file and read it all the way through. "I can't believe Mr. Davidson would do this."

"Have the Provost Marshal search his rooms," Gray said. "If he can deceive you in this matter, he can deceive you in other, more important matters."

* * *

There were five prisoners standing before the governor and members of the governing council. Behind each prisoner stood a soldier, musket polished and fixed bayonet glistening in the sun streaming through the windows. The men in uniform were handsome with their tall shakos, scarlet coats, white breeches, and black gaiters. Every belt, button, and insignia had been polished until it gleamed. In the heat of this lovely spring day, the soldiers' uniforms gave off a wet wool smell as well as odours the other occupants of the rooms tried to ignore.

By comparison, the prisoners looked drab and unkempt. Even Amos Skinner, who was an unusually large man, was somehow reduced in size by the nature of the surroundings. Each prisoner had heard the charge and had been given the opportunity to respond to the evidence presented.

The military and civilian men who made up the governing council sat behind a table at the front of the room. Officers were in full-dress uniform, their hats carefully placed on the table in front of them. Civilian members wore frock coats and cravats, and their hats were positioned as carefully as those of the military members' were. The men at the table were discussing their findings. The prisoners waited, shifting their weight from foot to foot. The soldiers were at "stand easy," feet apart and musket held close to the body in front of them.

Gray glanced through his notes as he waited for the governor to begin sentencing. He was standing at the rear of the room with some twenty or thirty persons who had crowded through the door to witness the proceedings. Despite the jostling, Gray had been able to make a fair record of the hearing.

Benjamin Storer had maintained he was not guilty of selling spiritous liquors without a licence. He said that Skinner had sought him out that afternoon just before he met with Sub-Lieutenant Gray. If he didn't lead Gray down to the beach, Skinner threatened to have him killed. He didn't know how Skinner found out about the rendezvous.

Mary Unick confessed she was guilty as charged; John Petty admitted he was a smuggler; and James Follin admitted he had been involved in smuggling.

Amos Skinner confessed he was guilty as charged. He had no explanation why Storer made up stories about him or tried to make things worse for him; he had always liked Storer. Skinner asked the governor to remember that he had tried to cooperate with the settlement's administration and had informed on all the smugglers presently before the council.

William looked up from his notes as, with a rustling of paper and a shifting of chairs, the council members turned to face the accused persons. In a loud whisper the corporal of the guard ordered, "Guard! Atten-*shun!*"

With an alarming clatter the five guards moved from stand easy to attention, feet together and weapon close to their rigid bodies, the butts of their muskets resting on the floor by their right foot. The soldiers' eyes were fixed at a point somewhere beyond the walls of the room. All other eyes were intent upon the governor.

"You have been charged with selling spiritous liquors by retail without a licence." The governor paused and looked at the first prisoner.[6] "John Petty, who confessed, is ordered to pay the penalty of ten pounds—five pounds to the poor of the settlement, to be administered by the chaplain, and five pounds to the informer—and to be whipped ten lashes."

There was no reaction from the prisoner.

The governor dipped a quill in the inkwell. He shook the pen lightly to clear the point and signed the judgment. He put the paper aside, and without looking up, read from the next judgement. "James Follin, who confessed, is ordered to pay the penalty of ten pounds—one half to the poor of the settlement and one half to the informer—and to be whipped ten lashes."

When he had signed the second judgment, Cornwallis took a minute to look at the next offender. The woman was short and slight with mousy brown hair. Her frightened eyes darted around the packed room, never resting anywhere more than a second. The governor read from the judgment: "Mary Unick, who confessed, is ordered to pay the penalty of ten pounds—one half to the poor of the settlement and one half to the informer. The whipping is remitted."

An audible sigh of relief, that somehow annoyed the governor, escaped from the woman. He dipped his pen and signed her judgment. Placing it aside, he read on: "Benjamin Storer, you have been convicted and ordered to pay the informer five pounds. For some reason the council has seen fit to remit any other punishment."

Storer's head bobbed up and down several times, and he swallowed heavily. He looked around the courtroom until his eyes met those of Lieutenant Gray. Then Storer dropped his gaze and contemplated his feet, and he maintained that posture throughout the rest of the proceedings.

"Amos Skinner," the governor continued, "who informed against himself, is ordered to pay ten pounds—one-half to himself as the informer—and to be whipped ten lashes."

Skinner stepped toward the governor, but the corporal ordered, "Prisoner, stand fast!" When Skinner resumed his position, the corporal said, "That's a good man."

The members of the council and all of the witnesses stood. "This hearing is adjourned. God save the King!"

The corporal made a smart about-turn. In a loud whisper he ordered, "Escorts, take charge of your prisoner." Each guard stepped forward and herded his prisoner through the witnesses and out the door. Outside, the corporal formed up the guards with their prisoners and marched them away.

Governor Cornwallis tidied up his papers and handed them to Lieutenant Bulkeley. He chatted briefly with other members of the council and then signalled Lieutenant Gray to join him. "Walk with me back to the mansion, will you?"

"Of course, sir."

The two men passed through the throng and down the street to the Governor's Mansion. When they were alone, Cornwallis heaved a big sigh. "That was good work, William. If it hadn't been for you, we wouldn't have caught that bunch."

"Thank you, sir," Gray said. "Perhaps it might put a stop to the smuggling for a bit." He paused before continuing. "I hate to ask this, but I haven't seen Mr. Davidson since the incident. Was there anything in his rooms that incriminated him?"

The governor stopped walking. He watched a harbour craft take on passengers at Fisherman's Pier; a business had sprung up transporting people around the harbour. "There's a group that wants the name of that pier changed, and I have agreed. From now on it will be called Market Slip. Things change."

They continued on, and when they reached the mansion Cornwallis opened the door and waved the young officer inside. They were soon seated in two chairs near the front window. "You asked about Davidson. We found a blood-spattered jacket. Davidson said the blood came from Skinner when he hit him on the nose. There was a naval pistol—he had a cock-and-bull story for it being there—but that's all we found in his rooms."

"You don't believe him, do you?" asked Gray.

"The Davidson problem will resolve itself. As you know, I've been criticized by the Lords of Trade for our handling of funds. Our written explanations failed to satisfy their concerns. In a personal letter, Lord Halifax suggested that to clear up the matter, I return to England with copies of all of our ledgers. As a friend, he warned me that this matter will not be easily resolved."

Gray was surprised. "I didn't know it was that serious."

"The sums involved make it serious." The governor stood up, and the young man followed suit.

"I want to thank you, William," the governor said. "This has been a very trying matter. Without your help, I might have had to return to England to explain things, leaving my staff to carry on in my absence." Cornwallis shook his head at the thought. "Instead, I've ordered Mr. Davidson to make copies of all of the ledgers and files, and to depart immediately for England to justify his accounts before the clerks of the Lords of Trade. No matter what the result, Davidson will not be returning to Halifax."

Gray moved toward the door and opened it. He turned to look at the governor. "There will be a new treasurer?"

Cornwallis smiled sadly. "Mr. Townsend will be the new treasurer. I picked him carefully; he has my confidence."

Sub-Lieutenant William Gray saluted the governor and walked the short distance home to Holles Street.

## Endnotes

1  Minutes of H.M. Council.

2  Holles. The spelling that was used at the time.

3  Davidson was sent home ahead of Cornwallis to explain colonial extravagance. The incident between Gray and Davidson probably didn't occur.

4  The question as to why so much wood was being cut at Dartmouth Cove and not being delivered to the other side of the harbour was raised in the Governor's correspondence. I have created a possible answer.

5  H.M. Council minutes.

6  The hearing and sentences are as recorded in the Council minutes. The actions and storyline are created.

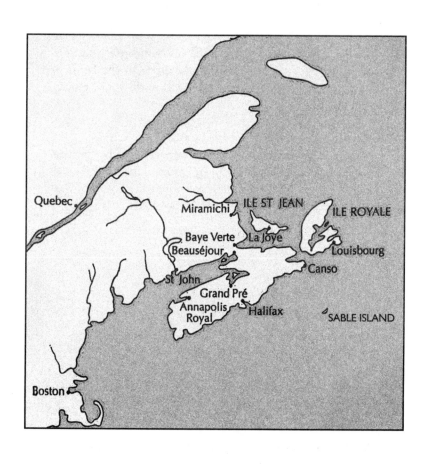

## Chapter Three

### *Spring 1751*
### *Near Sable Island*
### *Off Nova Scotia*

Morning twilight was a time of tension for the crew of His Majesty's sloop of war, *Albany*, John Rous, captain.

During the hours of darkness, vessels could approach each other without being aware of one another's presence. At sunrise unpleasant things happened to the ill prepared and the unwary. Captain Rous was neither. He always mustered his crew a half-hour before sunrise. Assuming battle readiness each morning was routine on *H.M.S. Albany*. Ship's guns were loaded, primed, and run out. Flintlocks were attached to the cannon touchholes, through which the cannon were ignited, and cocked. The lanyards snaked across the sanded decks to callused hands. Lit fuses hung over the sides of water barrels for quick use in case of a flintlock misfire. Arms lockers were open so personal weapons could be issued to the ship's crew at a moment's notice. England was not at war—at least not in home waters—but here, off the shores of Nova Scotia, a French ship was an enemy ship at all times. *H.M.S. Albany* was ready as the sun came up.

The deck was brightened by the rosy glow of the newborn sun. Captain Rous had appeared on the quarterdeck and was searching the horizon with the ship's bring 'em near. Rous was the slightest and shortest of the officers on the deck, often making it necessary for him to move more bulky bodies out of his way when he wanted to observe something. He did this now. As he pivoted on the spot, the officers moved quickly so as not to block his view.

The water at the point of sunrise had been scanned as the first points of light brightened the day. Now First Lieutenant Evans, assured the brilliance of the rising sun would hide no threat, ordered other quadrants searched for possible enemies. Evans held on to his hat as he leaned back and called to the seaman perched on the pedestal near the top of the mainmast.

"Lookout!"

"Aye, sir!" came the answer from aloft.

"Scan western quadrant," said Evans. Searching the quadrant that was the best possible escape route was prudent. *Albany* would want to retreat west to Halifax if she found herself confronted by a superior force.

"Clear, sir!"

"Continue search."

"Aye, sir."

The lookout called out, "A sail!"

"Say where!" Evans snapped his head back to see which direction the lookout was pointing. His hat tumbled off and plopped on the deck. Awkwardly, Evans contorted himself so he could pick up his hat and still keep his eyes on the lookout.

Raising his arm, the lookout pointed. "Starboard beam! Ten miles, sir!"

Rous turned to face southeast where the strange vessel was reported to be. "Secure guns for manoeuvring," Rous ordered. "Close gun ports."

Using colourful language the gunnery mate encouraged the gun crews, additionally applying several blows with a knotted rope to the back of a sailor who had lost his footing. When the gun ports were closed and there was no danger of seawater entering, Captain Rous ordered, "Port your helm!" He raised his glass, and adjusted the focus.

Sailing Master Izzard ordered the duty watch into motion. "Man the sheets!" The port watch hustled to lay hands on the ropes that controlled the sails. In mere seconds Izzard was satisfied that all was in readiness for the ship to alter its direction, and he gave the order, "Ready to come about!"

Rous spoke again. "Head straight for him, Mr. Izzard."

"Helmsman," called Izzard. "Port your helm!"

"Aye, sir!"

In the light breeze *H.M.S. Albany* heeled as she rapidly turned to the right and headed downwind to meet the oncoming vessel.

The lookout called, "She's a brigantine, sir!"

Rous had her in the glass now. "She's got a French look to her." He lowered the glass. "Show our colours, Evans."

The second lieutenant had anticipated the order and had already clewed up the Jack to the flag halyard.

"Raise the colours!"

As the English flag began snapping in the breeze, Izzard ordered the helmsman to ease. The helmsman reduced the rate of turn of *Albany* until she had regained an even keel.

"Steady." Izzard nodded to the helmsman, then he raised his voice, "Make fast your sheets!" He turned to face his captain. "On course, sir, steering east southeast."

Rous nodded, and studied the oncoming ship through the glass. "Either she hasn't seen us or she doesn't mind being intercepted by an English warship," he mused.

"Is she armed, sir?" asked Izzard.

"I can't see. She's hull down." Rous kept his eye glued to his glass. "There she goes! Raise all canvas! She's a warship and she's turning to make a run for it."

Once Izzard had all sails set, he stated the obvious. "She's bigger than we are."

"Yes, and she can probably throw more iron than we can, but for some reason she's turned tail."

"If she has more guns, sir ..."

Rous sent the second lieutenant to fetch the sextant and addressed Izzard, "Why are we chasing her? Because she's French and we're English." Rous, a New Englander, had a wry sense of humour. "Our first problem is to catch her. With her brigantine rig, she can sail downwind faster than we can. If she means to avoid us, this is the way to do it."

Second Lieutenant Foster returned with the astrolabe in his hand. He unwrapped it from its waterproof covering and stood waiting for the captain's orders.

"Measure the angle of the Frenchie's masts," Rous said.

Bracing his feet, Foster sighted through the sextant and found the angle between the horizon and the top of the other ship's masts: sixteen degrees, seven minutes, and fourteen seconds.

"There're her colours, sir. She's French." Foster pointed at the other ship. "A gun crew is working her stern chaser."

Rous replied, "They might try a shot or two, hoping to slow us down. Measure her again, Foster."

Foster braced his feet. He jumped and spoiled his measurement when the sound of the other ship's swivel gun reached *Albany*. None of the Englishmen knew where the shot had fallen. Foster sighted again. "Sixteen degrees and seven, sir."

The masts were getting smaller. The Frenchman was pulling away from them.

Rous gave the brigantine a last look, stamped his feet as if to get the blood circulating in his legs, and snapped out a series of commands: "Stand down the gun crews. Port watch, continue the chase. Ship's company to be fed."

Rous crossed the deck to the companionway hatch leading to his cabin. "You have the deck, Mr. Evans. Call me if there is any change." Then he muttered, "These boots are damned uncomfortable." The captain closed the hatch behind him.

Evans and Foster exchanged a knowing look because, from their experience, every time the captain had decided to put himself and his ship in harm's way, he complained about his boots and exchanged them for deerskin moccasins.

"Somehow, that Frenchie's gonna get it," said Evans.

Foster nodded his head in agreement.

* * *

By midday, the angle of the French ship's masts had dwindled to ten degrees and forty-six. When the port watch was relieved, there was no joshing between the sailors. There didn't seem to be much point in chasing this Frenchie since he could sail faster in this wind and direction. Besides, on this heading they were getting closer and closer to the graveyard of the Atlantic, Sable Island.

When Foster took noon sights on the sun, Captain Rous also took a sun shot. The two officers compared readings, and the crew strained to see if the captain was wearing his naval boots. It was difficult to tell; Foster was standing between the captain and the rest of the crew.

When Foster went below to plot the ship's position on the navigation chart using dead reckoning and the information from the astrolabe, the crew was able to get a good view of their captain. He was wearing moccasins. Suddenly an air of excitement and anticipation infused the crew; *Albany* was going hunting.

Foster returned. "Sir," he reported, "at midday we were ten nautical miles from the first of the Sable Island shoals."

"Our friend will have to turn soon," said Rous. "He's closer to them than we are. What do you think, boys? Time to cut him off?"

Without waiting for an answer, Rous gave the command: "Port your helm ten degrees, Mr. Izzard."

Izzard repeated the order. "Helmsman, port your helm ten degrees."

The helmsman, conscious that the ship's officers were watching his every move, made sure both hands stayed on the ship's wheel as he adjusted their course to a more southerly heading. *Albany* responded nicely, putting the target ship on her port bow about ten degrees.

Foster grinned when he realized what the captain had been doing. "You've been herding him against Sable Island. He's going to have to come starboard and run along the line of shoals." Foster did a little jig. When he noticed Rous's frown he stopped quickly. "I'm sorry, sir. Guess I got a trifle carried away."

Rous didn't seem to have noticed. "If I were that French captain," he reflected, "I wouldn't turn into the wind to run to the north because *Albany* sails better in that direction than he does. We'd catch him for sure."

"So he'll turn to starboard, and we'll get closer to him by the minute!" Foster was quite pleased with himself. He paused. "She has more firepower than we do."

"Yes, and if he takes a course parallel to us, he could cause us a great deal of damage before we bag him." Rous enjoyed developing the tactical skills of his officers; he was a patient teacher. "But he could have done that this morning. Why has he been running all day?"

Neither officer had an answer for him.

Rous studied the other ship through the glass. "She's reducing sail but maintaining her course into the shoals. Looks like she has anticipated our tactics. Mr. Evans, resume our original chase heading."

"Helmsman," ordered Evans, "starboard the helm, ten degrees."

"Helm starboard ten degrees, aye, sir."

Foster could see movement near the prow of the brigantine. "They have a man taking soundings. Damn! They're going into the shoals!"

"At least far enough in to cause us some concern," the captain said and rubbed his hands together. "Muster ship's crew, Mr. Evans."

The enemy had turned into the wind, her bow pointing northwest. When her sails luffed, flapping, the Englishmen could hear the chains of her bow anchor rattle. If *Albany* wanted to fight, it would be on the Frenchman's terms.

To make matter worse for *Albany*, the wind was dropping. Momentum was carrying *Albany* along but her approach to the other ship was slowing. In the meantime, the French had laid out a stern anchor. Men were over the side attaching spring lines to allow the ship's broadside to be directed through a wider arc by lengthening and shortening the spring lines on the anchors. Gun ports were open, and the French crew was serving the guns.

"With their spring lines and anchors," said Rous, "they'll be able to manoeuvre their ship enough to deliver a broadside effectively while we will have very little wind to sail and fight our ship. And they've anchored up against the shoals. Smart! They'll only have to defend one side. Because of the shoals, we can't attack from the other side."

Captain Rous was intrigued by the tactical problem facing him. Challenging a larger ship wasn't something Rous did on a regular basis, but he honestly believed that a determined show of aggression was worth an extra broadside in any encounter. This time, the opposing vessel had sought flight rather than confrontation, and Rous had begun pursuit of the ship almost as a reflex action. Now, going over the possibilities in his mind, he was wary of the larger ship.

It was true that Rous had forced the brigantine into the position she was in. However, he had anticipated a running fight along the edge of the shoals where the English ship could intercept the brigantine quickly. In such circumstances the French vessel would be forced to sail parallel to the shoals and *Albany*, by increasing the angle of approach, could have cut the brigantine off. Then it would have been up to the superior English gun crews to subdue the more numerous French guns. It was no small matter and fraught with hazard, but Rous had been confident of the result.

Now the French captain had tucked himself amongst the shoals and had rigged his ship so the hull could swing from left to right of centre, thus increasing by a large measure the field of fire for his broadsides. Rous likened it to a farmer trying to pick up a porcupine: the porcupine keeps moving its dangerous end towards the farmer. Somehow, the farmer had to pin the porcupine so he could grab its head and subdue the beast.

Rous's man, Wimper, brought the captain's battle sword and pistol and helped Rous strap them on. As Rous pulled the sword belt over his head he commanded, "Reduce sail! Break out the sweeps! Man the bow swivel gun!"

Wimper handed his captain a pair of leather gloves with metal studs on the backs. Rous slipped them on while the little man adjusted the pistol in the captain's belt. Then Wimper handed Rous a bandana. He took the captain's hat and stepped back to view the transformation. "Anything else, sir?"

Rous tied the bandana over his grey hair. "How many times is this, Wimper?"

"Seventeen battles, sir."

"It was at Louisbourg that bastard put up the white flag and then tried to trick us, wasn't it?"

"Yes, sir," said Wimper. "Tried to ram us at the last minute."

"How do you feel about this one, Wimper?"

"They aren't showing many men, sir. Maybe they're keeping them below and out of sight, waiting to surprise us when we attempt to board her."

Rous smiled at his personal servant. "You should have been the captain, Wimper. They *aren't* showing many men."

The captain took a chart from the first lieutenant. "They're settled in against the shoal. I bet their hull is touching bottom!" Rous stuck his finger on the map, "Think it's this one with the crescent shape?"

"It would be difficult to know, Captain."

Rous rubbed his chin thoughtfully. "Our French captain has taken careful soundings and approached the shoal slowly. On the other hand, we have to go in quickly under the threat of his cannon and take the distinct risk of touching bottom. If we get run up onto the shoal, he can adjust the angle of his ship with his spring lines and pound us to pieces. But ignoring that problem for the moment, when we're attacking we must ship our sweeps just before we fire, and while we still have momentum we must turn to present our broadside to him. As we turn, he'll rake us with his own broadside and cause us a great deal of havoc. He'll probably hit us with two broadsides before we'll be able to deliver one." Rous, regarding the doleful faces of his officers, laughed. "That's only what our Frenchie captain has *planned* for us."

Watching the crew install the sweeps, like very long oars, into notches in the bulwark between the guns, Rous decided to assign two men to each sweep, and ordered Foster to execute the plan. "Let's see if we can cause old Frenchie some heartburn. Evans, have Mr. Izzard lower all sails except one lower foresail."

"Aye, sir."

"Unship the sweeps and set up a measured beat," said Rous. "There's no rush about this. Frenchie isn't going anywhere."

"Aye, sir."

"Foster, I want a man with a strong voice on the mainmast. I want to be warned of any activity on the deck of that ship."

"Aye, sir."

Rous paused. "It is possible he ran from us this morning because he doesn't have a full crew? He might not have enough men to sail his ship and fight at the same time." Rous smiled. "Foster, make sure your lookout keeps me well informed about movement on the enemy's decks."

"Aye, sir."

"Helmsman, take us into the shoaled waters as close as you can about a half mile astern. On my command, mind you."

"Aye, sir."

"Evans, have the starboard guns loaded with grapeshot. Tell Guns to order his crews to fire one at a time as their guns come to bear on the Frenchie. Load the port guns with ball. Depress them so they fire into the bugger's water line; the range won't be more than a hundred yards." Rous gave his first lieutenant a grin. "If we don't get them with the grape, we'll reverse course and sink them where they stand. Half the gun crews will be manning the sweeps, so the remaining gunners will serve both port and starboard guns."

"Aye, sir."

Rous raised his voice. "Midshipman Stevens!"

The call was taken up. "Mr. Stevens to the captain!"

From amidships the sound of running feet preceded the appearance before the captain of a young lad with coal-black curly hair.

"You've been bragging how well you shoot," said Rous.

"I can take the eye out of a squirrel at a thousand yards, sir!" acknowledged the young man.

"So you have often said, Stevens." Rous knew when men were young like this one they were full of piss and vinegar. He had to give it to Stevens; he was an excellent shot. "I've ordered the bow chaser to be manned. I want you to take command of the gun and be ready to use it when we get into range of that Frenchie."

"I can put a hole in her before …"

Rous didn't have time for brashness from this young officer. He ordered, "You will be silent, Mister!"

"Aye, sir! Sorry sir. I didn't mean to …"

Rous gave the midshipman what the other officers called his "evil eye." Mister Stevens promptly shut his mouth.

"*Albany* is going to come up on that vessel from her stern," Rous said. "Your job will be to prevent any of her crew from adjusting the spring lines."

"Aye, sir," said Stevens.

"Use grapeshot," the captain instructed. "Be sure to eliminate any enemy crewman attempting to manoeuvre that ship so they can fire a broadside into us."

"Aye, sir!"

Rous waved off the midshipman. Stevens touched his forehead with his knuckles in salute and ran forward to where the gun crew was mounting the swivel gun on a bracket. Meanwhile, Lieutenant Foster was getting the sweeps into place. "Lift!"

Rous watched as the sixteen sweeps were lifted from the deck and turned by the sailors so that the blades were pointed at the sweep holes.

"Mount sweeps," Foster ordered.

The sweeps were pushed through the holes in the bulwarks until they had reached their balance point. Each sailor, standing amidships, held his sweep parallel to the deck so that the blade was clear of the water. Sixteen sailors waited for further instructions from the second lieutenant.

Foster informed Rous, "Ready to double the hands on the sweeps, Captain."

"Make it so, Foster," Rous said.

"Guns," Foster called to the gunnery mate.

"Aye, sir!"

"Second man to each sweep!"

"Aye, sir!" The gunnery mate was quick to obey. "Starboard gun crews, stand fast! Port gun crews, see to your secondary duties."

There was no confusion on the deck. The port crews stored their gun equipment where it could be rapidly acquired. Then a number of them reported to the arms locker and were issued personal arms. Sixteen gunners joined the men on the sweeps. When all was in readiness Evans called out, "Ship's company ready, Captain!"

*Albany*, with most of her sails furled, had been converted to a gunboat. Her purpose was to rain destruction on the chosen target, and when opposition had been suppressed, boarding parties would clear the enemy's decks and take possession of his ship. There would be no finesse and very little seamanship. Concentrated, accurate gunfire would win the day.

"Mr. Evans, take her in well to starboard if you please."
Rous smiled at his first lieutenant. "I don't want a plank of this
ship to be in the arc of his broadside."

"Aye, sir." Evans nodded to Foster. "Give us some way,
Mr. Foster."

"Unship sweeps!" Foster, nervous under the pressure, gave
an additional, redundant order, "Do not wet your sweeps!"

The men, two to a sweep and facing the rear of the ship,
extended the sweeps through the bulwark holes until they were
in the proper position—blades hovering a foot or two over the
water. When Foster saw the men were ready, he ordered,
"Sweep!" The men took two steps back.

Foster ordered, "Heave!" The sailors lowered the blades into
the water and put all of their weight and strength against the
oars. Foster counted out a cadence as the men moved forward,
straining against the weight of the oars. "One, two, three, four,
five, sweep!" On "sweep," the crews lifted the sweeps out of the
water. "One, two, three, four, five, heave!" At each count, the
men paced backwards. On "heave," they lowered the sweeps
and once again began the strenuous chore of pushing the oars.

First Lieutenant Evans waited until *Albany* had enough
way to answer the helm nicely, then ordered the helmsman to
port the helm thirty degrees. Slowly *Albany* turned to starboard, heading to a point about five hundred yards south of the
enemy ship.

Rous slapped his thigh. "We are committed now, Evans.
Foster! Work the sweeps as hard as you can!"

The tempo of the sweeps commands picked up considerably.

Rous observed the enemy ship though his eyeglass. He
wondered if the other captain would work his spring lines
right away. The French commander tried a broadside. It was
ragged but could have been deadly if *Albany*, with her hull
exposed, had been in range. Most of the balls fell short,
splashing harmlessly. Two balls ricocheted, bouncing until
they disappeared into the swells. The men of *Albany* heard the
hum of the nearer ball as it flew by.

Rous figured the French captain wanted to reload his guns
and start working his spring lines to change the arc of fire.

Since we can't hit him with our bow gun to stop his men work-ing the lines, Rous thought, *Albany* could be in a lot of trouble. Rous craned to see if his lookout was alert. "Lookout!"

"Aye, sir!"

"What are they doing?"

"Serving the guns, sir." The lookout added, "I see shoals, sir, dead ahead. Gettin' shallow!"

Rous heard concern in the man's voice. If the French cap-tain didn't change his arc, perhaps *Albany* could cut the corner and make the turn to the north sooner.

"Starboard the helm," Rous said.

"Aye, sir."

Rous considered before adding, "Twenty degrees."

"Aye, sir."

"Evans! Go forward and see if Stevens is ready. Don't let the little bugger fire too soon!"

"Aye, sir."

The lookout called, "Some of the crew are formed up on the deck like soljers!"

"Are they working the lines, yet?"

"No, sir!"

"Starboard the helm, seventy degrees!" This would bring *Albany* onto the stern of the enemy more quickly, but if they began working their spring lines the French wouldn't have far to turn their ship to hit *Albany* with a broadside. Rous hoped to make a stern approach and avoid that risk.

"They took a crew from their port guns," the lookout cried. "Manning their stern gun, sir!"

Rous made a mental note to ensure the man aloft received an extra tot of rum when this was over. Evans returned to his side.

"Is Stevens ready?" Rous asked.

"Aye, sir."

Rous glared at the enemy ship. The swivel guns of both ships were in range of one another now. There was still no sign of sailors working the brigantine's spring lines; Stevens should be able to take out the other gun crew. The French were still mounting and loading their gun, but *Albany* had been ready from the beginning. Rous could see Stevens hunched over the gun, babying it like a fowling piece, and expected to see smoke discharge from his bow gun. Why hadn't Stevens fired? The lookout must have been wondering, too. "They're ready, sir," he called down. "They're taking aim. No other movement on their deck."

Rous tugged his jacket down at his waist as if he was pulling on armour. "Why doesn't Stevens shoot?" Rous asked his first lieutenant crossly.

Evans's face expression turned ghastly, and he croaked, "Because I told him not to shoot until he saw sailors working the spring lines!"

Rous sprang forward, shouting, "Take out their gun, Stevens! Stevens, fire!"

Stevens's weapon discharged, and the smoke from the swivel gun blanketed the prow of *Albany*. From somewhere up forward, there was the impact of the French shot. In the almost still air, the movement of *Albany* would clear the smoke away shortly.

The lookout, above the smoke, called, "A direct hit, sir. Their gun crew is down!"

Rous smiled and said, "That little bugger has earned himself an extra rum tot as well."

*Albany* shuddered and then moved on again.

"Should we have a leadsman sounding the depth of water, sir?" Evans pointed starboard where about one hundred feet off the beam of *Albany* the water was a lighter colour. The swells were breaking as they passed over the shoals. Both officers realized *Albany* had just touched bottom. The next touch could spell the end of the ship and the death or capture of the crew.

"Sail on," Rous said with more confidence than he felt. "We need less water under us then the Frenchie does." Rous figured there was either enough water under *Albany*, or there wasn't. Measuring wouldn't make a difference. The captain gauged the distance to where *Albany* could turn to port and rake the decks of the other ship with grapeshot. It wasn't far now.

"She's *Saint Francis*, Captain."[1] Evans read the name from the stern of the brigantine.

From above came the news, "Their crews are working the spring lines, sir!"

Good man, that lookout, Rous thought. Now Stevens can do his work again. Our starboard guns will clear their decks, and we'll have a trophy to take into Halifax Harbour. The smoke had finally cleared from the bow gun. Stevens and his crew were down, their bodies torn and bloody from the grapeshot fired from the stern gun of *Saint Francis*. Both crews had fired almost instantaneously. The French gunner had been as accurate as poor Stevens.

"Evans, get a crew up there to man the bow gun." Even as he gave the order, Rous knew it was too late to bring the gun into play. "Belay that, Evans! Mr. Foster! More speed, if you please!" Rous could hear Foster calling the beat but couldn't see him. Two legs stuck out either side of the mainmast; the grape had hit Foster. He was down but still doing his job. The sweeps moved faster.

The French crew was working the spring lines. Slowly but surely the entire broadside of the brigantine was being brought to bear on the English ship as *Saint Francis* pivoted on its anchors.

Rous judged the rate of swing of the French ship to its best firing position. The Frenchie had fired early before, but at this range firing early could still have a devastating effect on *Albany*. He could see the gun ports of the other ship but refrained from counting them. For the effect Rous needed, he had to be at close range; *Albany's* guns were loaded with grape. Now he could look right into the mouths of the cannons. He held his breath to keep from giving the command to turn.

Evans put Rous's thoughts into words. "What is he waiting for? He could get us right now."

Rous nodded his head in agreement.

From aloft came the call, "They're finished with the spring lines. The crew is running to the guns."

So, that was it! The French ship was seriously under-manned. "Starboard your helm," roared the captain. "Port sweeps to backwater. Now! Starboard sweeps, ship your sweeps! Now! Starboard guns, fire as you bear!"

*H.M.S. Albany* turned rapidly, and her first gun fired seconds later. The French gun crews were hurt but they still served their weapons. Rous commanded, "Port sweeps, ship your sweeps! Now! Helmsman, steady on!"

The second *Albany* gun delivered a deadly cargo of iron balls that took out great chunks of anything in their paths. There were few French sailors still standing. A French gun fired. The solid shot passed through *Albany's* rigging but did very little harm. Again *Albany* fired; then again and again until the whole starboard broadside had been delivered across the decks of *Saint Francis*.

The ensuing silence was deafening. Both ships were covered with smoke.

"Unship sweeps," Rous commanded. "Bring us around, Mr. Evans, so our port guns come to bear."

"Aye, sir!"

Evans saw that Foster had been wounded; his white silk shirt was soaked with blood. It was Evans then who ordered the starboard sweeps to backwater, while the port sweeps rowed furiously ahead. *Albany's* port guns were brought to bear as quickly as possible. In a matter of minutes *Albany* was sitting about two hundred feet parallel to the enemy ship, all port guns loaded with solid shot and aimed at the brigantine's waterline.

Rous detected movement on the enemy's deck, and signalled to Evans. Evans, using a hailer, challenged *Saint Francis*. "We are His Britannic Majesty's warship *Albany*, Captain John Rous commanding. Do you yield?"

There was no response. Rous called to his sailor on the mainmast pedestal. "Lookout! What do you see?"

"They're waving a red flag, sir."

Rous shook his head in disbelief. "A red flag!" He quickly considered his options. He must not put *Albany* at further risk. "Mr. Evans! Fire your broadside!"

"Aye, sir!" Evans stepped forward where the gun crews could see him and raised his arm. Before he could signal, the call came from aloft, "She's struck her colours, sir!" The lookout pointed at the other ship. "The red flag was a white shirt covered with blood."

Rous breathed a sigh of relief; he hadn't really wanted to sink the brigantine. "Take us in, Evans. Put an armed party aboard that ship. Let's shake a leg. We don't want to be here when the wind comes up."

"Aye, sir," said Evans. "As soon as she's secure you mean to put tow lines to her, Captain?"

"Yes. We'll use *Albany's* sweeps to get both ships away from the shoals. Hopefully there'll be a breeze later this evening, and we can sail toward Halifax."

Foster, his face grey from pain and loss of blood, reported to the captain. "Sorry, sir. I didn't mean to let you down, but I picked up a piece of shrapnel. Bones took it out of my chest muscles. I can resume my duties now if you permit me."

"Good man, Foster," said Rous. "You did well. We all did well. I can't wait to sail that pretty brigantine into Halifax."

"Will they give us prize money, sir?" asked Foster.

"Since there's no war with France, perhaps not."

"The ship we took this spring was declared a prize. We got money for her."

"Aye, Foster," said Rous, "and it was good money. When she was sold, she brought a handsome price. It depends on the governor. He can direct prize money be paid or he can sell the ship and put the money in the government's coffers. But enough of this, Foster. If you're fit, get to work. Help Evans move both of these ships to Halifax."

"Aye, sir."

\* \* \*

Lieutenant Gray stood on Market Slip in all his finery; it was the first time he had worn his new uniform. In a letter to his uncle, Gray had asked that his new uniform accommodate a height of five feet, seven inches, a height he had anticipated he might reach by the time the uniform arrived from England. With increasing dismay, Gray had watched his height increase over the winter until he stood at almost five feet, nine inches. His lady friend, Molly Ferguson, a fisherman's daughter newly arrived from Massachusetts, had let out the seams of his old uniforms and added new material to the gaps caused by the increased breadth of his chest and shoulders. His britches had been the biggest problem. Molly had made him new ones that, while not the naval fashion, had not caused comment from the governor or his staff officers.

Gray was relieved, therefore, when he found that Uncle Charles, bless his heart, had allowed for the effects of a vigorous life and plentiful although not necessarily good food on a young man's constitution, and Molly had done the rest. Sub-Lieutenant Gray was smartly turned out for his inspection of the sawmill on the other side of the harbour.

It had been a nettlesome problem since the governor had personally picked Major Ezekiel Gilman to manage the sawmill and had also appointed him guard commander. The major had failed on both counts: there had been no production of planks and, during the massacre, the guard had been of no help to the attacked men. After the massacre, the governor had belatedly removed the regular troops and assigned Rangers to the blockhouse with Captain Clapham in command. Now Major Gilman was responsible only for the sawmill and the Rangers were expected to provide better protection for the settlement.

Gray frowned as he watched the harbour craft approach Market Slip to ferry him to Mill Cove, or Dartmouth as it was now called. He considered the situation. There was still no production of planks and the Rangers seemed to be more on the lookout for inspecting officers from the governor's staff than they were for raids from Indians. The Rangers had fallen into the habit of placing two or three sentries where they had a good view of the harbour while the rest of them performed duties inside the blockhouse. With the approach of any boat, the forest rang with the sound of axes, Rangers appeared at the entrance to the blockhouse fully equipped for patrol, redcoats paced their sentry walks, and tradesmen could be seen energetically inspecting the mill machinery for faults. Trees were being cut, but where was the timber going? Gray had been sent to find out.

The harbour craft was almost at the pier. Gray spent his last few moments before going aboard gazing up the hill at

Halifax. Near the old tree, Joshua Mauger had collected a crowd as he usually did once or twice a week at this time of morning. He was selling three Negroes: two men in chains and a young girl. With the bustle and noise around Market Slip, Gray couldn't hear any of Mauger's sales talk or the bidding, but he watched one of the buyers reach over and pinch the girl's chest. She stepped back and turned away, and Gray saw that her hands were tied behind her back. Without interrupting his sales pitch, Mauger took her firmly by her hair to allow a more thorough inspection by the prospective buyer.

Mauger was a lowlife if ever there was one.[2] The man was into everything. Gray could smell the half-sour odour from Mauger's distillery. The governor knew Joshua Mauger was a smuggler and meant to catch him. Good luck! The governor might have his whipping post, but Mauger had his rum. If smugglers were caught, they took their stripes because Mauger bought their continued silence with more rum.

The harbour craft had arrived at the pier. Two Dartmouth settlers disembarked even before the boat had docked. They were a sturdy-looking pair and seemed very familiar with boat handling; one of them took the sternfast ashore, made a quick knot, and hurried on after his companion. Gray suspected they were fishermen.

Boarding the shallop, a small boat used only in shallow waters, Gray continued his ruminations. The governor had gotten his wish. Cornwallis had begged the Lords of Trade for a better type of settler. The most recent arrivals were mostly fishermen from the English town of Dartmouth in Devon. Some three hundred colonists had arrived on *Alderney* in late August 1750, and Cornwallis hadn't known where to put them. There wasn't enough room within the defences on the Halifax side of the harbour, so it was decided to settle them at Mill Cove where there was a blockhouse and a guard of Rangers and redcoats.

Since the settlers had been kept on board *Alderney* until the matter was settled, they had streamed ashore without complaint and gone right to work, glad to be off the ship. They seemed like a hard-working, no-nonsense bunch—the kind of settler that Cornwallis had dreamed of. Consequently, the governor was pleased with the progress being made on the Dartmouth side of the harbour. Now, if the matter of the sawmill lumber production could only be resolved ... and that was Gray's job.

William looked across the harbour. He recalled that Charles Morris, the surveyor, had laid out a town plan of oblong-shaped blocks with building lots fifty by one hundred feet. Gray could see the resulting grid of the settlement on the side of the first low hill. He realized that when the houses were finished the sawmill would no longer be visible from the harbour. Gray settled himself on one of the boat's seats, called thwarts, and waited for the oarsman to get the shallop under way.

"Dartmouth, Lieutenant Gray?"

Startled, Gray turned to look at the oarsman. "I know you! You're Seaman Denham, from *Sphinx.*"

"Aye, sir. Able Seaman Denham, late of His Majesty's Service, now Issac Denham, if it pleases you, sir." He touched his forelock with his knuckle and then grinned. "Hard to break the old habits, sir."

"What happened, Denham, er, Issac? *Sphinx* left months ago. Are you adrift?"

Denham undid the sternfast and painter. He pushed the shallop away from the pier. Picking up an oar, he dropped it into the nick at the stern, and standing, began sculling. The boat quickly slipped away from the shore toward Dartmouth.

"Governor Cornwallis wanted volunteers to man some of the boats used to peddle provisions to ships anchored offshore. Bumboats we calls 'em, sir." With a huge grin, Denham added, "Captain Lloyd wasn't very pleased that I was recruited right off his deck, so to speak, but here I am, sir." Denham hauled a small sail up the mast set through a hole in the forward thwart. He used the oar as a boom held fast against the sail and the gunwale by pressure from the sheets. The sail filled and hardened, and the shallop continued briskly on to Dartmouth.

"That'll be a ha'penny for your passage, sir." While the officer searched for the money in his pockets and handed over several farthings, Denham talked about Dartmouth.

"Me and Mary Clark ... Mary's me woman,"[3] Denham gave another one of his big grins. "She has a double-building lot near the end of town." Denham pointed to the shore nearest to Halifax. "That's the town front. End of town is about two hundred yards from the sawmill down t' the cove. Mary and me are building a house close t' the beach where I drop me passengers. Most days a breeze blows up the harbour. Now that the trees have been cut down, the black flies and mosquitoes are blown away. Makes a good spot t' live."

Gray saw a chance to gain some information. "Most of the trees have been cut down. Where did the lumber go?"

Denham gave his big grin again. "That's why your visit this afternoon? You checkin' up on Major Gilman and 'is boys?"

Pulling the sheets a little tighter Denham steered around the point, and now Gray could see the whole cove. The two of them watched the activity at the end of the cove. Rangers travelled the path to the tree line. Two redcoats patrolled back and forth near the gate. Several woodsmen were sharpening axes, while in front of the sawmill three tradesmen were fitting a rope through a pulley and tying it to the end of a large saw blade. They were preparing to hoist the blade back into the sawmill as Denham ran the boat onto the stony beach.

"Welcome t' Dartmouth." Denham's easy grin made Gray feel especially welcome.

A pole had been driven into the beach just above the tidemark. Denham looped the painter over the top of the pole and gestured that Gray should follow him. There was a small rocky knoll overlooking the beach. From there it was obvious from the pattern of the surveyor's pegs that the street, if it were continued, would go right into the water and straight over the knoll. A cross street was staked generally parallel to the water toward the sawmill.

"That's our place over there." The walls were made of logs and saplings driven into the ground on end. Planks sheathed most of the front of the cottage, and the roof was steeply pitched so that rain or snow would not linger upon it. Two small windows in the front were covered with well-cured leather upon which oil had been spread to make it translucent. "Soon we'll have glass for our windows," Denham said with some pride.

"Mary, I'm back! We've company, woman!" Pushing his way through the leather strips that hung down over the open door, Denham was met by a tall woman wearing a leather apron. She kissed her man lightly, and stepped through the leather strips to welcome the naval officer.

"You're welcome here, sir. I'm Mary Clark."

"My pleasure, ma'am. Lieutenant William Gray." Gray reached out but she held her hand back.

"My hands are a mess," Mary Clark explained. "I've been moulding shot for our muskets. Come in, please. Issac, don't forget your manners. Offer the dear man some of Mauger's rum. We'll have supper if you'll but visit a while with us. I've made shepherd's pie. Excuse me while I put things away." She disappeared into the cottage.

* * *

After a good meal, Gray again brought up the matter that most concerned him. He said it was his duty to find out for the governor about the sawmill's lack of production.

Mary Clark unhesitatingly said that she would tell Gray everything he needed to know. With a devilish little smile, she began. "Governor Cornwallis gets all of the wood the sawmill produces. Every tree that's been cut in Dartmouth has been delivered to the governor."

"Not so," protested Gray. "He hasn't seen a stick of it! The governor has been forced to buy wood from the New Englanders at a hefty price."

"That's true." Mary slapped her knee and laughed as if at a grand joke. She waited for Gray to catch on.

While Gray puzzled over it, Mary gave him some help. "New Englanders arrive here with their load of lumber and sell it in Halifax. At night, they slip over here to our cove—which is plenty deep for their ships to come right to shore—and buy lumber from our sawmill at rock-bottom prices from Major Gilman."

Gray nodded his head in agreement. "Yes, I know it's a fine, deep cove."

"The ships leave Halifax Harbour," she explained, "but soon they're back with a fresh load of lumber for which the governor pays top price. Gilman gets to keep all the money paid on this side of the harbour, and the New Englanders make a big profit with hardly any effort by selling it on the other side."

"We're buying our own lumber back from the New Englanders?" Gray felt sick as he considered the implications of what he had just heard. He shook his head. "That might have worked while Major Gilman was in charge of the guards and the sawmill, but that changed last year. Surely, Captain Clapham and his Rangers can't be a part of this scheme, too!"

"Of course Clapham's part of the fraud! They all share in the loot," Mary exclaimed. "Even the settlers get something out of it. Just look at the front of our house, lovely planking we didn't pay a penny for."

Silence filled the cabin. Finally Gray asked quietly, "Why are you telling me this?"

Mary Clark leaned back against Denham's chest and stroked his arm. "I love this man and want us to be together for a long, long time. When the governor finds out about this scheme ..." She picked her words carefully. "The governor hanged a man for petty burglary last week. I don't want us hanged for a few planks."

They talked and enjoyed a few drinks until the afternoon shadows had lengthened considerably. Gray got up to leave. "I must be getting back to Halifax. Thank you for the meal and the drinks." He took Mary's hand and raised it to his lips. "Thank you, ma'am, for your hospitality."

Mary dropped a little curtsey. "Thank you, Lieutenant. I'll look forward to seeing you again."

"On the matter that we discussed, I'll gather proof of Gilman's scheme and present it to the governor. You'll be protected," Gray promised.

As they stepped outside, Mary pointed with pride to a little garden and said, "I've planted some chestnuts. Someday, our children will sit out here in the shade of a spreading chestnut tree and watch the boats in the cove, enjoying a breeze just like this one."

Denham gave Mary a hug. "And we'll be right with 'em."

Mary and the two men strolled to the knoll.[4] She sat down on the rock as Denham made ready to leave. "You won't try to come back tonight, will you, Issac?" she asked.

"I'll be back in about an hour," Denham said. "Leave a lantern on the knoll for me, darlin'." He lifted his gaze further up the hill. The Ranger sentries had moved down to where they could see Mary's cottage. "Ha! Take a look, Lieutenant. They're waiting for you to leave."

"They're keeping a watch on me?" asked Gray. "How many are there?"

"Three of them, but now I can only see two. Robert Carney, the one at the top of the hill, must have gone back to his regular post. Ferguson and Philipson[5] are a nosy pair. They'll hang around until we're gone."

The men saw movement further up the hill. "Must be hunters," Denham commented, dismissing both the guards and the strangers from his mind.

Gray continued to watch. A third hunter could now be seen walking down the hill toward the houses. The nearest hunter waved to someone at the front of the settlement. Gray looked and so did the guard. No one was there to return the wave. Gray looked back to where the man had waved. The hunter had run forward to the guard and was supporting him. The guard had dropped his musket and was clutching his throat. The hunter seemed to be helping the guard to the ground.

"Issac, something's wrong," said Gray.

"What happened to Philipson?" Mary, gathering up her skirts, ran up the hill to help the guard.

Denham dropped the boat ropes on the ground. "No, Mary!" He scanned the area. There was lots of commotion but no guards. He leaped up the bank and climbed the knoll, running as fast as he could. He didn't recognize the face of the man who stepped back as Mary reached the fallen Ranger. Denham kept running.

Mary knelt down beside Philipson. She made a small sound when the stranger struck the back of her neck with an axe. She fell across Philipson's body. He raised the axe to strike another blow but hesitated, as he became aware of Denham's furious charge.

"Acadians!" Denham cried as he threw himself at the intruder, knocking the man to the ground. Ignoring the Acadian, Denham lifted Mary to look in her face. Her head was nearly severed and kept falling away to one side or the other. There was so much blood. He was laying her down gently when the Acadian swung his axe at Denham's neck. Denham dodged the blow and the axe was pulled out of the Acadian's hand when it caught in the shoulder of Issac's leather jacket. The blade must have cut into flesh because Issac grunted and clutched his shoulder.

Gray hurtled at the enemy, smashing the Acadian on the side of the head with his pistol.

Denham jumped on top of the man. He looked once more at Mary's lifeless body and then drove the Acadian's axe into the middle of the man's forehead. Denham knelt and started to cry.

"Come on! There're Indians between the blockhouse and us. Make for the cottage!" Gray ran a few steps but could see the Indians were already inside the cottage. He returned to Denham's side.

"We have to make a run for the boat!" He pulled hard on Denham's arm to get him to stand. Denham didn't move.

Twenty or thirty Indians and several white men were running toward them. A musket was fired from the fort. One of the raiders yelped and suddenly sat down.

"Denham! Launch the boat," cried Gray.

Denham snapped out of it and moved quickly. His wounded arm flopping uselessly, he followed William as they raced down the hill toward the beach. Gray tripped but regained his balance. God! There were Indians running along the beach to cut them off! He could hear Denham right behind him. It would be close, but he thought they would get to the boat first. There was a roar of angry voices from up the hill. The enemy must have discovered their comrade with an axe buried in his face.

Gray and Denham had reached the knoll when Gray heard a screech right behind them. He spun around in time to see an

Indian throw himself forward, catch Denham's foot, and hold on. Denham went down hard with a grunt.

Without thinking, Gray ran back past the prostrate Denham and jammed the pistol into the Indian's chest. The man knocked the weapon out of the way, but not before it had discharged a ball into his armpit. The Indian howled with pain and fell back.

Grabbing Denham by the arm, Gray jumped to the beach. Fortunately the boat wasn't tied. Denham ran to the bow and began pushing the boat across the gravel. Gray pushed from the port side with all his might. When the boat was in the water and moving with the flow from the millstream, Gray threw himself over the gunwale. He was face down in the boat and felt the boat shift as Denham boarded too. They could make it!

Indians were in the water, grouped around the shallop, trying to stop it. Gray had to get the boat further away from the shore! He sat up to give Denham a hand with the oars but came face to face with the crimson-and-black painted face of a Micmac warrior! It wasn't Denham who had clambered on board!

The Indian stood up to get a better swing with his axe, rocking the shallop. A second Indian had been crawling over the bow but lost his balance and fell back into the water. Gray threw his pistol at the figure towering over him. The painted face disappeared over the side. Gray grabbed an oar and beat at the Indians in the water. He poled the oar against the bottom. The oar was wrenched out of his hand. Desperately he looked around for the second oar and found it just as another hideous face came over the bow. The man ducked and fell back into the water before Gray had a chance to complete his swing. Suddenly he was alone in the boat some distance from the shore.

Gray sat on the forward thwart. Splinters of wood flew into his face followed closely by the noise of a musket shot. He ducked down into the bottom of the shallop. Several more shots were fired, but none of them hit the boat. He raised his head.

A howl came from the beach. Twenty or more Indians were making violent gestures at Gray. He hastily searched the water for more of the enemy but found none. He returned his attention to the beach where the howling continued. He couldn't see Denham.

Mary's cottage was burning. In the light of the fire he could see a settler standing very still with his arms around his wife and child. The little boy had his face buried against his father's leg. Gray thought surely the Rangers would attempt a rescue of the family, but the blockhouse was dark and battened down, ready to repel an attack.

The Indians didn't go anywhere near the blockhouse. The largest group worked its way down the streets of Dartmouth burning and killing as they went. There was some resistance at each house, but the end result was always the same—fire—the settlers coming out or staying inside, dying in either case.

The small family standing by Mary's burning house looked pathetically helpless. The soldiers weren't coming to the family's rescue, although in the light of the fire the family was easily visible to those safely tucked inside the blockhouse walls.

Where was Denham? He had been on the stern of the boat. Gray checked the water again: no Denham, no Indians. Another loud howl from the beach caught Gray's attention. Denham, surrounded by Indians, stood with his hands tied in front and a pole threaded through his arms and behind his back. An Indian stood on either side holding the ends of the pole in place. Denham was trapped. One of the Indians reached up to Denham's face and made sawing motions. Denham screamed.

Extending his arm, the Indian held something out either for Gray to see or to offer it to him. The bloody object fell to the beach. The wound on the side of Denham's head told Gray it was an ear.

With ritual slowness, the Indian cut off the other ear and held it out. This time the gestures were defiant; he was taunting Gray to come and stop the torture. Gray tore his eyes from the ghastly scene.

Gray looked up again to see the Indian disembowel what was left of Able Seaman Issac Denham. The Indians stepped away, let go of the pole, and allowed Denham's body to drop. Before they left the beach, there was one last howl from the

Indians. One of them brandished what Gray assumed could only be Denham's scalp.

Now it was the small family's turn. Gray put the remaining oar in the stern nick and clumsily sculled the shallop toward the lights of Halifax. The screams of the child were the hardest to bear.

*Next morning*
*Dartmouth*

In front of one of the few Dartmouth homes still standing, a little boy stood stiff as a soldier reporting to his sergeant. "My name is John George Pyke.[6] I hid under the bed. Ma told me to stay under there until she came back. Then she went to help Da." John George Pyke's lip quivered, and he brushed his eyes with the back of his hand. "She went to help my da."

The soldier standing with the boy knelt down to the youngster's level. "I'm glad you waited until we got here before you came out. You were a good lad to do what your ma said." The soldier looked around. "I bet you're hungry. I've got a mate who never goes anywhere without some food in his pockets. Come on, we'll go get some."

The redcoat took the little fellow's hand and led him off to the beach. "We can come back later if you like. Right now let's get some food into that belly of yours."

"I'm not supposed to call it a belly."

The man laughed. "What are you supposed to call it?"

Lieutenant Gray and another soldier watched them go, the boy chattering away with the soldier. They looked at the crumpled bodies near the door of the cabin. The soldier asked, "Do you think he saw his parents?"

A commanding voice behind them made the soldier jump and quickly move off. "Look under the beds in the houses still standing. We might find more survivors that way." Gray didn't have to turn around to know it was Colour Sergeant Brown giving the orders.

"Permission to carry on, sir!" It wasn't a request; the sergeant was acknowledging the presence of an officer.

"Please do, Colour Sergeant." Lieutenant Gray returned the sergeant's salute.

"All right, you men, the boy says they are his mom and dad. Pick up Mister and Missus Pyke. Careful-like, now! Make sure the officer at the beach properly identifies them before you leave them. Report back here on the double when you're finished." The sergeant stuck his swagger stick under his arm. He made a smart right turn and saluted. Governor Cornwallis had walked up the street behind him.

"Thank you, Sergeant," said the governor. "Please carry on."

"Very good, sir." The sergeant pointed his swagger stick at one of the soldiers. "Don't just stand there, Cameron! No more harm can come to these people. It's all over for them. Now it's up to us to carry on. And smartly, Cameron! You search the Pyke home. Make sure the residence is empty. The rest of you men follow me up the street."

The soldier, a young lad with red hair and freckles, jumped to attention, "Yes, Colour Sergeant!" he said.

Governor Cornwallis and Lieutenant Gray were left standing in front of the Pyke house. The young soldier, Cameron, came out and hurried up the street after the sergeant.

"Dreadful scene, William," said Cornwallis.

Gray nodded his head but remained silent.

Governor Cornwallis put his hand on the young officer's arm. "You were here last night. I'm glad you escaped. Tell me what happened."

Pointing to the cleared area above the blockhouse, Gray related his tale. "Three white men walked past the blockhouse, each on a different path, toward the guards. The guards probably thought they were from the settlement and let them approach. They killed the guards, then my friends, and then the rest of the settlers." Gray turned away from the governor and gazed at the rocky knoll by the beach. With a choked voice he added, "They tortured Able Seaman Denham over there to try to persuade me to come ashore or to coax the soldiers out of the blockhouse. They tortured the Hayes family at the corner of the street, but the soldiers stayed inside the blockhouse."

Gray met the governor's sympathetic eyes. "Sir, I used my pistol on one of the Indians and threw it at another to knock him off the boat. I couldn't help Issac."

"He was a sailor," said the governor, "and knew the risks of war."

"There's no war! We aren't at war with France or any other country! This is peacetime!"

The governor regarded his officer with some concern. "Lieutenant Gray!"

Gray squared his shoulders and faced his commander.

"You couldn't do any more for Denham or these people." The governor watched as more bodies were carried to the beach. "Neither could I. This," the governor spread his hands indicating the destruction and death around them, "is warfare. I have seen this before, in Scotland. Identify your enemy, inflict as much of …" Cornwallis gestured again, "… this, as it takes to have them surrender."

Gray nodded his head. "Or until they are destroyed."

"Yes, yes." The governor studied the face of the young officer. "Yes. Until they are destroyed." He quickly looked away as he thought of Scotland. One of the clans his regiment subjugated was Gray? Could this man be … no, this man would have been a mere child. "Your father was a colonel?" He smiled as he asked the question.

"My uncle, sir. Retired in Nottinghamshire. I have him to thank for my position, sir."

Reassured, Cornwallis turned to watch Lieutenant Bulkeley as he made his way up the hill with long, loping strides.

Bulkeley saluted the governor. "The Pyke youngster is the only one we found alive. If any settlers lived through the attack, they fled or were taken prisoner. There's no one here but the boy."

Returning the salute, Cornwallis said, "William was witness to the attack. The Indian war party was led by Acadians." He took Bulkeley by the elbow, and they went downhill toward the beach. "Order the Rangers into the field. Tell them the bounty for enemy scalps is thirty pounds."

"That's almost double what we are paying for Indian scalps now!"

Cornwallis firmly replied. "Tell them the bounty is for *enemy* scalps."

Noting the absence of the young officer, Governor Cornwallis turned around and saw that Gray was still standing where he had left him. "Come along, Lieutenant!"

"Do you want a guard left at the sawmill?" Bulkeley asked the governor.

Cornwallis didn't answer but waited until Gray had joined them. "It doesn't much matter now, Lieutenant, but did you learn anything about the sawmill production?"

The young man hesitated, averted his eyes, and gazed at what was left of Mary's house. "No, sir," he said quietly.

Cornwallis ordered Bulkeley to leave the sawmill unguarded for the time being and to concentrate on getting the Rangers into action against the enemy. He finished his instructions with, "Lieutenant, signal for my boat."

"Aye, sir." Gray removed and waved his hat to signal the governor's cutter to return to the beach.

"Lieutenant Bulkeley, instruct Townsend to provide treasury funds for either you or Lieutenant Gates to travel to New England to recruit more Rangers. With a thirty-pound bounty we should have no dearth of recruits."

There was a growing row of bodies on the beach. A couple of sailors worked with canvas and string making bags so that the bodies could be transported to Halifax with some dignity. For the first time the governor spoke angrily. "Those Acadians are going to rue the day they did this to us!"

The governor's party halted next to a pole jutting out of a line of seaweed that marked high tide. They watched the collection and placement of the bodies on the beach. One member of the work party rose stiffly from his grisly chore and approached them. His body was bent and twisted, and his gait was awkward. Hesitantly he said, "Yer pardons, sirs."

Lieutenant Bulkeley, the tallest of the three and wearing the green uniform of the Irish Dragoons, confronted the little man. Bulkeley surveyed with disdain the rounded shoulders and the callused hands clutching the workman's tools of his profession: awl, needle, and twine. He demanded, "Why are you troubling the governor's party? You have your duties, man."

"Yer pardon, sir, I knowed I got me orders to make shawls for them bodies …"

"Then, for heaven's sake man," Bulkeley said impatiently, "get on with it or I'll find someone to discipline you."

The sailor touched his forehead and bowed his way backward. "I thought the young sir might help an old sailmaker do the right thing by 'em." He indicated with a shrug of his head and shoulders the bodies lined up behind him.

Bulkeley interrupted his scratching at black-fly bites and beckoned to Lieutenant Gray, whom the sailmaker had referred to as the 'young sir.'

Governor Cornwallis, amused by the old sailor's persistence in the face of Bulkeley's imperious behaviour, beckoned the sailmaker closer. Not moving, the little man said with a trembling voice, "I didn't mean no trouble, Yer Grace."

"I am not Your Grace," said Cornwallis. "I am the governor. Speak your piece, man!"

"I was tol' t'make shawls fer them was massacreed last night," the little man said. "I done that. But I needs a proper officer t'make his say. This is the first time I put landlubbers in shawls an' I don't know if'n I'm t'do it the seaman's way."

Cornwallis turned to the lieutenant. "You look into it, William, but don't take long. We leave as soon as the cutter arrives."

Gray moved off with the sailmaker to where several rows of body bags were aligned perfectly above the high-tide mark. The colour-sergeant was berating the freckle-faced soldier named Cameron for not lining up the bags properly. Cameron had aligned the bodies by their heads. The colour sergeant, terribly red in the face, bellied up to the freckle-faced soldier. "People are lined up by their feet, Cameron," the sergeant screamed, "never by their heads. That's unseemly! By their heads? Never! Do it right, Cameron!"

Sergeant Brown huffed away, leaving Cameron to correct his error. Spying the naval officer's approach, Cameron remained stiffly at attention until Gray indicated the soldier should continue his work. Gray stopped at the first of the body bags, and found himself staring down into the face of Mary Clark. She looked serene, almost smiling, in death. Someone had wrapped a cloth around her neck where the Acadian's tomahawk had almost severed it. Gray looked into the next bag expecting to see Issac Denham, but Denham wasn't beside his beloved Mary.

Gray tore his eyes away. Everyone in Dartmouth who had been living last night was dead this morning. No, he thought, that's not right. The soldiers lived; they had stayed safe in their fort. I lived; I ran for the boat with Denham, but they got him. Gray's flesh crawled when he realized he was almost at the spot where Denham had been tortured and died. Gray was breathing heavily and his mind whirled as he remembered all he had seen and heard last night. He shook his head to clear away the vile memories. "Well, sailor," he finally said, "what is it you want?"

\* \* \*

An English warship rounded George's Island heading for Dartmouth Cove.[7] The masts and sails of a second ship followed in the wake of the first. Governor Cornwallis asked the lieutenant of dragoons if he recognized either of the ships. Lieutenant Bulkeley admitted he didn't. "Lieutenant Gray could probably name them." Bulkeley preened his moustache and added, "I can never understand how those naval types tell one from the other."

"Ask him to rejoin us," said the governor.

Lieutenant Bulkeley raised his arm and waved to Gray.

Holding his sword close to his side, Gray double-timed back to the waiting governor and his aide.

"What ship is that, Lieutenant?" Bulkeley asked.

"She's *Albany*, sir." Gray screwed up his eyes as he tried to discern anything familiar about the second ship. "The other's a brigantine. She's suffered some damage. There're men on the foredeck lined up like ... lined up like prisoners."

"Look at the flags," he pointed out. "Captain Rous has taken another prize!"

"Prize," snorted Cornwallis. "That blighter Rous is a devil to tempt me so!"

Gray had no idea what the governor meant, but Lieutenant Bulkeley knew. No official state of war meant there could be no prizes. French ships on unfriendly missions apprehended in English waters were sold to the highest bidder, and the funds deposited in government accounts. If, however, the governor felt the circumstances were warranted, he could declare the ship a prize. In that case, each man serving on the English ship or ships involved in the capture received a portion of the sale price of the captured vessel, as did the governor since the conquest was within his jurisdiction.

Cornwallis searched for another topic. He scratched at some black-fly bites along his hairline at the edge of his collar. "There are fewer black flies here than on the Halifax side. It must be the effect of the breeze coming up the harbour."

Lieutenant Bulkeley murmured agreement as the governor's cutter crunched onto the gravel. Two sailors jumped out to steady the small craft in the wavelets.

Gray was distracted from the comment he was going to make because Lieutenant Bulkeley, unaware of naval etiquette, was moving to embark before the governor. The sailors put up their hands to deter him, but Bulkeley thought they were trying to help him and pushed away their efforts. He was still rocking the boat looking for a place to sit when the governor boarded. Gray fully expected one of them to land in the water but the boat's crew would never allow their senior officer to suffer a dunking, at least not from *their* cutter and not at the hands of an ill-mannered army officer. Two sailors quickly jumped into the knee-deep water, one on either side of the cutter, to steady the craft. Passengers settled at last, and the cutter moved swiftly away from the beach.

By this time, *H.M.S. Albany* had taken up mooring in the cove, and the governor's party made for the ship. The coxswain quickly signalled to *Albany* that the governor was coming their way. From across the water, Gray heard *Albany's* pipes play "All Hands" and smiled. Neither Cornwallis nor Bulkeley noticed the cutter crew taking a roundabout approach to the warship at a reduced stroke to allow the ship's company time to prepare and to give the proper salutes.

Governor Cornwallis asked the naval officer about the sail-maker's questions.

"It was just a matter of naval procedures, sir," said Gray.

"What was he concerned about?" the governor asked testily.

"When the bags, called shawls, are about to be closed," explained Gray, "a naval officer checks each shawl to make sure each person is in the correct bag. The officer can then attest, for the purposes of the Royal Navy's records, that a particular person was DD, discharged by reason of death."

"Well, there's no one left to check on the deceased of Dartmouth. I can understand the sailmaker didn't want to disobey regulations." Cornwallis pursed his lips. "Was that all there was to it?"

"No, sir. He wanted to know about the last stitch."

"Go on."

"Sailors are superstitious about waking up on the way to Davy Jones with no way of getting out of their shawl. So sail-makers always put the last stitch through the soft tissue at the base of the nose." Gray pinched the flesh together on his upper lip to demonstrate. "If that doesn't wake up the body, then nothing ever will."

The governor was noncommittal, but Lieutenant Bulkeley grimaced with disgust.

Gray hastened on. "I told him to carry on. I know Seaman Denham would have expected it. I didn't know which shawl he was in so I told the sailmaker to do the same to them all."

On that disquieting note, the officers continued in silence to *H.M.S. Albany*.

\* \* \*

By the time Lieutenant Gray reached the *Albany's* deck, the formalities between Captain Rous and Governor Cornwallis had been made, and the governor was seeking information about Rous's latest victory.

Rous was well into his story. "She's bigger than we are, but when she turned tail to run with the nor'west wind, I knew she would come up against the shoals of Sable Island. At that time we could easily anticipate her course, intercept her, and put her in the bag, so to speak."

Cornwallis was intrigued with this man. Rous had achieved recognition from the Lords of the Admiralty as being the only colonial appointed captain in the Royal Navy. "Unheard of, actually," had been Captain Lloyd's comment when Cornwallis and Rous had first met on the deck of *H.M.S. Sphinx* during the summer of 1749.

At that meeting, Lieutenant Gray had just returned to *Sphinx* with news of a good freshwater source on the west side of Chebucto Harbour. Based on that information, Cornwallis had decided to build the new fort around the water source. Captain Rous had disagreed. Looking at the little man today, Cornwallis recalled Rous's arguments.

"The fort should be at the harbour entrance where the fisher-men and the coastal traders can get easy protection from the guns of your fort. Tucking it 'way inside the harbour, where you pro-pose, means a much greater distance for them to travel to safety."

Lloyd, captain of *Sphinx*, had expressed a different opinion.

"The Royal Navy will want to use this harbour as a con-centration point for convoys. The best location for the fort is that which the governor has chosen. From there, the fort can offer protection to the fleet moored in the roadstead. No doubt a Royal Navy dockyard will be built, and the fort could extend its protection to that facility as well."

Captain Lloyd had then made reference to Rous being from New England and predisposed to protecting Yankee coastal vessels rather than His Majesty's ships.

Cornwallis had closed the discussion at that point by declaring sharply, "Lieutenant Gray has reported a good source of water on the western shore, and that, gentlemen, settles the location of the fort."

Standing aboard *Albany* twenty-two months later and lis-tening to the famous Captain Rous relate the capture of *Saint Francis*, Cornwallis considered the captain's reputation. Last

July he had taken eight French vessels into St. John's, and not a month later he had captured five French ships and brought them here to Halifax. Cornwallis smiled. He may not be famous, but he certainly is getting rich from his prize money. Making me rich, too. Now what's he saying, something about losses? "Pardon, Captain Rous, you said ..."

"It was at that point that we suffered our only losses: two sailors and one of my officers, Midshipman Stevens. They were manning the bow gun. It was their good marksmanship that made the operation a success." Captain Rous adjusted his sword belt and continued. "It is my intention to give their kin a double share in the prize money." He fixed the governor with a steady gaze. "I hope you'll approve this gesture from the crew of *Albany* to the families of their fallen comrades.

"Lieutenant Foster took a bit of grape in the chest, probably from a ricochet, but he wouldn't join the sick list." Rous smiled broadly. "*Albany* has a good crew, Governor."

It was the governor's turn to smile broadly. "And a Yankee trader for a captain. You'll need replacements. I can provide sailors, but you'll have to await the arrival of a junior officer from England. That won't be soon. There are a number of ships ahead of you requesting replacement officers."

"I appreciate whatever you can do for us, sir."

Cornwallis glanced around, taking in the sorry bunch of prisoners at the far end of the deck. "You took few prisoners?"

"They were sailing shorthanded," said Rous. "In fact, *Saint Francis* was on her way to Louisbourg to pick up crew replacements for their other ships at sea."

"They have extra sailors in Louisbourg?"

"No. Sometimes they use garrison soldiers as sailors on their warships."

"Does that make sense, Captain Rous?" asked the governor.

"Of course it does, sir," Lieutenant Bulkeley spoke up. "They're well disciplined and can adapt their training to ..."

Rous wasn't at all pleased that a junior officer had interrupted, and an *army* officer at that. "Balderdash!" he exploded. "Just because they're trained to obey doesn't mean they can perform as seamen."

Bulkeley was determined to voice his opinion. "Certainly, Governor, given good leadership, soldiers can accomplish any assigned task."

Captain Rous glared at the tall officer and said, "Excuse me, Governor, but during our encounter with *Saint Francis*, there was a moment when a few sailors and a well-handled gun could have caused us serious harm. Instead the deck hands fought the only way they knew how."

"And how was that?" Bulkeley looked down his nose at the Yankee naval captain.

"They grabbed muskets and formed squad around their wounded captain. Our cannon cut them down with a well-placed shot."

A red-faced Bulkeley muttered something about cannon against muskets, and leaned over to wipe some seaweed off his otherwise shiny riding boots.

Rous waited, but the dragoon officer apparently had nothing more to say. Rous had the feeling that this disagreement was merely the opening salvo of a long, long war between a haughty Irishman and a jumped-up colonial.

Cornwallis, unaware of the hostility between the two officers, turned on his heel. "I've heard your requests, Captain Rous. I'll see what can be done for you. Meanwhile, our congratulations." Pointing to the beach, Governor Cornwallis continued, "I would appreciate a working party from this ship to help clean up in Dartmouth."

The ship's officers regarded the shore as if seeing it for the first time. Rous immediately recognized the devastation for what it was. "Indian attack. Of course, sir, we'll send crews ashore. How bad was it?"

"At dusk," said the governor, "three Acadians, pretending to be returning hunters, killed the pickets. The Micmac did the rest. None of the settlers survived."

"None?"

"There was a small boy whose parents managed to hide him. Gray was there. Gray fought hand to hand with the bastards and managed to escape, but he was the only one to ..."

Gray interrupted. "The soldiers in the fort survived. They

closed the gates at the first sign of trouble and didn't lift a finger to help."

"Most of the men in the fort weren't soldiers!" Bulkeley was still smarting from Rous's rebuke. "They weren't redcoats! They were Rangers. You can't expect undisciplined half-castes to fight and protect the settlement like proper regulars."

Governor Cornwallis obviously didn't like the discussion. "Thank you, gentlemen, for your views and thank you, Captain Rous, in advance, for sending your crews to help." Without looking over the side of the ship, Cornwallis asked his naval officer, "The cutter is alongside?"

Gray had told the coxswain to hold his craft alongside and was able to answer without hesitation, "Aye, sir, she is."

"Well then, come along you two, and thank you, Captain Rous, for receiving us on your ship." With a nod to acknowledge the salutes from the *Albany* crew, Governor Cornwallis and his party descended to the cutter. The crew pulled her away smartly as soon as the party was settled.

With the visiting party gone, Captain Rous left the deck to Lieutenant Evans and retired to his cabin. Foster, leaning against the ship's bulwark, his face still deathly white, asked Evans quietly, "You think he'll declare *Saint Francis* a prize?"

"I think so," said Evans. "Our captain fixed it so the governor has an easy choice. He can declare her a prize, thereby rewarding dead heroes with a double share or ..."

"Or he can deposit the money in the colony's coffers," Foster completed for him.

"And the heroes' families suffer."

"Captain Rous sure set him up, didn't he?"

Both men chuckled. "Just like he set up *Saint Francis*," Foster said admiringly.

"Yes, that was well executed," said Evans. "How do you think he knew there was enough water under our hull on the final turn to attack?"

"Well, he did the noon sighting, with me. I couldn't tell which shoal the Frenchie had cozied up to, at least not for certain. Maybe he knew better'n me where we were."

Lieutenant Evans straightened his tunic. "The captain said

we would send crews ashore. We should send two boats to the beach, Foster. Make it so."

"Aye, Lieutenant."

## *Endnotes*

[1] John Rous did capture the *Saint Francis*, a French brigantine, off Cape Sable. I have moved the action to the vicinity of Sable Island because I was more familiar with that area. The French were using soldiers as crew on some of their undermanned ships but the details of the chase and capture are fiction.

[2] Joshua Mauger was involved in a continuous quest for money and influence. He was an earnest opponent of colonial authority and suspected of dealing with the French in time of war, smuggling, etc.

[3] Mary Clark owned a double lot near the corner of Dundas Street and Portland Street. She probably planted the chestnut trees that grew opposite my house. They are all gone now (2000).

[4] Doctor Martin showed me the area where the blockhouse was situated and the spot where the family could have been killed close to the houses and yet be in full view of the soldiers. There was an outcropping of slate rock there. I incorporated the knoll into the story.

[5] I used several of the actual names of the guards who were killed that night.

[6] According to town records, John Pyke was the only survivor of the people who were in Dartmouth that night. Gray's presence is, of course, fictitious.

[7] Rous did enter harbour with the *St Francis* during that period of time and could have provided assistance to the Governor's staff. Besides, I had to set up Gray joining Rous's crew.

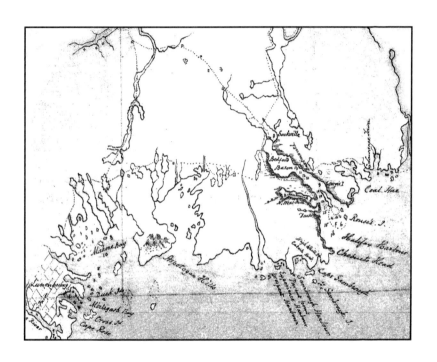

# Chapter Four

## Spring 1752
## Halifax

Lieutenant Bulkeley watched his valet pack his papers. "I'm staying in Halifax to work for the new governor. After all, Colonel Hopson is an army man. He'll treat his staff right."

Leaning against a table, Lieutenant Gates plucked remnants of dried food from the front of his uniform. He started to undo the buttons. "Have your man clean this, will you?" He slipped off and held out his tunic in the general direction of the valet.

"My pleasure, sir." The man carried the tunic out of the room.

Gates patted his belly. "I've gotten a bit sloppy this winter. Must get out and about more as the weather gets better."

Bulkeley scratched his moustache and glanced around the room. "It's a pity Colonel Hopson is bringing his own aides from his regiment. I was comfortable here." He moved to the dry sink and examined himself in the mirror. "Hopson won't make the same mistake Cornwallis made." Bulkeley spied something between his front teeth and picked at it with his fingernail. Reaching down into his boot, he pulled out his dirk and, using the point of the blade, extracted whatever was bothering him.

"What mistake?" asked Gates.

"Using the Rangers. Hopson will use regulars. This Acadian mess will be cleaned up in Hopson's first year, mark my words."

Gates leaned back on the table and grasped his knee with both hands. "I'm not going back with the governor, and I'm not going to stay here in the backwaters of the empire. No, as soon as Susanne and I get married ..."

"Susanne Scofield?[1] You think the Earl of Leeds will consider her a suitable match?" Bulkeley teased. He knew Gates's tendency to drop his father's title into any conversation he could and was in a good frame of mind to oblige. "Have you informed the earl?"

"The Earl of Leeds has been very kind, even promising a posting to New York after the wedding," Gates said absently. He was preoccupied with thoughts of his own packing; it would be terribly complicated and lengthy. He had to keep aside proper clothing for the betrothal party, the governor's reception, and the wedding. He sighed. It was all so difficult! He planned to ask Bulkeley for his valet's services, but had to wait for the right opportunity. He shoved aside his problems for the moment and turned his attention to the ex-governor's failings.

"You can't begin to say the old man is returning to England in triumph." This was one of Lieutenant Gates' favourite subjects: shortcomings—of the governor or the Crown, the food or the cook, the hounds or the hounds master—it didn't much matter, as long as they were someone else's and not his own. He considered Governor Cornwallis very fertile ground and had been practising his arguments leading up to the handing-over ceremony that was scheduled for today. Gates hurried on, fearful that the more articulate Irishman might steal his thunder. "Y' know, he was supposed to build an English fort to rival the French one at Louisbourg on Cape Breton."

"I think it would be more accurate to say Isle Royale instead of Cape Breton," Bulkeley corrected.

Gates made no response but filed away the information for future use. Of course it would be better. Isle Royale sounded so much more *je ne sais quoi*, continental. He continued as if there had been no interruption. "It was assumed that the lush lands of the Fundy would support a large settler population, that the settlers' crops would provide sustenance to the fortress, and that the settlers would breed strong sons for the provincial militia. Instead, Cornwallis settled at Chebucto, which has a fine harbour but inhospitable Atlantic weather. And the sour, rocky soil makes for …"

"Oh, come now, my good fellow," Bulkeley snorted. "There were no ship's pilots familiar with the Fundy. He couldn't take a fleet of transports into unknown waters."

"That may be so," Gates conceded, "but he was supposed to establish a *Pax Britannica* by making treaties with the Indians and obtaining oaths of allegiance from the Acadians."

"The Acadians and Micmac are natural enemies of the English," Bulkeley argued.

"It doesn't change the fact that there were existing treaties with the Indians," Gates insisted, "and understandings with the Acadians that could have been built upon."

"I think you're correct there," Bulkeley agreed. "Cornwallis was unable to effect a truce or a reduction of hostilities. I think we must admit, for an Englishman to go out of sight of Halifax without a guard of redcoats means a certain, miserable death." Bulkeley was suddenly tired of being a sounding board. He tried to change the subject. "Is Susanne looking forward to leaving?"

With a nod of his head, Gates continued, "The Lords of Trade know that there is no fortress here. Halifax is a tiny settlement clinging to the edge of the North Atlantic, besieged by cruel winters and implacable enemies." Gates enjoyed rolling that line off his tongue; it had a nice ring to it. He had borrowed the phrase from Susanne, who had uttered it the first time he raised this subject with her. He paused and then delivered his killing summation, "And that's why our esteemed Governor Cornwallis has been recalled."

Lieutenant Bulkeley found his associate a boor and had not yet corrected Gates' assumption. There were so many things Gates said that needed correcting. Perhaps this was the time to set things straight with the pompous ass. "The governor's problems were in the ships' cabins and Halifax offices where the business of the settlement was carried on. It took money to run the colony, and the money ran through the governor's fingers like quicksilver." Bulkeley, in a moment of rare candour, shook his finger at the other officer. "You had no notion of economy!"

"I was never dishonest," Gates protested. "Dammit, man! For you to suggest such a thing of a son of the Earl of Leeds is ..."

"No, old sod, you and I were not dishonest, but we prided ourselves on being simple military men. If there was a shortage of building supplies, fixtures, food, horseshoes, or wax, why, we bought it. And we bought enough so that we wouldn't run short again in the foreseeable future."

"Damn right! And a mighty good thing Cornwallis had us here to do it for him! There were others who bled the system of every farthing they could."

"Yes, well, whether honestly spent, inadvertently misdirected, or subverted to personal use, the settlement's budget has become a scandal for which the governor has been called home to account." Bulkeley immediately regretted his speech. He wondered if Gates had understood anything they had been talking about, or if he was just one of those talking birds—a parrot with not a brain in his head. He glanced at the portly figure. Gates had certainly let himself go to seed. Bulkeley smiled at his own pun, and smiled even more broadly when he pictured the other man on a horse. The stable master often refused him a horse, son of the Earl of Leeds or no. He made a snort of laughter as he thought of what a fuss that raised.

Mistaking the reason for Bulkeley's amusement Gates said, "Why do you laugh? Even though it was the treasurer who misappropriated all those funds, he was still Governor Cornwallis's man."

"I was just thinking that our mighty erstwhile ex-governor is going to have to stand in front of his old friend Lord Halifax like a naughty boy in front of a schoolmaster," Bulkeley said.

The valet returned with the tunic, and helped Gates shrug into it. "It came out nicely, sir."

Gates didn't acknowledge the man, but said, "Did you know our Sub-Lieutenant Gray has asked the governor for a release from his office? The young pup wants to stay in Halifax."[2]

"The 'young pup,' as you call him, is taller and broader at the shoulder than you, my dear Gates." Lieutenant Bulkeley leaned over and poked at the other officer's middle. "But you do have him in girth, my dear boy."

Gates drew in his stomach, tugged at the front of his tunic, and laughed uncomfortably. "Army officers' uniforms were not made with the mature figure in mind, but I truly thought my tailor would have anticipated the effects of garrison living. After all, he damn well serviced the Earl of Leeds throughout his career without allowing the fullness of his figure to interrupt the line of the tunic. I will complain …"

Tiring of the subject, Bulkeley asked, "What is Gray going to do?"

Through the window set in the door, Gates spied the naval officer approaching. "Ask him directly. He's at the door right now."

Gray knocked and entered without waiting for a reply. "Sirs, the governor is leaving the mansion in the next few minutes and he expects to see us on the pier as he leaves Halifax. I came to hurry you along."

"You little bugger!" Gates was angry at the offhand manner of the younger man. "Show the proper respect for your seniors!"

Not the least bit fazed, Gray continued. "I'm sorry if you find the words or my manner offensive but I'm complying with the wishes of the governor. 'Hurry you along' were his words."

"Ex-governor." Lieutenant Gates continued to bluster and complain. "He can't give us orders any more. Tell him ..."

"We're coming, Gray." Putting his hand on the shoulder of Lieutenant Gates, Bulkeley squeezed hard and started him toward the door. "We've been through a lot, the three of us. If we aren't on that pier, it will be like we farted in polite company. Everyone will remember the smell and nothing else we ever did."

They stepped into the sunlight, adjusted their uniforms and swords, and checked the set of their hats in the glass of the windows. Gates had difficulty adjusting his belt, and Bulkeley gave him some assistance. Gray took some care making sure that his white lace handkerchief was just visible under the cuff on his left wrist. Holding their swords and scabbards closely to their sides the three officers walked briskly down the street. The departure of Edward Cornwallis, former governor of Nova Scotia and founder of Halifax, was an event that not many of the settlement would miss. Bulkeley, Gates, and Gray had earned their places in the front row of the handing-over ceremony, which they hurried to without further delay.

The pomp and ceremony of the handing over of command was quickly finished. The honour guard was stood at ease while Edward Cornwallis spoke some kind words to each member of his personal staff.

His drawn sword flashing in the sunlight, the honour guard commander brought the redcoats to attention as Cornwallis boarded the cutter that would take him to the frigate anchored just off Dartmouth Cove. The crew of the cutter cast off, and the redcoats were ordered to present arms. The guard commander brought the hilt of his sword to his lips, and then, in time with the movements of the redcoats and their muskets, extended his sword forward and down to the right, its point almost touching the ground. Officers raised their right hands to their hats in a formal salute, and the civilians stood still in various versions of attention. Governor Edward Cornwallis was returning home to England, if not in disgrace, certainly not a hero.

If asked, Sub-Lieutenant Gray would have found it difficult to argue that Governor Cornwallis had made a great success of his Halifax adventure but, through a cloud of memories, he stared fondly at his former commander seated in the sternsheet of the cutter. He watched as the governor gazed up past the old tree where Gray had found the brook that had started it all.

On the pier not a person moved. The seamen of the cutter sat quietly awaiting the orders of the boat commander. All eyes rested on Edward Cornwallis.

"What's the old man waiting for?" Lieutenant Gates had begun to fidget.

Out of the corner of his mouth Lieutenant Bulkeley whispered, "When he salutes it's all over."

The cannons of the frigate began firing the salute. Edward Cornwallis made an informal salute to the honour guard commander, and the cutter moved away from the pier, the sailors bending to the oars in well-practised unison. The guard commander called the order arms, the guard responding with an impressive flourish. The officers smartly lowered their hands from the salute and watched as Cornwallis was rowed away for the last time from the settlement he had founded.

The frigate's cannons had almost finished the salute. Gray had lost count as the memory of the governor's complaint of being assigned to a sloop of war in 1749 pushed its way into his consciousness. In his mind's eye he could see the tiny cabin on board *Sphinx* with those air ventilators. Gray could hear the governor protesting he was entitled to a frigate, and questioning why he had been assigned a sloop of war instead. Lost in memories, Gray missed the question Lieutenant Bulkeley had put to him.

"Sub-Lieutenant Gray!"

"I'm sorry," Gray said. "Thinking about something else. What did you say, sir?"

"Did you actually resign?" Bulkeley repeated.

"I asked the governor to approve my request to become a harbour pilot for the port of Halifax. It meant that I had to give up my office. He arranged it for me."

The Halifax cannons fired the first shot of the salute for the departing Cornwallis. Gray began to count the rounds.

Gates was still rankled at the more junior officer and let it show. "Where are you going to live? You don't qualify as a settler so there won't be any free land or supplies for the likes of you."

"He offered me some land on Cornwallis Island, the big island near the harbour entrance. I thought to take it, but the pilots are stationed at the head of the harbour, Chebucto Head, actually. It would be better if I had some land at Samborough."[3]

As the last of the salute was fired, Lieutenant Gates harrumphed. "You should have taken up the offer, my young sir!" Gates' voice carried in the ensuing quiet and he drew looks of rebuke from several of the officials and spectators on the pier. The three officers returned stare for stare and were self-consciously silent.

Across the water, the governor's figure could barely be made out on the frigate's deck, until he raised his hat and waved at the gathering on the pier. Colonel Hopson stepped forward until he was directly in front of the crowd. He removed his hat and held it against his chest. "Three cheers for the governor! Hip, hip …" When the colonel extended his arm over his head, holding his hat stiffly upright, the crowd responded with a feeble "hooray."

Gray shouted in a loud voice, "Come on, lads! We can do better than that!" He wildly waved his arms as the colonel led the next cheer. The second "hooray" was louder, and the final one was tremendous, accompanied with cheers, shouts, and laughter.

The frigate's foretopsails were set and drawing. She had moved, and because of her angle, Gray could not see if the governor was still watching. In case he was, the young officer settled his hat properly and gave an informal salute to his former commander and former way of life.

As the honour guard went through the motions of re-forming line, the three officers returned to their quarters to finish packing. Gray was aware that Lieutenant Gates was not remaining at Halifax and had asked his father for a New York posting. Lieutenant Bulkeley, on the other hand, had asked his father for an increase in his already generous stipend and had great expectations for his future in Halifax. As for himself, according to regulations he should have returned to England with Cornwallis. His commission as a naval officer read that he had been assigned to the staff of Captain General Edward Cornwallis "at his pleasure." Fortunately, the governor had agreed to grant the sub-lieutenant's request, and Gray had been relieved of his duties. He was elated that he would become ship's pilot for Halifax Harbour.

"As I said, Gray, you should have taken Cornwallis's offer of land." Gates was out of breath and puffing slightly. He had drawn himself fully erect and made a mighty effort to hold in his paunch. "Now you'll have to pay good money. I didn't think *your* family had that kind of resources."

Gray's first impulse was to make an angry retort. He regarded the other officer, whose belly was quivering with his efforts to appear slim. Gates' London tailor had truly underestimated the effect of garrison living on the captain's waistline. "I beg of you, sir," said Gray, "to continue to manage your more ample resources or you might destroy that tunic beyond the talents of the most dedicated seamstress."

"By Jove," Bulkeley guffawed, "that was a good sally!" Bulkeley poked Lieutenant Gates in the ribs. "Totally unexpected, you'll have to admit." He threw his arm over Gates's shoulder and turned him so they continued up George Street. "When Gray becomes a civilian, you won't be able to take refuge behind your rank, Gates!"

Lieutenant Gates managed a croaking laugh. "So what are

you going to do, Master Gray?" Lieutenant Gates was struggling to restore his good humour.

"Cornwallis put me down on the settlers' rolls in Samborough in place of a family that had died. He arranged for me to get all that they were entitled to."

Lieutenant Bulkeley said quietly, "The old man had a soul after all."

Gates shook his head in disbelief. "Wouldn't have believed it of him."

"It was Mr. Townsend who drew up the papers and put my name on the roll," Gray added. "Maybe Cornwallis didn't know what he was signing."

"Wouldn't have been the first time," Bulkeley said with an ironic laugh.

As they passed the Governor's Mansion someone in the front window nodded his head at them: it was the governor of Nova Scotia but not *their* governor, Cornwallis. Bulkeley, nearest the mansion, threw a short, snappy salute in the direction of the window. Without breaking either stride or conversation, Bulkeley went on, "That takes care of the land and some provisions, Master Gray, but what are you going to do for money?"

"I have no funds," Gray said. "My mother can't help me. After my father died, she remarried and …"

From behind them came a voice, heavy with authority. "Hold, there!"

Gates and Bulkeley kept walking, but Gray looked back over his shoulder. Running up the slope was a corporal of Hopson's Regiment, musket in his hands, ammunition tabs and bayonet sheath flapping. "Hold, there, sirs!"

Gentlemen of rank might have ignored being accosted on a London street, but this wasn't London. The three officers stopped and waited for the soldier. "What is it you want, Corporal?" Lieutenant Gates asked irritably.

"The governor would speak with Lieutenant Bulkeley," said the corporal.

"I'm Lieutenant Bulkeley," Bulkeley said. "Inform the governor …"

"The governor said now, sir." The corporal stepped aside to allow the lieutenant to proceed down the hill.

Bulkeley looked at his companions questioningly. Gray said nothing but feared Governor Hopson had uncovered one of the many shortcuts in which Cornwallis's personal staff had been involved. Shortcuts made to get things done in a timely manner of course; but shortcuts nonetheless. His face reflected his concern for all three of them.

Lieutenant Gates' mouth flapped open and shut a few times. Finally he asked, "While you're away, Bulkeley, would you mind terribly if I used your man to help me plan my packing?"

It was a moment before Bulkeley responded. "Certainly not, old man." Bulkeley pulled his tunic taut, adjusted his hat, and turned to go down the hill.

Lieutenant Gates reached out and grabbed the sleeve of the other captain. "Bulkeley!"

"Yes, old man?"

"You said, 'certainly not.' Does that mean I can't have him?"

Gray flashed Bulkeley an apologetic smile as he took Gates by the arm, and the two of them continued up George Street.

Lieutenant Bulkeley marched resolutely down the hill to answer the unexpected summons from the new governor.

Lieutenant Gates complained, "Well, I don't understand! Can I have his man, or can't I?"

At the corner of Holles Street, William Gray, late of Governor Cornwallis's service, waved his hand—either in farewell or perhaps in disgust—at the bastard son of the Earl of Leeds and returned to his own quarters.

## Endnotes

[1]  Marrying a Scofield is fiction.

[2]  Church records show Gray at Sambro at about the time the governor returned to England. William Gray did become a ship's pilot.

[3]  On the accompanying map (circa 1755), Sambro was spelled Samborough: Samborough Harbour, etc.

# Chapter Five

## 1753
### Sackville River

The Mi'kmaq warriors and the Rangers played a deadly game at Fort Sackville. The Rangers sat in the woods some distance from the redcoat guard pickets, silent, ever watchful for an Indian attack. The Indians, knowing the Rangers were there, carefully approached the redcoats and attempted to capture them. If it was too difficult to effect the capture, the Indians scalped the redcoats and tried to return to the safety of the deep forest before the Rangers could intercept them. The Rangers played the game because Halifax paid thirty pounds apiece for Mi'kmaq, Acadian, or Canadian scalps. It meant a great deal of money with little risk to the Rangers. On the other side, the Mi'kmaq Indians sought scalps to gain tribal recognition and, of course, at Louisbourg there was a comparable bounty for English scalps.

The score for the last week in May was three to one for the Indians: one redcoat scalped, two abducted (one found mutilated and the other missing with no trace), one Mi'kmaq warrior scalped. It was a blood sport with scalps as trophy.

Private Robert Cameron had no knowledge of the games being played at Fort Sackville, but when he was selected to join a group of soldiers ordered to report there, he had a terrible feeling about it.

Cameron[1] didn't want to be a British soldier any more.

His disaffection had started with the massacre of the Dartmouth settlers in 1751. The evening of the massacre, he had been the first guard of the Dartmouth fort to see the attacking Indians. In fact he had fired off a shot and wounded one of a group of Indians chasing two Englishmen.

He recalled how he had reloaded quickly and answered the muster call at the fort gate. He had been astonished when the orders had been given to close and bar the gates, abandoning the settlers to the Indians, and had protested to the captain. "We must try to help 'em, sir!"

Captain Clapham had balled his fist and struck the unresisting private in the face repeatedly, until he had tumbled to the ground. "Pick up your musket, soldier," Clapham had ordered, "and man the wall!"

Private Cameron had stood at his post and watched the Indians destroy the settlement. By the flickering fires, he had witnessed it all: the mutilation and eventual death of Issac Denham; William Gray's close call and escape; and worst of all, the torture and death of the settler family.

In the time it took Cameron's right eye to swell shut from the captain's blows, the Indians had begun to torment the small family they had flushed from one of the homes nearest the fort. The soldiers in the fort had an unobstructed view of the family's death.

The Indians had started with the woman. Cameron had averted his head but couldn't block out her screams. The man had shouted and pleaded for his wife to be spared, but in time he had pleaded for her quick death. When it was his turn the man was stoically quiet. The little boy, the last to die, screamed for a very long time.

When Cameron had finally looked up, the Indians were gone, the fires were guttering out, and the officer in the shallop had disappeared into the darkness.

The next morning, Cameron had helped gather the dead and put out some fires. In the afternoon, Cameron had been accosted by Colour Sergeant Brown and put under arrest. His officer had ordered a punishment of twenty lashes for conduct unbecoming a soldier of the regiment.

On the day of punishment, when he was being tied to the wooden horse, Sergeant Brown had whispered in his ear, "I saved you thirty lashes, lad. I told our officer that you was raring to fight, but the Ranger officer was givin' other orders." He patted Cameron's shoulder and repeated, "I done you a favour. I saved you thirty."

After the lashing, it seemed Brown rode the private even harder, expecting more from him because of the favour, but better behaviour wasn't forthcoming. Cameron quickly found himself in the sergeant's bad books.

Now Cameron was being sent to Fort Sackville in the company of army miscreants: three thieves, an accused rapist, and several slackers and backsliders. No, Cameron said to himself, Fort Sackville was not going to be a good assignment.

\* \* \*

The rapist was the first to go. He had been assigned picket duty about five hundred yards from the fort. At dusk, Indians had attacked, taking him prisoner. The Rangers were swift to react, catching the Indians before they were able to escape the area with their captive.

It was the Rangers' story that, while the Indians had killed and scalped the rapist, the Rangers more than evened the score by lifting the hair of three of the enemy. One of the scalped Indians had slipped away into the forest with the help of his friends, which would explain why there were only three bodies found at the site of the melee: two Indians and one redcoat.

Cameron was part of the burial detail. He noted the rapist's bound hands and the gag, but questioned the scalping. To him it seemed there had been no haste in the cutting away of the hair. It was as neat a circle as he had ever seen. "Whoever did that," he said, "wasn't worried about gettin' caught."

One of the Ranger's guards overheard Cameron's remark, and chose to misinterpret it. "Yeah, they get pretty uppity, them Injuns. Ain't a bit scared." He spat in the direction of the rapist's body. "Anyhow, we're doin' better this week. Up three to one in our favour!"

A second guard laughed. "And it's only the first day of the week!"

The next afternoon Cameron was ordered to picket duty. As soon as he reached his post, he slipped into the woods and ran as fast as he could without a backward glance down the Sackville River Valley. He followed a well-trod trail without giving it a second thought or questioning who used the trail. The obvious answer might have given him pause and he might have returned to the fort, but Private Cameron of the Fortieth Foot was running away with no more thought of the future than where his next footstep should fall, and his feet took him along the easiest path.

Much later, when it was too dark to see, he left the trail to seek a hiding place for the night. Under an oak tree he kicked dried leaves into a mound. He stripped off his red coat and spread it over the leaves. Taking special care that his musket was close by and tucked under his coat, Cameron crawled onto his makeshift bed and pulled as many leaves over himself as he could. He had some trouble getting comfortable, but in the middle of cursing mosquitoes he fell asleep.

\* \* \*

Through his closed eyelids, Cameron could tell it was almost daylight. Suddenly something pulled at his throat, and in his state of half-sleep, he thought his mother was adjusting the collar of his jerkin. He pushed at the hands to leave him to his sleep.

Roughly wrenched from under the leaves by a stout rope around his neck, Cameron was tugged upright and then aloft by three Indians who had looped the other end of the rope over one of the lower branches of the oak tree. Another Indian picked up his red coat and musket. Cameron managed to kick him on the side of the head before, with a great roaring in his ears, he passed out.

Cameron's ears still roared so he knew he was alive. He realized he was lying on his side with his hands tied behind him. Oh, Christ! He remembered the Rangers' admonition, "If your hands are bound in front, they mean to take you with them. Bound behind your back, you're not going very far."

"Shit!" he said. "Not going very far!"

Cameron was rolled onto his back. One of the Indians leaned over, looked into his eyes, and pointed at the side of his head where Cameron's boot had left its mark. The Indian stepped back and took the end of the rope from the other Indians. Then he pulled, hard. Cameron scrambled to sit up to take his weight off his neck. The Indian kept pulling until

Cameron was upright and on tiptoe. Grinning, the Indian heaved on the rope.

Cameron's toes made little swirls in the leaves as they frantically sought firm ground. Cameron gasped and grunted. He struggled to breathe. This time there was no roaring in his ears. He was gone.

\* \* \*

Back again, sitting on the ground. Starting again. Pulled up by the rope. Gasping. Choking. Sitting. Choking. Dying. Damn it! Sitting again. Choking.

Lying on the ground, his chest hurt. Someone was kicking him. Rolling into a ball only seemed to increase the tempo of the kicking. Cameron pushed himself upright and brushed dirt off his face. His hands were tied in front! Instantly he was more alert. There was a tether tied to his wrist, and the Indian who had been torturing him was pulling on the end of it. He wanted Cameron to get up and walk! Well, he could certainly walk. His neck and chest were hurting; there was nothing wrong with his legs and feet.

Cameron forced his legs to move. He was almost on his feet when the Indian gave the tether a little tug, and Cameron fell on his face. The Indian behind him kicked him until he managed to get up again. This time the little tug didn't cause Cameron to lose his balance. Savouring the triumph only brought a kick from the Indian behind him. Robert Cameron learned quickly; prisoners of the Mi'kmaq Indians were allowed no pride, no dignity. He ran awkwardly as the Indians tugged him along.

Sometime during the hangings, Cameron had pissed himself. Shortly into the forced dogtrot, Cameron began to chafe; his crotch was sore. He motioned to the Indian behind him that he wanted to clean himself. Thereafter, anytime they stopped, the tether Indian, "Tether" in Cameron's mind, made sure Cameron couldn't use his hands. Eventually he messed himself as well. If it had been the Indians' plan to humiliate him, they gave no sign they were pleased with the results.

On the second day, the Indian following Cameron, whom Cameron had begun to think of as "Follow," said something to his comrades, who grunted in response. At the next brook Follow untied the thongs holding Cameron's wrists together and allowed him to clean himself and his clothes. The water stung Cameron's private parts, and his resulting antics made both Tether and Follow laugh. But the wrist thongs weren't so tightly bound after that.

On the fourth day they passed farms and hayfields, and stopped at a village with French-speaking white people. Cameron was fed and given homespun clothing. After a good night's rest, they continued on. Now he was accompanied by only Tether and Follow, the other Indians having remained at the village. Cameron was no navigator, but he thought they were travelling west. He worried about where he was going and what would happen when he got there, but he was still alive.

\* \* \*

The Bay of Fundy has the world's highest tides. Twice a day, the Fundy rises and falls as much as forty feet. When the water returns to the bay, and as the walls of the bay and then the banks of the rivers constrict the flow, the incoming water, or tidal bore, rises higher and higher. Meadows and flat lands would be inundated if it weren't for the system of sturdy dykes that the earlier generations of Acadians had constructed.

Of course, the dykes were in constant need of repair but it seemed to the present generation of farmers that the dykes had always been there ... would always be there for them. Despite the fact that once salt water spilled over onto the farms the land would be unusable for years, they had put off making the repairs, and put it off, again.

Abbé Jean LeLoutre had become fed up with this indifference to the condition of the dykes. He had demanded three weeks of labour from each Acadian. The farmers had said they would give him seven days and no more. They had made no apology; they insisted it was all the time they could spare from their farm work. Besides, the movement of the water was unpredictable, and, the farmers had reasoned, the dykes in their present condition had held back the tidal bore for decades. On the other hand, the movement of the seasons was entirely predictable and the time was right for planting. The farmers had little time to spare for Père Jean and his precious dykes; seven days was all the priest was going to get. So, it gave the priest a perverse sense of satisfaction as he watched his parishioners toil in the muddy soil, under the hot sun. He didn't feel the least bit sorry for them.

Abbé LeLoutre put his hands on his hips and surveyed the work done this day. His black frock was splashed with mud. He had frequently been forced to step aside and into mud to avoid losing a cartload of soil on the wrong side of the dyke. The farmers had apologized but he had seen their smiles as they went about their work. It wasn't often the French priest got dirty.

The mud and the sly smiles of the farmers were small aggravations to Jean LeLoutre. Not being able to relieve his feelings with strong language was a much larger aggravation. Not being permitted to kill the English was a real torment, but that was the way things had to be. Being a priest, he must keep a civil tongue and leave it to French soldiers to kill English. It was the role of French priests to pray for the French soldiers who killed the English.

However, LeLoutre didn't merely live the life of a simple priest; he schemed and planned for France's victory over the English in America. He had an agile mind, was well read on military matters, and was a long-time resident of the Bay of Fundy. Military commanders were frequently rotated home and consequently, each new commander relied upon LeLoutre for his knowledge of the Fundy and most often followed his advice, even on military matters.

Abbé LeLoutre considered the irony of the commanders who took his advice as orders while the Acadians, his spiritual flock, took his orders as advice, at least as far as the dykes were concerned. He needed to find some sort of lever to motivate the farmers to work harder on the dykes.

*"Il y a un groupe qui approche, mon père."* one of the farmers called. "There's a party approaching, Father."

Abbé LeLoutre looked up. Two Indians and a white man with carrot-red hair and freckles were some distance away. LeLoutre hastily brushed away the mud from the front of his frock. He straightened just as the approaching men came within speaking distance.

"*Bonjour, mes enfants.* Good morning, my children." He could see now that the redhead was tethered, and had a nasty rope burn on his neck. "You come from where?"

The Indians replied in French that they had just returned from Chebucto. They had captured the red-haired white man in the river valley above Chebucto, and had brought him to LeLoutre as expected. It was the custom that prisoners from the old French possessions had to be brought to the priest alive while prisoners from the English forts could be killed or ransomed at the raiding party's pleasure.

Cameron, not understanding any of the conversation, knelt and said in English, "Father, I am in sore need of your help."

LeLoutre struggled to work his tongue around the English words, but even with his heavy accent he spoke the language well enough. "Are you of our church, my son?"

"I am Catholic, father."

"And where were you taken prisoner?" asked LeLoutre.

"I was taken from Fort Sackville."

The priest asked the Indians how the Englishman had been captured. They answered him briefly. Looking down at the Englishman the priest said, "You deserted your regiment?"

"No, father," Cameron said. "I was on detachment at Fort Sackville. The Rangers put me in the field ..."

LeLoutre nodded his head. "*Oui, un des cochons dans le champ.* Yes, one of the pigs in the field." He continued in English. "What is your name?"

"Robert Cameron, father."

Abbé Jean LeLoutre studied him. "You're not even English, are you?"

"No, sir," said Cameron. "I mean, no, father. I'm a Scot."

Silently the priest considered his options. He could arrange for the deserter to be turned over to the English at Fort Lawrence ... there was a generous bounty for English deserters and that is what he would normally do ... but there was another possibility. He examined the Scot through slitted eyes as he fussed at a spot of mud on the front of his frock. The Scot seemed strong enough and could be put to work on the dykes. He thought, the good Lord knows I don't get enough work out of the habitants. Making a smoothing motion with his hands down the front of his habit, the priest made his pronouncement. "You will live here and work on the dykes." LeLoutre smiled thinly. "If you fail me, I will allow the Indians to do with you what they will. You do understand, don't you?"

"I do," Cameron said. "Thank you, father. I won't let you down."

"Good. Now go with Pierre. He will see that you're cared for." Turning aside, the priest called, "Pierre!"

"*Oui, mon père?*"

"*Tu l'emmène chez les LeBlanc.* Take him to LeBlanc's home. Explain that I want him to have their son's bed."

Pierre was glad for the excuse to leave early. He took the tether from the Indians and led Cameron away from the dykes. When they were out of earshot, one of the farmers asked, "Why send him to the home of LeBlanc, *mon père?*"

"Their son, Jean Pierre, was conscripted for Louisbourg. He won't be back any time soon." The priest smiled knowingly. "And LeBlanc has four unmarried daughters."

## 1754
### Point Pleasant

The young couple were "taking the air," drifting toward the point of land separating the entrances of Northwest Arm and Halifax Harbour. A corduroy road had been built from Barrington Street to Point Pleasant, making it possible for the citizens of Halifax to stroll along the harbour and escape the noise and smells of the settlement. Despite the presence of nearly one hundred redcoats patrolling the road, Gray was always uneasy and watchful for the Micmac. Almost daily, someone either careless or bold strayed beyond the picket boundaries and was taken prisoner. Sometimes they were held for ransom but usually they were tortured within earshot of the picket lines before being mutilated and killed. When troops searched the woods, the Indians became invisible. Whenever the redcoats did find signs of the Indians' presence, it was because the Micmac wanted them to.

Today had been peaceful. Their stroll was interrupted only by the distant wail from a lone piper's bagpipe. Even so, something caused the young man to stop slightly and whip his head around.

"What is it, sweetheart?" Recognizing the alarm in his wife's eyes,[2] Gray hastened to assure her he had seen nothing threatening. He took her hands in his and then lowered his lips to them in a soft caress.

"Oh, William," she protested. "Not in public!" She firmly withdrew her hand from his and lowered it to her side. An attractive woman with brown eyes and a heart-shaped face, Molly Gray was almost as tall as her husband was. In stocking feet, she and her husband stood eye to eye. Consequently, Molly was very careful not to wear shoes that augmented her stature. She gave him her most penetrating look. "Why did you turn like that?"

"I hadn't realized that I startled you, dearest," Gray apologized. "I'm truly sorry."

Molly pressed on. "Well then, what was it?"

"I just realized something."

"Tell me," she urged.

Gray took her arm again and they continued their walk. "In the beginning, when the redcoats paraded down this road, they marched with fife and drum. Last fall, when Captain Rous brought us back from Lunenburg, a lone piper led the redcoats. Rous said that even though the pipes had been outlawed in Britain, the change had been made from fife and drum to pipe because the Indians don't like bagpipes."

"That's interesting," said Molly. "I suppose the pipes can be heard further into the woods than the fife. But what startled you?"

"That piper isn't playing a regimental tune. He's playing a rebel song from Scotland about Bonnie Prince Charlie. If the tune is recognized, the piper will be flogged."

"Oh!"

Two riders were coming down the road toward them. Molly pointed at the rider in front. "Who's the big man in the green uniform?"

It was an officer of the Irish Dragoons. Tall, handsome, and dashing with an impeccable uniform on a splendid horse, it could only be one man—Richard Bulkeley.

"He's Governor Lawrence's aide, Lieutenant Bulkeley," said William. "I think they call him the provincial secretary now."

"Do you know him?" asked Molly.

"Yes. He came here with Cornwallis, then Governor Hopson chose him to be his aide, and Lawrence kept him on. He's a powerful man; he knows where all the governors' skeletons are buried."

When the riders came abreast of the couple, Bulkeley reined in his horse and slid easily to the ground. He tossed the reins of his horse to the other rider, his groom. "What ho! Sub-Lieutenant," Bulkeley called, and bowed politely to Molly. "My best wishes, Mrs. Gray!"

"Why, thank you sir," said Molly.

Bulkeley grabbed Gray and pulled him forward. "I was pleased to hear of your marriage. Congratulations!"

Gray, a trifle overpowered by the much larger man, felt smothered by the embrace. "You still don't know anything about the navy, Bulkeley! I'm a lieutenant, now."

"Oh, the sub-lieutenant was just for old time's sake, William." Letting go of his friend, Bulkeley stepped back a pace or two and grinned at the young couple. "Acting Lieutenant and Mrs. Gray. Isn't that just fine!"

Molly's very pretty face blushed scarlet. "Please excuse me, Mrs. Gray," said Bulkeley. "I don't mean to embarrass you. I mean no offence!"

"None taken, sir."

Indicating an approaching squad of soldiers, Bulkeley said, "They're heading back. I'll order them to delay enough so we won't have to rush our walk." Bulkeley spoke to his groom, who rode off, still leading Bulkeley's horse, to pass the command to the officer of the guard.

Offering his arm to Molly, Bulkeley chatted with her as they walked back to the settlement. The lamplighter was at work; twinkles of light showed from the lamps swathed in deep afternoon shadows under the citadel. "Do you like the street-lights, Mrs. Gray?" Bulkeley inquired.

"Oh yes, I do."

"I brought them from Boston in 1750." Bulkeley cocked his ear and listened to the piper. "What a noise! I can understand why the Indians don't like those things. I'm supposed to, you know. They're Irish bagpipes. Took me a while to find a piper. Nobody likes to admit they play the damned things any more."

"Anything that keeps the Micmac away ..."

"Yes, but it's the redcoats that will beat the heathen!" He changed the subject. "You were Molly Ferguson, weren't you? Your family came in 1750 from New England. I know your father; he's a fine man."

"Thank you, sir. I'll tell him you said so."

"You married young William at Samborough last year ..."

Molly put her free hand on Bulkeley's cuff. "We call it Sambro, now."

Bulkeley went on, "... and let him join Rous on his pirate expeditions."

Gray kept his tone jovial as he contradicted the most pow-erful man in Nova Scotia. "Not at all, Richard!" He hastened his steps until he was able to look into Bulkeley's face. "Captain Rous is Royal Navy, not a privateer. Last year Captain Rous didn't capture a single vessel, worse luck!"

"Yes, William," Bulkeley said. "I know. Last year he was on convoy duty escorting the transports that carried the German settlers to Lunenburg. He took a devil of a long time to set them ashore, didn't he?"

"We received intelligence the French had arranged an ambush," Gray explained. "Captain Rous wouldn't put the set-tlers ashore until he was absolutely certain there wasn't any threat to their lives."

"Good man, Rous. A bit of an old woman, but he does a good job. You joined him because?"

"Captain Rous was short an officer, and I thought there

would be a couple of prizes, but there haven't been any. There isn't much money in being a harbour pilot, at least not enough for Molly and me to get set up the way we want at Sambro."

Giving the lady on his arm a big smile Bulkeley said, "My spies tell me that you aren't living at Sambro, Mrs. Gray, but in William's old digs on Holles Street while he's away."

"Yes," said Mary. "That's so I can be nearer my family while my husband is gone."

Bulkeley signalled to his groom, who had returned to trail the lieutenant. "We're almost back, and I'm having guests at my estate this evening." He bowed to Molly and shook Gray's hand. "I must take my leave. I will arrange for you to be invited to my next evening."

The couple offered their thanks and said their good-byes as they entered the safety of the old stockade at the south end of the settlement. Molly shivered. "Would he have had the piper flogged if he had known?"

"Yes," said Gray. "He certainly would have."

*The Next Afternoon*
*George Street, Halifax*

"Good afternoon, ladies."

Richard Bulkeley and Miss Amy Rous[3] had been walking the boardwalk near Saint Paul's church. While it had been a poor summer, the last days of August had been gorgeous, and most of the settlement had turned out to take the air each day in the hour or two before sunset.

Molly Gray acknowledged the greeting and said, "We meet again, Lieutenant Bulkeley. May I introduce my good friend, Penelope Hay? Her husband is Ensign William Hay attached to the Fortieth Regiment of Foot."

Bulkeley gave a small bow and lifted his hat slightly. "Ah, Hopson's regiment! Good day to you, Mrs. Hay."

Bulkeley's companion thrust her hand forward and, taking Penelope's, shook it strongly like a man would. "I am so pleased to meet you, Penelope. I met your husband one afternoon on my father's ship, *H.M.S. Success*. As the captain's daughter, I am

unmercifully spoiled and get to meet all the nice young gentlemen. Your William certainly is a nice young man. He spoke
lovingly of his wife, so I am so very pleased to meet you. I
understand you plan to have a family as soon as …"

"Please, dear." It was probably the first time Richard
Bulkeley had ever been embarrassed in public; gentlemen did-
n't discuss such subjects with the fairer sex. He couldn't imagine what kind of an officer Ensign Hay[4] was, talking about his
personal affairs with an unmarried woman he had just met. But
then, Amy was quite open and disarming and people often
returned her openness with sometimes unexpectedly revealing
confidences. Bulkeley was often pleasantly surprised at the tid-
bits Amy passed on.

Bulkeley removed his hat. "Amy is my fiancée," he said by
way of introduction. "Amy, I would like you to meet Molly
Gray, the wife of an old friend of mine."

"Oh, I've met your husband, too," exclaimed Amy. "He's a
lieutenant. He seems enthusiastic about sea duty. I was at the
dock when Father came back from Lunenburg last year. Your
husband told me he had been stuck ashore and was enjoying
himself on the high seas." Amy Rous leaned forward as if giving a confidence. "Your man's much like my father, you know.
He's got a seaman's head is what my father says, although
Father wouldn't like it very much if he knew I had quoted
him." Amy looked sharply at Bulkeley, "And we had your stuffy
business associates at the soirée last evening. Why couldn't we
have had the Grays and the Hays? Oh my! That rhymes."

"I have promised William and Molly," he corrected himself with a nod to Molly, "Mrs. Gray, that we would have
them at the next soirée, my dear. I now make the same promise to Mrs. Hay."

"That's lovely, Richard," said Amy. "Here comes that
dreadful man who keeps taking you away from me. If you must
go, I tell you now, I will *not* re-enter any of these smelly buildings until the lamplighter comes." Amy Rous emphasized her
point with a stamp of her foot and pouted charmingly.

Seeing the instant concern on Bulkeley's face, Molly volunteered, "Penelope and I will see that she comes to no harm,

my dear sir. If you must go off to your soldier business, we'll look after Amy."

Huffing and puffing, the Corporal of the Governor's Guard ran up. He stopped to catch his breath before he spoke. Bulkeley seized the moment to make light banter in front of the ladies. "I daresay, Corporal, George Street Hill will be the death of you!"

The corporal was so out of breath he couldn't respond. Molly Gray, ever one to think of others, volunteered, "It's those dreadful uniforms. They're so tight fitting they cut off the circulation of air everywhere!" She smiled at the perspiring guard and added, "It must be so hard to run with that heavy musket, too."

"Uphill," Bulkeley added dryly.

"It's garrison living, ma'am," the corporal huffed. "Lieutenant Bulkeley tells Cook to make extra apple turnovers fer me supper."

Usually quite stiff, Bulkeley was pleased this social banter was going so well in front of his fiancée. In a jovial tone he asked, "I suppose Governor Lawrence has need of me, corporal?"

"Yessir. He said to tell you 'Tyrell.'"

Bulkeley was caught by surprise. Tyrell was the code name for the English spy at Fort Beauséjour. The spy took dreadful risks for each message so the subject matter must be very important. He began to discuss the conditions under which he could permit his dear Amy to continue the stroll without him.

"Sorry sir," the corporal interrupted. "Governor Lawrence said to tell you the fox was with the chickens."

Any annoyance Bulkeley felt at the corporal's interruption disappeared. This meant war! He made his apologies and briskly accompanied the corporal down the hill to the Governor's Mansion.

"Oh, la!" Amy Rous positioned herself between the two ladies, and hooking arms with each of them, resumed her stroll. "I wonder what the corporal meant?"

Penelope Hay thought he might have said "tie well," and guessed that something very important had to be pulled together. The ladies laughed, and after several more guesses the conversation moved on to something else. Mrs. Hay was closer to the truth than any of them realized.

* * *

Bulkeley burst through the doors into the front room of the mansion. "What is it, sir? Have the French declared war on us?" "Worse, Richard," Governor Lawrence said. "Tyrell[5] says they're planning a sneak attack on Fort Lawrence."

Lawrence held several pieces of paper in his hands. "When you read some of his earlier correspondence, it all fits together." He held up a letter to the remaining light from the window. "Tyrell told us that when the new French commandant, deVergor, assumed command, he reported back to Quebec that Fort Beauséjour was in very bad shape." Scanning the page, Lawrence read on, "deVergor despaired that the fort would ever be able to withstand a siege."

Bulkeley nodded his head in remembrance, "And when you told your friend Governor Shirley the details Tyrell sent describing the conditions of the fort, Shirley wanted to raise a horde of Massachusetts troops and take the fort."

Lawrence couldn't contain a smile. "My old friend, William Shirley, still wants to do just that—kick the French first off the isthmus and then off Cape Breton. He would do it too, but for lack of support from Lord Halifax." The governor picked up the most recent message. "Tyrell says that the French governor of Canada has ordered deVergor[6] to strike at us on the isthmus."

"And his reason for doing that?" asked Bulkeley.

"The French governor believes deVergor's assessment that if we attacked we could capture Beauséjour[7], so he has ordered deVergor to attack us first. The devilish part of this is that he has ordered that Satan priest, LeLoutre, to turn his Acadians and tame Micmac loose on us at the same time. He means to wipe out the English settlements."[8]

Bulkeley sat in one of the chairs. "Raids and massacres!"

"Yes." Lawrence sat down opposite him and lit his pipe. "We can't let that happen." When he had the pipe going

Lawrence blew several smoke rings and poked them apart with his finger. He leaned back and closed his eyes. "That's my part of the country, you know. Governor Cornwallis ordered me to build a fort on the English side of the Missaguash River[9] in the spring of 1750."

Richard had suffered through the governor's favourite story a number of times. He put on a good face and nodded, appreciatively, as the story began.

"When I got there, I saw that my fort would be better located on the long ridge between the Aulac River and the Missaguash, but Chevalier de La Corne was already on the long ridge with over four hundred men." Lawrence swept his arm in a wide circle, "Behind me, on the supposedly English side of the Missaguash, LeLoutre was burning everything to ashes; said he was moving the village of Beaubassin to the French side of the river. Said he was cleaning the place up." For dramatic effect, the governor slapped both hands on his thighs, "What he did was lay waste to the countryside so I had nothing to work with." He sighed, in remembrance. "They made a wily pair, La Corne and LeLoutre." Lawrence shrugged his shoulders. "As a result, I couldn't do anything that spring."

Lawrence examined his pipe and gave it a knock into his hand.

The governor's aide remained silent; he knew the story still had some distance to go before its denouement.

"I returned that September with all the provisions necessary to be self-sustaining. LeLoutre could burn as much as he liked, but I still had enough men and supplies to build my fort." He sighed, putting his pipe and the partially burned tobacco on a tray. "But ... he was there."

Bulkeley had lost track of where they were in the story line. "Who was there?"

"LeLoutre. He was there waiting for me. He had built a defensive dyke on his side of the river. When we tried to land on our side of the river, his Indians and Acadians opened fire on my men. Well, I wasn't having any of that shit!"

"No," Richard agreed but, by the look on the governor's face, not strongly enough. "No! Of course not! What did you do?"

"I jumped into a boat, and the boys rowed like hell to the shore." Lawrence smiled at the memory. "Fortunately, all of my men followed me. We assumed skirmish formation. I told the boys to hold their fire until the very last minute before we charged the dyke and drove them the hell out of there. We went back and set up camp on the Beaubassin ridge. Fort Lawrence is there to this very day." Lawrence stood. He paced back and forth in front of the desk and then went to the window. Looking outside, he watched as the corporal of the guard made some final adjustments to his own appearance before going on parade. Lawrence turned away. "So LeLoutre and I have some history, and that son of a bitch isn't going to push me off my isthmus!"

"What do you intend to do?" Bulkeley asked, rising also.

"Governor Shirley says he can raise two thousand New Englanders."

Bulkeley displayed the proper enthusiasm, "We can use the regulars at Fort Lawrence; that's three hundred more."

"Yes, and we'll need some support artillery, warships, transports, and a good army commander; Colonel Monckton will do."

After a moment's hesitation, Bulkeley cautiously suggested, "Rous is senior naval officer on station. I suppose he could command the naval end."

"Let's get it all pulled together! We'll knock on the doors of Fort Beauséjour and find out if our friend Tyrell was right." Charles Lawrence grinned. "Maybe all we'll have to do is blow a horn, and the walls will come tumbling down."

## *Endnotes*

1  Robert Cameron and his story are fiction.

2  I didn't find the name of the woman who married William Gray. She became Molly Ferguson from New England.

3  Amy Rous is an historical figure and her story is as close as possible to what is recorded about her.

4  Ensign Hay was captured at Fort Beauséjour. There are several accounts as to how he was captured; i.e. coming from the camp, proceeding to Halifax. He did die in the bombardment after having given his parole. For the sake of my story, I have made the giving of his parole later in the story rather than earlier.

5  Tyrell is an historical character who worked both sides.

6  DeVergor's activities are as correct as I can make them.

7  Fort Beauséjour is shown as Fort Cumberland on the accompanying map (circa 1755) because the map was drawn after the capture of the fort.

8  Taken from the copies of Governor Lawrence's correspondence, which were made available to the N.S. Archives and are now on microfiche. I used them extensively.

9  This was an actual incident.

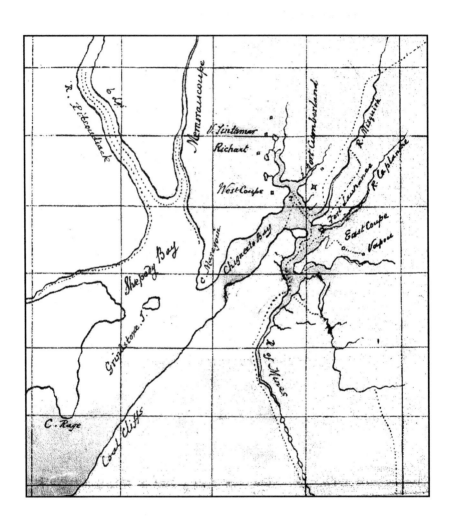

# Chapter Six

## 10 April 1755
## Boston Common
## Boston, Massachusetts

The soldiers of the Massachusetts Militia talked about driving the French out of North America. Even while they mustered on Boston Common—to receive their campaign kit, the remainder of their sign-up bounty, and wages from their sign-up date to April 14 inclusive—they spoke of the French as if they were animals to be hunted and killed. The talk made Jeremiah Bancroft uncomfortable.

Bancroft didn't pretend to like the French; nobody in their right mind did considering the heinous things the French and their Indian allies did to New Englanders. But he had listened to what his preacher had said about loving his fellow man, and the French, no matter how base their actions, were human beings. As well, if one's enemy were not a worthy opponent, what honour was acquired by a victory over something less than human?

"Ensign Jeremiah Bancroft of Captain Phenehas's company,"[1] called the adjutant.

Bancroft stood at attention and stepped forward. "Yes, sir!"

"Sign or make your mark."

Bancroft signed, and the adjutant counted out money into the ensign's outstretched hand. Bancroft saluted and stepped away to receive a mound of blankets and utensils that a sergeant piled into his waiting arms. Military etiquette decreed that a parting salute was required, but Bancroft found it rather difficult with both hands full. Instead, nodding his head in the direction of the adjutant, he turned and marched off.

Bancroft searched for the officers of his company and saw them gathered at the edge of the common. They're probably drinking, he thought. Not that he was against rum, but drinking had no place while serious soldiering was going on. Lieutenant Timothy Wheller was quick to put away his rum flask at

Bancroft's approach but, from the odour, Jeremiah could tell that the flask had made its rounds. Wheller was saying he wanted their company to be assigned to the second battalion; it was historical fact the second battalion of any army always confronted the enemy first. "I want to have a chance at them before they're all exterminated!"

Bancroft dropped his equipment on the grass next to other piles, standing slightly back from the circle with his arms folded across his chest. He had learned to keep his own counsel on both subjects—rum and the nature of warfare. Boyish boasting and bravado passed as professional comment in this regiment, and Bancroft didn't consider these men professional soldiers. He believed that many of his company didn't particularly care for army life; most of them had joined for the money. Of course the money was important to Bancroft, too. His wife, Elisabeth, and little Catherine could live quite well on the money he would leave them.[2] The difference was that Bancroft loved the profession of arms and wanted to be a proper soldier. This constant slander of a worthy opponent unsettled him more than he would admit, even to his wife.

Bancroft sometimes had a smug, self-satisfied air about him that irritated others, and they tended to avoid him. This evening, even though he appeared that way now, he found he was drawn unwillingly into the officers' conversation. Nathan Simons, the other company lieutenant, asked, "How did the musket drill go?"

Bayonet and musket drill was left to Bancroft because he was the best in the company and he had the knack of quickly passing on his skill to the men.

"Our company is the best in the regiment, Lieutenant," Bancroft said. "All they need now is sight of the enemy."

"That's good, Ensign." Captain Phenehas had come up behind the group and had overheard the last comment. "That's jolly good!" The captain pointed to the other side of the common. "Isn't that your Elisabeth?"

"Thank you sir, it is. May I be excused, now?"

"Yes, of course, Ensign. But, who's that with her?"

"That's her brother, sir," Bancroft replied. "I arranged to have an escort home this evening."

"Good thinking, Ensign," the captain said. "The purse-snatchers will be watching for men carrying an armload of military gear. They'll know he has a purse full of money."

Ensign Bancroft saluted, picked up his equipment, and skirted the edge of the common because, technically, the centre of the common was a parade ground and he was no longer on parade so he avoided crossing it. He was pleased with the captain's praise. Maintaining a brisk military step, he thought smugly, tactics! Everything was tactics. Discover the risks and plan for them; that's the road to victory. Remembering it was Elisabeth who had suggested the escort home this evening, his step faltered briefly. Oh, well! A good officer would recognize a good suggestion and implement it.

Elisabeth Bancroft spotted her husband. She waved, and then she and her brother cut across the common to join him.

*28 May 1755*
*Baie Verte village*

At first Abbé LeLoutre was surprised at the amount of hard work the English turncoat was willing to do but soon realized it was the man's nature. Cameron did so well, the priest used the ex-soldier to goad the farmers. "*Il n'est qu'un Anglais.* He's just an Englishman," LeLoutre told them scornfully, "and yet he does more than two of you in half the time. If you worked as hard as that lobster-back, we would be finished by now."

It worked. The Acadians spent more time on the dykes and managed to equal Cameron's output. Abbé LeLoutre fully appreciated the asset that was Robert Cameron.

Cameron had other qualities. He demonstrated, daily, his thankfulness for being rescued from the Indians by being obedient and helpful. He was a good Catholic and devoted to his church. (Abbé LeLoutre wished he could say the same about all of his parishioners.) And the man was a sponge; Cameron rapidly acquired the French language as well as an understanding of Baie Verte's politics.

It wasn't long before one of LeBlanc's[3] daughters chose Cameron to shower with affection and love, and in time he married her. Now, in 1755 he still ate and slept in the LeBlanc farmhouse whenever his duties on the dykes permitted him, but he and his wife, Reine, had already picked out a location for their own house and were making plans. The priest, as a grand gesture of appreciation for his best worker, constructed a new dyke that would enclose several new farms, one of them to be worked by the Camerons. Abbé LeLoutre was looking forward to a second generation of hard-working Camerons.

Abbé LeLoutre's new dyke was barely finished when all dyke work was stopped by circumstances beyond the priest's control.

Very soon after his arrival in the Fundy, the new commandant of Fort Beauséjour, Captain deVergor, had requested that the priest provide more habitants to work on the fortress defences. Over time, deVergor became aware that the priest was holding back large numbers of men to work on the priest's projects while the fort's defences languished. Abbé LeLoutre was forced to send all of his workers to Fort Beauséjour but not the deserter, Robert Cameron: he was to be kept far away from the fortifications. This day, for the first time in two years, Robert Cameron had been released from the almost daily drudgery of building new and renewing old dykes.

Cameron walked down the street of Baie Verte with his eyes open to its beauty. The priest's words had been music to his ears: "Get plenty of rest. Enjoy your family. Eat some good food. I don't want to see you back here until I call for you."

*Dieu, merci.* God was good.

*30 May 1755*
*H.M.S. Success*
*Offshore, Annapolis Royal*

Lieutenant William Gray had been ordered to take the jolly boat from the *H.M.S. Success* to one of the transports anchored off Annapolis Royal. Men and officers of a provincial regiment, second battalion, who had been taken on board at Boston on May 1, had come to find their ship confinement tedious. When what looked suspiciously like a bar-room brawl had broken out on her decks, Captain Rous had imagined the worst; the men had broken into the rum stores and were in mutiny! He considered sending an armed party but instead he ordered his level-headed lieutenant, William Gray, to make some innocuous enquiry and determine the state of affairs on board *Leopard*.

"What was the commotion on *Leopard*, William?"[4] asked Rous on Gray's return.

Gray saluted. "You were right about rum being the cause of the problem, sir."

"Ah! Does the captain still have control of his ship?"

"Aye, he does, sir. But the problem wasn't of the crew or captain's making. The men of the regiment were cut off their rum ration on Tuesday. The ship's purser said he had laid in a thirty day's supply, but it hadn't lasted that long."

"Pursers!" Rous spat out with disgust and loathing. "A captain can never tell if a purser is lining the hold of the ship with proper supplies or his own pockets with coin." Captain Rous cast a quick glance around, checking whether other members of his crew had overheard the remark. Reassured no tattle-tale would go running to curry favour with the purser of *Success*, Rous motioned for Gray to continue his report.

"Sir, the rest of this information was given to me by one of the junior militia officers, Ensign Jeremiah Bancroft. None of the more senior officers would speak to me about it."

Captain Rous waited impatiently for the lieutenant to get on with the report.

"Bancroft said it really wasn't the men's fault. He said they were goaded to it by ..."

"By God, Gray," Rous stormed, "I swear you're rewriting the Bible the way you're dragging this along."

"Aye, sir. Wednesday, May 28, being the Day of Ascension, some of the officers drank to the health of those they had left at home."

"Rum?" Rous interrupted.

"Yes, sir," Gray said. "One of the officers has his own supply. Once the men got a whiff, they became upset. The soldiers asked for their ration. One of the officers said they weren't drinking rations and, besides, there wasn't enough to go around. There was a disturbance."

"So it's an army problem," Rous said.

"Yes, sir. The soldiers' spokesman has been identified. He will be disciplined."

Both officers knew the soldier would be flogged. "Did you speak to the men, calm things down a little?" asked the captain.

"I did, sir. I gave them a message, from you, sir, that, once we were ashore, there would be enough rum for everyone." William gave his captain a half smile.

"Humph!" Rous stared at the lieutenant while the colour rose in the young man's face. When Gray's face reached a satisfactory rosy sheen, the captain relented. "Then we had better make arrangements to get their rum, hadn't we, William?"

Gray breathed a long sigh of relief. "Well, sir, we probably have more than enough rum in the fleet, but none of the captains will admit to the extent of their supply for fear it will be appropriated."

The captain smiled at his lieutenant. "Following your promise, I just might have to do that."

Gray shuffled his feet and fixed his eyes on the top gold button on the captain's chest as he tried to think of a proper response. Damn, he thought. If the other captains learn that a junior lieutenant promised their supplies of rum to the Massachusetts Militia …

As if reading his thoughts, Rous said, "Enough of this, William. You did well to defuse the situation. My man, Wimper, will undoubtedly drive our purser to distraction but we'll have rum for your militia friends."

Captain Rous regarded the sky for a moment. "These days there is a good possibility of morning fog." His mind seemed to be elsewhere as he asked absently, "How many men did you promise rum to?"

"A company, sir. Phenehas Company of the second battalion."

"I'm glad it wasn't the regiment," Rous snorted. "You are the watch officer this evening."

Lieutenant Gray was not surprised that the old privateer knew the details of the ship's operations; the crew believed that the eyes in the back of their captain's head were cat's eyes so he could see in the dark.

"Aye, sir."

Rous sniffed the air. "If we should have fog, place an armed guard, with musket and cutlass, every ten paces along the deck. I don't want any surprises. The password is "rum keg." The countersign is ..."

"Bone dry, sir?"

"Inform the officer who replaces you. You have the deck, Lieutenant Gray."

*1 June 1755*
*The Priest's House*
*Baie Verte*

*"Je m'excuse, Robert, pour te séparer de ta femme charmante,"* said LeLoutre. "I must apologize, Robert, for taking you away from the charming company of your dear wife. I've received word that a huge British fleet is off Annapolis Royal. They were making preparations to sail yesterday, most probably to lay siege to Fort Beauséjour."

Abbé LeLoutre was neatly dressed in his best frock and cap, complete with a gold cross, chain, and big gold ring, as well as his best shoes with the gold buckles. Unusual for the priest, he appeared agitated, unconsciously clasping and unclasping his hands.

*"Je suis au courant, mon Père.* I know, Father. Most of the men of the village are going to the fort."

*"Et toi?* You're not?"

"The soldiers won't let me near the fortifications."

"Then I have a job for you; the road from Fort Lawrence to Pont à Buot must be blocked. I want you to breach the dyke and flood the road."

*"Oui, mon Père."* After considering a moment, Robert said, "That will only block the road at high tides. At low tide it might still be passable."

"The English will want to use the road in the next few days, Robert. Pierce the dyke in as many places as you can."

*"Oui, monsieur."* For a minute it seemed as if the colour sergeant had been issuing orders. Robert smiled and corrected himself. *"Oui, mon Père."*

"I haven't been to the fort yet," LeLoutre said. "I suppose all is in chaos. I'll go there directly we have finished. You have your job to do. Report to me at the fort afterwards."

"I'll be shot if I approach," Cameron protested.

"I'll give them orders not to but, just in case, don't come within musket range of the fort until you see my gold cross."

Robert took the priest's hand and kissed his ring.

"Robert, don't tell the farmers what you're doing. They won't understand." The priest shrugged his shoulders. "They consider the sea a bigger threat than the English."

*"Oui, mon Père. Je ferai ce que vous demandez.* Yes, Father. I'll do what you ask."

*Morning*
*2 June 1755*
*Fort Lawrence*

"How many sail?" asked Captain Hussey.

"Thirty-eight, Captain," the ensign replied.

"Thank you. Come down, Ensign. I have work for you."

Ensign William Hay stood on the catwalk that bordered the palisade facing the bay. With the aid of his telescope and the fort's doctor who was taking notes for him, he was listing the British ships that had begun appearing before the fort that morning.

Hay recognized the three frigates: *H.M.S. Success, H.M.S. Mermaid,* and *H.M.S. Serene,* all with twenty guns each. He had his friend William Gray to thank for his knowledge of ships. In Halifax, Gray had scoffed at army officers who weren't able to tell one vessel from another. In a place like Nova Scotia, Gray had argued, where the army used the navy for transport and assault, it seemed self-defeating not to know something about the capabilities of naval vessels. The two Williams had made a game of it, identifying ships in the harbour until Hay was quite knowledgeable.

Ensign Hay went over the numbers in his mind so he

could make a complete report to the major. "Let's see, most of them are sloops. There're three schooners, one brigantine ..."

"Excuse me, Ensign," the doctor said, "I think you had better get down to see the captain. He sounded angry."

"I'll have this all done in a mo ..."

The voice from below was petulant, annoyed. "Ensign Hay, now! Not sometime after tea."

The Fortieth Regiment of Foot might have spent years on garrison duty here and in Gibraltar, but this commandant, Captain Thomas Hussey, thought himself Caesar—and the Fortieth Regiment a Roman Legion in Gaul. The man had no damned patience! Hay grumbled to himself all the way down, but when he appeared before his commanding officer, all traces of his disaffection had disappeared. "Sir, there are thirty-eight vessels. The majority of them are sloops and should be able to pass well inshore and up the Missaguash River to provide support to our troops if need be."

"That's fine, Hay," said the captain. "We're going to have to use the road along the shore to the bridge at Pont à Buot. The French have breached the dyke and flooded the road.[5] Take half a company to clean up the mess."

"Yes sir." Hay saluted and turned to go.

Hussey grabbed Hay's arm to stop him. "I expect the navy will get the provincials ashore by tomorrow." The captain took off his hat and scratched the back of his head. "If the French had meant to oppose the landings, they wouldn't have flooded the road, but I suppose they could always land below our fort." He smoothed his hair and replaced his hat. "Keep your eyes peeled, Ensign. Don't get cut off from the fort. It takes a long time to train an officer."

"Very good, sir."

*Morning*
*2 June 1755*
*Pont à Buot*

Monsieur deBaralon, a cadet officer, commanded the redoubt at Pont à Buot.[6] It wasn't much of a command; there were only three buildings. The redoubt, built of logs, stood about halfway up the hill from the banks of the Missaguash. The shanty known as the officer's house was about twenty feet from the redoubt and further up the hill. And, off to one side, was the shed that served as living quarters for the eight soldiers of the detachment.

About mid-morning, Cadet Officer deBaralon heard English voices and the sounds of construction on the other side of the river. In response to the English activity, deBaralon sent seven of his men to dig trenches along the edge of the river. He and the corporal installed extra swivel guns on the flimsy walls of the redoubt wherever they found sufficient strength to bear the recoil of the weapon.

"*Monsieur, quelqu'un descend la colline.* Sir, someone's coming down the hill. Perhaps it is a messenger from the fort."

Wiping his brow, deBaralon checked the rear of the redoubt. The corporal was right; someone was indeed approaching. He slipped on his tunic, affixed his sword, and ran his fingers quickly through his long hair. He firmly pulled on his hat, using his hand to measure the width above his eyebrows to make sure it was squarely placed. He had been expecting a messenger from the fort with orders, but he was surprised to see the messenger was the redheaded English deserter. DeBaralon laughed aloud when the redhead stopped far enough away to shout for permission to enter the redoubt. "You are not the fool, my little Englishman. You have few friends on either side of this river," deBaralon said to himself.

The corporal knew *Fanne de Carrotte,* Carrot Top, was one of LeLoutre's men and gave him permission to advance. Even then, the redhead approached cautiously, seeking cover wherever he could. Still wary, he trotted through the open gate at the back of the redoubt and quickly scaled the ladder to the parapet. He handed the officer a skin pouch.

As deBaralon broke the seal on the message, he asked, "*Pourquoi est-ce qu'ils vous ont envoyé, Fanne de Carrotte?* Why did they send you, Carrot Top?"

In passably good French Cameron replied, "*Je ne suis pas entièrement l'acceuil vers le fortifications.* I am not entirely welcome around the fortifications."

"But trustworthy enough to bring me my orders. Humph." The cadet officer smoothed out the letter and began to read.

"Abbé LeLoutre said to tell you that the road to Fort Lawrence on the other side of the river is flooded."

Without looking up, deBaralon asked, "The dyke?"

"Yes. I breached it yesterday."

"I heard a commotion over there this morning. The English must have sent a party to repair it."

"I could break it down again tonight," Cameron offered.

"No, my orders are to burn the bridge and fortify this position." For the first time the cadet officer looked at the deserter's face. "Do you now consider yourself *un Habitant*, an Inhabitant?" deBaralon used the term the European French called the Acadians.

Raising his chin, Cameron said with pride, "*Oui, je suis Acadien*. Yes, I am an Acadian."[7]

"Then you're under my command," deBaralon said. "I've been ordered to take command of all *Habitants* in the area and to oppose the advance of the English. I need you here. Go down to the edge of the river and help my men dig that trench."

"But, sir, I can't go down there. If I'm cut off by the English and taken prisoner, I'll be flogged until I'm dead, and my body hung for the crows."

The cadet officer wasn't pleased at being defied by a deserter, but deBaralon had other problems at that moment and ignored Cameron. He shouted to his men, "Quickly, burn the bridge! Those English might take it into their minds to cross right now. Burn the bridge!"

Using old slash from the days of clearing the approaches to the redoubt, they had soon set the bridge ablaze. By mid-afternoon deBaralon was feeling more secure, since the bridge was gone and the detachment soldiers had brought about one hundred Habitants to the redoubt. Cadet Officer deBaralon ordered the Habitants to deepen and extend the trenches along the river. The work was well along when one of the older farmers noticed that Cameron was not working in the muck with the rest of them.

Cameron explained his logic to the Habitants.

These farmers had formerly lived in the Beaubassin area that had been assigned to the English by treaty. Abbé LeLoutre had moved them to the French side of the Missaguash River and scorched the land in the English territory. Now, if these farmers were cut off at the river, with guns raised against their former English masters, would they not also be flogged and hung out for the birds?

After hearing Cameron's persuasive arguments, the farmers refused to work on the trenches for fear the English might cross the river and cut off their retreat.[8] Because of that, the cadet officer was forced to build a defensive line farther up the hill. The soil was harder to work, and the entrenchment progressed very slowly.

Toward the end of the day, stumps and branches from the old slash were added to cover the shallow trenches. It was a decidedly weaker defensive line than the trenches along the river would have been. Cadet Officer deBaralon was forced to make the best of the situation, and mounted four swivel cannon on the larger tree stumps.

Just before sunset, fifty Mi'kmaq joined the French forces. Not quite knowing what to do with them, the officer left it to the corporal to assign them to positions in the woods. When it was dark, Cadet Officer deBaralon retired to the officer's house content in the work he had accomplished that day.

*Evening*
*2 June 1755*
*H.M.S. Success*
*Offshore, Fort Lawrence*

"Fog's as thick as pea soup,"[9] said the lieutenant. "Will you postpone disembarkation, sir?"

"The tide's right," Rous responded. "We're off Galop's Cove where the beaches are good. We can't see any of the enemy so our army friends shouldn't be upset by the thought of open boats approaching a hostile beach. No, we'll proceed."

"Aye sir. The signal gun to be discharged as planned, sir?"

Captain Rous regarded the small circle of ship's officers, and considered the thick fog and the fact that he would need the first and second lieutenants on the *Success*. Captain Rous made up his mind. "Have Midshipman Stewart come forward."

The first lieutenant called out, "Mister Stewart to the captain!"

"Aye, sir," sounded almost immediately from the stern.

The sound of running feet preceded a young officer with coal-black hair who presented himself to the captain with a salute. The young man waited, but Rous didn't return the salute. For a haunting moment Rous was back on the deck of *Albany* and the enemy had taken refuge up against a shoal. So many years and so many young men gone. All dead under his command.

Rous finally nodded at the boy who dropped his salute. "I have an important task for you, so listen carefully," Rous said to Lieutenant Gray and Midshipman Stewart. "*Mermaid's* north of us a thousand yards, almost at the mouth of the Missaguash. I want you, Gray, to take the jolly boat and tell Captain Washington you need *Mermaid's* jolly boat plus an officer and crew. Stewart, you take the cutter and do the same thing with Captain Probey of *Serene*; she's about eight hundred yards south of us. Any questions, so far?"

There were none.

"You'll each take five hundred yards of line, with floats attached, to keep in your boat and another five hundred yards of line with floats to hand to the officer of the other ship's jolly boat. Tie your line to the frigate's anchor cable and row for Galop's Cove in close company with the other jolly boat. When you come to the end of your line, tie yourself to the end of the other jolly boat's line and send her to shore."

Young Stewart thought it was a grand idea. "Like making a corridor to the shore."

"That's right," said Rous. "If we keep all the ships' boats between the lines, we won't lose any of our precious soldiers."

Rous gave Gray a penetrating look. "Gray, if any boat goes across your line, they won't just get lost."

"I understand, sir," Gray said. "They'll either run aground

under the guns of Fort Beauséjour or continue up the river where they'll be fired upon by the French troops at Butte à Roger."

"I'm glad you understand, Gray. First Lieutenant!"

"Aye, sir."

"Is the signal gun ready?"

"It is, sir."

"When you hear the gun, gentlemen," Rous instructed Gray and Stewart, "you'll know that disembarkation has begun. The ships' crews know nothing of the lines to shore that we have just devised. I sincerely hope you can make it work."

"It will," the men promised. "We'll make it work, sir."

* * *

So far, so good, thought Lieutenant Gray. He looked at the line that trailed off to starboard into the fog and eventually to the bow of *Mermaid*. Over the other side of the boat, another line trailed into the fog and hopefully to the shore at Galop's Cove. It was a good plan and would probably work, but Gray prayed the fog would lift, anyway.

From somewhere in the fog came a splashing sound followed shortly by the bow of a boat about ten feet away, heading across the line.

"Go starboard, coxs'n," Gray warned. "Go starboard hard!"

The bow of the other boat swerved to the right. It was loaded with soldiers who sat as still as statues. As they disappeared into the fog, Gray shouted after them, "Steady on that course. Five hundred yards to the beach. From what ship?"

Gray thought the answer was "*Fortunatus.*"

Two more boats came out of the fog moving in close company. "Coxs'n, starboard twenty points. There's a line in the water to your port. Don't cross it. What ship?"

"*Fortunatus.* Thanks, mate."

Boats from *Phoenix, Seaflower,* and *Prosperous* passed Gray. When the fog finally lifted, he saw the convoy sitting serenely in the bay and a multitude of boats and men on the beach at Galop's Cove. By seven that evening Colonel Monckton's army was safely lodged in and about Fort Lawrence.

*Early morning*
*4 June 1755*
*Fort Lawrence*

"William," asked Hay, "what are you doing here?"

"I'm supposed to maintain ship-to-shore signals with *Success*." Gray put his arm around Hay's shoulder, shoving a crumpled piece of paper under Hay's nose, but then quickly pulled it out of his friend's reach. "Besides, I wanted to give you this."

"William, I don't have time to fool around!"

"It's a letter from Penelope."

"Penelope? How wonderful!"

"Yes. She's getting along fine. The doctor says she's as healthy as a cow and the baby should come soon without any complications."

Hay regarded Gray and the seal on the letter suspiciously. "How do you know all that?"

"The letters came on the supply ship, *Warren*. I had a letter from Molly; she told me. Isn't it great? You're going to be a father!"

"And soon! First we have to get this little campaign out of the way." Ensign Hay stuffed the letter in his tunic and buttoned it up carefully. "It's quarter of six. The advance party moves off on the hour."

"Do you know the order of march?" Gray asked.

"Captain Adams is the advance guard with sixty men," Hay said. "I'll be with them since I've already travelled the road to Pont à Buot."

"Good for you! I wish I were in your shoes."

"My shoes will be pretty muddy. The Frenchies broke the dykes. I took a work party out to repair them on Monday but, this being only Wednesday, the roads are still very wet."

"Lieutenant Colonel Monckton?" Gray asked.

"He's next with his three hundred regulars from the fort, followed by Lieutenant Colonel George Scott and the second battalion. The first battalion with Lieutenant Colonel John Winslow will be in the rear."[10]

Both men watched the organized confusion of an army

readying itself for its march. A twinkle of light from the other side of the river caught Gray's eye.

"They're watching us form up!" Gray pointed so his friend could see it too.

Hay announced in an aggrieved tone of voice, "A Frenchie has an eyeglass over there, and he's watching everything we do."

\* \* \*

Ensign deLangy, stationed at the observation post on Butte à Roger, lowered his eyeglass while speaking quietly to his sergeant. "I want to send a runner to the fort, Sergeant."

"I could send Fortier, sir,"[11] the sergeant said. "He's smart and in good condition."

In short order Fortier stood at attention in front of the ensign. "At ease, soldier," deLangy said. "Can you use a spyglass?"

*"Oui, m'sieur."* Fortier took the glass and trained it where the ensign told him to.

"See? There are about sixty soldiers in the advance party. They have four short brass field guns. They won't be able to travel any faster than those guns. I figure it will take them six hours to get through the flooded marsh and along the road."

Fortier, still examining the scene through the spyglass, said, *"Pardonnez-moi, m'sieur.* The English seem to have assigned a large number of provincials to haul the cannons."

The ensign took the glass and carefully surveyed the scene. "Yes, they have indeed ordered a body of New Englanders to pull the cannon. Perhaps they will reach Pont à Buot in four hours." He continued to stare through the glass while Fortier fidgeted beside him.

"Relax, soldier," deLangy said. "As soon as they begin their march ... ah! They are moving. What is the hour?"

"0600, Ensign."

"Fortier, go to the commandant and tell him there are four short brass cannon in the advance party being hauled by a special contingent. I figure four hours en route, so he can plan for an assault at Pont à Buot after 1000. Got that?"

"Yes, sir. Do you want me to tell him the advance party is sixty men?"

"*Bonne idée,* Fortier. Now run with the wind, soldier."

"*Oui, m'sieur,*" and he was gone.

\* \* \*

Atop the rampart of Fort Beauséjour and inside the compartment that stored the fort's artillery, Abbé LeLoutre was arguing with deVergor, counselling the commandant against using the Mi'kmaq warriors in defensive positions. "They will not stand against the cannon, commandant. We should send them on raids. Let them harass the English from the cover of the woods."

The priest's harangue was interrupted when the outside guard knocked respectfully with his ring of keys on the iron door at the entrance to the grand casemate. "There is a soldier outside with a message from Butte à Roger, Commandant."

Commandant deVergor answered sullenly, "*Faites-le entrer.* Send him in."

"*M'sieur,*" said the messenger. "I have a message from Ensign deLangy. "The English began their march along the swamp road to Pont à Buot at 0600."

Commandant deVergor held up his hand to halt the soldier's report. Without looking at the priest, he said, "I thought you said the road was flooded."

"*Oui, Commandant,*" said LeLoutre. "*Oui, il l'était le dimanche.* Yes, it was on Sunday. My Mi'kmaq children tell me the English have restored the dyke. The road is very wet but passable."

"Humph," the commandant snorted. Private Fortier continued with his report. "The advance party of sixty English regulars has four short brass cannon. The cannon are being hauled by a contingent of provincials. My officer believes that because of the condition of the road and the presence of the cannon the advance party will not reach Pont à Buot until 1000."

"Is that all, soldier?"

"*Oui, m'sieur.*"

"*Attendez dehors.* Wait outside."

When the casemate door had closed, LeLoutre was quick to speak. "Turn the Mi'kmaq warriors loose! I will order them to cross the river to harry the English from the swamp. We still have time! The English will reconsider trying to cross the river with hostiles behind them."

"How many do you have?"

"I could put a force of two hundred into movement behind the English."

DeVergor paced the length of the casemate from the heavy door to the masonry wall. He returned to the middle of the domed room and sat down on the chair before the table that served as a desk. He opened the sketches of the terrain around the fort, using his sword scabbard to hold down one end of the papers. Jabbing at the map with his finger, he said, "The redoubt at Pont à Buot is our first and most important defensive point for Beauséjour. It must be defended."

"*Oui, Commandant,*" LeLoutre said. "I agree with you. However, we should use our forces in the most effective manner possible. Mi'kmaq warriors are best suited to hiding in, and fighting from, the woods. They shouldn't be expected to stand and face the English cannon and bayonets."

Shaking his head, deVergor stood up. "We sent couriers to River Saint John, Québec, and Louisbourg asking for reinforcements."

"You forget, we also sent couriers to Isle Saint Jean and Chignecto. They are closer. We should have heard from them by now if they were coming."

Disregarding the priest's comments, the commandant continued. "When the reinforcements arrive, we should be able to contain this English force and even take Fort Lawrence if their losses are great enough in their attempt to cross the Missaguash River."

"Commandant, I don't advise …"

Interrupting the priest for probably the first time in their relationship, deVergor said, "I understand we've destroyed the bridge and established a defensive line at the crossing."

"*Oui, Commandant.*"

"Then, when the English attempt their crossing, I want to meet them with concentrated fire from every cannon and gun we can bring to bear on them."

Without waiting for the priest's response, the commandant called for the runner from Butte à Roger.

\* \* \*

It had been a busy morning for Cadet Officer deBaralon. The very first thing was to check his defences. The trenches with breastworks looked substantial. The ground had been cleared from the river to where his shallow trenches—strengthened by tree stumps, branches, and boulders—formed the defensive line. His frontage was perhaps one hundred and ten yards, and both ends of the trenches were anchored in the trees. The defensive line should have been dug into the dyke at the edge of the river with flanking defensive positions in the trees, but that couldn't be helped now. His immediate thought was to put Indians in the trees, and he ordered his corporal to make the appropriate arrangements.

When deBaralon surveyed the approaches from the parapet of the redoubt, he was content with his efforts. What he needed now were more men. He was pleased when a mixed force of soldiers, Habitants, and Indians showed up at the redoubt. DeBaralon worked to correct the fields of fire for the swivel guns while the corporal assigned positions to the new recruits.

Around 0930, a troop of soldiers marched down the hill and entered the redoubt from its single gate. DeBaralon descended from the parapet and noticed there was a more senior officer in charge of the troop. His emotions were in conflict; he was resentful that another officer would have the glory of a successful defence and relieved that he could no longer be held responsible for the defence of such an important position.

"Are you the officer here?" the new officer queried.

"Yes, Ensign."

"I'm Levraux deLangy, Ensign of Foot from Isle Royale. I relieve you of command, Cadet Officer ..."

"DeBaralon."

"Why did you locate your defensive line so far from the crossing?"

"The Habitants wouldn't occupy the position for fear of being cut off and captured," deBaralon reported reluctantly. "They fear being flogged and hanged as civilian insurgents."

The ensign didn't comment but climbed the parapet and studied the terrain. Finally he said, "I have orders from Commandant deVergor. At the first opportunity, I am to subject the English to concentrated fire from every weapon at my disposal. Pass the word and position our men accordingly."

"I've posted the Indians in the woods on either side of the clearing."

"Will they be able to bring their weapons to bear in accordance with orders?"

"Yes, I think so. I'll ask the corporal."

From the other side of the river came the kind of noise an army makes when it's on the move. There was no doubt about it; the English had arrived.

"Pass the word, quickly," deLangy said. "Everyone is to watch for my signal. From here everyone should be able to see me. I'll raise my sword, and when I lower it, every weapon is to be discharged and reloaded. Volleys will be at my command until I give the order for independent fire."

"Yes, Ensign."

* * *

The English advance guard came within sight of the bridge ruins. When Captain Adams saw the breastworks on the opposite shore, he gave orders for his men to take up a defensive position to the left where there was some shelter. While they were still three hundred yards from the river, a tremendous volley came from the breastworks, the trees, and the redoubt. Adams saw his sergeant spin and fall. Otherwise, the men of the advance guard were untouched. Adams was now established on the left.

Some of Adams's men helped the provincials unlimber the

four six-pounders.[12] Gunners set their guns and opened their caissons. They were serving their weapons when Colonel Monckton's three hundred regulars came off the road and up the slight incline to the crossing. They changed formation from column of route to line and, as they advanced majestically to the edge of the river, they were met with a crashing French volley. There was no discernible effect on the arrow-straight lines of redcoats.

Monckton moved his men to the right, leaving room for the second and first battalions.

\* \* \*

Ensign deLangy ordered two volleys. Smoke and flame had engulfed his whole line, but when the noise had died and the smoke had drifted away, the English line stood pristine and unaffected by the fury of the French arms. In the comparative silence, he could hear the English officers giving orders to their men. His sergeant spoke softly from his side; "Our men are shooting too high because they're aiming downhill."

DeLangy seemed bemused by it all. "What are the English doing in the centre of their line?"

The sergeant glanced sideways to see if his officer was all right. Deciding that he was, he said, "The English are preparing to fire their six-pounders."

"Independent fire! *Independent fire!*" DeLangy was surprised by the strength of his voice; it had carried well. The French defenders began peppering shots at the English; however, all of the French swivels discharged with one voice.

The English troops returned fire. Part of the parapet near where deLangy was standing disappeared, along with one of the swivel guns, as an English six-pounder scored a direct hit.

\* \* \*

Ensign Jeremiah Bancroft was in his glory. He had gone forward with his company to protect the engineers who were laying timbers for a new bridge. His boys were holding up well.

Lieutenant Timothy Wheller had been directing the company fire when he dropped his sword and seized his chest. The men of the company assumed independent fire.

Bancroft dashed over to Wheller who was kneeling, still clutching his chest. The ensign detected the strong odour of rum as he helped the stricken officer lie down.

"I think the flask stopped the bullet, Jerry," Wheller smiled at the ensign. Then blood gushed from his mouth. Both men looked down at the gory mess on the front of Wheller's tunic. When Bancroft looked into Wheller's eyes again, the lieutenant was dead. A soldier from the front rank of the company fell over Bancroft's shoulder and slid off; he didn't look to see who it was.

Bancroft laid down his musket and picked up Wheller's sword. "On me!" he shouted, and led the company to the side of the near-completed bridge from where he could see a group of French soldiers running from the breastworks to a half-completed trench near the dyke. He raised his sword. "There! Take them down!"

\* \* \*

DeLangy's corporal realized the English engineers were going to finish the bridge unless muskets could be taken close enough to be more accurate. He gathered a small group of soldiers from the redoubt and led them at the run to the breastworks. Once there, he realized the damned Habitants, who had been defending the breastworks, were rapidly retreating beyond the range of the six-pounders! He noticed movement in the trees; the Indians were doing the same thing, but that wasn't his worry right now. He had to leave that to the officers. He motioned to several other soldiers to join him in the forward dash. One of the men shook his head no, and the corporal lifted the muzzle of his musket slightly. The soldier changed his mind.

Through the smoke, the corporal saw a provincial officer waving his sword. As the smoke lifted, he saw a line of Englishmen with muskets levelled at him. They fired. All of his men went down.

The corporal went down too, hit in the shoulder. He

checked the soldier on one side of him, dead. He squirmed the other way and was confronted with a smiling face. "*Mon Dieu!* Why are you smiling?"

"The Fortier family always smiles into the face of disaster, so we are always smiling! We have to get out of here, Corporal. Get up!" Fortier pulled him upright, and they staggered back to the breastworks. There were no Habitants or Indians in the trench, only the soldiers from Butte à Roger. Fortier didn't hesitate. "Move out boys. Head for the redoubt."

It was then Fortier noticed a cloud of smoke up the hill; the redoubt was on fire, the officers' house was burning merrily, and the shed had been demolished. It certainly looked as if the French were abandoning the crossing. He looked back at the river. Lobsterbacks and provincials in their blue uniforms were everywhere, streaming across the completed bridge.

\* \* \*

"Company! In skirmish order! Ad*vance!*" Bancroft swung the sword in a circle over his head and pointed it forward. He jumped down from the new bridge, ran along the dyke, leaping over the incomplete trench work where his men had cut down the line of Frenchmen trying to reach the trench. Odd! Only two bodies! A musket ball plucked at the sleeve of Bancroft's tunic. He ducked down, searched for the enemy, and caught a glimpse of him as he darted through the trees in a running retreat. Was it his imagination or did the enemy have red hair? If Bancroft had only had his musket he might have been able to bring him down. Ensign Bancroft checked his arm for blood. Nothing. He rested a moment or two and then followed after his company.

When Bancroft reached the ruins of the redoubt, the French and the Indians had disappeared.

*5 June 1755*
*Fort Lawrence*

William Gray stood at the entry port of *H.M.S. Success.* He saluted the quarterdeck and took his sea bag from the sailor who had hoisted it aboard for him. The watch officer acknowledged him with a nod. William nodded back, but he remained there, his bag over his shoulder, as he sensed something special, comforting—it was almost like he had always imagined going home to Scotland might feel like. That was it! He was home, back home on *H.M.S. Success*. He realized that he had missed the neat, naval way of living. Army tents lacked the reassuring solidness of the ship's deck planks that had been holly-stoned clean so often that they were almost white. The sea air, even the sunshine, was a refreshing change from the smelly fort. He breathed it all in and stepped away, heading for the galley. The first thing he would do, get some hard biscuits from Cookie and then catch some shuteye. He might have a chance to write a letter to Molly, but there was no real rush for that; *Warren's* next trip wasn't until the ninth.

Gray had a happy thought. Captain Rous always sent his letters and reports to Halifax by hand on *Warren*. He had yet to choose an officer for the next run. It could very well be him! He could see Molly.

"Is that you, Lieutenant Gray?" asked Rous.

Of course it's me, old mother hen! Who else would it be, Gray thought. Aloud he said, "Aye, sir! 'Tis Lieutenant William Gray back from the wars."

"Feelin' a bit cocky are we now, Lieutenant?" Captain Rous beckoned for Gray to join him on the quarterdeck where Wimper was fixing a ribbon to one of the captain's pigtails. Pigtails were an old-fashioned naval style and more suited to a privateer than a captain of the Royal Navy, but Rous had been a privateer in his earlier days and the old habits died hard. Rous was silent as Wimper put the finishing touches to his hair.

Gray took the opportunity to regard the man who was his captain. He wore his dark blue uniform with grace; his cat-like movements were always fluid and restrained. The gold epaulettes of his rank looked bigger on this man than on any other captain Gray had met. Gray wondered if he saw it that way because Rous was his captain. He had a large head, a beak nose, and eyes so deep brown they were almost black. And his hair was rapidly changing from grey to white. When Gray had first met the captain on board *Sphinx* in 1749 at the founding of Halifax, Rous's hair had been steel grey. Gray wondered now at Rous's age.

Wimper startled William from his reverie: "Your lieutenant is taking a good look at you, Captain."

Captain Rous cackled his strange little laugh. "If Wimper wasn't responsible for my turnout, there wouldn't be much to see, Gray."

After joining in the laughter, Wimper finished his task and left the two officers alone.

"I used my glass to try to see what the Frenchies were doing," said Rous, "but there's too much smoke coming from near Beauséjour. D'you know what's going on?"

"Aye, sir," Gray said. "Lieutenant Colonel Scott's men captured an Inhabitant and he told the tale. The French commandant gave orders to bring all supplies and any cattle that could be found inside the walls of the fort. Then the Frenchies destroyed all buildings in the vicinity, including their church. We could see 'em from the palisade. They burned everything."

"Couldn't Monckton's men stop them?"

"The provincials of the second battalion were nearest to the fort, about a mile and a quarter away, but they were busy setting up a camp and building breastworks to protect it."

Rous looked toward Fort Beauséjour; the smoke was dying down. Colonel Monckton couldn't do everything at once, he thought, but it was too bad the French had been given the time to empty their external storehouses into the fort.

"I have some other information from Ensign Hay," Gray said. "He said Colonel Monckton has started looking for a suitable site for his cannon. Hay figures the fun will start in five or six days."

"Why so long?"

"The French broke the dykes last week. We patched them, but the road from Fort Lawrence is very wet, and that makes moving supplies and the bigger cannon difficult. It's slow work."

"I see. Well, you, Lieutenant, will have a piece of work to do soon, probably tomorrow."

Gray's heart sank. He knew for a fact that *Warren* was sailing on the ninth; there was no possibility of her sailing tomorrow. So taking the captain's mail aboard *Warren* was not the "piece of work" he had in mind. Gray had a strong feeling that he wasn't going to get a chance to see Molly in Halifax. He waited for the captain to break the bad news.

"Captain Cobb has been collecting some particular supplies throughout the fleet," Rous said. "When he has sufficient cargo, he'll take it up the Missaguash. I want you to ensure its delivery to the proper soldiers."

"The rum! That's it, isn't it? The rum for Bancroft's boys."

"Yes, Lieutenant. Please hold yourself ready. As soon as *Yorke* hoists the 'prepared to carry out your orders' pennant, I expect you to be ready to board her." In a surprisingly fatherly gesture, Captain Rous put his hand on the lieutenant's shoulder. "Make sure the armourer issues you with a pistol before you leave. I do believe you'll be going in harm's way." Rous removed his hand from Gray's shoulder, and clasped both his hands behind his back. Turning away from the young officer to face the enemy fort, he stated, "Commandant deVergor undoubtedly still considers the Missaguash a French-controlled river. As soon as he sees the sloop unship her sweeps, he'll guess where she's going. He won't let *Yorke* pass unchallenged."

"We'll get through, sir. Bancroft's boys earned their rum."

Rous was momentarily distracted. He had been feeling somewhat melancholy during the last weeks. Over the years, so many men had died that he had become more and more reluctant to risk his crews. The sight of young Stewart crumpled on the deck of *Albany* haunted him. No, it wasn't Stewart; he had sent Stewart out in the fog, and he had come back—this time. It was Stevens who had died! Christ! The young officers of his command, who seemed to be getting younger, were so brash and daring. And here was another one; Lieutenant Gray, who only knew life and adventure and believed himself immortal. Had he, Rous, ever been like that?

Captain Rous regarded his shoes. *I used to take off my shoes when going into battle because it felt right; it felt lucky,* he thought. Now I take them off because my feet hurt. I don't know what year I was born, but I must be in my fifties; my feet feel like they're fifty. Two fifties make a hundred. I feel a hundred. Suddenly remembering the lieutenant's presence, Rous asked, "What do you want, William?"

The lieutenant was standing quietly, waiting to be dismissed. On the spur of the moment Gray asked, "Sir, *Warren* goes to Halifax on Monday, and you usually pick an officer to hand-deliver the mail to the governor. Could it be Ensign Hay this time, please? His wife is in Halifax. She's pregnant with their first child and expects to deliver shortly. It would be a good ..."

The look on the captain's face told Gray he had stepped over the line, and he let his words dribble to a halt. Christ! How could he have been so stupid? The captain would crucify him!

Captain Rous regarded the young man. He considered the request and what had prompted it. These boys think of life, he thought, while I'm engrossed with death. We must make more room for life. "If he can arrange with his commanding officer to be absent from his post," said Rous, "then he can be the courier this time."

"Thank you sir. I'll send a message ashore right away. I know Captain Adams can spare him. Thank you sir."

"You're dismissed, Lieutenant."

*6 June 1755*
*H.M.S. Yorke*
*Missaguash River*

The river had narrowed quickly, and if the French were going to interfere with the passage of *H.M.S. Yorke* upstream, they would have made their presence known by now. Thus, in traditional naval terms, Captain Sylvanus Cobb was beginning to "lose his pucker"; he was beginning to feel safe and comfortable with the situation.[13]

"Lieutenant Gray," asked Cobb, "do you know which company gets resupplied?"

"Aye, sir. The Phenehas Company."

"What kind of a name is that?"

"I truly don't know, sir," Gray said. "The officer I had some dealings with was Ensign Jeremiah Bancroft. If he's still alive, I should be able to spot him from the ship, he's such a tall fellow."

"Good. I don't like taking my ship too close to shore in hostile country. The sooner we finish this business, the better I'll like it."

A spout of water raised about ten yards off the stern, and a cannonball passed through the rigging, smashing into the bushes on the opposite bank of the river, followed closely by reports of the two cannon. "Damn," said Cobb. "I knew it was too good to be true!" He quickly searched for the location of the enemy's guns while simultaneously giving orders to his first lieutenant. "Increase the stroke on the sweeps! Move us out of here!"

Cobb spotted the French guns when they next fired. "Swivel! Target is astern, in the bushes just beyond the field. Return fire!"

The first lieutenant joined his captain. "Captain, I'd like to ship the sweeps and return fire from our main guns."

"Just move us out of here, First Lieutenant!" Cobb shook his fist at the two cannon that fired again. "The bastards were smart! They waited until we passed. We'll have to pass them again to return to the bay. They're trying to bottle us in!"

"No, captain." Gray looked ahead to a point where the river narrowed. "I think they mean to board us."

On the enemy's side of the river was an overhang where French soldiers held their muskets at ready, waiting for *Yorke* to come within range. A second group, Inhabitants armed with muskets, pitchforks, and homemade pikes, were sheltered behind large trees. Several of them held grappling hooks that had been attached to trees with ropes.

"Sweeps! Hard astern!"

As soon as *Yorke* lost her forward momentum, Cobb ordered the crew to resume stroke to hold her where she was against the flow of the river. "We're trapped!"

\* \* \*

Ensign deLangy was delighted. "We have them! Corporal Fortier!"

"Yes, Ensign."

"Signal the artillery to bring down one cannon to support us in our assault."

"*Oui, m'sieur.*"

Several French soldiers fired their muskets at *Yorke*. "Hold your fire!" deLangy ordered. "Do not waste ammunition. As soon as the cannon arrives, we'll charge the ship."

Several of the French soldiers looked physically ill at the thought of running into the mouths of the ship's cannons.

"No, no! The English won't be able to use their cannon because their crew is rowing. If we move quickly, they won't be able to get their cannon ready in time." Ensign deLangy pointed up the hill. "Look! Our cannon is ready and the other cannon prevents them from leaving the trap. We will have them! *Allons, les gars!*"

With a loud cheer, the soldiers ran along the bank of the river toward the trapped *Yorke*.

\* \* \*

"Christ!" Gray saw the soldiers running toward them. "Captain, they're going to attack us!"

Captain Cobb could see the danger. "First Lieutenant, drop the port and starboard anchors. Quickly, if you please."

"Aye sir!"

"Sweeps!"

The second lieutenant responded, "Aye sir!"

"Continue the sweeps until the anchors are set. Ship your sweeps at your discretion."

"Aye sir!"

"Swivel gun, disregard the cannons," Cobb ordered. "Target the attacking party. Load grape! Remainder of ship's company, prepare to repel boarders!"

Gray accepted a cutlass from the armourer. He gripped his navy pistol in his right hand and the cutlass in his left. His mouth twisted into a grin. If he was going to die here, he planned to take some of the bastards with him.

With a tremendous crash, one of *Yorke*'s cannon was knocked off its mount, and part of the bulwark was smashed by a direct hit. The sailor who had been working that sweep simply disappeared. Gray was thrown back. He lost his footing and fell over the body of the armourer. The French soldiers fired a volley. Splinters from the bulwark, deck, and mainmast flew in all directions. Another sailor went down with a scream, a long, thin piece of wood sticking out of his leg above his knee.

Gray staggered to his feet. He saw that the attackers had stopped to load their muskets. Big mistake, Mr. Frenchman! Gray remembered some soldierly advice his uncle had given him as a boy. Uncle Charles had said, "When assaulting a defended position, put the defenders to the bayonet as quickly as you can. Don't stop to reload."

Gray screamed out loud, "Big mistake, Mr. Frenchman!" He lifted his pistol and, sighting on an opposing officer, pulled the trigger.

\* \* \*

Ensign deLangy looked down. His right hand stung. He had been holding a musket. Now it was gone, and he seemed to be missing some fingers. With his left hand he unbuttoned his tunic and jammed his injured hand inside. He waved his good arm. "Let's finish this, fellows. Onward!"

Corporal Fortier was shouting into his face. What was he saying? DeLangy pushed him away. "Come on! Follow me!"

"… more English, sir," Fortier shouted. "We must move to cover our cannon so they can withdraw."

Provincials! They were coming along the shore of the river. The Habitants at the overhang were fleeing. His flank was exposed to the attacking provincials! He must retreat to the cannon.

\* \* \*

Gray thought his pistol ball had hit the French officer, but the bastard was still standing! Now the Frenchman was waving his troops on.

"Reload," Gray told himself, "before they swarm the bulwark!" He hunched down and methodically went through the business of loading his weapon properly. He was always afraid a damn navy pistol might misfire. When he looked up, the French were retreating and taking their cannon with them. A tall, skinny man was leading a company of provincials in hot pursuit. The man saw Gray and, as he trotted by, waved. Jeremiah Bancroft! Gray managed to work his features back into a grin. "Good luck, Jerry!" He noticed that Bancroft had been promoted. War was good for promotions, he thought. Suddenly weary, Gray sat on the bulwark and checked to see if he had any wounds.

Cobb watched the tall New England lieutenant trying to reform his company. It wasn't an easy task; the New Englanders' blood was up, and they were ready to chase the Frenchmen to the walls of the fort. But hearing the lieutenant's orders, they started to straggle back.

"Who are they, Lieutenant Gray?"

"They're Phenehas Company, sir. I think they've come to collect their rum," he added, dryly.

*7 June 1755*
*Fort Beauséjour*

The guard at the grand casemate watched as Abbé LeLoutre strode down the corridor and knocked on the iron door.

The response from inside was swift. *"Entrez."*

As the guard swung open the heavy door, LeLoutre could see the commandant was alone, smoking his pipe. LeLoutre grimaced. He hated the stench of French tobacco. He didn't mind a pipe of Virginia tobacco now and again (he wasn't above asking his warriors if they had been able to find any when they returned from raids), but what passed for French tobacco was ghastly.

LeLoutre indicated to the guard that he wanted the door

left open as he entered the casemate. "I have bad news, Commandant."

"What could be worse than the English have finished their road and are moving up their heavy cannon?" deVergor asked.

"I sent out a party of Habitants under deBoucherville last night to harass the English road builders."

"I gather it wasn't successful."

"They didn't come back."

"*Mon Dieu!* All of them captured?"

"They went home to their villages, Le Lac and Baie Verte," said LeLoutre.

"How do you know?"

"Cameron, the English deserter, the one we call Carrot Top, was the only one to return. Carrot Top said the Habitants didn't want to run the risk of being hanged." LeLoutre pulled up a chair and sat down. "The British had announced that would be the fate of any Habitant who took up arms against them."

"How many deserted?" the commandant asked.

"Fifty."

"*Mon Dieu!* Has deBoucherville returned?"

"I think so."

"Then, send deBoucherville to Le Lac and Baie Verte to order them back."

"I don't think it will do any good." LeLoutre adjusted his gold chain and cross so that it was centred on his frock. "I suppose we could tell them we received reinforcements from Isle Saint Jean. Perhaps they would take heart at the news."

"Did we? Did we receive reinforcements?"

"*Oui, Commandant.* An officer of the Isle Saint Jean garrison arrived with sixteen Habitants."

"Arms? Ammunition?"

"None."

Commandant deVergor took his pipe out of his mouth as if he suddenly didn't like the taste any more. He put the pipe down. "Do what you think best with the Habitants, Abbé. I'm counting on getting reinforcements from Quebec and Louisbourg. Some real soldiers! Do what you think best with the Habitants," he repeated.

"I'll send deBoucherville to bring back as many as he can."
Dispirited, the commandant replied, "Good. That's fine."
LeLoutre could hear the despair in the other man's voice.
Something positive must be done, he thought. Waiting for
reinforcements to come, waiting for the English to finish the
road, and waiting for the fighting to begin wasn't good for
morale. On the other hand, attempting to capture that sloop of
war had done wonders for the garrison's morale. The men had
returned to the fort in high spirits telling stories of their bravery. It hadn't stopped the Habitants from deserting, that's true,
but the Habitants were a special matter. What the troops of
Beauséjour need is another effort to tweak the nose of the English! LeLoutre outlined a plan. "I'll send Beau Soleil with his
warriors to raid the English lines and pick up a prisoner or two.
It will be good for morale to have a couple of English prisoners, and we'll learn the problems *they're* having."

"*Oui.*" The commandant smiled and picked up his pipe.
He knocked the ash and struck a match to relight it. "I think
that's an excellent idea. *Occupez-vous-en, mon Père.* Please see to
it, Father."

That night just after dark Beau Soleil, a Habitant who had
taken up Mi'kmaq ways, slipped out of the fort leading a raiding party of thirty Indians. They took up positions outside the
English camp and waited.

*8 June 1755*
*English camp*

Ensign William Hay presented his papers to the officer at the
gate for inspection.

"Goin' to Halifax, Ensign?" The officer of the guard could
not keep the envy out of his voice.

"Yes, Lieutenant. I'm the courier on *Warren* this trip."

"Yer papers are in order. Good luck t' yuh." He handed
Hay's orders back to him.

Hay gave a casual salute and left the camp. Dressed in his
campaign uniform Hay felt slightly dirty but, he consoled
himself, he would have plenty of time to clean up at the fort.

Tonight while he was sleeping, his man would lay out his parade dress and polish all of his accoutrements. This campaign uniform would disappear and reappear in his travel trunk, cleaned and pressed. He looked down at his boots as he walked. These boots had to be worked on before looking presentable again, but he had no doubt that his man could accomplish wonders.

Hay planned to wear his parade dress when he boarded *Warren* just for appearance's sake. "Have to show the navy what a real officer looks like," he said to himself. Once on board, and after he had made a good first impression, he could slip into his newly cleaned campaign uniform and these boots, hopefully restored close to their former splendour.

And wouldn't Penelope be surprised to see him! He realized that he would be forever in debt to William Gray for arranging this. Have to hand it to Gray, Hay thought. He knew all the right people. And because of Gray, Penelope had been invited two or three times to tea with Molly Gray and Amy Rous. It was nice of Amy to arrange for a covered coach to take Penelope to tea. Certainly there was no social life for an army wife in a garrison town while she was "in confinement." Most often, women in Penelope's condition remained in seclusion, at least women of breeding certainly did.

Instinctively, Hay knew he was being watched. He cast a quick look back over his shoulder. He was far enough along the road to be out of sight of the sentries at the camp gate and not yet seen by the guards at the bridge. He hurried his step. Hay didn't actually hear anything but rather felt a presence behind him. He turned his head in time to avoid the swing of a war club. He jumped back several paces and drew his sword on the Indian who had swung at him. He should have armed himself with a musket as Captain Adams had advised. But of course he hadn't done any such thing; a musket simply wasn't an officer's weapon. He had to handle this savage with his sword. Hay thrust and felt the blade strike. "Ah, ha! Got you, my friend!" Unfortunately Hay didn't see or hear the second Indian until his club struck Hay's sword arm. He almost dropped his weapon from the pain. He faced the new threat.

The second Indian feinted and weaved to encourage the white man to commit himself to battle. Hay looked around. The first Indian was no threat; he stood off to one side holding the spot on his body where blood seeped through his fingers. He made no move to either interfere or leave. He was an interested spectator, as were the dozen or so other Indians who had quickly formed a rough circle around the two combatants. More Indians poured out of the woods, putting Hay in mind of ants scurrying about.

"Some ants' nest," he said to himself. Hay shook his sword arm to bring back some feeling, and immediately regretted it because of the renewed pain he felt. He made a big show of being in pain, clutching at his arm where the club had landed. Then he suddenly thrust at the Indian. The Indian was quick, but the point of Hay's blade slashed his arm. The Indian yelped, more in surprise than in pain, and jumped back, disregarding his wound.

Another Indian stepped out of the circle and took his place. Hay ignored him. Instead, he turned in the direction of the bridge and slashed at the Indian who was in his way. Since the Indians appeared to be taking him on one at a time Hay thought he might have half a chance to fight his way to the bridge. He shouted, hoping the camp sentries might hear him, "That's all William Hay needs, boys! Half a chance!"

One of the Indians shouted something, but Hay ignored him and continued his slashing attack on the surprised man who stood between Hay and the bridge. Again he drew blood, this time from the man's hand and cheek. Hay felt good. He had gained seven or eight paces toward the bridge. The circle of Indians moved with him, keeping him in their centre. The Indian he had just bloodied had stepped back. He glowered at Hay but made no effort to return to the fight.

Another Indian took his place, holding a short javelin-like spear in one hand and a club in the other. Hay didn't hesitate. He attacked hard, driving his sword down on the spear, breaking it in half. At the same moment, the Indian landed a strong blow to Hay's left shoulder. Hay staggered back with the Indian following closely, hitting the Englishman twice more before

Hay's sword delivered a slashing cut to the Indian's chest, drawing blood.

The next Indian didn't wait for the wounded brave to withdraw. He stepped in and knocked down Hay's sword. With a backhand swing, he caught Hay on the side of the face.

Hay went down on one knee. He tried to raise his sword but the Indian bludgeoned Hay's sword arm. This time he hit the Englishman on the back of his bowed head. Hay fell. With shouts of triumph the Indians closed in on the fallen officer.

*H.M.S. Success*
*Offshore, Fort Lawrence*

Removing his hat, Lieutenant William Gray wiped the sweat from his brow. Glancing at the handkerchief before tucking it back into his sleeve, he grimaced at the wet, black smudge. He was down in the ship's hold supervising a work party and getting very dirty in the process.

It was not only filthy but also boring duty moving the ship's stores to check on their condition and then ensuring proper stowage. During the long morning, every crate, case, box, bale, and barrel had been lifted at least twice; first to examine its condition and second to stow it properly, bearing in mind the ship's centre of gravity. With the cargo tentatively stowed, Gray climbed out of the hold and boarded the jolly boat to be rowed around *Success* to gauge her attitude, her trim, in the water. When Gray returned to the hold to have part of the load rearranged, the sailors worked with a will until the young officer climbed out for another visual inspection. With the officer gone, the sailors relaxed and talked as sailors always do about the immediate things in their world: their captain, their officers, and their ship.

"I'm tellin' yuh, that lieutenant stood up to them Frenchies, bold as brass, when he was defendin' *Yorke!*" said Jake Fink.[14] He was perhaps the tallest sailor in the fleet and enjoyed a measure of respect because no one could get in close enough during a brawl to do him any harm. It was his arms; they were so long that he could knock down every belligerent patron at his favourite Water Street pub with one swipe of his cudgel.

Fink, on the other hand, believed he was entitled to the respect of his mates because he had two brains: one in his head like everyone else, and a second and larger "brain" to digest his food and release evil-smelling gases when it had the notion. The lower brain was easily affronted, and revenge was deadly. So with little fear of contradiction, Big Jake went on, "I got it from the *Yorke* work party yest'day. They said the Frenchies' cannon blewed away Tommy Quick who was workin' the sweeps. Our officer stands up, bold as brass, mind you, points his ship's pistol at the Frenchie general and orders him t' surrender."

"Did he?"

"Surrender? Nah! T'ain't possible for them Frenchies t'do a thing yuh tells 'em. They's so stupid they can't understand the King's English." Fink paused to scratch his belly while his audience waited for him to continue. "So the general points his sword at our lieutenant and orders 'is men to charge 'im."

His scratching finished, Fink inspected the binding on the nearest bale and waited until one of the sailors asked the question. "Then wot, Jake?"

Raising his hand Jake pointed his finger at an imaginary general. "Bang!"

"Shot him down, I bet he did. Didn't he, Jake?"

"Shot the sword right out of 'is 'and. Didn't want t' kill the general, mate. Our officer just wanted t' save *Yorke*."

"Why didn't he kill the general, Jake?"

"Think about it," Fink said. "If he killed the general, there'd be no one on the French side t' surrender the fort when the time comes. Got t' have a general with a sword when it's time t' surrender."

The men heard the cutter alongside. Lieutenant Gray was returning to the hold.

"But the lieutenant already had the sword, Jake." From the dirty look Fink gave him, the doubting Thomas knew he courted a lingering death. He looked away.

"Our officer used the sword t' drive off the soldiers," Fink said.

The buffer in charge of the work party ordered the men to stand to. "Lieutenant wants us to move these six chests to starboard. Shake a leg!"

"Besides, when Lieutenant Gray got them Frenchies t' run," Fink continued, "he threw the sword at them."

"You got somethin' to say, Fink?"

"No, Buffer, I ain't."

"Get to work then."

The lieutenant watched every move the work party made. Getting the cargo stowed properly was vital. The last thing Gray needed right now was Captain Rous complaining about the "trim of my ship," because, somehow, Gray had slipped into the captain's bad books. Something he had said or done had earned him this dirty assignment. For the life of him, he couldn't figure out where he had erred.

He had been telling Captain Rous about the defence of *Yorke* on the river. He had noticed a spark of interest, or was it something else? Anger? Concern? Anyhow, the captain's eyes had flashed with something and then, as quick as he could say Barrington Street, Lieutenant William Gray had been sent into the blackness of the ship's hold. Counting beans. Coughing from the dust.

That was it! He had been saying that things weren't looking good for *Yorke* when Jeremiah Bancroft had brought his New Englanders to the rescue! Maybe the captain didn't like the thought of being beholden to the army for saving one of his ships. "I shouldn't be the one counting beans! *Yorke* was Captain Cobb's responsibility, not mine," Gray muttered.

"Excuse me, sir." The buffer was watching the lieutenant. "Did you say something for my ears, sir?" The buffer was used to working with the officers since his job was to reissue officers' orders to the sailors in terms they could understand. He found that most officers talked to themselves at one time or another, and he mostly ignored them. This lieutenant didn't have that habit so the buffer had questioned him.

"No, Buffer."

"Very good, sir. The chests are stowed on the starboard side, sir."

"Right-o, Buffer. Let's go topside and see how close we are to a proper trim this time."

"Aye, sir."

Jake Fink was the first to sit down the minute the buffer's back was turned. "I bet we gets orders to go to the River Saint John."

"That's French Territory. Why go there?"

"They're a real threat to us now that we're here at Beauséjour."

"How would you know that, Jake?"

"I heard it through the ventilator when we was waitin' t' take the captain's mail over t' *Warren*."

"What did you hear?"

"A French schooner run aground on the Point La Tour shoals," Fink said. "She was loaded with cannon and stuff bound for the River Saint John fort. One of our ships took her t' Halifax as prize." [15]

"There ain't no war. There ain't gonna be no prizes, not with this New England feller Lawrence as gov'nor."

"May be true about the prizes but I still believe we goes t' River Saint John soon. I heard him through the ventilator. 'It is a safe and convenient harbour for the enemy's ships, and the river itself provides a grand inlet by water from Canada to this country. We must secure it to our own use.'" Fink did a fair imitation of the captain's New England twang. "Them's his very words."

The work party heard the lieutenant's cutter return to the side of the ship.

"Wonder if we got her trimmed right this time?"

The doubting Thomas spoke up. "I heard Gov'nor Lawrence has hundreds of New England friends ready to settle in the Fundy. Least, as soon's we takes the fort."

"Nah. All the good land's already took by Inhabitants. What's left ain't worth the Yankees comin' fer." Jake shook his finger at the smaller man. "I don't know where ya gets these stories."

The buffer came down the ladder. "Lieutenant wants those four barrels moved to the port side."

Jake smiled. "The moves is gettin' smaller. We's almost done!"

"Fink! Less talk, more work."

"I'll be quiet, Buffer."

The work party heard pipes sounding on the main deck. The captain was returning to his ship.

"Move smart, boys! The old man is back," said the buffer.

Lieutenant Gray reached the bottom of the ladder. "It looks good, men. I think this is our last adjustment."

"The lieutenant says secure the tie downs, boys. Move it, now." The buffer saw a shadow at the lip of the hold. It was Wimper, the captain's man.

When he heard him speak, Gray didn't have to look up to know who it was. "Lieutenant Gray, sir, Captain requests the pleasure of your company aft. Now, sir."

Gray quickly scaled the ladder. When he reached the deck, Wimper smiled and handed the young officer a piece of clean, damp linen. Gray quickly wiped his hands and face as the captain's servant spoke softly. "I overheard him to say *Success* was well trimmed."

Gray leaned back over the hold and spoke to the buffer. "Have the work party stand down, Buffer. Well done."

Wimper gestured at the ship's hold. "You wonder why the captain was hard on you. Well, Captain Rous has moments of self-doubt. He felt bad he sent you on *Yorke* as a whim."

Gray whispered, "He sent me on *Yorke* to make sure Phenehas Company received their rum ration."

"It was a whim, sir," Wimper replied firmly. "He regretted it muchly when he heard about the attack. He suffered pangs of worry."

"And I got the dirty duty?"

"Yes, sir." Wimper seemed uncomfortable as he related, "He doesn't have a son, you know. Just a daughter."

"Officers to the captain's cabin." The command came from the stern of the vessel.

"Thank you, Wimper." Gray handed the soiled linen to the man. After a moment's hesitation, he said, "Wimper, why me?" Gray was flustered as he tried to explain himself. "You told the armourer …"

"I told the armourer to ensure your personal weapons were in good order and your pistol primed."

"And here you are today with a damp linen."

"You're going in front of the captain and should be presentable. Understand me, sir. I try to tend to the small matters that might prove a distraction to the captain. He's got more than enough on his plate to worry about than the young officers he's obliged to send in harm's way."

"I understand, Wimper. Thank you." Gray hurried aft to the captain's cabin.

It took a moment for Gray's eyes to adjust from the bright sunlight to the dim confines of the captain's cabin. The deck-head beams of the sloop of war were low enough to be hazardous to a man of his height. He made his way carefully through the crowded room to a vacant spot near the captain's desk.

Captain Rous acknowledged his presence with a nod. "Now that we're all here, I'll get started. I thought I'd better tell you about my concerns for this enterprise." Rous pulled out his pipe. "You may smoke, gentlemen."

No one made a move to smoke while in the captain's cabin but waited while the captain stoked his pipe and lit it. When he had it going he said, "First the good news. I spoke to Colonel Monckton. He expects to have his parallel trenches dug soon. That will allow him to bring his heavy artillery into play. After that, the fort will resist, but it will eventually—in a week or two—fall to us."

Captain Rous knocked the bowl of his pipe on the side of the desk. He examined the pipe minutely and then tamped the tobacco with his forefinger. "As naval officers, you are aware that every moment we spend against this shore we're vulnerable to attack from the bay." He struck a flint and lit a taper. "The bad news is I fear we have no choice but to stay and wait for the success of Colonel Monckton's artillery."

The officers shifted uncomfortably. No naval officer liked to think his ship was exposed to danger.

Drawing on his pipe Rous continued, "We sit here at the end of the bay and up against an inhospitable shore. Meanwhile, the word from Halifax is there are two enemy frigates in these waters. One of thirty-six guns and the second of at least twenty." He blew out the taper, leaned back, and enjoyed his pipe.

The first lieutenant looked anxious, and his comments betrayed his concern. "If they come upon us they'll have the advantage! We should leave and search them out." He looked around at the other officers for support. "They're probably at River Saint John drawing fresh water. We could come upon them and drive them onto the shore or force them to sail into our guns."

"A good plan if we didn't have to leave our transports here undefended to accomplish it." Rous took a somewhat fatherly tone with the first lieutenant. "The troops and cannon will have to be returned to Halifax, and there are other problems that increase the importance of the transports over and beyond the possible loss of a few sloops. You will please wait until you have all the information."

"Aye, sir. I'm sorry, sir."

"Fort Beauséjour will fall. The French commander doesn't know it yet, but there will be no reinforcements from Louisbourg or Quebec. Admiral Boscowen is stationed off Louisbourg with twelve ships-of-the-line. Both Quebec and Louisbourg are too busy looking after their own skins to worry about Fort Beauséjour."

The officers smiled at the news.

Captain Rous shuffled a couple of sheets of paper. "Since the Inhabitants have taken up arms against us, Lord Halifax considers them a threat to any peace we might establish in Nova Scotia. What we need is a stable loyal population here; one that cannot be riled up by French priests like LeLoutre. Governor Lawrence thinks it's possible that a large number of the New England soldiers might be encouraged to stay in Fundy. If that should happen, there will be a need for transports to bring their families and possessions here."

"Another good reason for the sloops to remain here at Fort Lawrence?"

"Yes, to protect the transports. Finally, if there is a good response from the New Englanders, it may be necessary to displace some of the French Inhabitants."

Gray nodded his head. He had just understood something. "And give that valuable land to New Englanders."

"Yes," Rous confirmed. "We'll need more transports if Governor Lawrence means to move some of the Inhabitants around in the Fundy."

"Lock, stock, and barrel, sir? That would be a huge job."

"You're right, First Lieutenant, it would be a huge undertaking."

Sailing master Scott spoke first. "I can position us further out into the bay. If there was a picket ship on the horizon to warn us of approaching frigates, we might be able to manoeuvre enough to sting 'em. That would take some doin', captain, against a thirty-six!" He rubbed his chin. "But we could sting 'em!"

"My gun crews can sleep on the deck. It's milder now, sir, so they could do it." The first lieutenant used his hands to emphasize his promise. "Our response time would be cut by two-thirds!"

"Fine. Gentlemen, implement your plans. At least you now know why I'm willing to place us at risk. The transports are vital to the final success of our enterprise. Thank you. Gentlemen, you are dismissed."

Captain Rous bit on the stem of his pipe and waited until Gray had reached the door of the cabin. "Lieutenant Gray, would you please stay behind?"

"Certainly, sir."

"Close the door. There was a raid near the bridge at Pont de Buot this morning. Your friend Ensign Hay was taken."

"Christ, no!" Gray burst out.

"He was travelling alone from the camp to the fort," the captain continued. "I don't know if he survived. There was no body, but there was a fair amount of blood and his broken sword at the scene. An old-fashioned Micmac weapon of some sort was also found. It was cut in half."

"Ensign Hay is a professional, sir. I'm sure he gave a very good account of himself."

"Yes, well, Commandant deVergor is a professional as well. If he has your friend in custody, he'll advise us. I'll let you know if I hear anything."

"Thank you, sir."

"You're dismissed, Lieutenant."

Gray saluted and left the cabin.

*Main Casemate*

*Fort Beauséjour*

*"Entrez."* Commandant deVergor was at his desk smoking. A man dressed in a priest's habit sat on a campaign stool some distance from the commandant. A blue tobacco haze had settled to just about eye level and little swirls of smoke spiralled up from the lanterns' chimneys.

Ensign William Hay saluted Commandant deVergor. He stepped across the threshold and then stood at attention just inside the open door. The two armed guards that had brought him from the main gate to the grand casemate maintained a careful watch of the English prisoner from outside.

The commandant spoke. *"Voulez-vous me donnez votre parole, m'sieur?"*

When the English officer failed to respond, the priest asked the same question in English. "Will you give the commandant your word that you will not attempt to escape custody?"

In fluent French Hay answered, "Your pardon, priest. I understand what the commandant asked of me. I cannot give my parole that I will not attempt escape." [16]

Commandant deVergor shrugged his shoulders. "I can't afford to have guards assigned to you, and I have no space to lock you up." He looked to the priest for guidance.

"I am Abbé Jean Louis LeLoutre," the priest said. "Your name is?"

"Ensign William Hay of His Majesty's Fortieth Regiment of Foot."

"Well, Ensign William Hay, where were you going when my people ran across you with only a sword to defend yourself?"

"I was walking along the road from the camp to the fort. I really didn't expect to find hostiles behind our lines."

The commandant smiled. "Your pardon, Ensign. We didn't expect to have an English camp behind *our* lines." He leaned forward to better see the Englishman's face in the uncertain light. "The leader of our raiding party expressed admiration for your swordsmanship. It's a dying art among younger officers."

"I come from a military family, sir."

"And that's why you acquired French?"

"Yes, sir, and Dutch and German."

The priest was a trifle annoyed at what he considered military talk. "Where were you going when my people ran across you?"

"To the fort. I planned to catch the mail ship to Halifax; my wife is having a baby."

"There we are, commandant," LeLoutre said, indicating the English officer, "he was leaving the area of confrontation. If he writes a letter to his colonel, we'll pass it along seeking to exchange Ensign Hay for one of our men who is missing since last night." LeLoutre gave Hay his most pleasant smile. "Give your parole. Since you do not intend to participate any further in this conflict, it should be of little actual consequence."

"I regret, priest, that I am unable to give my parole. My colonel might understand my motives, but my family? Never."

The priest grasped his gold cross and spoke coldly. "My son, understand this. You survived your encounter with my Mi'kmaq friends because I asked them to acquire a prisoner. If my request places the commandant at a disadvantage, I might have to return you to your captors." He made an agitated gesture with his cross in the direction of the Englishman. "Hopefully, you would have a safe passage back to your camp."

Obviously discomfited, deVergor hastily intervened. "We'll find some sort of answer to our dilemma short of sending you back to your captors." Indicating the only other chair in the room, roughly hewn with a woven seat, deVergor said, "Sit down, Ensign. You might be interested to know that your regiment chose to take possession of a little hill this afternoon. They seem to be preparing that site as a place to establish their batteries."

Hay settled into the chair and crossed his legs. "You failed to contest the ground, sir?"

"My infantry fired on them, and we continue to bombard." The commandant inspected his pipe with great care. "I have a mind to say your regiment made a bad choice, but I hope they persist in developing the site. We harass them at this stage, but not too much." He struck a match and held it to his pipe.

"Just opposite your main gate would be a better location for artillery," Hay said. "I understand the rise is called Butte à Charles."

"Ah!" Commandant deVergor slid a glance at the priest. "Our visitor wasn't blindfolded when he was brought in."

"No matter, sir, that I saw it. If Butte à Charles is a better site, our engineer will see it."

"Your engineer? Who might that be?"

"Engineer Tonge.[17] It won't take him long to site his cannon and ..."

"There are so few cannon?"

"No, sir. You're mistaken. We have thirty-two heavy cannon and twenty-two large mortars. I assure you that Engineer Tonge will bring them to bear when they arrive at the site. You will be well advised to remain in this casemate." Hay looked around at the construction. "I think this room could withstand the eight-inch and the royals, but a direct hit from the thirteen-inch mortars would probably ..."

LeLoutre interrupted. "I apologize, Ensign Hay. Our manners are terrible. Someone should look at your wounds."

"Yes, that's a nasty cut on your face, and there's blood at the back of your head." deVergor waved at the guards. "Take the ensign to the officer's mess. See that he is well fed. Corporal?"

"*Oui, m'sieur.*"

"I don't recognize you. What's your name and who's your officer?"

"Corporal Fortier, sir. I came with Ensign deBaralon from Pont à Buot."

"Please inform Ensign deBaralon that I want you assigned to guard this officer. Ensign Hay has not given his parole. You will guard him accordingly. Ask one of the other guards to fetch the doctor."

"*Oui, monsieur.*"

After Fortier and Hay had left, the priest and the soldier sat quietly digesting what they had learned. DeVergor was the first to speak. "He's a little mine of information, isn't he?"

"Yes, a real gem. I didn't want to milk him too quickly."

"You were wise, Abbé, to interrupt."

"We can talk to him again later this afternoon."

"In the meantime," deVergor said, "use your good offices to persuade him to write his note to his colonel. I'll order Ensign deBaralon to take it to the English camp under a flag of truce. We'll use Hay's capture as an excuse to get one of our officers inside their camp. DeBaralon can try to arrange an exchange of prisoners and observe as much as he can."

"You wouldn't release this Englishman, would you?" LeLoutre asked.

"No." Commandant deVergor smiled. "Ensign Hay has walked across the hill that is the best location for artillery. I wouldn't want him to be able to tell his colonel what he saw. No, Ensign Hay will be a permanent guest of Fort Beauséjour."

DeVergor put down his pipe. "In the meantime, tell our Indian allies to blindfold any prisoners they bring to the fort."

"They won't be bringing any more prisoners to the fort."

The soldier regarded the priest through slitted eyes. He picked up his pipe and began to fiddle with it. He made no further comment. After a few moments the priest rose and, saying good afternoon, left the casemate.

\* \* \*

The French doctor, a talkative little fellow, was roughly kind to the Englishman. As he bound Hay's wounds he complained about the conditions inside the fort. "They drove all the livestock into the fort. I suppose that's all right in a way; we'll eat well because there isn't enough water for the livestock and the extra people. Cows, chickens, goats, Indians, Acadians, and Canadians as well as the regular garrison are all jammed into this little space." The doctor stopped and cupped his hands together. "See? A little space where we must rid ourselves of human and animal waste. So! The animals will be disposed of quickly." He resumed his task. "And the water! There used to be good water inside the walls, but now it's a dark brown colour. I won't drink it and neither should you, my young patient." He flipped open his case and produced a leather-covered flask. "Here, this wine has no water in it."

Hay gratefully accepted the drink.

"That should take away some of the buzzing from between your ears. You were hit really hard! War club?"

"Yes," said Hay. "At least I think it was. I didn't get to see it at the time."

"*Mon Dieu*, you speak French like a Parisian! I close my eyes and I am at home." The doctor gathered up his things. "Are the *maudits Anglais*, cursed English, going to take our fort?"

Hay smiled. If one spoke French well enough, it was like belonging to a club or a society where there was a certain acceptance of values.

"I said, are the *maudits Anglais* going to …"

"*Pardonnez-moi, monsieur le docteur*. It is just a matter of time. The guns will destroy the walls, and once the walls are down, the regulars will advance and take the fort."

"*Mon Dieu!*"

"Find a safe place," Hay instructed the little man, "and stay there until the bombardment is over and the redcoats have raised the Jack."

"Where would be safe?" asked the doctor.

"The grand casemate looks strong enough."

"That's the commandant's office."

"You have a wise commandant."

Corporal Fortier stuck his head into the room. "Are you finished, doctor?"

"*Oui, merci, Corporal.*" The doctor picked up his bag, retrieved the flask, and hustled out of the smaller casemate. "*Bonne chance, Anglais,*" he called back as he departed.

Corporal Fortier handed the ensign some parchment, a bottle of ink, and some quills. "I took the liberty of sharpening the quills for you, sir. Since you haven't given your parole I couldn't let you have the knife, as small as it was."

Laughingly, Ensign Hay went about the task of composing a letter to Colonel Monckton. He had a sudden thought: certainly the priest spoke passable English, but perhaps he couldn't read it. Perhaps a hidden message could be sent to the colonel telling him there was a better site for the cannon. Hay hadn't given any parole. He was an active soldier with important information for his commander. How to do it? He crumpled up the first piece of paper and started again.

> Dear Colonel Mmonckton:
> I am thankful to Good to be vvery well treated heree. My wounds are not serious and have been seen to by a ggood doctor. Uunder these circumstanncess, I have not givenn my paroole, and no further prressures have put upon me in thatt regard. Hopefully, you will be able to affect an exchange so that I might be able to resume my duties forthwithh.

Hay had just finished writing when LeLoutre entered the casemate followed by a short plump man. "You have your letter ready, Englishman?"

"Yes, priest, I do. I suppose you must check it." Hay held out the letter to the priest.

Taking the parchment in his hands the priest said, "I don't read English that well. I asked Thomas Pichon, commissary of stores, to join us. He learned the language from his English mother."

The newcomer entered the circle of light from the lanterns, and Hay's heart fell. Thomas Pichon looked every inch the English squire.

"Thomas," the priest said by way of introduction, "this is Ensign William Hay."

Pichon inclined his head toward the Englishman but made no attempt at pleasantries. Looking at the letter, LeLoutre said, "The ensign wrote a letter to his colonel. I would want you to check it." A small smile played around the priest's mouth. "There mustn't be any hidden meanings or underlined portions, Thomas."

Pichon adjusted his spectacles and, holding the letter near a lamp, Pichon read the contents aloud to the priest. When he had finished reading, he removed his spectacles. Placing the letter on the desk, Pichon removed the top from the inkwell. He dipped the quill and, leaning on the table, scratched a few letters on the bottom of the page. "My initials," he said, handing the letter back to the English officer. "I think you should add your signature and date it." Turning away, he excused himself from the room.

Hay hid his amazement. Pichon surely had the language skills to see through Hay's crude attempts at hiding a message. He must have seen it, but why hadn't he said anything? Hurriedly, Hay signed the letter. After folding the parchment in four, he took the stick of sealing wax and held it against the candle, and waited for the wax to drip onto the parchment where its edges met. Wetting his ring with his tongue he pressed it into the hot wax. He blew on the wax for a moment, and passed the letter to the priest. LeLoutre took the sealed letter and left the casemate.

Hay sat alone and puzzled over Thomas Pichon's mysterious actions. He shook his head and instantly regretted it; he had a massive headache. Some more of the doctor's wine would be appreciated. He leaned back in his chair, his eyes closed but his mind active. If his exchange wasn't arranged in time, he would have to find some way to live through the bombardment. As far as he could see, the commandant's office was the only place with walls thick enough to resist the thirteen-inchers' bombs.

## *Endnotes*

[1] Jeremiah Bancroft was a New England soldier who kept a diary. It gave a very personal view of the Nova Scotia campaign. Most of the New England names and ranks used in this story are taken from this account as well as the dates and the nature of the operations. Although Bancroft never mentions his rank, he might have been an NCO. NS Archives.

[2] Information is drawn from a letter from Elizabeth Bancroft. NS Archives.

[3] LeBlanc is an Acadian family I knew as a child in New Brunswick. The characters and mannerisms are theirs adapted to fit the historical setting. I drew from the Bourgeois Family Book much of the detail concerning the Acadians and their feelings about 'the English.'

[4] The ships and captains are correct, taken as they are from the order of battle. The incident of the rum on *Leopard* is fictitious, being used to set up the meeting between Bancroft and Gray. It leads to the sortie of the *H.M.S. Yorke* up the Missaguash River on a resupply mission that did in fact happen.

[5] "Progress was slow over the marsh owing to the dykes having been destroyed in places," said Lieutenant Colonel Winslow. The dykes were breached (not by Cameron) and were repaired (probably not by Hay).

[6] Jacau de Piedmont's account. Also, I obtained a description of the redoubt during a visit to Fort Beauséjour.

[7] I used the then-current terms for the various peoples. European-born French used 'Les Habitants' to denote French speakers born in the Fundy to differentiate them from 'Les Canadiens.' The English used 'Inhabitants,' 'Canadians' and 'French.'

[8] The habitants did refuse to work for the reasons quoted (Jacau de Piedmont) but not at the instigation of Cameron.

[9] The fog was real. The incident of Gray and the longboats in the fog is fiction. The landings were made at Galop's Cove.

[10] Information concerning the movements of forces came from the accounts of Jacau de Piedmont, Lieut Col John Winslow, the diary of Jeremiah Bancroft and "A Narrative and Structural History of Fort Beauséjour 1751—1755" by Barbara M. Schmeisser, Parks Services historian.

[11] There was a fleet-footed messenger, but the name is fiction.

¹² Description of the attack from the diary of Jeremiah Bancroft. "Set out for the French forte and having a bridge to lay over the river in order to go over to them opposite a block house where the French had placet 6 canon also a battery they had and we marcht in Batalion form to the place where we war met by a great number of french and indians who made a hideous yelling and then firing upon us with there canon and small arms. We had 4 field pieces which ware six pounders which we or at least our guners got ready and returned shot as good as they sent and much better, then a smart engagement began between the two party our men firing and husaing that within an half hour we drove them forward.." According to Jeremiah's diary, there was at least one New Englander killed. I selected the man who would give Bancroft a promotion.

¹³ "Captain Cob came up river at which ye french fire 2 canon and running down to the marsh, firing with there small arms intending to bord him but they were soon obliged to return by reason our men ran upon em firing also Capt. Cob fireing his swivel." That is how Jeremiah Bancroft reported the encounter in his diary.

¹⁴ Fink is a fictional character.

¹⁵ From the letters of Governor Lawrence. NS Archives.

¹⁶ Hay eventually gives his parole in the story. In real life he gave it, readily.

¹⁷ Information about and actions of Engineer Tonge are according to records.

# Chapter Seven

*8 June 1755*
*English Camp*

The sergeant of the guard rapped on the metal tag attached to the flap of Colonel Monckton's tent.

"Enter!"

The sergeant briskly pushed the flap aside and entered. He assumed the position of attention and, looking straight ahead, stated, "Captain Adams begs to inform the colonel a French officer has come under flag of truce."

"Where is he?"

"Bein' brought blindfolded up the path, sir. He should be here forthwith, sir."

Colonel Monckton buckled on his sword belt and attached his scabbard. He reached for his hat and stepped through the tent flap into the light breezes of a fine Nova Scotia morning. He could see the approaching party, two French soldiers escorted by a section of redcoats.

The group halted about twenty yards from the colonel. Captain Adams raised his voice so the colonel could hear him over the distance. "Sir, they carry a letter from Ensign Hay. They wish to discuss an exchange of prisoners. May we approach, sir?"

Colonel Monckton nodded his head, and the party advanced. When they stood in front of the colonel, Captain Adams removed the blindfolds from a junior officer and a soldier bearing the flag of truce. Colonel Monckton spoke to the officer. "Good morning, Ensign."

"Ensign deBaralon at your service, Colonel. I have a letter from one of your officers. I've been instructed to tell you he's in good health and under the protection of the French Army."

Thinking of the ferocity of the Micmac, Monckton said, "That's good to know." Monckton accepted the letter and turned away. Inside the tent he said to the sergeant, "Inform

Captain Adams to entertain the ensign. Walk him around the camp. Make sure he sees as many troops and guns as possible. When the little ensign has seen enough, take him to the officer's mess tent and feed him well. Then send for me. We'll discuss the terms of the prisoner exchange." Colonel Monckton allowed the flap of the tent to fall. He broke the seal of the letter and put on his spectacles. The first thing he noticed was his name was misspelled.

The bottom of the message was signed Tyrell.

*12 June 1755*
*Fort Beauséjour*

Ensign deBaralon clattered down the corridor to the grand casemate. "Commandant! The English are approaching Butte à Charles! Commandant!"

Commandant deVergor stepped into the corridor. "Show some decorum, man! So, the English are attacking our forces on Butte à Charles. We expected that!"

DeBaralon was breathing heavily. He stood at attention, his eyes bulging. "No, sir! Our Habitant and Indian force has retreated in the face of the New England Militia."

*"Mon Dieu! Les laches!"* deVergor looked back into the casemate. "You told me, priest, that your people would defend the butte!" Before Abbé LeLoutre could respond, deVergor was shouting orders. "Sergeant of the guard! Assemble the garrison!" DeVergor ran down the corridor toward the gate to see what was happening on the slopes of Butte à Charles.

Ensign deBaralon followed the commandant. As he stepped into the bright sunshine he said to himself, "So much for showing some decorum, Monsieur le Commandant!"

From the raised entrance to the casemate, deBaralon could look over the heads of the commandant and the assembling troops. The blue uniforms of the New Englanders could be easily seen forming up on the south slope of Butte à Charles. There was movement on either side of the larger formation. Even without a spyglass, deBaralon could see other militia companies advancing in line of skirmish. The English were coming in force! He sensed someone standing beside him and moved to let the man pass. It was the English prisoner, Hay, with Corporal Fortier close behind.

Ensign Hay stopped alongside deBaralon and gazed upon the activity.

"Come to see the fun, Hay?" asked deBaralon.

"It looks like Colonel Monckton plans to put his artillery on Butte à Charles."

"We're sending two companies from the garrison and our entire force of Habitants and Indians. We'll push them off."

\* \* \*

Captain Phenehas led his company out of the bushes on the right flank of Lieutenant Colonel Scott's battalion. Giving hand signals to his two lieutenants, he waited for his men to resume formation.

Lieutenant Bancroft turned around to face his men as they straggled out into the open. He held his arms wide, indicating the line he wished them to take. "Hurry on, men. We don't have time to enjoy the view!"

When his sergeant took the proper position at the right of the line, Bancroft walked forward to chat with the other officers and left the form-up in the hands of his non-commissioned officers.

"That's a magnificent view, Captain!" Bancroft removed his hat and wiped the sweat from its band. He slipped the hat back on to its most comfortable position before measuring with his fingers to make sure it was aligned properly.

Nathan Simons, the other lieutenant of the company, stood with his hands on his hips in a most unmilitary manner. "You can see right down into the fort. Look!" He pointed. "There's a redcoat standing in the doorway!"

"That would be the ensign from the Fortieth who was captured the other day." The captain liked to gossip, and he continued with what he considered a juicy story. "They say the ensign sent a secret message to the colonel telling him Butte à Charles was a better position for our guns than the one originally picked by Engineer Tonge. Tonge didn't want to move the guns this far north."

"Why would he not want to use this spot? It's magnificent!" Bancroft swept his arms from left to right. "We can see everything."

Simons used his personal spyglass to inspect the approaches to the fort. "The French are still trying to fortify the gate! We caught them unprepared." He handed the glass to his captain.

Rather than look at the fort, Captain Phenehas adjusted the glass so he could see the facial features of the two officers standing in front of the redcoats. "Engineer Tonge is arguing with Colonel Scott. Tonge's face is red."

Simons was dying to see what was going on, but he felt he couldn't ask the captain to return his glass. Instead, he said, "Engineer Tonge estimated he would have to build four or five more miles of road to bring the cannon to this location."

"And it's all uphill," Bancroft added. "I bet he doesn't want that. Look! French regulars are coming out the gate!"

Captain Phenehas handed the glass back to Lieutenant Simons. "And I am summoned to receive our orders from Scott." The captain tucked his sword in close to his side and strode purposefully across the field to report to the colonel.

Simons and Bancroft returned to supervise the positioning of their men. As Bancroft watched the men forming up, he considered the engineer's problem. This was an excellent artillery position, but it meant miles of new road. Once the road was built there was the problem of dragging the cannon to this site. When the English cannon were eventually established in full sight of the fort, a determined enemy could overrun the position and capture the cannon—particularly if that enemy had Indians to slip behind the English pickets to clear the way for the French regulars. Bancroft shuddered at the thought.

The captain was returning. Phenehas gave a hand signal, and Nathan Simons as the senior lieutenant immediately gave the command. "Phenehas Company, form skirmish line right!"

\* \* \*

By this time, deBaralon had assumed his position with the fort's gun crews, leaving Ensign Hay and Corporal Fortier alone at the entrance to the casemates. Hay watched with interest as two companies of French regulars formed up and marched through the gate. The effect of the uneven ground on the column of soldiers gave them a wobbly appearance. Not the least bit inspiring, he thought. On the other hand, the rockfirm line of New England Militia was awesome. They were in two lines: officers in front, sergeants behind. That meant the colonel planned to advance. Hay cast his eyes first to the left and then to the right flank. Other provincials were assuming a line of skirmish on the flanks. He peered down at the French forces to see what they were doing.

The French regulars were on the open ground at the bottom of the slope. the Habitant and Indian auxiliaries were just leaving the gate. There was a moment of hesitation, and then all of the auxiliaries moved to the left flank where there was a fence, some bushes, and the remains of some burned buildings. Hay smiled. Those farmers and Indians were looking for cover from which to fight.

A French officer ran from the fort to convince the Habitants to move to the right of the regulars, to protect that flank from attack. Hay watched with interest. Would the Inhabitants, untrained in warfare, move to the more exposed right of the line? He watched the officer argue with the farmers. Although several looked like they might be willing to go where they were ordered, in the end, none of them did.

The officer returned to the fort, obviously disgusted with the performance of the auxiliaries. Now, if the French regulars attacked, their flank would be exposed to English militia skirmishers. For the French to advance then would be a fatal mistake. Hay was not surprised when the French regulars were ordered to assume skirmish order. Each soldier sought cover, and began to harass the English line with individual musket fire. Almost immediately there was a break in the solid line as a soldier fell. The hole was filled quickly by a soldier from the second rank. Another soldier in the blue wall fell to his knees clutching his musket. Long arms pulled the wounded man behind the wall. The breech was filled.

Rapid gunfire came from the left of the French regulars' position. Phenehas Company was forcing the Habitants and Indians to withdraw. Soon, the New Englanders would threaten the left flank of the regulars.

Several loud bangs inside the fort startled the ensign, and he flinched. He was embarrassed when he saw it was deBaralon's cannon firing on the English troops. Hay guessed the shots would fall short of the New England lines. As it was, they fell quite short and close enough to the French regulars in the centre to make them pull back. Once the French movement downhill started, it continued until the New Englanders were no longer subject to musket fire.

By sunset the battle was pretty well over and the English had gained control of Butte à Charles. At last light, Colonel Scott ordered his force to break ground for the entrenchments.

\* \* \*

"The sun's goin' down. When do you think the bastard will let us stop?"

Lieutenant Simons overheard Wyman's remark. Solomon Wyman was a good soldier; he just had a big mouth. Simons decided to make light of it this time because the boys had behaved well this day. "Never you mind, Wyman. You could be over there with the other boys diggin' them trenches …"

Another voice joined in, "Or like Engineer Tonge with a bullet in his chest."

Simons recognized the next voice as Sergeant Pollard's. "Yes, I don't think he'll make it. Looked like death! And they had to carry him all the way back to the camp."

They were moving rocks and logs to form breastworks at the edge of the hill. The sun was almost down, and they were almost finished, but Wyman wasn't going to let it go. "We'uns did good. It's time to have a break."

The lieutenant gave up being nice. "Private Wyman, pick up your load and keep your mouth shut for a while." Just a bit more and then they could stop to eat. "Keep movin', Wyman!"

Lieutenant Simons heard Wyman mutter something meant only for the men working near him to hear. Simons was ready to take the soldier to task when Jeremiah Bancroft joined the work party.

"Almost finished over t'other side." Bancroft good-naturedly struck the sergeant on the back. "What were you doin' this afternoon?" He turned to include the rest of the men. "I was standing just over there when I saw this here sergeant stand up like a scalded cat and take off down the hill into the Frenchies like he was going t' chase them all t' hell! I couldn't let him do that all by himself, so I went after him."

Sergeant Pollard stopped working to wipe his eyes. He was laughing so hard tears ran down his face. "Doggoned if I had to follow Major Prebble," Pollard said. "He was standin' there tellin' us what brave lads we wus when some Frenchie shot his britches off. He turned to see who had done that to his pride, and I could see his pink little arse hangin' out about two cheeks wide."[1]

"Was he hurt?"

"Nah! I don't think he was hurt so much 'til he saw me laughing. Then he drew his durned sword and charged down the hill lookin' for the Frenchie that had done it. I followed ... couldn't lose sight of him what with his pink bottom winking at me all the way down the hill."

Bancroft added, "Well, he must have been a sight from the other end as well, because the Frenchies didn't wait to see what he had in mind. They skedaddled to the fort and closed the gate tight."

Most of the men were laughing, and good humour had been restored. Wyman lifted his head. "I smell food."

Lieutenant Simons waved his men to the direction of the top of the hill. "Solomon Wyman can always be counted on to find food. Let's go, men."

*13 June 1755*
*Fort Beauséjour*

It was a good breakfast. One thing about being a prisoner of the French, a man got lots to eat. Ensign Hay took his time over his meal, waiting for the commandant or the priest to join him in the officer's mess. He wanted to hear them explain away the militia's possession of Butte à Charles but, up to this point, he only had the company of the good doctor and deBaralon.

The other ensign had been pumping the Englishman for "intelligence." Hay hoped he wasn't laying it on too thick. "All last night and today, Engineer Tonge would have had his men making a trail up to the butte so they could mount cannons. The first cannon you hear will be the eights."

"What do you mean, the eights?" Dr. Favreau worried the English activity might mean the destruction of the fort and injuries to his colony of patients.

"'Eights?'" deBaralon answered. "He means the eight-inch mortars."

"Yes," said Hay. "The eight-inch mortar is lighter and doesn't need much of a road. They'll be the first to arrive. I think the bombardment will begin soon."

"Why don't the English attack? Why wait for the cannon?" Dr. Favreau queried.

The ensigns smiled knowingly at each other. It was Hay who answered. "Why send soldiers to attack a walled fort when in a few days the cannon will knock down the walls and soldiers can just walk in."

The doctor's face showed the depths of his concern. "While the English are knocking down the walls, what will happen to us?"

Hay made a show of examining the walls of the second casemate. "I don't think this casemate will survive, but the grand casemate will probably withstand the impact of a bomb from the thirteen-inch mortars."

"How will we know when the big mortars are coming?" The poor doctor's face was deathly white.

"There will be a few shots from the eights, probably in an hour or two. Then as the road improves, there'll be more ammunition available and more eights being fired. Then the royals will arrive. They're heavier, but you shouldn't worry until the first thirteen is fired. Bang! The earth will shake and the bomb will be thrown high," Hay raised his hand high above his head. "High in the air." Keeping his hand aloft, he continued. "There might even be time for the sound to travel all the way here before …" he lowered his hand ever faster as it neared the table until he slammed his open palm on the tabletop, rattling the utensils and bowls, "… oblivion!"

DeBaralon joined in, "We have no hope unless we are in the grand casemate?" He winked broadly at Hay, but the doctor didn't see it.

Hay shrugged his shoulders in a very French manner. "Who really knows?"

"But there is a chance?" Dr. Favreau grabbed Hay's arm as a mortar bomb exploded against the north wall of the fort. The bowls rattled.

The three men rose from their chairs as the commandant entered the room. "Good morning, gentlemen. Your comrades are not very accurate, Ensign Hay." He seated himself at the next table, and the mess steward brought his breakfast almost immediately. "I trust you had a good night's sleep." He picked up a sausage with his fingers, wrapped dark bread around it, and took a healthy bite.

A second bomb exploded. Commandant deVergor pushed his food to one side of his mouth. "What will be their rate of fire, Ensign Hay? How many bombs will they be able to throw a day?"

"When the road is improved enough to allow rapid delivery of artillery stores," Hay responded, "they should be able to throw a hundred and forty or a hundred and fifty a day."

Dr. Favreau could contain himself no longer. "Commandant deVergor, if the officer's mess was moved into the grand casemate, your officers would be better able to digest their meals. DeBaralon says it is the strongest of the casemates. It would be the best location to have our food prepared and consumed."

"That's an excellent suggestion, doctor."

"I give this opinion as your medical officer and think such an action would be in the best interests of …. It is, sir?" A big grin of relief was plastered on Dr. Favreau's face. "Thank you, sir."

DeVergor dipped bread into the sausage grease, and smiled at the officers at the other table. "I learned to eat like this when I went to stay with my aunt in Rastatt. She was very German."

The doctor stood and excused himself. "I'll go to the grand casemate now, if I may. It would be a good idea to move my medical supplies there as well." He didn't wait for comment, but quickly scurried away.

Commandant deVergor watched the little man go. "You gentlemen have been teasing the poor doctor?"

Ensign deBaralon chose not to reply. Ensign Hay tried to look properly contrite but couldn't hide a smile. "I'm afraid so, sir."

"Judging by the look on your face, you think we should have pushed the English off the butte yesterday, or, at least raided them last night." The commandant stopped eating and gave the English officer a hard stare.

"I believe," Hay said, "that with the butte in English hands—and if we are able to deliver our cannon to that site— Fort Beauséjour is lost, sir."

DeVergor continued to stare hard at the Englishman, but a trace of a smile crossed his face. "You speak French so well, it's hard to remember that you are *Anglais*." He wiped his hands on a piece of linen. "You saw that I can't rely upon Habitants or Indians to stand and fight, and I would be foolhardy to take my garrison troops into the open against a superior English force on terms that are advantageous to the English."

Ensign Hay interrupted the commander. "Then, sir, your cause is lost."

Annoyed, deVergor abruptly rose from his chair. "You fail to realize that we expect hundreds of front-line troops, not garrison troops, from Isle Royale. They'll appear behind your guns on Butte à Charles in full battle array. You'll lose your guns and your position here at Fundy," he gestured toward Fort Lawrence, then spread both hands wide and said, "and that little cesspool you now call Halifax."

Commandant deVergor stormed out of the casemate. He stopped in the corridor. His face mottled with anger, he barked new orders to Corporal Fortier. "Corporal, take the English prisoner into the grand casemate. Now! He will remain there and take his meals there. Stay by his side at all times."

He turned to glare at Hay through the open door. "I expect my reinforcements from Louisburg within the next day or two. You can sit in here and wait. When your guns fall silent, you'll know it's the beginning of the end for the English in North America!"

*13 June*
*Evening*
*Butte à Charles*

It was a beautiful sight. The sun had just gone down and the sky was draped in rose-tinted shades of pink and blue, while the diminished light had coloured the water slate grey. From either side of the Missaguash River, lanterns twinkled cheerily in both Fort Lawrence and Fort Beauséjour. A French guard issued a challenge and his voice carried to the slopes of Butte à Charles. "*Qui est-ce qui va?* Who passes?"

Jeremiah Bancroft listened but could not hear the reply. He turned his attention back to his troops. They were restless, hungry, and tired. Mosquitoes were bothersome. Any moment now, another New England company would replace them. The new company was supposed to have arrived an hour before sunset, but ...

"Have our boys start down the trail, Bancroft!" Captain Phenehas called. "Put Sergeant Pollard in charge. You remain behind."

"Yes, Captain." Bancroft turned to the sergeant. "You heard the man, Sergeant. Take the boys to the camp, and see that they are fed. Before any one beds down, I want every weapon, belt, and harness cleaned and inspected. Every man is to wash all his socks and hang 'em out on the bushes to dry. It's a good, dry night for it. When you get to the camp, check to see if Lieutenant Simons is back from the fort. There might be mail from home."

"Yes, sir."

The men within earshot murmured their approval and shuffled off in the direction of the new road.

Bancroft left to join a knot of officers. Behind him, Sergeant Pollard cussed the men of the company for not waiting for the order to move off. The cussing continued until the round of the hill cut off the sound.

The whole second battalion was being relieved. They had worked all day digging a main trench across the slope. The deep shadows made the trench look enormous. Bancroft was impressed by the amount of work that had been done. A major of the first battalion was giving instructions to the officers. "The replacements will dig the lateral trench toward the fort by the light of lanterns tonight. Have them stack their arms every twenty feet along the line that's been marked out for the trench. You officers make damned sure your men know where they are in relation to their weapons at all times. If the lanterns have to be doused in a hurry, the men must be able to find their muskets quickly."

The order made the officers uncomfortable. Putting down weapons to dig on the side of a hill facing a fort filled with enemy soldiers and treacherous Indians was bad enough. Doing it in the glare of lanterns was damned hazardous!

"This replacement company will guard the diggers." The major pointed at a line of militia whose men were occupying the positions vacated by Phenehas Company.

"Sure they will!" One of younger militia officers spoke up, voicing the opinion of his fellow officers. "They'll be well lit and blinded by the lanterns, and won't be able to see the Indians coming!"

"Steady on, there," the major retorted. "When I want your comments I'll ask for them!" In an undertone, he added, "And you'll be a long time waiting, m'lad." He knew exactly where the officers' sympathies lay.

"I've asked the officers of Phenehas Company to stay behind," the major continued. "They covered that ground quite thoroughly yesterday and should be able to give us some valuable intelligence. Are your officers here, Captain Phenehas?"

"Just me and one of my lieutenants, sir. I sent my other lieutenant to check for mail from home."

"Ah, yes," the major said acidly, "you colonials ... you

colonials did well," he sputtered on. "I thought a certain mad militia major was going to breach the fort all by himself."

The comment generated shouts of laughter; the story of bare-assed Major Prebble chasing some French soldier had made its rounds throughout the army.

"Good thing you caught up to him or he would have had the honour of capturing the fort all by himself." The major waited for the laughter to die and continued briskly. "Now m'boys, we have to finish this thing we've started. Although Governor Lawrence believes no reinforcements will be sent to rescue Fort Beauséjour, at least not in time, the danger persists. On top of that, if a French naval force should catch our ships against these shores, well, I'm told there's little room to manoeuvre. We must work night and day to subdue these laddies. Captain Phenehas, what do we have in front of us?"

"The slope has a few bushes, some high weeds, two fences, and several burned out buildings."

"How would you position the pickets?"

The captain gestured to Bancroft, who said, "Just past the first fence. That's about half way to the fort. If they stand up, they'll be silhouetted against the working party's lanterns so I'd order them to lie down facing the fort. They'd have to be sure not to look at the lanterns but always toward the fort."

"How many men?"

"Fifty, maybe sixty. If there's no activity, I'd sound recall just before first light so they could slip back to our lines in semi-darkness."

"Thank you, Captain, Lieutenant. Rejoin your men at the camp."

*14 June 1755*
*Fort Beauséjour*

Corporal Fortier climbed the ladder to the parapet. He hesitated at the edge of the platform before waving to someone below. Quick as a wink, Ensign Hay joined him. They ducked around the corner and were immediately confronted by Ensign deBaralon.

"What is this, Corporal? I heard the commandant order this prisoner not to be permitted out again until we had captured the English guns." DeBaralon was upset the corporal had disobeyed a direct order.

"Ensign, I know what it looks like but ..."

"You'll earn a ride on the wooden horse for this."

"Please, sir, understand ..."

"You'll get fifty lashes but I, as an officer, will be shot!"

Corporal Fortier indicated that they should discuss the matter without the Englishman overhearing them. DeBaralon ordered Hay to the other end of the parapet where they could still keep an eye on him.

"Well?" deBaralon challenged.

"It was indicated to me," Fortier explained, "that the commandant prefers the prisoner not be present when he takes his meals."

"Indicated by whom?"

"Abbé LeLoutre said I should take the prisoner to the latrine, or anywhere, so the commandant could not be annoyed by the presence of the Englishman." Fortier shrugged his shoulders. "I tried the officer's latrine, but we met the commandant on the narrow path. We went to the chapel, but the commandant came ..."

"Why bring him here?"

"The commandant never comes here."

It was deBaralon's turn to shrug his shoulders. "So how long will he be here?"

"Only twenty minutes, Ensign. The cook will tell me when the commandant has finished his meal."

"Bring him to the north side," deBaralon ordered. "I wish to interrogate him."

Hay wasn't long in doing as he was ordered because he was curious to see if the thirteen-inch guns were in place yet. When he looked over the parapet, he was astounded. The main trench was finished and the lateral trench had been extended out nearly one hundred and twenty yards toward the fort! He squinted against the glare of the midday sun but could not see any thirteen-inch mortars. Two eight-inch mortars were mounted and crews were serving their pieces. One of the mortars belched a cloud of reddish smoke, and Hay thought he caught a fleeting glimpse of the bomb as it rose in the air. Instinctively, he crouched down and hunched his shoulders. He became aware of the French ensign standing upright beside him.

"No need to seek cover, Englishman. They've been firing on the main gate this morning."

A sharp explosion followed the dull boom of a mortar almost immediately. Just inside the stockade, chickens squawked and fluttered in the ensuing silence, but as far as Hay could tell there was no interruption in the daily activity of the fort.

Hay looked over the parapet in time to see the second gun crew assume the firing position around their mortar. This time there was no reddish smoke. When the grey smoke had cleared, two of the gun crew lay very still on the ground, and a third writhed in pain. The gun itself was split and destroyed.[2]

DeBaralon explained in the dispassionate voice of a gunnery officer what had happened to the English gun. "They've been throwing solid shot from that mortar, not bombs. Their rate of fire was too brisk. Perhaps they became careless and failed to check the shot when they introduced it to the mortar. It was probably 'out of round,' no longer spherical. Too bad about the crew." He watched soldiers drag the wounded and dead away from the ruined gun. DeBaralon sighed. "It takes a long time to train a gun crew."

"I'm amazed the main trench is finished and the lateral so close to the fort."

Sighing again, deBaralon replied, "*Maudits Anglais!* They set up lanterns and worked all night."

The men were silent as three of the fort's cannon barked their responses to the English mortars. DeBaralon sighted his glass on the trenches, and noted the fall of the shot on a pad. He grinned at the English ensign, "Not much effect but it keeps English heads down! Sergeant! Tell the men to go down for a hot meal. I'll remain here."

DeBaralon leaned against the parapet and studied the butte. "In response to your unasked question, the enthusiasm for making sallies from this fort has waned considerably." He held up his hand and counted off on his fingers. "One, the garrison soldiers aren't much good at it. Two, when the Habitants get out of sight of the fort, they desert to their homes. Three, the Indians don't like night work; they'd rather attack at dawn or at dusk and work at night only when we insist. The commandant didn't insist."

He shrugged and collapsed his hand. "The commandant has his own strategy. He's waiting for the rescue troops to come from Louisbourg."

The two young officers leaned against the parapet and enjoyed the warm sunshine, to all appearances not as enemies but as casual acquaintances. Corporal Fortier, his musket held loosely at his side, was standing some distance away out of earshot, picking at some dinner that had stuck between his teeth. He would have been surprised at their innocuous conversation.

"Looks like we might have rain tomorrow," Hay offered.

"I thought it was going to rain today."

"Ever been to Halifax?" Hay asked.

"You mean Chebucto?" deBaralon replied.

"We call it Halifax now."

"No, I haven't been there."

"I was going … there … when I was captured. My wife, Penelope, is having our baby."

"Penelope. That's a nice name."

A gust of wind caught Hay's hat and almost carried it over the parapet. He lunged and managed to capture it. He tried several times to smooth his unruly mane and put the hat on properly but finally gave up, letting the breeze ruffle his hair. He noticed some figures on the marsh. "What's going on out there?"

"We saw loose cattle on the marsh," deBaralon said. "I sent out a work party to herd them to the fort. I figure each man eats about seven pounds of meat a week. Doesn't take long to eat a whole cow."

Hay leaned further over the parapet to get a better view. He pointed to the far side of the marsh. "That looks like a really big cow!"

DeBaralon leaned out to see what Hay was pointing at. "It's an ox." At that moment he glanced down, let out a surprised yelp, and pulled Hay back into the shadows.

"What's the matter with you?" Hay asked, annoyed.

"The commandant was below on the esplanade. In another moment he would have seen you."

Corporal Fortier marched over to the two officers. "The commandant has left the mess. It's time for us to return, Ensign Hay."

Hay descended from the platform. He nodded to deBaralon and disappeared below.

*Lateral Trench*
*Butte à Charles*

Jeremiah Bancroft scratched his crotch. Last night he had only thought he had fleas; now he was sure of it. His mother had a harsh liniment she used to get rid of them. Maybe the doctor had something similar. As soon as possible, he would jump in the river and scrub away as many of the little devils as he could. He stopped scratching when Sergeant Pollard approached.

"The mortar blew up in their faces, Lieutenant," the sergeant reported tersely. "Killed one of 'em. The other two are pretty bad. We had three of our men in the area. Nobody hurt. Taylor's cartridge box was tore right off his side and his bayonet broke in three pieces. He weren't hurt none, though."

Lieutenant Nathan Simons came up behind the two men and handed his spyglass to Bancroft. "Take a look, Jeremiah. There's our captured redcoat on the parapet. You can almost make out his face through the glass."

Bancroft took the offered spyglass and sighted on the parapet. "He's waving to us. Now he's pointing to the marsh. Christ! Someone came up behind him and knocked him down!" Bancroft continued to search the parapet for further signs of the English officer. "He was trying to tell us something and got knocked about for his trouble."

"The man has balls!"

Bancroft scanned the marsh with the glass. "There're French soldiers and Indians on the marsh." [3]

"I'll go get 'em!" Simons called for the sergeant to return on the double.

"I feel like it was me the redcoat was signalling. I'd like to go, if you don't mind, Nathan," Bancroft said.

Simons nodded his head in agreement.

"Yes, sir?" Sergeant Pollard ran up and sensed the men's excitement. Usually Lieutenant Bancroft scratched himself behind his ears or on the side of his neck when he was planning some devilment. Now he was scratching in several places with both hands. Must be something wild.

"There're Frenchies out on the marsh rounding up some fresh beef. Call for volunteers. Tell 'em we're going after roast beef."

"Yes, sir, Lieutenant Bancroft! I'll get you enough volunteers to take the fort!"

In a matter of minutes, Bancroft had fifty volunteers armed and ready to go.

"Form skirmish line. By the centre, advance!"

The New Englanders waded through the straw-like marsh grass. They were soon wet to their knees, and the line was ragged but advancing at a good clip. A corporal, who was taller than even Bancroft, called out, "They're gettin' off with the cattle. We won't reach 'em in time to cut 'em off from the fort! Some Indians over t' the left are butcherin' an ox!"

"Which way, Corporal Steeves?"

Steeves pointed, but Bancroft couldn't see anything from where he was standing. "Call it out, Steeves."

"Yes, sir. Skirmish line advance on the double!" The company moved forward quickly. As the soldiers passed a copse of alder bush, the Indians were in plain sight to the left. They could see that the French had already reached dry land at the fort. The corporal had been correct; it was too late to catch them. Catching the Indians, though, was still a possibility.

"Left section, skirmish left! Right section, advance by the right! Double time!"

The Indians took one look at the enemy soldiers running through the marsh—knees up high, faces red with exertion, bayonets at the ready, hollering like mad—and fled across the marsh. Bancroft and a dozen others chased the Indians to a tributary of the Missaguash River where the Indians escaped by diving in, swimming underwater with the current until out of sight.

Suddenly very tired, Bancroft dragged himself back to the ox's carcass. The meat had been cut and divided so it could be carried back to the butte. With fifty men available, carrying that amount of meat was not a daunting task.

Simons thought the group of men was a strange sight as they approached the English lines. They were covered with blood, carrying indescribable hunks of flesh over their shoulders, and loudly singing Protestant hymns extolling the triumph of good over evil. They seemed more like gory monsters from some witch's tale than the happy boys they were, returning from a lark and packing their own dinners to feed their ravenous bellies.

That night, after everyone had eaten their fill of meat roasted over an open fire, Bancroft repeated the story of the brave English ensign who, while a prisoner of the French, showed their army where to place the cannon for the conquest of Fort Beauséjour. This very afternoon, that same ensign had pointed out an easy conquest for Phenehas Company. There was a hush as Bancroft related how he had seen the unknown French hand strike down the brave ensign, to what fate he knew not.

Some of the younger lads began the chant, and soon even the older men were shouting it. "En-sign Hay! En-sign Hay! There's none braver!"

Bancroft was quick to join in. He hoped that if the company shouted it loud enough, the ensign would hear it inside the fort.

Of course, Ensign William Hay was protected behind almost fifteen feet of earth, solid timber beams, and a foot of masonry that not only protected everything inside the grand casemate, but also kept out anything as frail as human voices.

*15 June 1755*
*Fort Beauséjour*

Commandant Duchambon deVergor paused at the entrance to the officer's mess and beckoned Ensign deBaralon to join him. Most of the previous evening and early that morning, there had been a furious artillery exchange between the fort and a newly arrived thirteen-inch mortar in the English trench. The French artillery, personally sighted by deBaralon, had driven the English from the trench and damaged the big mortar. DeVergor was pleased. He wanted the ensign to know just how pleased he was. "Why don't you join Abbé LeLoutre and me for breakfast, Ensign."

"I would be pleased, sir, but I must return to my guns."

"Have you eaten?"

"I had some food earlier on the parapet. My sergeant tells me the English have resumed work on the trench and have brought up another big mortar. You can understand, sir, I must continue."

"Yes, yes. I understand, Ensign." The commandant saw a delegation of Habitants gathering at the end of the corridor. "Carry on," he said to deBaralon. With some difficulty deVergor pasted a pleasant smile on his face until he had entered the grand casemate and the door had closed behind him. He cringed as the knock he feared sounded. "Find out what the Habitants want," he said to LeLoutre.

Abbé LeLoutre remained seated and said impassively, "You know what they want, Commandant. They want you to tell them what was in the courier's bag."

"In good time."

"I think 'in good time' is probably right now." The priest wiped his mouth, and rose to open the big door. "*Bonjour, mes enfants.* Good morning, my children. You wish to speak to me?"

"We wish to speak to Commandant deVergor."[4]

"There isn't enough room for all of you in the officer's mess at the same time. Perhaps it would be better if only three men represented you."

"There are only seven of us, Father," protested one of the Acadian farmers.

"Three will have to do."

With a bit of pushing and shoving, three men followed the priest into the grand casemate. Their leader, Joseph Bourgeois, spoke. "Commandant, we want to know if a rescue army is coming from Louisbourg."

Indicating the leather pouch on the table, the commandant replied, "I received word this morning ..."

"Last night, Monsieur le Commandant." Bourgeois insisted. He was intent on establishing the proper atmosphere for this delicate meeting. "You received word by courier last night."

DeVergor sighed. "The governor of Louisbourg states that he will not be able to send any assistance."

Bourgeois showed no surprise. His face remained impassive as he said, "If there is no hope of help, Commandant, may the Acadians be permitted to return to their homes? For us to remain in the fort is a useless sacrifice."

Commandant deVergor stared at the three men. "You know what you ask?"

*"Oui, Monsieur le Commandant."*

The commandant waved his hand in dismissal. After the Habitants had left, the commandant raised his voice and called to the guard at the door to the casemate. "Summon the officers for a council of war!"

Later, when Chevalier deVannes, the second most senior officer, entered the grand casemate, he asked, "Do we have good news or bad, Duchambon?"

DeVergor shook his head negatively. "My old friend, the Habitants want to go home."

Officers dePiedmont, de St. Laurent and Falaise came through the door in time to hear the commandant's remark. DePiedmont had more bad news. "Over eighty Habitants left last night and this morning."

Officers Laverandry and de Langy had comments to make. "They should have been shot in the back as they walked away from the fort. They are not Frenchmen!" As these two sat at the second table, Laverandry added, "The remaining Habitants should be rounded up and shot."

DeVannes made a calming motion with his hands. "Of course we will do no such thing, eh, Duchambon?" He didn't wait for a response. "We can't be seen executing our own people."

DeVergor looked into the eyes of his old friend, checking to see if any truth was hidden behind his aristocratic mask. Slowly, deVergor looked away, unsure as to what kind of support he would receive from deVannes at a court martial if this fort should be lost to the English.

Ensign deBaralon knocked, entered, and stood at attention. "I apologize for my tardiness, Commandant. I heard the big farmer, Bourgeois, talking to the Habitants. I stopped to listen."

DePiedmont, deBaralon's immediate superior, leaned forward in his chair. "Well, what did you overhear?"

"Bourgeois said all is lost. He said that after the English overrun the fort, any Acadian still alive would be hanged as a traitor. He said he demanded permission from you, Commandant, for his people to leave."

Up till now Abbé LeLoutre had been quiet. "*Peuple à lui!* His people," he roared. The gathered officers thought the priest might choke on his own spit. A similar outburst came from the commandant, who was as outraged as the priest. "*Il a exigé la permission?* Demanded permission from me!?"

DePiedmont spoke first. "Your pardon, sir. I can have an order written prohibiting such statements from being made by the Habitants under penalty of being shot or of having their land and property confiscated."

"Do that!" deVergor choked out. He loosened his collar and took several deep breaths.

In the quiet interval, deVannes spoke softly. "We should think about our options. I suggest we get an administrative officer ..."

"Ensign Raimbault," deVergor gasped. He added with a stronger voice, "He composes all the administrative orders."

DeVannes looked around. "Where is he? Why isn't he here?"

"He's at the commissary helping Pichon with the inventory. We forgot them."

"I suggest we adjourn for now and allow Raimbault to devise an order."

LeLoutre volunteered, "He usually consults Sieur Fermand on syntax and spelling."

Gesturing impatiently, deVannes said, "Have Sieur Fermand provide his usual support. We want this thing done right."

Speaking normally, deVergor took command of the meeting. "Notify Clerk Billy to report here. When Raimbault and Fermand have determined a draft, they will require his fine hand to put the order in good form."

Commandant deVergor stood up. "We will meet here at midday to determine our course of action. Good morning, gentlemen. You are dismissed."

### 16 June

Corporal Fortier knocked timidly on the iron door. When no one answered, he pushed against the door and called, *"Monsieur le Commandant?"* He stuck his head in and, seeing no one, gave the "all clear" to the English prisoner, who slipped past the corporal into the empty chamber.

As far as Ensign Hay was concerned, he was getting very tired of the farce. He was supposed to stay in the grand casemate at all times except when the man who ordered him kept there didn't want him there. Then he had to be moved without causing any embarrassment to the man who was relieved he wasn't there when he should have been there. Ah, the French! He sat down dispiritedly in the chair so very recently vacated by the commandant that it was still warm.

The corporal looked uncomfortable.

"You have to go again?" Hay asked incredulously.

"Yes, sir," said Fortier. "I must ask you to accompany me to the latrine and to wait for me."

"Oh, Corporal, just go ahead. I'll sit here. I'm tired of being a shadow."

"Please, sir. I can't leave you here unattended."

Ensign Hay started to get up but changed his mind and sat down again. He heaved a big sigh. "I give you my word, Corporal."

"Your parole?"

"Yes. And I promise I won't move from this room until you come back."

When the corporal hesitated, Hay said, "I promise on my word as an officer that I will not attempt to escape."

Corporal Fortier left the grand casemate. The door banged shut behind him. Ensign Hay tilted back in the chair and put his feet on the table. He laced his fingers behind his head and closed his eyes. It wasn't long before there was timid knock on the iron door. Ensign Hay didn't feel it was his place to invite anyone in so he maintained his silence.

Three men, one of them in a religious habit, entered. They were obviously startled to find a redcoat relaxing in the grand casemate. One of them spoke. "I am Ensign Raimbault."[5]

"I'm very pleased to meet you. I'm Ensign Hay."

"I know who you are, Englishman. We have important duties to perform for the commandant, and you cannot be a party to them. I must ask you to leave the casemate."

"I'm sorry, but I must remain here."

"No, you must leave."

"I gave my word." Hay folded his arms across his chest.

The floor of the casemate suddenly trembled. A smile crossed Hay's face, and he said in English, "I bet that was a thirteen-incher!"

The French officer was annoyed. "*Où est votre guardien?* Where is your guard?" he asked.

Hay stood. He had just heard the belching roar of the big mortar. He threw himself under the table to gain some protection, meagre as it might be.

The bomb landed directly on top of the grand casemate and tunnelled into the first four feet of solid earth. Ensign Hay heard and felt the impact. The bomb exploded, pushing through the remaining ten or eleven feet of earth. The timbers withstood the force for an instant before they collapsed inward, carrying the masonry down, and crushing everything below.

If there were a God in that awful place, He would have heard the cry. "Penelope!"

\* \* \*

Joseph Bourgeois whispered to the throng of Acadians gathered at the western end of the stockade. "The Englishman is dead! He was in the grand casemate."

One of Joseph's nephews said, "What does that matter to us? Just another dead Englishman."

"My dear sister was a sweet soul," Joseph threw his hands in the air, "that she died giving birth to such a donkey! Didn't you hear the English calling the prisoner's name around their campfires? They'll expect to find him here. We won't even be able to produce a body!"

"That's right! Their bomb buried him in the casemate."

"Guillaume!" Joseph realized that some of the other villagers didn't understand the trouble they were in either. "The commandant will sign a document giving the terms of surrender. After the surrender is signed, the soldiers are protected by the Rules of War."

"Because they're soldiers."

"*Oui, c'est vrai.* And when the English discover Ensign Hay is dead, they'll be mad as a bull stung by wasps."

One of Joseph's farmer cousins said, "They'll want to hurt somebody."

Joseph nodded his head in agreement. "They'll punish the only people not protected by the Rules of War."

When he realized what Joseph was saying, Guillaume became agitated. "We must dig the prisoner's body out so the English will see he was killed by one of their bombs!"

"No." Joseph contradicted his nephew calmly. "We must get out of here before the English arrive."

The Acadians grew silent because Commandant deVergor and Abbé LeLoutre had appeared on the parapet flanked by several senior officers.

"You wished to speak to me?" deVergor called.

There was some muttering from the farmers, but Joseph silenced them. "Commandant, we must be permitted to leave the fort, to return to our homes and families."

LeLoutre surprised the officers for the second time that day with another outburst. *"C'est impossible!"* The priest distanced himself from the officers and grasped the handrail with both hands. He leaned forward in much the same way he had often leaned from the pulpit. "We must not surrender to the English," he thundered.

"You would have us die here, Father?" Joseph Bourgeois called up to the priest.

"I would rather bury myself under the ruins of this fort then give up to the *maudits Anglais!*" [6]

Bourgeois regarded his priest with hooded eyes.

Commandant deVergor hoped perhaps the priest's declarations had convinced the Habitants to continue fighting. He was disappointed.

Bourgeois pointed an accusing finger at the commandant. "Another bomb like the one that destroyed the grand casemate could find the ammunition magazine! Then Père Jean will have his wish, but we would all join him under the ruins of this fort!"

Commandant deVergor straightened his shoulders, and said coldly, "I will not surrender my fort ..."

"If you will not surrender," Bourgeois shouted down the commandant, "we will be obliged to turn our guns on anyone who tries to stop us from leaving the fort."

There was silence. Bourgeois looked down at the ground and then back up at the shocked officers. "We will fight our way out of here if we have to."

Chevalier deVannes stepped forward. "You make a good point, monsieur." Addressing the commandant he continued, "If the English cannon ever find the magazine, there would be no one left to surrender." Without waiting for the commandant's reply, deVannes said to the Acadians, "We will hold a council of war and decide ..."

"In the terms of surrender, Commandant," Bourgeois persisted, "you must obtain protection for the Acadians. You must say we were ordered to take up arms under threat of death!"

DeVannes turned to lead the officers from the parapet, but Bourgeois wasn't finished.

"Those of us who choose to withdraw to French Territory

must be granted time to gather our belongings and ..."

Without turning around, deVannes said, "We will do whatever we can."

The officers were almost off the parapet.

Abbé LeLoutre, all but ignored by everyone present, protested vehemently. "the Habitants shall be free to enjoy their own religion, to have priests ..."

All motion ceased. The officers regarded the priest with disdain. The Acadians waited patiently for the priest to continue.

"... and no harm shall come to them," LeLoutre finished weakly.

Commandant deVergor waved his arm in the general direction of the priest and the Habitants. "We will do what we can." He turned abruptly and disappeared from the parapet.

*1000 Hours*
*Butte à Charles*

"Look at that, Jeremiah! Frenchies with a flag of truce!"[7]

Jeremiah Bancroft poked his head above the edge of the trench. "They're heading to the main trench!" He looked around quickly. "Sergeant! Send a runner to warn Colonel Scott!"

"Yessir, Mr. Bancroft!"

Nathan Simons continued to study the truce party through his glass. "It wasn't necessary to send a runner, Jeremiah. He probably saw them."

"Probably isn't good enough, Nathan! Wouldn't want us to shoot while there was a flag of truce on the field, would you?"

"I guess you're right."

Bancroft squirmed for a minute and then announced to no one in particular. "I'm goin' along to hear what they have to say." He took off like a rabbit across the open field to the post of the militia colonel, Lieutenant Colonel Scott. About twenty yards from the colonel's post, Bancroft dropped into the trench and nonchalantly walked the rest of the way.

A redcoat captain asked the New England lieutenant where he was going.

"To the nearest latrine, Captain. I've had the shits all

morning." Bancroft clutched at his middle and half jogged along the trench. He wasn't challenged again.

As Bancroft approached the colonel's position, the senior officer of the French party, a very aristocratic looking man, introduced himself as Chevalier deVannes, second in command of Fort Beauséjour. He was speaking on behalf of Commandant Duchambon deVergor, état major in the service of the King of France.

Colonel Scott was coldly polite. "I am Lieutenant Colonel Scott." Not a man to mince words, the colonel asked bluntly, "Are you ready to surrender?"

"I'm authorized to offer a cessation of hostilities for forty-eight hours."

"For what purpose?" Scott interrupted. "If you're inclined to capitulate, I will grant honourable conditions provided there is no great loss of time. You have until two o'clock to submit terms and arrange for the exchange of hostages."

"Two o'clock?" deVannes's mouth dropped open. "Two o'clock?"

"Yes. At two o'clock I will resume the bombardment." Colonel Scott gave the chevalier a half-salute. "Until then, sir."

Bancroft watched the stiff-backed aristocrat march back the way he had come. "That didn't sit well with him," he said with a smile. He hopped over the side of the trench and trotted back to his own men. He waved as he approached the line. "It's goin' to be finished at two," he announced to scattered cheers.

Soon the New Englanders had campfires going and had begun the serious business of cooking hot meals. Where before had been sounds of war there was now laughter and a violin playing plaintive, civilized music. The New Englanders didn't see the second French party cross the edge of the marsh and take the old trail to the English camp under a flag of truce.

### 1145 Hours
### English Camp

"What could they possibly want?" Colonel Monckton looked up from his dinner and gestured with his fork. "They have their ultimatum from Scott." The beef slipped off one of the tines and dangled precariously from the other. "What do they want from me?" The meat fell into his lap. Monckton didn't notice until his pet hunting-dog retrieved the morsel.

"They brought a list of terms, Colonel." Major Prebble said. "They want you to read 'em."

Monckton speared another piece of meat and took a bite. He pointed at the other chair. "Sit down. Tell me what their terms are."

Prebble read the proposed articles of surrender. "Item number one. Blah, blah ... march out with arms, baggage, drums beating, fuses burning."

Speaking around the meat in his mouth, Monckton said, "Army baggage and drums. Nothing else. Next?"

"Two. They will take six cannon of the largest calibre, one mortar and fifty charges for each piece."

"No. Next?"

"We shall furnish whatever supplies are necessary for the transport of this force to Baie Verte where the garrison shall embark in a French ship to go where they please. They will take two hundred quarters of flour and one hundred of pork."

"The garrison shall be sent directly to Louisbourg with enough supplies to last until they get there. Next?"

"The Inhabitants were forced to take up arms under pain of death and ..."

"Balderdash! The Inhabitants are traitors!"

"The Inhabitants shall be free to enjoy their own religion, and shall suffer no punishment."

Colonel Monckton stood while Prebble continued to read. "The French will be permitted to furnish the Inhabitants with all that is necessary for their withdrawal during the current year."

Not unkindly, the colonel said, "That's enough, major. I'll see them now."

"What about the Inhabitants, sir?"

"Inasmuch as the Inhabitants have been forced to take up arms under pain of death, they shall be pardoned. Nothing else."

"There are other articles," Prebble said.

"No more. Write those up while I speak with them. Who's the senior officer?"

"DeVannes."

"I'll meet them outside. Bring the terms to me when they're written. Oh! The traitorous Inhabitants call themselves Acadians. Use Acadian instead of Inhabitant so there can be absolutely no misunderstanding." Colonel Monckton left the tent. He stood for a moment adjusting his tunic and belt, then walked the short distance to where the truce party waited.

Without any preliminary comments, Colonel Monckton asked, "You have something to add to the terms Lieutenant Colonel Scott gave you?"

"I am Chevalier deVannes. I am authorized to speak on behalf of ..."

Monckton interrupted. "I demand you give up your fort. You will do so on honourable terms that my officers are now preparing."

The chevalier stepped back as if affronted. "We shall defend our fort to the last bomb, sir!"

Monckton continued speaking as if he hadn't heard the French officer. "If you choose to put my men to the test, I will hoist the Bloody Flag ..."

"But sir, we have proposed terms that ..."

"... and not take it down till we have destroyed you all."

Moments passed while the enemies regarded each other silently.

An English officer joined them and handed a paper to Colonel Monckton. Monckton read it briefly and passed it off-handedly it to the nearest French officer. "You have two hours to comply."

### 1300 Hours
### Fort Beauséjour

"They're going to surrender." Abbé LeLoutre had gathered his Mi'kmaq band and the remaining Habitants at the western end of the stockade. "I have just returned from the council of war. The commandant seeks delay although I do not know why.

The English have threatened to raise the *pavillon rouge* if there is any resistance."[8]

Robert Cameron couldn't believe what he had just heard. "The red flag! That means if we fight, the English will give no quarter. Everyone found in the fort will be killed."

"Oh, don't worry, my son! Our illustrious commandant means to save his hide and the hides of his officers. Asking for a delay serves no purpose because he does not intend to resist." LeLoutre shrugged his shoulders. "The fort is lost. I suggest all Habitants slip away now."

There was no argument or discussion. Several of the Habitants knelt before the priest and kissed his hand. Soon only Robert Cameron and the Indians were left.[9]

"Robert," LeLoutre said, "I want you to go to Baie Verte. Prepare a vessel. I will come shortly. There must be enough food and water to take us to Isle Royale."

"*Oui, mon Père.*"

"Leave now." LeLoutre grabbed a toque from one of the Indians and pulled the knit cap over Cameron's red hair. He smiled at the Scotsman. "Go with God." The priest made the sign of the cross and then turned to speak to the Indians.

Cameron hesitated but thought better of arguing with the priest. He quickly slipped over the wall and followed in the footsteps of the escaping Acadians.

Some of the zealot's fire returned to the priest's eyes as he spread his arms to encompass the band. "It's now up to you."

"What would you have us do, Father?" Beau Soleil was armed with a club and musket. He shook them in front of the priest. "These have not tasted English blood. When the New English took our ox they made us swim the river. I lost my club and musket in the waters. I suffered shame. I will fight."[10]

"My son, you must not be found in the fort. The conditions of surrender do not protect you." His eyes swept the members of the band. "You must all leave."

"*Et vous, mon Père?*"

"*Moi, aussi.* I, too, must leave." The priest smiled at Beau Soleil. "If you attack the New Englanders before the truce is signed, it might force the cowards in this fort to finally fight.

There would then be honour at Fort Beauséjour."

Beau Soleil's eyes were hard and cold. "We'll make the New English bleed for you, Father," he vowed.

The band bowed their heads as the priest blessed them. Each brave in turn touched the priest's robe before slipping over the wall into the marsh grass.

*1800 Hours*
*Lateral Trench*
*Butte à Charles*

Lieutenant Jeremiah Bancroft perched on the lip of the trench enjoying the fading rays of the afternoon sun. He mopped up the last of the stew from his mess tin with a piece of bread. "Pretty good stew!" He looked down into the trench where Corporal Steeves leaned against the thirteen-inch mortar sucking on the last of the tobacco in his pipe.

Steeves spit over the lip of the trench in the direction of the fort. "Wonder who'll get to march in at seven o'clock?"

"Scott, I've been told. He'll march a company or two through the gate. He's got some boys he taught to march real smart."

"Impress the Frenchies with our parade square bashing?"

Bancroft scratched his chest absent-mindedly. "Mostly ceremony now. Hand over his sword. Hand over his fort. March out tomorrow with his flags and drums."

"So we beat 'em at fightin', now it's spit-and-polish time."

"Yup. And we can do that better'n them. Leastwise, Scott's boys can."

Bancroft leaned back, supporting himself on his elbows. "Come on up here, Steeves. It's warmer and there's a view."

"I dunno, sir. I find it hard to sit out in plain view of the enemy's fort. I'm more comfortable down here in the trench." Steeves knocked the ash from his pipe. "You never know who's out there, watchin', waitin'."

\* \* \*

One hundred yards beyond the first of the old fences, Beau Soleil signalled his band. He watched with satisfaction as they melted into the grasses and approached the trenches of the New English.

Beau Soleil planned to attack the lateral trench at the point where the New English raiding party had taken his ox the day of his shame. Perhaps the same men who had stolen his meat and driven him from the field in disarray might still be there. He prayed to his god, make them be there, especially that tall, skinny New Englishman.

Lying in the grass, waiting for his men to get in position, Beau Soleil's face burned as he remembered the shock of seeing the New English in such large numbers so near the ox carcass. He had signalled his men to scatter because they were out-numbered and caught in the open.

His band had scattered, but Beau Soleil had not figured on the close pursuit. That tall, gangly New English, yelling and running like a deer, had led his men to cut off their retreat. Perhaps Beau Soleil might have been able to turn and rally his braves—there were much fewer New English in the pursuing party—but the tall demon breathed on his back. He heard the rasp of the tall one's knife as he drew it from its sheath. In two or three steps, the blade would have done its business and brought about the end of Beau Soleil. In two steps Beau Soleil had reached open water and disappeared into its depths.

Today Beau Soleil would find Tall One and kill him. On his belly, he crept closer to the New English trench.

\* \* \*

Bancroft sat forward and crossed his legs Indian style. He had just heard a bird. There hadn't been any birds in the area for several days, certainly none doing any singing. This was a sign of peace. Of the two, growling cannons or singing birds, he preferred the cannon. Bird songs didn't make vacancies in the ranks allowing for rapid promotions. "I saw the French truce party running down to the camp to meet their deadline. It's all over, Steeves. Besides, there's a flag of truce."

"I know, but something in my gut …"

"Probably the meat in the stew." Bancroft stood and extended a hand to Steeves to help him out of the trench. "Couldn't recognize what it was, but the vegetables were good."

Steeves took the proffered hand and hauled himself up. "The sergeant says he traded gunpowder with the Inhabitants and got some butter too."

"Didn't see any butter."

The two men stood on the lip of the trench. Corporal Steeves agreed with the lieutenant: the view was much better from up here.

\* \* \*

The bird signal! His braves were in place. Now they would wait until Beau Soleil selected his target.

Beau Soleil had chosen a traditional weapon to kill the tall one. Ritual was necessary if there was to be redemption. He fingered the feathers of the arrow and prayed for success. Then the soldier stood; he was taller than most white men were. Beau Soleil thanked the spirits. The time for prayer was over.

The warrior gauged the wind. The arrow must pierce the throat of the tall one. By giving Tall One minutes to contemplate death, Beau Soleil could reach the doomed soldier and mock his fading eyes. He notched his arrow and sighted along the shaft. It wasn't a difficult shot.

A second man appeared at the top of the trench, but Beau Soleil disregarded him. Taking a deep breath, he drew on his bow. Something disturbed his concentration and, from long experience, he knew he must trust his instincts and re-evaluate his attack.

Pausing, Beau Soleil saw nothing unusual: two Englishmen standing in the open, looking at the bay. The second man was taller! Tall One must be the second man! He sighted carefully, drawing his bow until he had the comfortable, tense feeling that told him the shot would be true. He resumed his preparations and released the arrow.

\* \* \*

"I might bring my family here, sir. Colonel Winslow says there will be free land for those of us who choose to stay."

"Yes, I heard that. Me, I'm going home to Boston." Bancroft caught sight of quick movement through the air. The birds are coming back, he thought. Maybe they sense the war is over.

\* \* \*

Beau Soleil lowered his bow. The first man must have seen the arrow's flight but there had been no time to warn Tall One. Tall One would begin his death throes. Beau Soleil moved forward through the grass. He wanted to be there before Tall One pumped the last of his life's blood on the raw earth of the trench.

\* \* \*

Bancroft pointed to the left. "See, Corporal! Scott's men are forming up. Looks pretty fancy!" Hearing a gasp, Bancroft turned in time to see Corporal Steeves suddenly sit down on the lip of the trench with his mouth open, eyes wide, and nostrils flaring. His face turned red, blood welled in his mouth and spilled down his shirt. It was then that Bancroft saw the arrow that pierced the corporal's throat.

Musket fire sounded all up and down the marsh side of the trench. The lateral trench was under attack! Several balls plucked at his shirt. One hit Steeves with a thwacking sound and knocked him backwards into the trench.

\* \* \*

Beau Soleil watched Tall One fall into the trench. There was no point in going forward. The Mi'kmaq god had given him the tall one's death but hadn't allowed him a personal vengeance. Crawling, he backed away from the trench. Now he would lead his band. Abbé LeLoutre wanted the New English to be provoked into attacking the fort. So be it. Maybe the French, belatedly, would show courage and leave the walls. White men liked walls. They hid behind their walls and died of sickness. It was much better to die as Tall One did today, in the open, as part of a ritual, even if that ritual was for the cleansing of an enemy warrior's life spark. Death should have meaning. Dying behind walls was like being buried in a box. Beau Soleil reached for his musket. He stopped thinking about the tall white man and the white man's walls, and began the business of killing. His musket joined in the fusillade against the New English trench.

* * *

"The sons of bitches got Corporal Steeves!" Bancroft peeked over the edge of the trench. "Return fire! Fire low! Indians crawling in the grass."

Bancroft picked up the fallen corporal's musket. He aimed at a clump of grass and fired. An Indian jumped up and ran in a zigzag pattern away from the New Englander's guns. Several muskets fired in rapid succession, bringing the Micmac down on his face. He lay there, still and unmoving.

Bancroft reloaded and carefully aimed at the Indian. He fired. The body didn't move. Either he missed or the Indian was dead.

* * *

The returning fire from the New English was deadly. Already Beau Soleil could see that three of his braves were down and several were wounded. He gave the signal to retrieve the casualties and to withdraw. His second in command, a small brave with an English name, Captain John, signalled back that he was going to help the brave lying in the open.

Beau Soleil signalled agreement. He watched Captain John put down his musket and crouch in preparation to run into the open. Then Beau Soleil jumped into the air, beating his breast and shouting at the New English. A number of muskets fired at Beau Soleil, who took cover before any musket ball could reach him.

Immediately, Captain John ran to the right and jogged quickly to the left. Beau Soleil and two other Mi'kmaq warriors stood and aimed their muskets at the trench. They sought cover just as the New Englanders returned fire.

Captain John had reached the downed brave. He hauled him across his shoulders and started back the way he had come, this time not jogging to the left or the right; he was just trying to get out of range of the English muskets.

All the raiding party stood to draw the English shots in their direction and away from Captain John. They might have been successful but, at that moment, Scott's parade party joined the fray. Forty new muskets fired almost in unison. Beau Soleil and his braves sought what cover they could from the hail of musket balls. When the smoke cleared, the only sign the Indians had been there were two bodies lying in the scrub grass. Beau Soleil and his band had melted away.

### Fort Beauséjour

"*Mon Dieu! Qu'est-ce que c'est?* My God! What is happening?" Commandant deVergor was beside himself with fear. Peering cautiously over the parapet, he could see the English forces mustering on Butte à Charles. "Who's doing the shooting?"

Ensign deBaralon lowered his eyeglass. "Sir, the Mi'kmaq attacked the New Englanders and are now withdrawing." He raised his glass and carefully examined the scene. "And, sir, the English gunners are charging their pieces."

"Does that mean they're going to bombard again?"

"Yes, sir. I can see their matches."

"Do something, Ensign! Tell them we're resigning!"

"Surrender, sir?"

"Yes! For God's sake, go tell them."

### Butte à Charles

Colonel Scott waved his sword in the air. "Batteries will commence independent fire!" He brought his sword down and levelled it at the fort. "Batteries ... independent ... fi—" [11]

"Wait, sir! Colonel Scott, sir! Wait!" It was Captain Speakman, a professional soldier from a long line of professional soldiers. He had been most disturbed that shooting had occurred during a period of truce. Warfare wasn't played that way. In his opinion, it was time both sides remembered they were, after all, European.

"Colonel Scott, sir!" Speakman pointed. "There's a French officer running from the fort waving his hat, sir!"

Somewhat haughtily Colonel Scott asked, "And that means, Captain?"

"I don't know exactly, sir, but he's no real threat to us. Should we not see what he wants?"

Colonel Scott looked up and down his lines and nodded. "Hold your fire!"

The order was repeated down the line. Meanwhile, the French officer climbed the embankment of the trench and held out both hands in supplication. He said something in French.

"Can anyone parlay-vous this chap?" Colonel Scott was exasperated.

"Sir," Captain Speakman called out, "he says the attack was made by renegade Indians. His commandant is prepared to hand over the fort as agreed."

"Now?"

Captain Speakman repeated the question to the French officer. The French officer nodded his head in agreement, and there were cheers all along the English line. A voice shouted above the cheering, "Where's Ensign Hay?"

Ensign deBaralon shrugged his shoulders. *"Il est mort."*

"What did he say?"

Captain Speakman exchanged words with deBaralon. He approached the colonel so that his words could be as private as possible. "Colonel, he says Ensign Hay was killed by our bombardment."

A nearby English voice repeated the news. "The blighter says Ensign Hay is dead!"

The word passed quickly down the line. "Our ensign is dead!"

"Raise the red flag," some of the men shouted.

As one, the New England Militia rose from the trenches and headed for the fort. Two of the soldiers near the French officer shouldered him out of the way. The next rank knocked him down.

"Officers! Control your men!" Colonel Scott was not the least bit perturbed. "Tell the Frenchie that the men are a trifle antsy."

Down the line the command was given. "Hold!"

The sergeants could be heard above all other voices, "Second battalion will stand steady! Steady, I say!"

Captain Speakman spoke with the French officer. DeBaralon unsheathed his sword and handed it to the captain, who carried it to the colonel. "He offers himself as hostage to the good conduct of the French garrison of Fort Beauséjour."

The colonel gave a curt nod to the French officer and dismissed him with a wave of his hand. "Colonel Winslow!"

"Yes, Colonel!"

"Have the parade party get on with it!"

"Yes, Colonel!"

"Fife and drums, Colonel Winslow."

"Yes, Colonel."

### On the Road to Baie Verte

Abbé Jean LeLoutre stood in the deep shadow the trees had created on the side of the road. From there he witnessed Captain John's attempt to rescue the fallen brave from under the noses of the English guns. LeLoutre liked Captain John and was sorry to see him cut down. The rest of the Mi'kmaq band got away, and for that he was grateful. Now he must wait to see what the English reaction would be.

It wasn't long before a French officer came running out of the gate. Most unseemly, LeLoutre thought. Arms flapping, waving his hat … it was that little snip deBaralon. LeLoutre smiled when the officer's sword got caught between his legs, almost tripping him. If I had a rifle, the priest thought, I could shoot down that imbecile; the cowards in the fort would blame the English. Maybe then the Beauséjour garrison would fight for the honour of France and the glory of Mother Church. *Merde!* They're going to talk! What must he do to make these English react? He thought of the possible loss of all his work in the Fundy. So many years, so much effort. He had asked the Habitants for sacrifice, and they had responded. His eyes misted when he remembered with pride the day in 1750 when he had ordered the villagers of Beaubassin to destroy their village and move to the other side of the Missaguash. Not all the villagers were willing to burn everything they owned to deny the English shelter while they were building Fort Lawrence, but eventually the village and the fields had been destroyed. Even that Bourgeois fellow, Joseph, had agreed.

A blue wall of soldiers rose from the trenches and marched toward the fort. They struck down deBaralon! Wonderful! The Mi'kmaq attack had worked. The garrison must defend the honour of France now even if they hadn't attacked for the honour of France before. Abbé Jean LeLoutre felt absolutely magnificent. I will go down in history, he thought, as the man who …

The New Englanders stopped. The priest could see the officers harrying the soldiers into a proper line. Surely they would continue the attack. Over the distance he heard the command, "Dress right!" He didn't quite know what that meant, but he recognized the movement of the troops. The English were not going to attack.

LeLoutre heard the fife and drums and watched the smart movements of the parade party as they marched to the gate of the fort. He hoped and prayed for a volley of musket fire to rip the proper lines of soldiers to shreds. Instead, the gate opened and the fife and drums led the English into Fort Beauséjour.

When the gaudy English rag rose above the parapet, the priest's eyes filled with tears. He shook the tears out of his eyes. Robert Cameron would be waiting for him with a boat. He must assemble what priests he can, he thought, and embark for Isle Royale. He furtively rubbed his cheeks with the sleeve of his habit. Once sure he had removed all traces of his tears, he adjusted his cross, hitched his skirt to keep the hem from dirtying, and stepped out on the road to Baie Verte. He turned his back on Fort Beauséjour and Acadia.

*17 June 1755*
*Baie Verte*

"We should have gone with Abbé LeLoutre, Robert." Reine and Robert Cameron stood just outside the village at the edge of a field where they had planned to build their home and raise their children. Reine had just realized that it was not to be.

Robert Cameron passed his hand through his wife's hair where the breeze off the water pushed it forward over her face. He held her close and nibbled on the tip of her ear. "The Abbé couldn't wait for me while I came to get you, Reine. The boat was ready, and he had to leave because the English were searching for him. There's a bounty for his scalp, you know."

"So what did he say? Is he sending the boat back for us?"

"If he can get past the English." Cameron decided to change the subject. "I want to take one last look at my hard work." He took Reine's hand and led her down the side of the dyke to where a stream of water flowed from the farmland under the dyke to the sea. He gazed at the mud flats. The ebb tide was finished. Very soon the sea would return, quickly covering the flats. The salt water would push the freshwater stream back under the dyke, and try to sneak in to flood the farmlands.

"What do you mean by one last look, Robert?"

"The English are here, and this time they won't be leaving. If they find me, they'll hang me."

Reine studied the landscape. Just three years ago this land had been covered by water. Hours of hard work and careful engineering had pushed back the sea and reclaimed the land. After a few more years, the rains will have flushed the salt from the reclaimed soil and washed it under the dyke and back to the sea. She sighed; they would have had bountiful crops. "It's so beautiful here, Robert."

Cameron slipped back into English. "Aye, lass. 'Tis a bonnie place, but not for a Cameron. Not with the English here."

Reine didn't understand him, but she didn't question him.

They walked to the small rise where they had planned to build a small, one-room house with a loft, a thatched roof, and walls filled with straw and marsh mud. Robert would haul stones for the hearth and the lower part of the chimney, and build the rest of the chimney with sticks plastered over with clay. They intended to have a single window for the wall opposite the fireplace so that the rising sun would shine through. If there had been good years, they might have been able to purchase real glass. They had laughed while discussing their dreams. "It never hurts to have a dream," Reine had said.

"Where will we go, Robert?" She snuggled into his arms. It caught his heart the way she said his name: Roe-bear. Robert kissed her light brown hair and hugged her tight. Looking down, he could see she was a LeBlanc, all right. She had the square LeBlanc jaw with a small cleft on her chin, which was emphasized by her large white teeth. Reine had a beautiful smile. She was smiling now but tears filled her eyes.

"Where can we go, Robert?" she repeated. Reine smoothed the dark green wool of her husband's jerkin against his chest. "I would rather we stay in Acadia. It's our homeland."

"We'll try to do that, dearest. First, we'll go to one of the larger villages away from Fort Beauséjour. Perhaps the English will leave other villages alone."

"Yes!" Reine kissed him on the lips. "Yes! The English always stay in their forts and leave the fields to Acadians. All they really want is to trade for our cattle and farm products." Reine turned away from their home site. She took her husband's hand and led him back the way they had come. "Where should we go?"

"I have to discuss it with Joseph Bourgeois now that Father LeLoutre is gone."

"Père Jean won't come back for us?"

Cameron stopped and took his wife's face in his hands. He looked into her deep brown eyes. "Bourgeois always warned us if we were to survive in Acadia we had to stay neutral. Now I agree with him. It was a mistake for us to support the French. Abbé LeLoutre was working for the good of the French, not for the Acadians." He released her face and took her hand in his.

They started walking again.

Cameron stopped and cocked his head to listen. "The tide is coming in." He smiled.

"What do you hear?" Reine waited to learn what it was her husband was listening for.

He pointed inland. "When it rains, the water wants to run to the sea, but my dyke is in the way. So I built a little canal, an *aboiteau*, under the dyke for the rainwater to run to the sea. But at high tide, the saltwater wanted to come back through my little canal and claim my lands. That's why *l'aboiteau* has a one-way valve."

Reine smiled. "You forget *chéri*, I am Acadian. I grew up knowing about *les aboiteaux*."

"Well, this one is mine. Look, the tide is filling the trap."

They watched as the tidal bore, a wave of some eight or ten inches, washed against the dyke. Reine listened and said, "I didn't hear the valve close, Robert."

"That's right, Reine. You didn't hear it close because this is my *aboiteau*. I made everything to fit perfectly. This *aboiteau* will still be working one hundred years from now."

Reine could see his pride, and gave her husband a hug. Taking one last look at their dyke, the Camerons walked away.

*18 June 1755*
*Fort Cumberland*
*(Formerly Fort Beauséjour)*

The eleven o'clock sun beat down on the backs of the provincials. A slight breeze moved the regiment's flags but it wasn't enough to provide any relief to the soldiers on parade. Four of the companies on the square were dressed in full marching gear—muskets, ammunition pouches, and water bottles—carrying sacks and backpacks. The heat was particularly wearing for these soldiers.

Colonel Winslow, standing at the head of the parade, read aloud from a piece of parchment. "Private Amos Weatherby, drunk and disorderly conduct. Twenty lashes to be applied by the tallest man of the next company." [12]

A corporal and a sergeant led a soldier to the front of the parade square. Leather thongs were attached to his wrists and ankles. The soldier assumed a bowed position over a wooden, barrel-like object called the horse, to which his wrists and ankles were quickly secured. As the corporal stepped back, he grabbed the collar of the loose shirt the soldier wore and ripped it off his back.

Lieutenant Jeremiah Bancroft, standing in the front rank of the first company, could see that the man had been whipped before. Raised scars crossed the man's back from his shoulders to his waist.

A soldier was selected from the next company and handed a whip. The sergeant gave him instructions. "Lay it on 'im, to the left and then to the right. If you miss one, you will lay it again. If you miss two, you'll take his place at the horse."

The big man took the whip in both hands. "Yes, Sergeant," he replied. He positioned himself seven or eight paces from the horse. He stood with his legs spread and waited for the order to begin. Bancroft determined that this wasn't the first time the big man had been selected for this duty.

The colonel nodded his head, and the sergeant ordered, "Punishment begin."

The man with the whip cocked his arm back and delivered the first stripe. The corporal called, "One!"

The soldier flinched but uttered no sound. Bancroft looked away.

Bancroft knew that an idle army quickly devolved into a nest of drunks, thieves, liars, and cheats, and if the idleness persisted long enough, into murderers, rapists, and deserters. He had no particular opinion about the whip as a form of punishment. Murderers were hanged, and drunks and thieves were given stripes. He looked up again. The count had reached eleven, and the man was no longer conscious. Checking the condition of the man's back, he wondered how a mess like that ever healed. He remembered a regular who had so many scars on his back he wasn't able to bend or twist properly. It didn't interfere with his use of his bayonet or otherwise prevent him from being a good soldier. Bancroft didn't look back again until he heard the sergeant call out, "Punishment delivered, sir!"

Colonel Winslow beckoned to a smallish man wearing a black suit and a black hat. Parson Phillips stepped forward. He cleared his throat and announced that the day's homily came from Numbers 23, verse 10. He opened the Bible and slowly read, "Let my soul die the death of the upright ones, and let my end turn out afterward like theirs."

He pursed his lips and rocked back and forth—heel and toe, heel and toe—several times. He began to preach. Jeremiah Bancroft didn't hear a word of the little man's sermon. The sun beat down on his back and he began to feel dizzy. He scrunched up his toes and then uncurled them inside his boots. He flexed his knees slightly, tensing and relaxing his muscles, in an effort to move the blood around. It was no good; he was going to pass out, fading, fading …. He was startled back to alertness when he heard a loud moan. That couldn't have been him! God, no! Not in front of the men—and not on parade! He moved his eyes from side to side. All the men were watching Private Weatherby who was no longer unconscious.

The parson glanced at the defaulter. He finished what he was saying, snapped the Bible shut, and removed his hat. He raised his right hand in benediction and, closing his eyes, intoned, "May the good Lord be with you this day." Phillips nodded at the colonel.

Colonel Winslow stepped forward and called, "Detachment stand fast! Remainder, dismissed to your duties!"

From a dozen throats issued the series of orders sending the dismissed companies to their duty or off-duty areas. Three soldiers stepped forward to help the unfortunate Weatherby back to his tent.

The colonel, disregarding the men at the horse, spoke to the companies still on parade. "We have exchanged terms of capitulation with the officers of the French fort at Gaspereau. You will march to Fort Gaspereau to take possession and to assist in the departure of the French forces. They are to be provided with carts to transport their baggage. Your officers have copies of requisition orders to give to the Inhabitants if required."

Winslow paused. He regarded the assembled men sternly. "You may supply yourselves from what you find at Gaspereau."

There was a rustling in the ranks and several men made remarks that couldn't be heard at the front of the parade. The sergeants bawled, "Steady up! Quiet in the ranks!"

Winslow continued, "I make it clearly understood!" He raised his voice, "There will be no plunder!"

No one moved or uttered a word.

In a more normal voice the colonel said, "I'm glad we understand each other."

Stepping away from the front of the parade square Colonel Winslow ordered, "Move them off. Company order of march."

Major Prebble gave the order, "Detachment will move to the right in column of route." The major paused to give the junior officers time to pass the order to each company.

Bancroft picked up the order. "Phenehas Company will move to the right in column of route." He paused and waited for the major to give the execution order.

"Riiight," said the major.

"Right," repeated the junior officers. After a beat they all ordered, "Turn."

The detachment of two hundred men turned as if one. The major marched to his position at the head of the first company, Phenehas Company. Bancroft placed himself immediately behind the major. When all of the officers and men had assumed their proper places, Major Prebble ordered, "Detachment will move off in column of route, Phenehas Company leading."

Bancroft gave the order, "Phenehas Company, quick march!"

In turn, each company was given the order to move and marched out the Fort Cumberland gate, up the hill, and turned onto the road that would eventually take them to Fort Gaspereau.[13]

* * *

Bancroft picked his canniest woodsmen to act as point for the company. It was their job to scout ahead of the column and sniff out trouble before the column was exposed to it. Solomon Wyman was in the lead with two other men. He knelt on one

knee and peered through some bushes. He raised his arm to signal the other two to join him.

"Jack," Wyman said, "take word back to the lieutenant that
there's water off to the right. I can smell it. Tell him the way the
land's leanin' we should be comin' to a river or a brook most
any time now. If'n he's lookin' for a place to rest, this be it."

Jack didn't question Wyman's nose. Wyman's nose never
failed when it came to scenting food, water, wine, or redskins.
He took off at a trot back over the small rise that separated the
soldiers on point from Phenehas Company.

Wyman stood and motioned for the other man, Willie, to
stay where he was. Wyman trotted down the cart road and out
of sight.

Willie leaned on his musket and waited for Wyman to
return. He closed his eyes and listened to the chattering of the
birds and the buzzing of the flies. God, it's hot, he thought. We
been on the road three hours. Time for a break. Trust ol'
Wyman to time it just right. Willie heard something from up
the road. He relaxed when he saw it was the first of the column
cresting the little hill with Jack trotting in the lead.

Christ, Willie thought. Where does that Jack get all of his
energy? Too hot to run. Willie looked the other way. There was
no sign of Wyman. Senses alert, he lifted his musket and walked
down the hill, looking for Wyman or trouble, whichever he
came across first.

The cart road bore left, and as Willie rounded the bend
he saw Wyman moving toward him, his boots and leggings
covered with mud.

"It's wet through here," Wyman reported. "Tell Bancroft
to leave the road at the bend and cut through the trees.
There's a large clearing at the edge of a brook. Did he say he
wanted to stop?"

"Dunno. Jack ain't here yet."

Wyman and Willie both looked back for Jack. Jack gave
the woodsman's signal for near camp, and the other two grunted at the same time. Without speaking they took off through
the trees to check the immediate area for hostiles.

* * *

When the main column reached a clearing at the edge of a brook, Bancroft led the company to the far side near the woods.

"Pickets," the lieutenant called. He pointed out five of his men and the nearest corporal. "About fifty yards out, corporal. Keep all men within sight of each other." He turned to Sergeant Pollard. "Form a flying squad of five men. Have them stand easy about twenty yards out."

"Yessir."

"Don't let them put their muskets down. Stay alert! Sooner or later, the Micmac will have a go at us. At the first sign of trouble, form skirmish line and advance to the sound of the muskets."

The rest of the company had spread out. Some were lying down with their packs still on their backs. Others had stripped off their packs, tunics, and shirts and were in the stream splashing their upper bodies with water. Bancroft's boots and leggings were soaked from the water-filled ruts of the cart road. He pulled off his boots and socks and waded into the stream. It felt good. The stream was cold and clear like those at home, except this one was teeming with fish. If there was enough time he could sure catch himself a mess of fish. He dried his feet and pulled on fresh socks. As he was lacing up his boots, the warning for formation was given. Bancroft quickly relieved the pickets and flying squad so they could refresh themselves in the water.

When they resumed the march, Captain Adams's company was in the fore and provided soldiers at the point. Phenehas Company assumed a more relaxed position in the middle of the column. Captain Phenehas, who had been doing duty as adjutant for Colonel Winslow, returned to the company and Bancroft was able to mix in with the men. He enjoyed their good-natured give and take, and time passed quickly.

On the Missaguash River, about three miles from Baie Verte, the column came upon a once-fine bridge that had been demolished by the French. There was some delay while the New Englanders laid a new one, but they were soon marching on. The cart road grew wetter as it neared the bay until, close to shore, the column was forced to leave the road and make its way through the trees. Not unpleasant, Bancroft thought. The trees gave some shade, and there was a breeze from the water. At least there weren't so many flies.

Word passed down the ranks that Captain Phenehas was calling for Bancroft. The lieutenant dodged out of the ranks and trotted outside the column, occasionally slipping on the grass and giving the troops something to laugh at. He was slightly breathless when he reached the head of the company and fell in with the captain. "You have orders for me, sir?"

"Yes. Look ahead. You can see houses."

"I see them."

"That's the village of Baie Verte. As we march through, I want you to take some men to search for Abbé Jean Louis LeLoutre. He's said to be lodged with a priest named Menac."

"How will I know which house to search? There must be twenty-five houses."

"If the villagers won't identify the priest's house, start with the finest looking house. Damn it, Lieutenant, search them all if you have to! The colonel wants that priest."

The column of New Englanders moved through the village and out the trail to the fort. When the colonel saw the one-and-one-half-mile-long causeway before them, he ordered a halt. He examined the situation. If a determined enemy caught them on the causeway there would be no hope; the detachment would be destroyed down to the last man. The darkening sky decided for him. The detachment advanced without incident. When they arrived at the fort, the French garrison was lined up at the front gate. Noting the white flag amongst the French colours, Colonel Winslow approached the fort with his soldiers in parade formation. The New Englanders put on a brave show of their formal parade skills on the desperately rough ground.

The hand-over was brief. Colonel Winslow accepted the French sword of surrender and then returned it in a gesture of chivalry. With flags flying and drums beating, the French marched down the same trail the New Englanders had just used, disappearing over the causeway in the direction of the village.

* * *

Bancroft waited on the trail while his men searched a house that was significantly larger than any other house in the village. With his back to a wall, he watched carefully for any sign of hostility from the Inhabitants. He lumped the Inhabitants and Micmac together, an implacable enemy that had attacked during the truce period at Fort Beauséjour and would attack here and now given the smallest opportunity.

"Sergeant Pollard! What have you found?"

" 'Tis the priest's house all right, sir, but they's gone for sure. A cleaning woman here says they left the same day Fort Beauséjour fell. By boat, she says."

"Is there a chest or papers?"

"Took all of their things with 'em, she says. Carrot Top helped 'em, she says."

"Who? Carrot Top?"

At the edge of the village came the sound of many soldiers marching. Over the eaves of a shed Bancroft saw the French flag fluttering as if it were being carried into action.

"Reassemble! On the double!" He drew his sword and pointed to the space between the priest's house and the next. There was room for a line of about a dozen men; he had fifteen. At least his flanks wouldn't be turned! He cast a hurried glance over his shoulder. Christ! It looked like an entire regiment coming his way. They hadn't seen the New Englanders yet. Surprise would help, but he and his men were in sore trouble.[14]

"Fix bayonets," he whispered. "Front rank kneel." The second rank, including himself and the sergeant, numbered six men. Both ranks would shoot since it was unlikely they would have time to reload before the enemy overran their position.

He thought about his dear Catherine who would be four in February. "Ready!" His mouth was dry. So this was how it felt. When he was leading the attack to rescue *Yorke*, he had been excited because the enemy had begun running the moment they saw him. These Frenchmen weren't going to run; there were too many of them. He lifted his chin. This was as good a place to die as any.

A last, stray thought: maybe when the priests came back, they would say a prayer. Not LeLoutre! He wouldn't say a prayer. He was a devil!

"Hold your fire, sir! They carry a white flag!"

"Hold your fire," Bancroft repeated.

The French had seen them but made no attempt to break parade formation. The sergeant was right. A white flag was next to the French colours.

"The boys must have relieved the garrison!" Bancroft thought his knees were going to collapse, but he held on. "They're marching to the shore to board ship for Isle Royale." He stuck his pistol back into his belt.

"Atten*shun*," he ordered as the French commander came abreast of their position. The commander saluted smartly. Bancroft returned his salute somewhat more casually.

As soon as the commander had passed, Bancroft led his men around the back of the priest's house and along a path to the long causeway. In fifteen minutes they were at the fort. Five minutes after that, the lieutenant was sipping his first French brandy. He licked his lips, savouring the strange, strong taste. "Better'n being dead," he said to Captain Adams.

"It's not as bad tasting as all that," said the captain, not quite understanding.

*25 June 1755*
*Halifax*

"My dear Bulkeley, do come in." Governor Lawrence stood in the centre of the room holding a sheaf of dispatches in his one hand while waving his other in the direction of Smythe, his personal clerk. "Leave us, Smythe. I would speak with First Secretary Bulkeley." Softening his abrupt manner, he smiled at the clerk and said, "We won't be but a moment, thank you."

When Smythe had softly closed the door behind him, Lawrence sat in the clerk's chair. He indicated the other to the first secretary. "What brings you here at this time of night?"

"I had a very successful afternoon," Richard Bulkeley reported.

"Your horse won?"

"All of my horses won." Bulkeley shrugged his shoulders in a what-can-I-do gesture. "I was returning home when I saw your lamp through the window. I expected you would be working on the Fundy situation."

"Governor Shirley is pressing me. He has friends who see the Fundy as a grand enterprise where, just by doing their duty for the king, they'll emerge rich and powerful. I must accede to Shirley's wishes or lose his support." Lawrence threw the papers on the desk, scattering a few to the floor. "I cannot afford to lose the support of the governor of Massachusetts."

"Is it so difficult to do what he wants?"

Governor Lawrence didn't answer. Instead he called out, "Smythe!"

Clerk Smythe returned almost immediately. He saw the papers on the floor, retrieved them, and held them out to the governor.

Lawrence took the papers and stood. He pointed at the desk and motioned for the clerk to take his seat. "I wish to send a letter to Colonel Monckton." Lawrence waited until the clerk had checked the points of his pens and chosen the best before he began.[15]

"My dear Colonel Monckton, etc. I am very happy with the capture of Fort Beausejour and so little loss of life."[16] Lawrence nodded to the clerk to stop writing and looked at Bulkeley. "Do you know the man Hay?"

"Ensign Hay? Yes. His wife gave birth last week."

"Boy or girl?"

"Stillborn." Governor Lawrence paused and then continued. "Ensign Hay died at Fort Beausejour. He was in the bombproof bunker when one of our thirteen-inch mortars made a direct hit." He held up the sheaf of dispatches. "At the time of this writing, his body had yet to be recovered, but the man is dead." Lawrence cast his eyes down and studied the dispatch.

Bulkeley took the cue. "I'll see that his wife, Penelope, is informed."

Nodding his head, Lawrence asked the clerk, "Where was I?"

"And so little loss of life, sir."

"Er, yes. And so little loss of life. Honours will be given where due." He held up his hand in a stop signal to the clerk. "Richard, you saw the terms that Monckton gave the French?"

"Yes, sir, I did."

The governor shuffled through his papers until he found the one he wanted. "'Article Four: The Acadians, inasmuch as they have been forced to take up arms under pain of death, shall be pardoned for the part they have taken.'" He waited expectantly for some comment from the First Secretary.

"It's Monckton's signature on that piece of paper, sir, not yours." Bulkeley spread his hands in an expansive gesture, "It was merely Monckton's way of promising not to execute the Inhabitants for their insurrection."

The governor pulled on his lower lip with his forefinger and thumb, and spoke to the clerk. "Take this down, Smythe: I am as yet far from determining the fate of your rebellious Inhabitants. Their pretending to have been forced to take up arms is an insult upon common sense. As it deserves the severest treatment, I am glad to find you have carefully avoided granting anything in our articles of capitulation ..."

Bulkeley had been perusing a file that had been open on the clerk's desk, and interrupted. "Your letter of January 29 warns him not to grant anything."

"Yes!" Lawrence slapped his thigh. "I remember!" He indicated to Smythe to continue. "You may remember I told you in my letter of 29 January to avoid granting anything to the Inhabitants that might entitle them to future enjoyment of their lands and habitations. I am too well satisfied that should they be allowed to remain, they will prove forever a thorn in our side. With their help the French may be able to do much against us; without them, I think nothing of much importance."

Governor Lawrence looked very pleased with himself. "When is the next meeting of the council?'

"The end of July, Governor. By that time, with the official approval of the council, you can give new orders to Monckton."

"And in the meantime?"

Bulkeley indicated to the clerk that he should write. With

a nod from the governor, Bulkeley went on with the dispatch. "Though for the present it may ease your people to use the Inhabitants for performing such labour as you will, I must have some very convincing proofs of their sorrows and repentance for what is past before I can prevail myself to think of their continued possession of those lands ..."

"Valuable lands," the governor interposed.

"... those valuable lands such as Chippody, Memeramcook, Petitcoudiack, Shediack, etc., all of which, being scattered at such great distances and divided by large rivers, and consequently not under the influence and command of our fort, the Inhabitants there will forever give intelligence and all manner of assistance to our enemies."

"That's long-winded, my dear Richard, but let me continue." Governor Lawrence paced back and forth as he dictated to his clerk. "Commandant deVergor has destroyed everything within two miles of the fort, which points out very strongly to me the propriety, if not the necessity, of destroying everything beyond. There may perhaps be time enough to do this when we are well established upon the isthmus, and it will be always easy to find a stick to beat a dog, especially such dogs as they are. Do not allow them to take the oaths of allegiance ...."

Bulkeley held up a file to get the governor's attention.

Lawrence nodded his head and continued. "You may remember I forbade that in my letter of 29 January lest they should claim title to the lands under that."

"You had better tell him what to do about the Micmac, sir."

"If the Indians are disposed to be well with us," Lawrence dictated, "give them all due encouragement. If we can make them our own, we shall find various advantages from it. I remain, faithfully, etc."

Governor Lawrence ushered Bulkeley into the anteroom. "Thank you for your advice, Richard. We will have long days until this matter is settled. I should excuse you so you may return home. Are you settling in nicely in your new house?"

Some small talk followed, and soon Bulkeley found himself in the courtyard accepting reins from his man who had been waiting for him. He patted the muzzle of his horse and whispered to the stallion to quiet him. "I wonder what the old man has in mind for the Inhabitants? If he means to deport them, do we have enough soldiers to do it?"

He mounted the stallion and rode to his house on Prince Street.

### 25 June 1755
### Fort Cumberland (Beauséjour)

"Well, hello, Lieutenant Church Steeple! Remember me?"

There was only one man who called him a church steeple: the lieutenant who had promised his men the rum and then delivered it himself on *H.M.S. Yorke*. Jeremiah Bancroft turned to face an English naval officer. What was his name? "Lieutenant Gray?"

"You have a great memory. Yes, I'm Lieutenant Gray of *H.M.S. Success!*"

Bancroft extended his hand. "How are you? What are you doing here? Your ship is gone."

"Yes, *Success* left yesterday for River Saint John to burn the French fort."

"Fort Natchouak and anything else they can find, I hope."

"Yes, that, too. I'm here to gather up whatever French and Inhabitant vessels are salvable, arrange crews, and have them sailed to Halifax." [17]

"What will happen to them?"

"The Admiralty Court will hold an auction, and the proceeds will probably be declared prize money." At this point, Lieutenant Gray rubbed his hands together. "That's why I'm still serving in this man's navy."

"For the prize money?"

"Yes. My wife, Molly, and I want to build a house at Sambro." With immense pride, Gray added, "I know Halifax Harbour and its approaches. I'm going to be a Halifax Harbour Pilot. At least, I will be as soon as we get enough money to settle at Sambro."

The army officer looked around. "There must be somewhere we can get out of the sun and have a chat. I know! Come to my tent." He took Gray by the elbow and steered him in the direction of the New England camp. "I think I have something you might consider a treat."

As they walked to the tents Gray asked, "Where have you been?"

"I was with the detachment that took possession of Fort Gaspereau. I found it to be a very pleasant place, and more so by our finding some quantity of brandy and wine for our comfort."

Bancroft pulled up the flaps on the tent. He set two camp-stools in the resultant shady area and Gray sat. Bancroft opened his kit bag and retrieved a flagon of brandy. Judging by the sounds, there were several others in the bag.

"When last we spoke, I had the understanding that you didn't drink spirits."

"I do now." Bancroft wiped the inside of two metal cups with the edge of the blanket. He poured a generous amount of brandy into both cups. "I had me some action at Baie Verte."

"Was it as hot as our time at the river with *Yorke*?"

"Nope." He took a sip of the brandy, swallowed, and sighed. "It wasn't the actual fighting." He hesitated and picked up the flagon. He pulled the cork and topped up his cup. He took a long swallow before continuing. "It isn't the fighting that ..." He paused again.

Gray understood the problem. "You were scared? We all fear being maimed or killed. A man must be scared to get his dander up." He gave Bancroft a big smile. "I will always remember you charging those Frenchies at the river. That French officer was gettin' set to kill me." He reached over and clasped the New Englander's knee. "If it hadn't been for your bravery, I would be dead now."

"I wasn't never scared before, but when the Indians attacked us during the truce period in front of the fort ..."

Gray's silence encouraged his friend to speak. He sipped his wine.

"We were sitting in the sun, the corporal and I. It was the same corporal who was with me the day I took the ox from the Micmac and chased their leader into the river."

Gray grunted. "What would you have done if you had caught him?"

"Exactly! I wasn't scared of nothing! That Indian was there to be got, and I tried my damnedest to get him."

"So you've changed?"

"There was a truce. No one was supposed to be fighting." Bancroft looked into the distance and said, "We were talking about home. I had just coaxed Corporal Steeves out of the trench into the open. He said he thought he would bring his family t' live here, and the arrow went through his neck."

Bancroft took another sip.

"I didn't even see an Indian! One second we were talkin' of settlin' in the Fundy and the next he was sittin' down with that queer look on his face. Took a while for him to die." Bancroft took a deep draught of brandy. "All the way to Fort Gaspereau, we didn't see Indians. They could've been there, but we didn't see any. I put my best Indian fighters in front, but we didn't see any."

"You said you had some action at Baie Verte."

"I had fifteen men with me. I'd been expectin' Micmac, all the way from Fort Beauséjour."

"How many were there?"

"There weren't none. There were two hundred French regulars."

"Two hundred! What did you do?"

"We stood firm. They surrendered."

"My God! You captured two hundred …"

"No. They had already surrendered to the colonel. They was on their way t' board ship for Louisbourg."

"But you thought …"

"Yes. That's what I thought."

Gray started to laugh. "You stood firm before two hundred regulars!" He laughed so hard tears ran down his cheeks.

Bancroft regarded his companion with some annoyance. "My men stood fast. I don't think it's funny. We thought we was going t' die!"

"I bet you all shit your pants!"

"Probably." Bancroft smiled and then grinned. "Not my

trusty Sergeant Pollard. He saw the white flag and stopped me from givin' the order to shoot."

"Good man!" Gray lifted his cup. "Here's to all good men."

Bancroft raised his cup. "Here's to sergeants and corporals who keep their officers outta trouble."

"Who keep their officers alive," Gray added.

They drank in companionable silence for a few minutes.

Gray chortled. "Facing two hundred regulars I would have pissed m'self." He forced a serious look on his face. "But first, I would've checked the direction of the wind."

"The wind?"

"Yup. Naval officers never, *never* piss t' windward ... It blows back on you!"

Careful not to spill any of his brandy, Bancroft doubled his fist and knocked Gray backward onto the cot. Gray set down his cup, and the two men engaged in some good-natured fisticuffs during which they dislodged a packet of letters from a table at the side of the cot.

Gray gathered them up. "Letters from home?"

"Yes. Neither of them good news." Bancroft held up one of the letters like it was something dirty. "A cousin of mine, Elkanah Smith, writes that the Province of Massachusetts will raise an army to clean the French outta Crown Point. That's where I wanted to begin my soldiering, goin' to Crown Point with the Boston boys, but instead I came here. I just couldn't wait to get started as a professional soldier so I came here." He grinned and took another long drink. "I got nothin' 'gainst the Inhabitants, or Acadians as they call themselves." He took another swallow. "And the Micmac have done us New Englanders no harm. Crown Point is where the bastards are ..."

"You haven't seen what the Micmac can do." Gray stood up and scratched his bottom. He sat down again. "I was at Dartmouth when they killed everyone 'cept a little boy. They woulda killed him, too, if they'd found him."

"Oh!"

"I watched as they tortured and then gutted a sailor from my first ship, *Sphinx*. I had escaped to a shallop just offshore.

They tortured him for a long time trying to get me to return to the beach to help him."

They gazed silently into the bottom of their cups. Bancroft was the first to speak.

"I wanted to fight an honourable war 'gainst an honourable opponent." He put down his cup. "But there is nothin' honourable 'bout murderin' a man." With a half-smile he added, "Must be the brandy talkin'. I usually keep my 'pinions to m'self when it comes to soldierin'."

Gray understood his friend was uncomfortable so he tried to change the subject. "When d'yuh expect to return home?"

"I don't know." It was Bancroft's turn to move and adjust his body as he gave himself a little scratch here and there. "Home is Harwich, Massachusetts, but right now m' family's in Boston. We moved there so I could get some military schoolin'." He separated another letter from the stack and held it out like it might bite. "That's t'other piece of news. Bad earthquake in Boston. Lots of damage." [18]

"Your family all right?"

"Yes, but the shake knocked over lanterns, and the house is gone." He waved the letter as if it was hot and he was trying to cool it. "Burnt down to the front step, she wrote. Lost near everythin'." He dropped the letter on the cot. "C'mon. We kin go to the cook tent. Cook should have some biscuits made b'now." Bancroft stood and extended his hand to Gray.

Gray waved aside the helping hand. "What can you do to help 'em? Can you get leave to return to Boston?" He struggled to his feet.

Bancroft smiled at his friend's efforts to control his legs. The brandy had done its work well. "I'm tryin' t' put together a few pence t' send t' Elisabeth this afternoon." He reached over with both hands and pulled on Gray's arms. He accepted the assistance this time.

"How much will she need?"

"Elisabeth's goin' home t' Harwich. My family and friends will help."

"But you have to send her some money." Without hesitation Gray added, "I can let you have three pounds."

Bancroft snapped a quick look at the other man's face. He moved his lips to say something but couldn't think of the right words. Instead he stood with his mouth flapping and his hands moving in helpless little circles.

Gray smoothed the rumples out of his white waistcoat. He didn't notice the brandy he had spilled on the sleeve of his blue jacket. "I owe you my life." Gray gave his friend a big smile. "You can owe me a couple of pounds."

"But, I can't do that! Besides, where'd you get that kind of money?"

"Captain Rous advanced me ten pounds on the prize money for the French boats I'm goin' to be sendin' to Halifax. I sent seven of it home t' Molly." William grasped the tent pole to steady himself. "Now, let's not talk about it. I'll get you the three pounds, and you send it t' Elisabeth." Gray took the New Englander's arm and pulled him out of the tent. "Maybe we should get somethin' t' eat t' soak up ..." he burped, "the brandy."

Both men laughed and walked arm in arm past the officers' tents. It was now late afternoon, and the shadows were long. They stepped aside and waited for a squad of men to march past on their way to relieve the pickets at the edges of the camp. Several of the soldiers' faces were just as flushed as the two officers' were. One man in particular staggered, but it could have been the uneven ground. The squad passed quickly, and Gray and Bancroft continued unsteadily to the officer's latrine.

Bancroft regaled his friend with a couple of army jokes. Gray didn't have any navy jokes to speak of so he proved an appreciative listener. The one-sided flow of jokes continued through a meal in the cook tent, which included some Acadian beer.

"They call it *bière d'épinette*," the cook told the officers as he served two generous portions. "It's got a bite to it. Helps pass the time."

Agreeing with a nod of his head, Bancroft thanked the cook for his gift. "It's not as if we need any more drink," he muttered to Gray out of the corner of his mouth.

Gray's grin was a bit lopsided. "I don't know how you stand the boredom of army life. You sit 'round and eat ..."

"n' drink ..."

A shot, fired somewhere off in the trees, was followed by a bloodcurdling scream. A sentry called, "Indians!" [19]

Two more shots brought the officers running out of the cook tent. Gray was armed with his pistol and sword, but Bancroft was unarmed. Gray pulled the pistol from his belt and tossed it to his companion. "What shall we do?"

They stood in the circle of light from the lanterns of the cook tent, their eyes momentarily blinded and unable to peer into the darkness. It was several moments before Bancroft thought to order the cook to douse the lanterns. His eyes were adjusting to the darkness when a large figure came charging toward them. He was distracted by a number of shots from the woods—a fight was going on at the edge of the camp—when he looked back, the dark figure was much closer and pointing a long spear directly at him. He was going to be impaled!

Bancroft raised the pistol and pulled the trigger. The weapon misfired, and he braced himself for the attack.

"I brought you muskets, gentlemen," the assailant called. It was Sergeant Pollard, and they had almost killed him.

"I noticed the lieutenant had no personal weapon with him." Sergeant Pollard handed them muskets. "I know you prefer the musket, Lieutenant Bancroft, but if the naval officer would prefer not to use one, I'd understand, sir."

"Thanks, Sergeant!" Bancroft handed the pistol back to Gray. "I don't need your pistol now." He knelt down to check his weapon as best he could in the darkness. A cold sweat bathed his entire body. "I'd check the prime of that pistol, William, if I were you."

Gray stuck the pistol in his belt, and took the musket from the sergeant. He knelt on one knee and faced the direction of the attack. The farthest sentry was still making a fight of it. The remainder of the pickets were silent. The Indians were attacking the camp perimeter at only one point.

Bancroft marshalled a group of men to go to the aid of the beleaguered sentry. It was difficult to bring things together in the darkness, and the lieutenant felt all thumbs. He grimaced when he thought of how many of his men might be in the same condition. The soldiers hurried; they could hear the voice of the sentry swearing as the enemy swarmed him. It would be over in a moment if the men in the camp didn't respond faster.

"Cookie, light the lanterns! We don't have much time if we're going to help that man!"

In the sudden light, Bancroft got his men into good order. There were fifty or sixty volunteers, most of whom had gone ox hunting with him. Quickly assigning the men to sections under non-commissioned officers, Lieutenant Bancroft ordered squads to flank either side of the disturbance, and sent the largest group of men right into the middle of the fight. Bancroft was with the middle group. "Make lots of noise, boys! Let 'em know we're comin'!"

The lone picket was still putting up a brave fight. With the volunteers whooping and hollering, he was sure to know that help was on the way. If they could scare off the Micmac, they might be able to save the sentry's life.

Another shot sounded. The New Englanders paused in their approach, each man listening, hoping. There were no more sounds of conflict in front of the middle party.

The men resumed their advance, but much slower and more cautiously; there was no sense rushing into trouble now.

Bancroft cautiously parted pine branches with the barrel of his musket. He hoped they would find a body. That way, the regiment would know the sentry wasn't somewhere being brutalized by the Indians.

Moaning and cursing sounded off to the right; it was a New Englander all right. Sergeant Pollard was the first to find the sentry. "It's Brown, Lieutenant! He says he's been shot in the balls!"

"Form a perimeter, boys, while we get Brown out of here!" The lieutenant and the sergeant hoisted Brown onto the shoulders of a heavy-set man who then pushed his way through the branches with ease and headed back to the camp.

Bancroft carried both the big man's and Brown's muskets as he followed behind. The branches slashed his face as they were released by the big form in front of him, but pride didn't let him fall back, and the burden of three muskets didn't allow him to protect his face. He didn't much care. He just wanted to get back to the camp where it was safe. Or safer, he thought.

Brown cursed the Indians for having shot his private parts. "I can't be no good to no one without me peter," he wailed.

"Oh shut up, you crazy bastard," the big man told Brown. "You ain't expected to fight out there! All you had t' do was raise the alarm!"

"There wuz fifty of 'em! I was loadin' and fighting 'em hand to hand. I wuz drivin' 'em off, too! I might have saved the whole damn camp!"

The big man carried the chattering Brown for thirty yards without making any further comment. Brown talked and talked. "I got off the first shot." Brown's voice was calmer now as the lights of the camp became visible. "The slimy bastards were sneakin' up on us. I saved the whole camp. Fifty ... or more of 'em. They would have made mincemeat outta us if I hadn't drove 'em off!"

Under the cook tent's lamplight, Bancroft recognized the soldier carrying Brown as the same man who had whipped the defaulter. Sarcastically the big man observed, "I thought your peter was shot off. You sure are doin' a lot of hero talk for a man with no peter." He dropped his load on one of the cook tables.

"Oh! Oh!" Brown writhed in pain, clutching his crotch. "I should get a regimental bonus and honours! Instead I get dropped like a sack of potatoes in the cookhouse! I want the surgeon!"

Sergeant Pollard pushed his way into the tent. "Dr. Thomas said to leave you here where the light's good. He's gone to get his bag."

The lieutenant surgeon came into the tent, glanced at the man on the table, and approached Bancroft. "What happened to your face, Jeremiah? It looks painful."

"The wounded man's over there, John. See to him, will you?"

"He doesn't look like he's in bad trouble. What happened to you?"

"I got whacked by a couple of branches. No real harm done." Bancroft waved his hands at the other men. "Move out, boys. Let's leave room for the doctor to work on Brown." He spoke softly to the doctor. "Brown's one of my men, so I'd like to know how he is when you're finished. He says his peter's been shot off."

"Not enough blood for that. I don't think you'll have to worry about him being on the sick list."

Bancroft left the tent and joined Gray, who was leaning against his musket. "Was that fun," Gray asked. "Chasing the bad guys through the woods?"

Gray picked up the musket and the two of them walked back the way they had come earlier in the evening. When Bancroft didn't answer, Gray continued, "I'm glad I'm in the navy. Grabbin' hold of a popgun and running off into the night isn't my idea of ..."

"William, why don't you just stuff it!"

Dr. Thomas called from the cook tent, "Lieutenant Bancroft!"

"Coming, Surgeon Thomas." Bancroft turned and headed back to the cook tent. To Gray he said, "That was quick."

Approaching the grinning surgeon, Bancroft asked, "How's his peter?"

"No sign of injury to his private parts." Thomas put his arm around Bancroft's shoulders and drew him to one side to speak privately. "You'll find there was no sign of Indians, either."

Bancroft started to ask a question, but the doctor shushed him. "Our friend Brown dropped his musket and the thing went off between his legs. He's got the powder burns to prove it."

"The Indian attack?"

"The Indian attack was undoubtedly the story of a man drunk." The lieutenant surgeon swiped his hands over his face to hide his grin.

"No Indians?" Bancroft was incredulous.

"Brown was quite simply drunk. In the dark, on sentry duty, he was anxious and fumbled his musket, injuring himself. Responding to the sound of Brown's musket and screams, the nearby sentries fired at shadows. Brown shot back. You and a hundred men ..."

"There were no more than fifty, doctor."

"You and fifty men went running through the trees, looking to kill something." Thomas turned his head away from the lamplight to hide his broad smile. "It was a good thing Brown had already done himself and was lying down or ..."

"Doctor, you don't have to report a story like that to the colonel?"

"If you can think of another one, I'd be glad to use it."

*29 June 1755*
*Fort Cumberland (Beauséjour)*

For the first time since the New Englanders arrived in the Fundy, Lieutenant Jeremiah Bancroft was the only officer available for Sunday morning parade. The captain was still away acting as the colonel's adjutant and First Lieutenant Nathan Simons had departed down the trail even before first light or the cook tent had opened. He had left a message that he had been ordered to report to the fort. That left Bancroft to face the ire of his colonel.

Puffy-eyed with a red, badly abused face, Bancroft formed up the men of Phenehas Company and marched them to the parade ground. The other companies were already there.

As Phenehas Company wheeled into position, a faint but unmistakable Indian war whoop emanated from the gathered men. Snickering and muffled laughter swept the ranks of the other companies.

"Steady up!" Major Prebble gave the order but didn't turn to attempt to enforce it. He carefully kept his expression blank.

A high falsetto voice cried, "Phenehas Company ain't got no balls."

This time the laughter was widespread throughout the ranks of the men.

The major brought the companies to attention, and turned the parade over to the colonel, who ordered the companies to form hollow square for the church service. Parson Phillips, all dark and solemn, walked to the head of the hollow square and cleared his voice. Reading from a sheaf of papers he began his sermon, quoting from Ecclesiastes 6, verses 11 and 12. His voice rang with righteous tones, rising and falling, as he stressed the words to give depth of meaning to their message: "Seeing there be many things that increase vanity, what is man the better?"

Phillips paused, studying the group of men directly in front of him. He looked down at his papers and read verse 12: "'For who knoweth what is good for man in this life, all the days of his vain life which he spendeth as a shadow? For who can tell a man what shall be after him under the sun?'"

The parson allowed a long period of silence before he turned the page and read again. "And from Ecclesiastes 11, verse 9, Rejoice, O young man, in thy youth; and let thy heart cheer thee in the days of thy youth, and walk in the ways of thine heart, and in the sight of thine eyes: but know thou …"The parson raised his chin and stared at the men of Phenehas Company. "But know thou you that for all these *things* God will bring thee into judgment."

What followed was a sermon the parson began with, "Fighting the good fight in the service of our Christian Monarch." He ended with, "Indulging in foul habits that seduce even the bravest Christian heart; that reduce the most dedicated and well meaning servant of the King of Kings and our most Christian Monarch, to a slavering tool of the fallen Arch Angel."

Bancroft groaned. There was no doubt about whom the parson was talking and why.

The parson concluded his sermon with a dramatic flourish. "Know ye, men of Massachusetts, ye shall be brought to judgment!"

Phillips bowed his head. He raised his right hand and recited the Soldier's Prayer: "I fight the good fight with all my might for God and King. I vanquish my foe in thy name, God, and for the glory of the King. Guide my arm straight and true that I might do good service this day."

After a moment's pause, Phillips stepped back and allowed Colonel Winslow to assume the position at the head of the hollow square.

The colonel fixed his eyes on the red face of the officer leading Phenehas Company. He took a deep breath. "I have seen," he proclaimed, "better soldiering than last night. Indeed I have." He clasped his hands behind his back and rocked on his toes. "I have seen worse soldiering, but not much worse." The last man on the parade square could hear Colonel

Winslow's quiet voice. "We are sons of Massachusetts, proud of our homeland and willing to die for her. Well, I'll see that you do just that—die for her—if there is any more drinking around this camp! The next man who is drunk will be whipped and shipped out in irons to Halifax where the governor has the authority to end his miserable life."

Winslow took several steps in the direction of Bancroft. He examined that officer's face carefully. "I know you, Lieutenant."

"Yes, sir!"

"I will still know you when the effects of your drinking have faded from your face!"

"Yes, sir!"

"You and your men are denied rum ration until further notice!"

An audible groan rose from the ranks of Phenehas Company. If the colonel heard it, he gave no sign. "Major Prebble!" he called loudly.

"Yes, sir!"

"Dismiss the companies ... all save Phenehas. Have Phenehas clean out the officer's latrine."

That evening, a tired and smelly Phenehas Company stood at attention while the rest of the companies received their ration of rum.

*30 June 1755*
*Fort Cumberland (Beauséjour)*

On the second day without rum rations, tempers in Phenehas Company had short fuses. There were three fights and a stabbing. Four men were sentenced by their officers to ride the wooden horse. Twenty lashes were meted out for the fighters and thirty lashes for the man who had wielded the bayonet.

*1 July 1755*
*Fort Cumberland*

The Phenehas men had been ordered to stand at attention in full parade dress, with empty ammunition pouches and muskets, while the rest of the New Englanders drew their rum ration. The smell of the dark, molasses-like rum enveloped the square.

Private Brown spoke from the rear rank. "It's not fair!"

Lieutenant Simons ordered Sergeant Pollard to find out who was talking so the man could be punished.

"Stay away from me, Pollard," Brown cried hysterically. "I haven't had a drink in two days!"

"Leave Brown alone," someone else called. "He's right. We does all the work around here and we don't get no rum like the others."

Sergeant Pollard marched down the line. As he approached Brown, several men who held their muskets like clubs confronted him. In a very steady voice Pollard called, "The men have broken rank, Lieutenant Simons!" [20]

Simons, standing at the head of the formation, ordered, "Lieutenant Bancroft! Your assistance, please!"

"Yes, Lieutenant." Bancroft moved forward from his position at the front right flank of the company and tapped Sergeant Walker on the shoulder. "No weapons," he whispered. "Get the corporals."

When Bancroft rounded the end of the ranks he saw three soldiers facing Sergeant Pollard. As he approached, two more broke ranks and joined the troublemakers. Several more had turned to watch what was going on, but hadn't as yet broken ranks to join the mutineers.

Mutineers! Thinking that, Bancroft realized that he was in the midst of a mutiny. Nothing he had ever been taught prepared him for the situation where his own men were the threat! With a sense of shock, he watched several more men move out of their ranks to face him, as he got closer. There were now about ten men waving their muskets like clubs and making threats. He saw Wyman, always the troublemaker, and Brown. Brown would have started it, and Potts was full of lip, but who would believe this?

Brown spoke. "You shoulda got our rum, Lieutenant. But then you don't drink n' you don't miss it."

"I never did like you, Bancroft, with your fancy Lutheran talk," Wyman sneered.

Bancroft looked crossly at Wyman. "Wyman, you don't have to like me; just do as you're told. Get back in the ranks."

Someone moved up behind Bancroft, but he couldn't turn to see who it was. He was relieved when he heard Sergeant Walker whisper, "I got four corporals here, sir. The other companies are loadin' their muskets now. Won't be but a minute. Keep 'em talkin'."

"Get back in the ranks. Get back in the ranks," Brown jeered. He threw his musket to the ground and pulled out his bayonet. "If I don't get some rum right now, I'm gonna feed you this little sticker, shithead!" Brown held his bayonet on a level with Bancroft's throat and stepped forward.

Because Bancroft was so much taller, Brown had to extend his arm to threaten the officer's throat. Seeing his chance, the lieutenant grabbed Brown by the wrist and lifted the man off the ground. With his other hand Bancroft twisted the bayonet out of Brown's grasp and let it fall. Bancroft now held the struggling Brown with two hands. He pivoted and handed Brown to the corporals, who quickly subdued him.

Wyman abruptly placed his musket properly by his side and stepped back into the ranks. "Yes, sir," he said. "I'm gettin' back in the ranks. Sorry, sir."

The rest of the mutineers shuffled a bit as if they weren't sure what to do next. Sergeant Pollard, backed up by twenty men from another company bearing loaded muskets, gave the order. "You men! Step back from the officer and put your hands up. Now!"

The mutiny was over. Eleven men were taken into custody, including Wyman. Within the hour, all the mutineers were sentenced to be whipped twenty stripes each.

\* \* \*

The morning of the whippings, Parson Phillips took the text of his sermon from Proverbs 15, verse 21. "Folly is joy to him who is destitute of wisdom: but a man of understanding walketh uprightly."

As far as Potts and Brown were concerned, after they rode

the wooden horse that morning, they were placed in irons and shipped to Halifax. There they faced the gibbet at the north-west corner of Halifax Common.

On their final day, they were served a double portion of navy rum before they were hanged, for whatever comfort that brought them.

*18 July 1755*
*Halifax*

Richard Bulkeley, First Secretary of Nova Scotia, studied his fingernails. He looked the epitome of composure; however, he was seething with anger at the governor who had told him to keep the Inhabitants waiting. That was very fine for the governor who sat comfortably in his office. Due to a lack of space, Bulkeley on the other hand was forced to keep company with the farmers, one of whom smelled like he had just come from a pigsty. Bulkeley wrinkled his nose. I'd wager that if I turned up the fat fellow's heels, I'd find raw shit, he thought. I'll have to give them this much though, they've been waiting for nigh onto an hour and have shown no signs of impatience.

Bulkeley gazed out the window at the passing scene on George Street. Soon the government would have to provide better arrangements for the governor. There should be an anteroom where undesirables could be kept waiting. Bulkeley should be able to tell them to wait and then leave them. He should be able to sit elsewhere while petitioners cooled their shit-covered heels.

He tapped the folder he held in his hand. Paperwork begets more paperwork. He sighed and shook his head. During the siege of Fort Beauséjour, Governor Lawrence had issued a proclamation ordering all Inhabitants to surrender their firearms. There had been protests; the Inhabitants had insisted on keeping their weapons saying they needed them for hunting. Petitions followed the protests, and now a party of petitioners had arrived at the Governor's Mansion. What a bother! It should be plain enough even for Acadian farmers to understand: guns could not be left in the hands of the enemy.

To pass the time, Bulkeley opened the file folder. He idly scanned the list of names. Funny names, he thought. Joseph ... what? Bore-go-zee, Bulkeley mouthed the man's name. French names always looked so ... foreign. The next name was easier, Le-blank. Le blank was almost English! Imagine going through life answering to Arse-nault! The governor's door opened. Bulkeley motioned for the Inhabitants to follow him.

Governor Lawrence remained seated. There weren't enough chairs for the entire party, so the Inhabitants stood in a little straight line in front of the governor. Like recalcitrant schoolboys, Bulkeley thought.

Bulkeley sat in one of the available chairs and opened the file. Clearing his throat he began, "Your Excellency, these gentlemen are from ..."

"Do they understand English?" Lawrence interrupted.

Bulkeley said very slowly, "Do—you—speak—English?"

One man with an air of authority stepped forward. "*Je*, uh, I am called Joseph Bourgeois. I speak a little."

"Your insolence is insufferable!" Governor Lawrence hit the palm of his hand with his fist. "You question me, Lieutenant Governor of Nova Scotia, with your protests and petitions?"

"*Quoi?*"

"Bulkeley, get someone to translate. Now!"

Bulkeley went to the door of the office and spoke to someone outside. The governor became impatient. "No, never mind! I don't care if they understand me or not." Governor Lawrence continued angrily. "Will your people swear an unqualified oath of allegiance?"

Joseph Bourgeois's face was a study of concentration and concern. "We ask to keep our guns for hunting."

"The matter of your guns has been settled! They will be surrendered immediately."

"We need them for hunting," Bourgeois persisted stubbornly.

"You will make an oath of allegiance, or we'll consider you an enemy of the realm."

A timid knock on the door momentarily halted the proceedings. A Ranger officer entered. "You need me, sir?"

"If you speak French," Bulkeley responded, "tell the Inhabitants that they must take an unqualified oath of allegiance. Now."
The Ranger spoke rapidly to the Inhabitants. Bourgeois answered resolutely and the Ranger translated. "He says they've taken an oath of fidelity in the past, and they would be willing to take it again. They will not bear arms against the French. Sir, he's more concerned about losing his guns so he can't go hunting."

"You tell him that he'll take an unqualified oath of allegiance or I'll put him in prison," warned the governor.[21]

A look of genuine surprise appeared on Bourgeois's face as the officer translated. He answered as soon as the Ranger had finished speaking. "An oath of fidelity is all we are obliged to give you. We have given the same oaths in the past. The other governors accepted them."

Governor Lawrence pressed his lips together and was silent for a moment. "Conditional oaths are of no use to me. You have until this time tomorrow. If you continue to refuse ..." He waved his hand in dismissal. "Call the guard. Keep them under arrest. They have until this time tomorrow."

Bulkeley and Lawrence remained silent as the Inhabitants filed out. The last man politely closed the door of the governor's office.

"Well," said the governor. "What do you think, Richard?"

"They won't take the oath of allegiance," Bulkeley predicted.

"You think not?"

"No. They consider you to be just another English governor who'll back down like Cornwallis and Hopson did. They expect you to bluster and threaten, but in the end accept the usual horseshit about Acadian neutrality and their not being obliged to bear arms."

"The usual horseshit, is it," stormed the governor.

"Well, sir, if they refuse to take the oath tomorrow ..."

"They're actually saying they refuse to become English subjects."

Bulkeley took it one step further. "They could be classified as rebels and considered a serious threat to the Crown. And, sir, if you tolerate their insolence, you'll most likely incur the Crown's displeasure. At the very least, the Lords of Trade would be dissatisfied with your actions and make their opinions known to the king's ministers."

Lawrence winced and nodded his head in agreement. "Thank you, Richard. I will seek other opinions, but please understand that I value yours highly."

"Until tomorrow, sir."

"Yes, Richard. Until tomorrow."

*5 August 1755*
*Fort Lawrence*

Colonel Robert Monckton and Captain John Rous sat in the officers' mess. Two half-finished glasses of sherry sat on the table before them. They were quite alone, having dismissed their staff officers before they began to discuss the contents of the letters they had received from the governor.[22]

Rous asked, "Your letter is the same as mine?"

Monckton sighed and opened his letter. He perched his glasses on the end of his nose and began to read: "'My dear Colonel, I was delighted to hear that' … mmm, yes, here's the business part …"

Rous placed his letter on the table. "Let's compare them, side by side."

The colonel put his letter on the table.

After a few moments Rous commented, "The only difference between the letters, is that I'm ordered to ensure that the transports all have full water casks." With a grim smile, he noted, "The governor doesn't leave much to chance, does he?"

Monckton's smile was just as grim. "No, he doesn't." He took his glasses off and placed them on the table. "You know, recently, some Acadian leaders petitioned Halifax seeking relief from the proclamation that all Inhabitants are to turn in their firearms."

The New Englander shook his head. "I can't imagine anyone thinking that a farmer can go to his fields without a gun!"

"Well, you can't leave weapons in the hands of the enemy," the army man countered.

"How would a man put meat on the table without a gun?" Rous tipped back his glass and drained it of sherry.

"Our dear governor refused to discuss it. He ordered the Inhabitants to take an unqualified oath of allegiance and gave them twenty-four hours to think it over. When they refused ..."

Rous put his glass down and looked around for the mess steward. "Shouldn't have surprised him; they've always refused."

"He had them locked up," Monckton said. "He's sending them back to France on the very first ship."

"What do you mean, 'back to France?' None of those people came from France!"

"No matter. That's where they're being sent. Probably gone already." Briskly, Monckton folded his copy of the governor's letter and placed it in his file folder. "Should make our job a mite easier what with the Acadian leaders out of the way."

Monckton, too, had finished his sherry. He raised his voice. "Steward!"

Almost immediately a head poked through the doorway at the far end of the officers' mess. "Yes, Colonel?"

"Bring two more sherries."

When the steward had brought the sherries and had left the room, Monckton lowered his voice as he said to Rous, "Secrecy is the key to this operation."

Rous nodded his head in agreement. "Yes."

"No one should know the purpose of the operation until it is accomplished."

"Not even our staff officers?"

"Not even our staff officers."

*7 August 1755*
*Grand Pré*

Reine Cameron served her husband a thick slice of bread hot from her great aunt Matilde's oven. "I know you don't like it so hot, *chéri*, but I had to wait my turn at the oven." She pushed wisps of hair off her forehead and stood with her hands on her hips looking down at the meal she had prepared and served. "There was no meat."

"I'm sorry, Reine. You know I haven't been able to go to the woods."

"No, no, *cher Robert*. I understand about the proclamation." Robert Cameron made a shushing motion with his finger. "We still have guns. They're hidden near the church, but if the English found us in the woods with weapons they'd probably hang us."

Cameron pulled Reine to him. He hugged her hips, and buried his face in the front of her dress that was still warm from the heat of the oven. She ran her fingers through his hair. His voice muffled, Cameron said in English, "I love you, my Queen of Hearts."

*"Quoi?"* Reine had not understood all of his words. She grasped his hair, pulling his head back to look into his eyes. Using English, she asked, "You love only me?"

*"Je t'aime."* Cameron stood, kissed her, and slipped his hand over her left breast.

The large figure of Great Aunt Matilde filled the open doorway. "You should let your man finish his meal or he won't be much use to you, child."

Not the least embarrassed, Reine pushed her husband back into his chair. "My Robert is always good for me."

Matilde chuckled. "My man was good."

The sound of running footsteps on the stone walk froze the three of them into silence. There were few English soldiers in the area, a small detachment near the shore, but Robert Cameron could never forget he was a deserter. If the English came this way, he and Reine would have to flee. So far, they had been untroubled by the English at Grand Pré, and they had begun to feel safe. The three in the kitchen breathed a collective sigh of relief when the big round face of a Bourgeois peeked through the doorway. "We need you up valley, *Fanne de Carotte*."

"Who needs me, André?"

"A war party near Fort Sackville captured a Ranger officer. He seems to know what happened to our leaders."

Robert filled his mouth with vegetables. Shaking his head, he chewed to make room before speaking. Finally he said, "I'm no good at making men tell their secrets when they don't want to."

"I don't know about that, Carrot Top. The French officer with the raiding party, Charles Des Champs de Boishebert said I was to bring you as soon as possible. So, come!"

Robert filled his mouth again. Apparently he wasn't going to be given time to eat. He had to shovel in as much of his meal as he could. Speaking around his food he asked, "How far to where the Ranger is being held?"

"I've travelled since yesterday."

Another mouthful. "So it's almost two days ..."

"Yes! You are to come right away!"

"Did you see signs of English patrols?"

"Boishebert must have killed some because he gave the Mi'kmaq warriors some English muskets, powder, and ball."

Swallowing, Cameron said, "If Boishebert killed some, there will be patrols out looking for revenge. It's dangerous for me to travel. If I'm found, I'll be hanged."

André Bourgeois lost patience. "If you don't come right now, Boishebert will kill you anyway!"

Robert Cameron had no doubt in his mind about that. If he wasn't Carrot Top, the hard-working, willing, relative-by-marriage of Georges LeBlanc, he would be the English deserter, and as good as dead. He took one last mouthful. Reaching around Reine, he took a jacket off a peg. Slipping it on, he allowed Reine to hug him before he and Bourgeois shuffled out the door. Once outside, he took a deep breath of the early evening air. "Wait for me, here, Reine. No matter what happens with this Boishebert fellow, wait for me here."

"I will, Robert. I will be quite safe here with Tante Matilde."

Three more men waited at the bottom of the path. They turned without speaking, and Bourgeois and Cameron joined them in an easy trot along the path leading out of the village.

Tante Matilde put her arm around her great niece. "He will be all right, Reine." They stood in front of the old house and watched until the party passed out of sight.

*10 August 1755*
*Fort Lawrence*

Lieutenant William Gray dismissed his boat's crew and turned to walk up the beach. The tall New Englander was waving at him from the top of the path leading from the beach to the fort.

"It's good to see you again, Lieutenant Church Steeple," Gray said when he caught up to Bancroft.

They grasped each other's hands in greeting.

"Likewise, William Grubby White," said Bancroft. "What've you been doing?"

"I've been gathering a dozen sea-worthy Acadian and French ships. I found some crews and sent most of the craft to be auctioned in Halifax."

"Had any trouble with the Micmac as you travelled around?"

"No." Gray's voice took on a very serious tone. "Has there been trouble?"

"Yep. At Fort Gaspereau. They took one of our boys and chopped him up."

"While he was alive?"

"Appears so. The colonel sent out a party of two hundred men but ..."

"But they found nothing. I know." Gray gave a little shiver. "At Halifax, back in '49, I ran across some Indians in the woods. Didn't see them until they wanted me to."

"They let you go?"

"Oh, I was leading an armed party," Gray said with a faraway look in his eyes. "But yes, I think they let us go." He changed the subject. "Why are you here in Fort Lawrence?"

"Something's up. Four transports came in from Boston this week. They're parked in the bay."

Gray smiled at the thought of ships being "parked" in the bay. "Maybe you're being sent home."

"Some of our sick will be sent home," Bancroft said. "But, no, the rest of us have been warned to be ready to move at an instant's notice. In fact, Captain Lewis took a hundred men and marched off to Cobequid the day before yesterday."

"Well, for what it's worth, I agree with you: something's up. My captain ordered me to find good sources of timber. He wants me to be ready to build large pens, like for cattle. When I saw the transports I thought it was ships' victuals to take the New England Militia home. But you think not?"

Bancroft shook his head negatively. "We're not going home, William." Giving his friend a quick smile he gestured down the path. "The mess tent is open. Want to eat?"

"I'm glad you asked. I was going to drop into the mess at Fort Cumberland, but the harbour-master directed my boat here. Any idea what's going on at the other fort?"

"All I know," Bancroft said, "is between four and five hundred French were imprisoned there, locked up inside the fort."

"French? I didn't think there were any French left around here!"

"Maybe I should have said Acadians. Acadian farmers were locked up. Colonel Monckton told them their lands and livestock were forfeit to the king."

"What did they do to deserve that? Armed insurrection?"

"I don't know, but the farmers are prisoners in the fort, and we're allowed to butcher any livestock we see." The taller man rubbed his hands together. "There's real good eatin' at the mess tent right now."

"Well, I can smell the beef from here. I'm starved."

Like the good friends they were the officers walked along chatting about this and that. At the mess tent they had a choice of several cuts of beef. While they waited for their meals to be prepared, they sipped strong tea. The jug of *bière d'épinette*, on the table well within their reach, was left completely untouched.

### 10 August 1755
### Cinq Maisons

Seated near the fireplace in one of the Acadian houses that gave the village its name, the French officer looked up casually as Robert Cameron was pushed into the low-ceilinged room. The sun had just set and the room was quite dark. The door closed behind Cameron who stood alone just inside the room.

"I'm Charles Des Champs de Boishebert. I'm leader of a war party that plans to drive the English out of the Fundy." He selected a candle from a package near the base of the hearth. Checking the wick, he lit it with a taper. Methodically, he dropped wax on the arm of his chair and affixed the lighted candle. He regarded it while he continued. "If we have to kill some of our friends to accomplish the removal of the devil's spawn from French territory," he held his hands up in a gesture of helplessness, "then we shall."

Boishebert preened his little moustache and stroked his goatee, then lowered his hand to the scabbard of his sword. He sat back as if relaxing after a successful day of hunting before he began again. "You're the English deserter known as *Fanne de Carrotte.*"

Cameron didn't respond.

"Are you one of us, or do I have you killed," Boishebert asked calmly.

Cameron hadn't been invited to sit. He shifted from one foot to the other as he replied, "I chose to be Acadian. I'm married to ..."

The French officer interrupted. "You will be loyal to our king?"

"*Oui.*"

"More loyal than you were to the English king, Englishman?"

Cameron's eyes flashed with anger. "I'm a Scot! And if we're going to chat about loyalties, why did the French garrison at Beauséjour abandon us to the English without a fight?"

The French officer's face darkened. He furiously preened his moustache without responding.

Cameron looked around the room. "I'm tired. I've been travelling without rest or food. I need to sit down. I need a drink."

Boishebert waved a hand. Someone who had been hidden in the room's shadows placed a chair and small table in the middle of the room. Cameron sat.

"We've captured a Ranger," Boishebert said. "He has information about the Acadian leaders who went to Halifax to petition for removal of the gun proclamation. The English governor locked them up. We need to know where. We think the Ranger knows."

"Could I please have something to drink? Something to eat?"

"In good time. Will you help us get the information we need?"

"If I can, yes."

"Good."

A pile of clothes was placed on the table. It was a corporal's uniform from Cameron's old regiment, the Fortieth. "Put them on."

"Now?"

Angrily, Boishebert said, *"Immédiatement!"*

Cameron stood and began to disrobe. He hesitated when he came to his underclothing.

"Take off all your Acadian clothes," Boishebert ordered. "I want you to be a lobster-back again. You'll be put in with the Ranger and gain his confidence. Find out where the Habitant leaders are imprisoned and you can return to your pretty wife."

Cameron, almost finished dressing, looked up quickly. "Is that a threat?"

"No, of course not. It's merely a statement of fact. If we don't get those leaders back, then it's unlikely the Acadians will have the will to resist further. If they don't resist, there will be few places in the Fundy where we can safely rest our heads." Boishebert paused and regarded the figure in the English uniform. "There'd be no place for the likes of you."

Cameron gave an understanding nod to what Boishebert said.

Several men entered the room. One of them walked over to Cameron and stared at him critically. He fingered a bullet hole in the sleeve of the red tunic a few inches down from the shoulder. He drew a knife and, with a few quick cuts, tore off the sleeve. He stepped back and regarded his work. He rubbed his hand under the mantel of the fireplace and smeared soot over the fresh cut and down Robert's arm. He spoke for the first time. "You were captured near Fort Edward several days ago. You were on patrol. There're initials on the collar of your tunic, HM-Herbert Miles, Bert for short. The Indians brought you here for Boishebert to interrogate. He asked you about the Acadian leaders. You passed out."

Someone standing behind Cameron asked, "You have any questions?"

"No, I guess not," Cameron replied.

Boishebert stood up. He was slim and surprisingly slight. He took two quick steps and struck Cameron's face with his fist. Cameron staggered back but didn't fall. "What the hell!"

The man holding the red sleeve in his hand hit him again. Cameron went down.

Nursing his hand, Boishebert complained, "He's got a jaw like iron."

"Is he out?" The man holding the sleeve ignored Boishebert and kicked Cameron's chest. "I don't think anything's broken," he said with a tone of disgust. Without waiting for a reply he motioned to one of the other men. "Break something. He must be in pain if the Ranger officer is to believe him."

"Break one of his fingers," Boishebert suggested.

Cameron groaned when his finger was broken but failed to waken.

"Hit him in the face a couple of times," the man with the sleeve suggested. "The lip. Do the lip better."

Boishebert, sucking on his bruised knuckles, ordered the men to lift Cameron. They dragged him to his feet and held him so Boishebert could get a good look. "How does he explain the blood on the tunic?"

"Cut his face."

One of them took a knife out of his belt, and made a cut about two inches long.

"Deeper."

Boishebert winced. "Not so close to his eye. We want his wife to be able to recognize him, don't we?"

After a few moments, Boishebert said, "I think that will do. Throw him in with the other Englishman. Don't show any lights. We want the blood to dry on his face before the Ranger sees him."

## Endnotes

[1] From the Bancroft diary. "... in ye skirmish they wounded Major Prebble in his ( ? ) which affronted so that he ordered his men to run upon them ..." The wound probably wasn't serious because the major reappeared in the Bancroft narrative soon after.

[2] From Bancroft's diary. "... one of our eight inch mortars was split by a cannon ball ..."

[3] The incident of the encounter on the marsh is mostly true according to Jeremiah's diary. "A number of french and indians were on ye marsh akillin catle which our men spied on. Sent out 50 men which drove them off and tuck ye ox they had killed and brought away."

[4] Jacau de Piedmont reported that the habitants chose a spokesman to make their case with the commandant. I gave the man a name: Joseph Bourgeois.

[5] "Killed in the casemate with Hay, the English Officer, M Raimbault, officer, Sieur Fermand, interpreter, M Billy clerk, by a bomb." The Forts Of Chignecto, NS Archives.

[6] "Father leLoutre, a priest, the most zealous worker in the interests of France, strongly opposed surrendering, stating he would rather bury himself under the ruins of the fort than give it up to the captors." From a paper titled, "One of the Forts of the Chignecto Peninsula," on microfiche at the NS Archives.

[7] The negotiations for surrender in the story are very close to those reported by de Piedmont's account. I only simplified them slightly making them, hopefully, easier to read.

[8] Jeremiah Bancroft wrote in his diary that, "the Col demanded ye forte and told them if they did not give up soon he would hoist his Bloody Flagg ..."

[9] This meeting is fiction.

[10] "Soon after the truce was on the Indians fired upon our centrays ..." Bancroft reports an attack on the sentries and that is the basis for the fiction of Beau Soliel's revenge on the 'tall one.' Having LeLoutre incite the Indians is fiction but the details of Captain John's death are: "... one Indian that we wounded that was calld Capt. John and many of ye English knew him he was mortally wounded ..."

[11] Bancroft diary. "... Col Scott hearing ye engagement thought ye truce was only a trick ordered all ye mortar to be loaded and was aputing the

match to when Capt. Speakman standing on the bank of trench calld out a truce."

[12] Details such as this are based on the Bancroft diary.

[13] "Ordered a party of 200 men to proceed to the village of Baie Verte to search for M. Le Loutre's chest and papers." There was detail about stopping at a stream, fixing a destroyed bridge, and finding a well-appointed priest's house. From the diary of Colonel Winslow.

[14] This confrontation is fiction.

[15] I made a point of using the very words of Governor Lawrence's letters wherever possible because they were so significant to our history. From microfiche at the NS Archives.

[16] Whoever was writing Governor Lawrence's letters did not use the {é} in Fort Beausejour (Fort Beauséjour) as perhaps he should have.

[17] I found references to an unnamed naval officer doing this so made it our man Gray.

[18] I changed the date of the earthquake so I didn't have to have a second meeting between the two men.

[19] "... was beset by about 50 indians which shot at him and wounded his hand. But he continued firing at them getting behind the Dykes and beat them off and made his escape as he relates the story whereupon a party of 50 men ware sent out. But could make no discovery of the enemy and afterwards the doctr dressing his wounds perceived his hand to be burnt with powder which makes it appear to be the story of a man drunk." From the Bancroft diary.

[20] Bancroft mentions a mutiny but not in detail.

[21] Lawrence wrote with satisfaction to Sir Thomas Robinson on July 18th, "we gave them a 24 hours' time to deliver their answer, and if they should then refuse, they must expect to be driven out of the country; and though they should afterwards repent of their refusal, they would not be permitted to take the oath."

[22] There is no record of such a meeting but the quotes from the governor's correspondence are accurate.

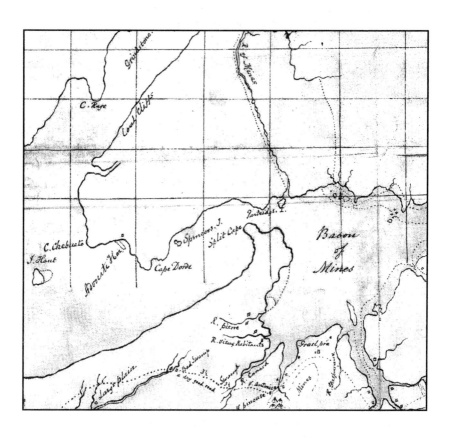

# Chapter Eight

His Majesty's Ship *Yorke*, Royal Navy sloop of war, pulled gently at her moorings. All was quiet, her decks fairly deserted. Visible were the officer of the watch, the helmsman, two marine guards, and the buffer. Although the crew had been dismissed below on 'make and mend,' servicing their personal gear, the buffer still patrolled the deck and operational areas searching for any oversight, untidy lashing, or improperly stowed gear that might label *Yorke* a slack ship.

The captain had made it very clear; *Yorke* would be told about her next mission with no warning. When operational orders did arrive, *H.M.S. Yorke* would be expected to respond at once. Captain Cobbs had ordered that everything be ready. Since it was the buffer's job to translate the captain's order into specific tasks, he had been busy. When the buffer was busy, the men of the crew were very busy indeed.

Finally, with the work done and the ship in readiness, the captain had given permission for the crew to service their personal gear. Usually the crew spread themselves throughout the vessel to complete their personal chores, but not today. Everyone had been sent below. Therefore, to any passing vessel, *Yorke* appeared unsullied and uncluttered like a newly commissioned sloop of war. She was ready.

Shortly after the midday meal, the officer of the watch sent word to the captain that a longboat bearing a naval officer was approaching from *H.M.S. Success*. Hurriedly, Captain Cobbs slipped on his tunic and tucked his hat under his arm. When he reached the deck, he accepted the telescope from the watch officer.

"Any signals from the fleet commander's ship?"

"No, sir."

If the visitor was a senior officer, or the fleet commander himself, *H.M.S. Success* would have flown the message, "Royal Navy Ship #248 (*Yorke*), prepare to receive visitors."

"Who is it?" Cobbs demanded as he adjusted the focus on the glass.

"It's Lieutenant Gray, sir. I saw him go out to *Success* from the fort several hours ago. The boat waited for him. I watched through the glass. He's bringing his sea bag with him."

"And he's clutching a dispatch case. Goddamn, Frederick! We just might be seeing some action!"

It was the first time the captain had addressed Sub-Lieutenant Frederick Marsh by his Christian name, and the officer's face beamed with pleasure. "Should I pipe general quarters, sir?"

Cobbs watched the longboat through the glass. "No. The longboat's taken a leisurely stroke. They're giving us time to prepare our decks for company." He nodded his head. "Pipe the duty watch."

"Aye, sir."

"Give me a call when he arrives," Cobbs said over his shoulder as he descended to his cabin.

Ten minutes later, the longboat was close enough to be challenged by Lieutenant Marsh. "Ahoy the boat!"

The coxswain for the longboat responded, "Aye, aye, sir! Lieutenant Gray requests permission to come aboard!"

"Carry on, the boat!"

Ten minutes later, Lieutenant William Gray stood at the entry port of *Yorke*. Saluting the quarterdeck he said in jovial tones, "Hello, Frederick. Please inform Captain Cobbs that I bring orders from the fleet commander."

Marsh nodded to one of the marines. "Inform the captain, Marine."

The marine gave the duty officer a snappy butt salute on his musket and clomped off.

Marsh and Gray shook hands.

"Are you going to give me a hint?"

"'fraid not, Frederick. You'll have to wait for your captain to inform you." Gray cast his eyes up and down the ship's deck. He noted a new bulwark, cannon, and stanchions had replaced the damage where the French cannon had made a direct hit. Now it was new and fresh. He took several steps to the other bulwark.

Behind him, Marsh commented, "Most of the damage is gone. There are still musket ball grooves just to your right that were too deep to get out."

"I was standing about here," Gray mused.

"Captain on the deck," the marine ordered.

Both officers turned and saluted.

"Yes, Gray, and that French officer had you dead in his sights, too." Captain Cobbs returned the salutes of the two officers and continued. "I thought you were a goner."

Gray grinned. "That afternoon on the Missaguash River is one I'll never forget, sir."

"Experiences like that make life so very sweet, gentlemen." Cobbs extended his hand for the dispatch case. "Any idea where we're going, Gray?"

"Yes, sir." Gray's face displayed his pleasure as he added, "And, with your permission, I have orders to go with you."

"Then come below, Lieutenant." Cobbs glanced at Marsh. "You have the deck, Lieutenant."

"Aye, sir."

Once below in the captain's cabin, Cobbs tossed the dispatch case onto his desk. Motioning for Gray to take the only other chair, Cobbs sat behind his desk. "How much do you know about it, William?"

"I know the details of the enterprise, sir, but I'm not aware of the objective."

"Tell me as much as you know. Is the objective in here?" Cobbs tapped the dispatch case with his finger.

"No sir, it's not. The details are: you are to embark four companies of New England Militia and transport them in very good order to arrive at Les Mines on the nineteenth."

"*Yorke* is to be a damn transport?"

"Aye, sir. She's able to protect the troops against anything she might run across."

Wearily the captain interrupted, "And she has shallow draught so she can go in closer than any other type vessel to support the troops with her cannon. Yes, I know the kind of rationale Captain Rous would use."

"Don't forget, sir," Gray reminded him, "your crew has some experience with this kind of thing, having acquitted themselves very well on the Missaguash. Captain Rous probably took that into account."

"Well, it was a near thing on the Missaguash. We almost lost it all that afternoon."

"Good thing the militia came to our rescue."

"It wouldn't happen to be the same boys we're transporting, would it?"

"Yes, one of the companies is Phenehas Company."

"That tall, long-legged officer still with them?"

"Yes, sir. I was talking to him just the other day. He said they had been warned to be ready to move at a moment's notice."[1]

Captain Cobbs broke the seal on the orders. "When will they be coming?"

"They're receiving their orders right now. Boats from the rest of the fleet will be heading for shore in the next hour to bring them to us." Gray rose. "I'm terribly sorry, sir. I must go. It's my duty to be mother hen and see that these chicks get to wherever they're going so they can do whatever they're meant to do."

"Yes, of course, Lieutenant. Carry on." With a wave of his hand, Cobbs dismissed the junior officer and began to read his orders.

Lieutenant Gray saluted and left.

*16 August 1755*
*Cinq Maisons*

"God, it smells bad in here!"

The Ranger officer didn't reply. He held his hands out toward the single shaft of light that found its way into the cellar where they were imprisoned. He didn't look into the dark corner where Bert Miles was lying on the dirt floor. Now that he could see his wrist with the help of the sunlight, he picked at a scab.

"Don't pick it," Herbert Miles said. "If there's no pus now, there will be if you pull it off."

The Ranger, George Ritchie, still didn't answer.

"What did they ask you?" Miles persisted.

Ritchie pulled at the scab. It came off, and he turned it over and studied the design in the crust. He put it in his mouth and chewed.

"Oh, Christ! You've gone out of your mind!"

Ritchie swallowed.

Miles sat up. "They keep asking me the same thing over and over. It was the same today as it was the first day."

The Ranger dropped his hands into his lap and let his head droop. To Miles it looked like he was in prayer. The man spoke for the first time in several days. "They're going to kill you."

Miles crawled to face the other man. "What do you mean?"

Ritchie gazed at the face of the soldier. It's funny, he thought. The hair is redder than the tunic. Now, isn't that something? The red on his face is not as red as the tunic. The dried blood on his tunic isn't red any more. Red doesn't last. Red won't last. Red's going to die. "You're going to die," Ritchie said, "because you don't know."

"Of course I don't know! I tell them I don't know," Miles cried. "I tell them I don't know!" He slid down until his head rested on the Ranger's lap. The Ranger stroked the red hair.

In the voice of a small child, George Ritchie said, "I speak French."

Miles said nothing.

"I speak French very well." Then, in the manner of an adult he said, "These bastards haven't found that out."

Miles lay very still.

The little-boy voice spoke again. "I heard them. They think the Acadian leaders are being kept somewhere near Fort Edward. That's why they think you should know." He cackled. "Me? They want to know about the Halifax fortifications. They ask about ships and guns." He rocked back and forth humming a lullaby to Miles, stroking his hair. "And you, they ask about the Acadians." He patted Miles's head and pushed him away. "Red doesn't last." He began humming again, but Miles didn't think it was a tune; it was more like the noise the wings of bees or hummingbirds made.

Despair overwhelmed Bert Miles. He would never see his wife again. She was waiting for him at Grand Pré. No, wait a minute. She was waiting for *Robert Cameron* at Grand Pré! That was it—not Bert Miles. Robert, not Bert. Aloud he said, "My name is ..."

"Your name is Miles and you're a good soldier. I'll remember that when I make my report."

Bert Miles froze. It was now or never. "How do you know the Acadian leaders aren't at Fort Edward?"

"They were sent to France."

*My God!* There it was. "How do you know that?"

"The governor and that prig, Bulkeley, sent them out to the ships and the ships left."

"To France?"

"The stupid bastards were still arguing for their guns while the governor called them rebels and ordered their deportation. I was the interpreter. They didn't understand until it was too late. I tried to tell them it was their last chance to see their families."

"What does that mean? Never see their families again? They can come back sooner or later."

"Oh, there's a grand plan. They talked in front of me as if I were a piece of furniture."

"Who talked in front of you?"

"Bulkeley and the governor."

"Tell me about the plan."

"I'm not supposed to know about the plan. Nobody knows about the plan."

The Ranger officer rocked back and forth. "Red doesn't last, you know," he said. "You'll have to change your colour." The last words Bert Miles was to hear from George Ritchie were, "I was a piece of furniture." Then he lapsed into the humming.

When Bert Miles was removed for questioning the next morning, he told Boishebert that the Acadian leaders were gone. There was now little hope of any Acadian resistance. Miles mentioned the grand plan, but the French officer made no further effort to interrogate the Ranger before he had him killed.

After several days' rest, Robert Cameron was given warm clothing and a gun. He was supposed to find his own way back to Grand Pré.

*Monday, 18 August 1755*
*H.M.S. Yorke*
*Sailing off Pisiquid*

Two naval officers were at the taffrail of *Yorke* enjoying a beautiful late summer's day—warm sun and a strong, following wind. The deep Fundy swells caught the ship astern and moved her directly forward so there was little seasickness among the four companies of militia crammed into the ship.

"It doesn't get any better than this, does it, sir."

"We'll be early at Les Mines, Lieutenant."

William Gray pursed his lips. "Well, sir, the colonel informed us he must disembark at Les Mines tomorrow morning."

Captain Cobbs pointed to a spot on the shore. "Les Mines is around that point, not more than three leagues." He studied the shoreline for a moment. "Have the watch officer ask the colonel to join us, if you please."

When the colonel arrived, the officers exchanged pleasantries. Captain Cobbs indicated the location of Les Mines on the coastline.

Colonel Winslow expressed surprise. "We have come thirty-six leagues since Saturday night?"

"More than that by sea but, yes, if you had travelled from Chignecto by land you would have travelled thirty-six leagues." Cobbs waved his hand at the sails. "With such a pleasant gale, it's hard to hold *Yorke* back," the captain said with some pride.

"What do you propose, Captain? My orders do not allow me to begin operations until early tomorrow."

"I suggest we anchor here in the lee of the point and wait until morning."

"Your pardon, sirs." The senior officers regarded Lieutenant Gray politely.

"If I may make a suggestion." The lieutenant waited to see if either officer would object and then proceeded. "We can land the men and give them a rest. I've been talking to your men, colonel. They're cramped and bored. Some of them suffer from nausea. If we have the better part of a day to wait, they should be put ashore where they may get some rest." [2]

The colonel seemed receptive to the idea, but Captain Cobbs didn't hide his displeasure.

Lieutenant Gray made direct eye contact with the captain. "Captain Cobbs, sir, I don't know what these men will be asked to do once they get ashore, but my orders are to ensure they're delivered to Les Mines in very good order. I know that *Yorke's* crew will have to break out the ship's boats, and there is some risk moving that number of men to an unknown shore, but …"

Colonel Winslow cleared his throat. "According to my orders, that part of the operation, the handling of the militia, is very clearly in the hands of the lieutenant."

Without breaking eye contact with Gray, Cobbs said, "There should be no trouble landing at Pisiquid; fishermen do it all the time." He smiled slightly. "*Yorke* is the transport; they're your men, Colonel, and by my orders also, Lieutenant Gray is the liaison between the army and the navy."

Gray asked, "Then, sirs, we put the men ashore at Pisiquid?"

"Return them to *Yorke* at eventide."

"Agreed."

* * *

"Why is the water so bloody cold?"

Jeremiah Bancroft was standing in the surf to his waist. William Gray had also waded into the water to his chest, but he was somewhat closer to the beach. Looking at Bancroft, Gray could swear the tall New Englander was turning blue.

Shouts and loud laughter stretched for a distance of a half-mile or so along the waterfront as the New Englanders cavorted on the beach and in the water. Guards had been posted on the bluffs, but the majority of the men were playing like truant schoolchildren.

"The tide is forty or fifty feet sometimes," Gray said, "and the water is changed from top to bottom twice a day. Fundy waters never have a chance to get the least bit warm."

"Well, I've had enough." With a great deal of splashing, Bancroft started for shore.

"Wait for me, Jerry!" Gray tried to keep up but his legs were much shorter than the New Englander's. By the time Gray reached the beach, Bancroft had begun dressing and was laughing at the half-frozen naval officer.

"Th-the s-salt w-water m-m-makes m-me f-f-feel so g-g-grubby," Gray stuttered.

"Take a sip of this." Bancroft held out something that looked suspiciously like a dirty sock.

"W-w-what is it?"

"When the tot was rationed, I kept mine." He offered the sack again. "Don't drink it all now, mind."

"B-but we drank the t-tot in the p-p-presence of the purser. W-w-we're not allowed to s-s-save it!" Gray put the sack to his lips and swallowed once, then again.

Bancroft grabbed the sack away from Gray. "Christ, William! I'm as cold as you are, and there's more of me to warm."

Gray ignored the complaint. "So how did you do it?"

"I took the tot in both hands and poured it down the sack in my vest. Most times I use it to trade since I don't drink."

Gray rubbed his hands. He could feel a small glow growing from the rum. "I'm glad you had it with you today."

"Me, too." Bancroft rolled his tunic into a ball. He lay down on the red sand, stuffed the tunic under his head, and closed his eyes. "Don't bother me, little man. I have some serious dreaming to do."

"Not a chance, Jerry. The colonel has ordered assembly."

"How do you know that?" Bancroft sat up and looked around.

"I had a friend who was an ensign in the regulars. I taught him about ships; he taught me army hand signals."

"I'll have to be careful what I signal around you, my friend. Never thought I'd have a navy type peeking in on my signals." Bancroft stood. "You're right. The colonel has called assembly." He gathered his things and trotted off to the assembly point.

* * *

"Company officers to the front! Companies stand easy."

Colonel Winslow jumped up on a provisions box. "Relax, men. You may smoke."

There was a stir while men dug in their packs or in their clothing. After a bit, all was quiet, and a haze of smoke filled the air above the gathered men.

"You know my thoughts on drink," the colonel began. He put his hands on his hips and stared at the men and officers of Phenehas Company.

"Yessir!" Phenehas Company responded, accompanied by laughter from the three other companies.

"So you couldn't expect to get any rum from this commanding officer, could you?"

"No, sir!"

"So, Phenehas Company! Why were you drinkin' rum when I came on the beach?"

There was an immediate hush. The colonel cast his eyes over the men and raised himself on his toes. "Well, it certainly wasn't *my* idea; it was the navy's. The men of *Yorke* shared their rum ration with you!" He raised both hands above his head. "Let's hear it for the navy!"

Wild, heartfelt cheers erupted. Colonel Winslow had to wave his arms to quiet the men down so he could continue. "Had a nice relaxing afternoon?"

More cheers accompanied the cries, "Yes! Yes!"

"Who do you think suggested it?" Some of the men began shouting out the names of various army officers.

"It was the navy that suggested our afternoon at the beach," the colonel informed them.

Loud cheers again echoed up and down the beach.

"Who brought us to shore without any wet feet?"

The men were onto it now. "The navy!"

"Who served up the hot meal?"

"The navy! The navy!"

The colonel raised his arms to stop the noise. "Yes, the navy has done very well. And they'll have more to do, some of it not very nice." He lowered his voice so that the men had to strain to hear him. "Now it's our turn. We start doing things tomorrow. Listen carefully."

Colonel Winslow stepped down from the provisions box and Major Prebble jumped up. From somewhere in the gathering someone called, "Be sure to cover your ass, Major!"

Good-naturedly, Prebble grinned and waved at the men. When the laughter had died down he said, "I didn't have any rum, so it was the only way I could get Phenehas Company to follow me."

His statement brought on another round of laughter, and Major Prebble raised his arms for quiet. "At 0700 hours tomorrow, our navy friends will put us ashore at Les Mines. The first company on deck will be Adams. The other three companies will stay below. Adams Company will follow the orders of our navy friends and board the boats as they are told to. No arguing. No discussion. The boats will head straight for the beach. Captain Adams?"

"Yes, sir." Adams stood up and continued the briefing. "Officers, one to each boat. Men, this is important! Even if you're taking fire from the shore, don't shoot from the boats. Do not fix bayonets in the boat. Once ashore, form up on the nearest officer and move up the beach. Establish a perimeter. Do not try to take any objectives; we want a beachhead."

Major Prebble spoke up. "The boats will return to the ship. By this time Hobbs Company should be on deck prepared to get into the boats."

Captain Hobbs was sitting with his men. "Same drill, men," he said. "Do exactly what our navy friends tell you to do. Get ashore and enlarge the perimeter."

"Osgood's company is next. Anything to add, Captain Osgood?"

"Get ashore. Enlarge the perimeter."

"Men, as soon as Osgood Company reinforces the perimeter, follow your officer's orders to suppress anyone who annoys you or poses a threat to the beachhead. Take whatever objectives are appropriate. That leaves Phenehas Company."

Someone from the crowd remarked, "They do better in the woods at night."

Colonel Winslow raised his voice to be heard above the roars of laughter. "Phenehas Company will land and form up in column of route as quickly as possible. Ignoring any enemy activity, they will pass through our perimeter and move off from Les Mines[3] to the village of Grand Pré. There they will take possession of the mass house."

Captain Phenehas asked, "By mass house you mean the French church, sir?"

"I do. A guide will meet you. I'll give you the details of meeting him later, Captain."

"Right, sir."

"All of you, this is extremely important! If all the Acadians in the area decided to attack us, we wouldn't have enough balls and powder or the time to reload before we would be overwhelmed. We must give them no reason to resist."

"For that reason, there are additional orders." Major Prebble read from a sheet of paper. "Captain Phenehas, your men will enter the church with weapons lowered. No bayonets, no shooting. If the church is occupied, allow whoever is there to finish whatever they're doing. Then help them to leave peacefully. Post guards. Allow no intrusions. Weapons are not to be displayed. The only time weapons are to be raised is in response to a physical threat and as a consequence of a direct order to do so by you, personally.

"Osgood Company, take the western approaches to the village. No raised weapons unless ordered personally by Captain Osgood. Do not interfere with the life of the village. Do not disturb anyone on lawful business. Do not take anything from the Acadians—even so much as a fowl.

"Captain Hobbs, Hobbs Company to the east. Same restrictions. I want all companies to watch the normal business of the village. Don't interfere in any way.

"Adams Company will be at the beach at Les Mines. The navy will be bringing supplies to us. You, Captain Adams, will keep the beachhead clear and help the navy any way you can." The major paused. Then he folded his paper. "Anything to add from the navy side, Lieutenant Gray?"

"The first supplies will be wagons," Gray said. "They'll have to be reassembled. The next load will be timber. We'll need help to load the timber on the wagons and take it to the church." Gray saluted the colonel. "Sir, with your permission I'll signal for the boats to return."

"Granted, Lieutenant."

Major Prebble brushed sand off his uniform and ordered, "Phenehas Company, move out. Last off, first on. You're first to go back to *Yorke*."

### 21 August 1755
### Grand Pré

"What are they doing now, Aunt Matilde?"

Aunt Matilde shushed Reine Cameron. Matilde was peeking through the open door at two English officers—one army, the other navy—and she didn't want them catch her watching them. They did.

"Bon-jour, Madame," the tall one said. The naval officer touched his hat with his forefinger and smiled.

"*Voulez-vous acheter quelque pain, monsieur?* You want to buy some bread, monsieur?" she asked as she stepped into the front yard. She made motions of eating bread with her hands to her mouth.

"She wants us to eat something?" William Gray asked Jeremiah Bancroft.

Bancroft looked past the old woman to the door where he was sure someone was watching from the darkness. "I've heard she's got a daughter I wouldn't mind trying to eat. I wonder if she's there."

Bancroft took his hat off and made a sweeping bow the way he thought a French officer might do for a beautiful woman. It worked! The old dame blushed and wiped her hands in her apron.

"Reine," she called. "Reine, come out and speak your English with these donkeys. Bring some bread for them to buy."

Reine Cameron came through the door holding two loaves

of bread wrapped in homespun. She held them out to the men, smiling as she did so.

"No harm in buying bread," Bancroft said as he smiled broadly at the beautiful young woman. "Pay her, William."

"You're getting the smiles. You pay her," Gray protested.

"I don't have any coin." Bancroft took the bread, being very careful to touch the young woman's hands. She blushed.

Gray handed Reine a coin. Her face very serious, Reine said, "More money ... for the ..." She made a wrapping motion with her hands and then pulled on the homespun around the bread.

Bancroft's mouth dropped open. "M' God! She speaks English!"

"And she wants more money for the damn bread." Gray unwrapped the bread and handed the homespun back to the old woman.

"You speak English?" Bancroft couldn't believe his luck.

"A little."

He pointed at his chest. "Jerry." He then pointed at her beautiful bosom, "You are?"

"Reine."

"I am an officer of the fort." Bancroft pointed down the street where his men were enclosing the mass house and two other houses in a timber stockade.

Reine shook her head. She managed to smile, as she said, "Not fort. C'est church of Saint Charles." She looked up at the tall Englishman and said firmly, "A church."

Bancroft forgot that Reine's English was probably very limited. He blurted, "Your priest was allowed back to take out anything sacred to him. Now it's where the garrison is going to be. In the fort."

Gray thought Bancroft was being too defensive about occupying the church. Maybe Jerry felt guilty billeting his soldiers in a house of God, even if it was a papist God. He looked closely at his friend. Bancroft had those kinds of feelings? Gray examined his own thoughts as his friend flirted with the woman.

The Acadians are plain people, much like us Scots, he thought, but we have to remember they are French and

Catholic; we really don't have much in common. Idly, he watched his friend trying to impress the younger woman and then, after a while, he glanced down the lane toward the centre of the village.

I'm not surprised the army took my timbers and built the stockade around the Mass House because it's the strongest, best-built building for miles around, right in the middle of the settlement and on the best defensive position. He sighed. Back in Scotland, we wouldn't have let the English invade our church without a fight, but here ... he sniffed his disdain.

Well, the English came into our churches anyway and my people died by the thousands.

On the other hand, these Acadians have survived; not one of them hurt.

For a moment he felt a sense of kinship to this woman who was saying 'no' in two languages to an officer of an occupying army. When she smiled, coyly, seeking some sort of additional gain from the encounter, William's sentiments quickly changed.

"Women," he muttered. "They'll turn your head every time, if you let them." He began to listen to the flirting. Bancroft was promising her something.

"I'll bring you English linen to cover your bread." Jerry reached over to finger the homespun to show her what he meant, but the young woman pulled out of his reach.

"Flighty little thing," said a disappointed Bancroft.

"Smart little thing," Gray said. "She probably has a husband, and you have a wife."

"When the cat's away, the mice will play," Bancroft said as he leered at Reine.

Reine might not have understood all the words, but the leer and tone were unmistakable. "Good day, sirs," she said and, turning on her heel, returned into the house.

Bancroft sighed. "There's one I'm sorry got away." He looked Matilde up and down. "Maybe I should try the old girl!"

"Oh, for Christ's sake, Jeremiah. You're a married man!"

"If you can't be near the girl you love, you love the girl you're near!"

Gray looked up into his friend's face. Was the man joking? Bancroft threw his arm over Gray's shoulder and led him toward the fort. "William! You're so straight-laced! What's a guy to do with you?"

Matilde put her hands on her ample hips and watched the officers walk away. She knew what the game was. Too bad it didn't get played out.

### 26 August 1755
### Grand Pré

"Come on, William. Let's go for a walk up by Reine's house." Bancroft ran his fingers through his hair. He had put on his cleanest tunic.

"Not a bad idea. I need some air. This fort is starting to smell."

Bancroft leaned over and spoke very softly. "Probably the men's fault. At night, they piss against the stockade instead of going out to the latrine."

"Shit!"

"That, too, maybe."

"I don't know which is worse—the smell or your humour!"

Bancroft gave Gray a good-natured shove, and they went out into the fresh, early evening air.

"I intend to bring it up at the next company assembly. The men should use the latrines."

The distaste showed on Gray's face. "Now that the fort is finished, I think I'll take quarters at the beachhead. At least the sea air is fresh."

"Yes, but considerably colder near the bay."

"I hope I'm back in Halifax soon. I miss Molly."

"What do you have to do next?"

"Don't know. I've been ordered to remain here until further advised."

Bancroft turned around and looked back at the fort. The Union Jack flew from the church steeple. Sentries paced the perimeter. It looked so neat, so … English. As soon as it got dark the sentries would call out "all's well" on the quarter-hours.

He had been very proud of that innovation; he thought it sounded right and proper, just like the Boston Foot Patrol. "We got us a fort to be proud of," Bancroft said, but then he was thoughtful for a moment. He leaned closer to his friend and lowered his voice before he spoke again.

"I told the captain of my concerns for the design of the fort. He ordered me not to mention it again."

"Shortcomings?"

"Yes."

"What shortcomings, dammit! It's my fort, too. I found the timber and got it here."

"Shh-h-h. I've been ordered …"

"Jeremiah! You knew when you mentioned it that you were going to tell me, so get on with it!"

Bancroft plucked a long grass straw and stuck it between his front teeth. "There are no gun ports, no firing platforms, there's no parapet, no ladders and no defensive screen for the main gate."

"What does all that mean, Jerry?"

"The fort wasn't built to keep people out."

"Oh!"

"And tomorrow, you'll be told we need more timber."

"What for?"

"As soon as we have the timber, we're going to build a wall around the burying place."

"Enclose the cemetery, too?"

"Yes."

"We're not going to let the Acadians bury their dead?"

They heard a commotion near Reine's house, and a man's voice called, "We need some help here!"

The officers ran to aid the owner of the English voice. They rounded the corner of Reine's house and discovered two sentries from Hobbs Company. One sentry carried three muskets while the other was trying to support an Acadian man who was barely able to walk. The man was injured; his face was puffed up with one eye swollen shut.

"We found 'im at the edge of the trees," one of the sentries reported. "'E was leaning on 'is musket. Looks like 'e been usin' it as a crutch for days 'cause it's no good as a musket no more. Didn't run when we got to 'im. 'E fell down, sirs."

The other sentry had a frightened look in his eyes. "We didn't hurt 'im, sir," he said nervously. "Honest to God, we didn't lay a finger on 'im. Just tried to help, sirs."

Bancroft nodded his head. "That's all right, sentry, I understand. I'll tell Captain Hobbs that you were doing the right thing, that you were following orders."

"Thank'ee sir. We're much obliged."

"Put him down." Bancroft pointed at the smaller of the two sentries, "Go along to the fort and say that Lieutenant Bancroft needs two more men to help with …"

A scream from the yard behind them interrupted him. "Robert!" Reine ran out of the yard and threw herself over the man on the ground, her hands fluttering over his wounded face. "*Que faites-vous?* What are you doing?" She looked with fierce anger at the English. "You … hurt … my man!"

Aunt Matilde was not long to follow. She pushed the officers out of the way, and with Reine's help, picked up the inert form, and carried him into the house. Reine ran after them slamming the door behind her.

The four Englishmen were startled into silence. Gray was the first to speak. "Well, despite our best efforts we're the bad guys."

Bancroft dismissed the soldiers. "You did the best you could. I'll tell your officer. Go along, now."

Bancroft and Gray gazed at the silent house where a light shone in the single window. Bancroft thought of his own homecoming and welcome in Boston, while Gray wondered where he had seen a head of hair like that before.

From the fort came the first call of the evening. "Eight o'clock, and all's well."

"Let's go back. That's as much fresh air as I needed." Bancroft cast a last glance at Reine's house and began to walk back to the fort.

"That Frenchman had red hair," Gray said.

"Yes. I saw that. Rather unusual."

"A person remembers redheads; they're so seldom seen. The last time I saw one, he was a soldier on the beach at Dartmouth

Cove. It was the morning after the massacre in '50. Or was it '49? Anyway, he was a private in the Fortieth, and he was getting the settlers' bodies ready for the sailmaker to put them in shrouds."

"To bury them, you mean?"

"Yes." Gray looked back at the house. There was no sign of life other than the light in the window. "The redhead on the Dartmouth beach was not a happy soldier. He was a Scot just like me, except I was an officer on the governor's staff, and he was a private being chewed out by his colour sergeant."

"What happened to him?"

"I don't know, but I think I just saw him again."

Bancroft stopped abruptly. "That means he's a deserter and turncoat."

Gray put his hand on Bancroft's arm to stop him from going back. "I'm not entirely sure, Jerry. That man's face is badly swollen. He might not be my Scot." Gray gave Bancroft a droopy smile. "If he is, let's give him a while with his family before we turn him in to be hanged."

"Why not? By the looks of him, he's not going anywhere."

"Besides, it might stir up the village if we take a sick man away from his wife."

They entered the fort. Gad, Gray thought, that *is* a pissy smell. "Let's wait until I come back from the beachhead. We'll know better what we're doing here by that time."

"Are you leaving tonight?"

"Yes, and I can't wait!"

Gray wasn't long gathering up his sea bag and weapons. Bancroft assigned him a four-man escort and Gray was off to Les Mines. By the time he returned to Grand Pré on Thursday, the fourth of September, he would know finally what the objectives of the expedition were.

*27 August 1755*
*Grand Pré*

Reine Cameron nursed her man. A foul-smelling poultice that Aunt Matilde made up was the best she could do for his swollen eye. As for the rest, cutting away the dirt-encrusted homespun, she had been surprised to find that most of the wounds and bruises were superficial, more colourful than harmful, but they had been left unattended and had become infected. Those English were beasts, she thought. Why, Uncle Maurice had died as a result of fewer wounds when he had been dragged over the side of the boat. Maurice's death occurred despite old Dr. Bourgeois's finest care. She shook her head as she looked at the thin body of her unconscious husband. Her Robert had been badly handled by the English and left somewhere to putrefy! Beasts!

Reine wrung her hands in frustration. Last night, she had been quite sure Robert had been feigning unconsciousness when the two English were talking about him. Bless Aunt Matilde! She had been very quick to spirit him away. But now, Robert was in a deep sleep, or perhaps he was unconscious. He must waken soon! What if the English came for him? Despite how much weight Robert had lost, the men of the village would not be able to carry him very far, and the English were everywhere! If Robert were to get away, he must be able to walk.

Clank! Clunk! Clank! Clunk! A patrol! It was easy to know where in the village the English were; they made so much noise. She resisted running to the doorway to see where they were going. If they were coming here, she couldn't do anything about it. She sat by the bed and lifted her man's head to her bosom, clutching him tightly. As the patrol approached she intensified her hold on his head.

Robert Cameron spoke. "Easy, lass! I know you missed me, but give a man space to breathe!" He pushed against her breasts.

Reine covered his scarred face with kisses. "Oh, Robert, you are back! There are soldiers outside," she whispered and continued to kiss him.

Repeating his request for air, Cameron convinced Reine that he wanted to sit up. They both listened to the English patrol march past to the outskirts of the village.

Cameron was now very alert. "What are the English doing in Grand Pré?"

"Nothing, Robert. They came about a week ago. The soldiers

are not allowed to do anything bad. One of them was whipped in the square for putting his hands on Madeleine."

"Putting his hands on Madeleine?"

"You know, Cousin Richard's daughter, the one who flirts with all the boys. Well, the soldier who was found with her was whipped." Rushing her story she said, "Another was whipped for stealing a hen. The English soldiers have been very well behaved."

Cameron listened to the sounds coming from the village. Every now and then he heard an English voice.

"They have been so nice to us here," Reine said. "I can't understand why they treated you so badly. Is it because you are English? Where were you? Aunt Matilde says your cheek was carved with a knife. Why did they do that?"

Cameron shook his head. "It wasn't the English. It was that Frenchman, Boishebert, at Cinq Maisons. He wanted me to trick an English officer into telling some secrets."

"What kind of secrets would you know?"

"I didn't have any secrets; it was the Ranger officer. The French dressed me like a lobster-back. They cut me up to make me look like a real prisoner. I talked to the Englishman until he told me that … I must be getting stupid! What *are* the English doing here? You didn't tell me!"

Cameron freed a hand from his wife's embrace. He tilted her chin until he could see her face with his good eye. "Reine, what have the soldiers done here? Please start at the beginning."

"Well, they marched to the church and asked the priest to leave. They raised the English flag on the steeple. Colonel Winslow bought bread, wine, and chickens in the village and had a dinner for his officers that first evening."

"No fighting?"

"No. In fact, they allowed the priest back into the church the next day to remove *le calice et le ciboire*, the chalice and the ciborium. The English have been very thoughtful."

"So what else?"

"Just the other day, when they finished turning the church into a fort, they brought more timber and made the fort bigger.

The fort now has a back door by the burial mounds." She thought for a minute and then added, "I suppose the front door of the fort is the front door of the church." Reine traced the line of the bandage holding the poultice on his eye. "Jerry says the fort is as fine as any fort in Boston. The patrols call out in the night." She raised her head and imitated the patrol's call softly. "Nine o'clock, and all's welll-ll." She wiped away some liquid that was leaking from his cheek. "Just like in Boston, Jerry says."

"What have the village elders been doing?"

"They went to Halifax to ask for our guns back."

"Does anyone know where they are?"

"No, but they are expected back soon."

Cameron bit his lip to keep from telling his wife that the elders weren't ever coming back, that there was some sort of English plan that boded ill for the families of the elders. Cameron felt sick. What if the plan boded ill for everyone?

"We must get out of the village." He tried to stand, but Reine easily pushed him down.

"Tomorrow, Robert."

"But the English!"

"They have orders to be nice to us. Sleep, *chéri*. We don't have to worry about the soldiers. Go to sleep now. You will feel better tomorrow."

Cameron decided to tell her the English governor planned to send the elders to France. "Reine, you must listen to me. The elders are gone...."

"I know. I know, *chéri*. They will be back soon."

"You don't understand."

"I do. You rest, now. Tomorrow is another day."

"But ..."

Reine wasn't listening. She knew what was good for her man. She stroked his hair, watching the worry lines disappear as he sank into a deep sleep. She listened to the night sounds. She heard the English patrol sing out, "All's well!" Then she slipped off her clothes and slid under the quilted cover. Afraid that she might touch one of his many wounds, Reine contented herself with snuggling her nose into her husband's neck. "*Je t'aime,*" she whispered. "*Tu es mon coeur.*"

Reine Cameron lay quietly waiting for sleep to overtake her. If Aunt Matilde allowed her more time at the ovens, she could make more bread to sell to the English; they paid in real coin. Tomorrow she would tell Cameron about the cache of coins she had buried near the barn door. Her last thoughts before she drifted off to sleep were of how comforting it was to have the English soldiers in the village.

### 3 September 1755
### Grand Pré

"Where is your husband, Madame?"

Reine Cameron looked into the eyes of Lieutenant Bancroft, and smiled shyly. "Oh, Jerrie-e-e. We 'ave no doctor. 'E go to village for 'elp."

Bancroft pointed to another officer standing in the shade of a tree some ten paces away. "Would you mind speaking to Lieutenant Simons? He speaks French, passably well." Before Reine could form an answer, Bancroft had waved Simons over. "Ask her, Nathan," he said as the other officer approached.

Lieutenant Nathan Simons touched his hat and gave the woman a small nod. "*Où est votre mari?* Where did your husband go?" He listened as Reine explained that since the old doctor had died, there were no remedies in Grand Pré. Her husband had gone to the next village for help.

"Tell her he didn't look well enough to travel alone, so who went with him? How did they get past the pickets without being seen?" For some reason, the deep brown eyes and broad, open smile and the lovely accent of the French woman irritated Bancroft. He almost didn't wait for Simons to tell him what she had said, but he managed to bite his tongue in time.

"She says he left early one morning ..."

Reine put her hand on Simons's arm to stop him. She leaned forward, and avoiding Bancroft's eyes, added something as if in confidence. Simons blushed as he translated. "He was well enough to perform on her before he left. She was resting, afterwards, must have fallen asleep, so ..."

Bancroft pictured the redhead crawling all over her;

spewing his seed into ... he was suddenly aware of something else—Carrot Top! The cleaning woman at Abbé LeLoutre's house had said that "Carrot Top" had helped the priest get away! Carrot Top could mean redhead.

"... so she didn't get to speak to him before he left." Simons saw discomfort and anger in his fellow officer. He tried to lighten up the situation by saying, "Sounds to me like he was well enough to travel alone." Simons smiled up at the taller officer and was startled by the fury in Bancroft's eyes.

Bancroft stormed down the street toward the fort leaving Simons to bid the Acadian matron a good day. Simons caught up with him at the entrance to the church. Out of breath from his chase he puffed, "What ... is the ... matter with ... you?"

Bancroft looked down at his companion. "William Gray thinks Robert LeBlanc is an English deserter and turncoat." He put his hands on his hips and looked back at Matilde's house. "I do, too. I believe he helped Abbé LeLoutre escape. She's lying when she says their name is LeBlanc. The villagers pretend not to understand when I ask what her family name is." He turned away from the village and walked up the three steps into the fort. "She's been lying to me."

Simons gave a short laugh. "What did you expect?" He grabbed Bancroft's arm and pulled him around. "If what you say is true, wouldn't you expect the woman to lie to protect her husband?"

Bancroft unhooked his scabbard. He clutched it in his hand. "I suppose so. She's one of them."

"And you're one of us. We have orders not to become involved in the village. We can't start anything," Simons reached up and punched his finger into Bancroft chest for emphasis, "and we can't get involved with Acadian women."

"Righto." Bancroft regarded the village thoughtfully. In a pensive voice he said, "Hobbs and Osgood are taking their companies out to view the surrounding villages. Would you ask them to ..."

"I'll have it put right into their orders to be on the lookout for a red-headed deserter."

"Good!"

*4 September 1755*
*Grand Pré*

William Gray rode a black mare into Grand Pré. He hadn't been looking forward to the hot, dusty walk from Les Mines, so he was grateful to Captain Rous for arranging the horse for him.

He stroked her neck to quiet her, as she became aware of the meaty sounds of another whipping taking place in the village square. She had been an army horse, probably belonging to one of the French commandants. She would have been trained to tolerate gunfire and the screams of humans and horses in mortal pain, but the noise of a whip was always sinister and frightening no matter how well trained the horse. His mare, now called Shadow, was very unsettled by the sound of slapping leather; Gray didn't like it either. He slipped down and led her by the reins into the square where the garrison was standing witness to the punishment.

The soldier being punished was unconscious. Gray listened for the count.

"Twenty-five!"

Three soldiers, two on crutches and another with his arm in a sling, had gathered near the front steps of the church. Gray smiled at himself as he repeated the words under his breath, "Front steps of the church." Even Lieutenant William Gray, Royal Navy Liaison Officer assigned to Colonel Robert Monckton's army, the man who had provided the materials that had turned the church into a fort, still thought of it as 'the church.'

"Twenty-six!"

He joined the men of the sick list by the front door as unobtrusively as a man leading a horse could, and waited for the parade to be over. "Once a church, always a church," he muttered.

"Beg pardon, sir?" The soldier with the sling had overheard him.

"I'm sorry. I didn't mean to speak out loud." He glanced at the soldier. "On sick list?"

"Twenty-seven!" The count of the lashes was an unsettling underscore to the peaceful day.

"Yessir. Since yest'day. Did somethin' t' my wrist. Doctor says I got seven days light duty."

"How many will ride today?"

"There's Tom. He got thirty for stealin' from the French."

"Twenty-eight!"

"Bill already got his twenty for givin' hisself to a French woman."

Gray looked around. The men of the garrison were drawn up in hollow square. Most of the villagers were there—he saw Reine and Matilde—but there was no sign of his Scot. He had heard at Les Mines that all companies had been instructed to be on the lookout for an English deserter with red hair. Gray sighed. It wouldn't be long before he was caught.

"Twenty-nine!"

The soldier had continued talking to him. He caught enough of the man's comments to understand that two men had been shipped out to Halifax to be hanged. He wasn't much interested and didn't pursue the subject.

"Thirty!"

The colonel dismissed the men to their duties.

Gray tied his horse in the shade of a tree, and patted her neck. He wanted to get her some water, and looked around for something to put water in. He realized that the parade had been dismissed without the usual sermon from Parson Phillips. The sanctimonious little bastard must be really sick to miss moralizing after two whippings! He smiled at the thought of Parson Phillips writhing on his sickbed as countless soldiers beat him with long strings of Biblical verses.

* * *

Tante Matilde shook her head and took Reine's arm to walk back to the house. "Look!" she said. "Look at your fine naval officer, the one you like. He came back in time to watch the beating. I understand the English navy whips their men more than the English army. See? He's smiling. He enjoyed it!"

Reine Cameron glanced at Gray, then quickly down at the ground to avoid catching his eye.

Tante Matilde wasn't about to stop. "Imagine what he would do to Robert if he caught him."

Reine sighed. "Robert told me. They would flog him and then hang him until he was dead. *Maudits Anglais!*"

"Not really, Aunt. The English punish their men for breaking any rule. They made a rule not to cause us any harm. Some men broke the rules and they were punished. In the village, the English buy whatever we are willing to sell and they pay us in coin, more than the French ever did." She squeezed her aunt's arm. "What Robert did before he came here was bad in the eyes of any army, French or English. Now, Robert must hide in the forest until the English go back into their forts." Reine gave the older lady a kiss on the cheek. "Then we will build our home and have lots and lots of children for you to play with."

Both women fell silent as an Englishman passed. When he was safely out of earshot, Matilde asked, "Perhaps we can both go tomorrow to take Robert his supplies?"

"No. Not tomorrow. With the naval officer back, he will be looking for us. We will go see Robert in a couple of days."

Tante Matilde nodded her head in agreement. "Then tomorrow we will send your cousin, Sylvie."

"I'll ask the priest to write a note for her to take." Reine Cameron pulled her arm loose and ran ahead. "I must get started now. I have so much to say!"

Tante Matilde stood in the middle of the street. She searched the crowd for someone to walk with. Ah! There was Abel. "Abel!" Matilde could sound very imperious. "Abel! My dear, dear nephew! Come, walk me home."

With a flourish, Abel Comeau took his aunt's arm. "*Avec plaisir.* With pleasure, Aunt Matilde. It is my honour to be seen with you."

"You are such a nice boy, Abel," the old woman gushed.

"I am not a boy any longer, aunt."

Matilde stopped in the street so she could get a good look at Comeau. He was tall for his sixteen years. His dark-brown eyes were always filled with mischief. He was broad-shouldered like all of the LeBlancs, and his muscled arms and chest were the envy of many an older man.

"Don't you worry, dear Aunt. Your Abel will always be here for you."

She pulled him to her and hugged his arm. "I know, my dear."

*5 September 1755*
*Grand Pré*

Colonel Winslow gave the sign. Sergeant Pollard and two corporals closed the doors to the church and quietly barred them from the outside. Guards, who had been lined up just inside the doors, moved through the crowd of Acadians until they were standing by the colonel at the front of the church. Their weapons were loaded but held seemingly casually at their sides.

Colonel Winslow, standing where the priest might have stood, took a deep breath. "Pay attention!" he said.

There was still commotion and noise in the room. The colonel waited until there was comparative quiet. Colonel Winslow cleared his throat. "The governor in Halifax has determined that you are rebels."

The crowd in the church became absolutely silent.

"He has ordered that you be transported from this land …"

There was a great roar as many voices were raised. The loudest was Tante Matilde's. "*Le petit salaud, qu'est-ce qu'il dit? What is that little shit saying?*" Matilde looked at Reine Cameron for the answer.

Reine shrugged. "He said 'alifax and rebels. I do not know what he means by it." She stepped forward to where she could see Nathan Simons. "Monsieur! Repeat what the colonel has said in French, if you please."

Lieutenant Simons looked to the colonel for guidance, but of course the colonel hadn't understood the French the woman had spoken. The colonel continued with his orders. "Your land, your homes, your cattle …"

These were English words that a number of Acadians understood. Abel Comeau, Matilde's nephew, pushed through the crowd and stood in front of the colonel. He was so aggressive, standing there with his hands on his hips, that the armed guards raised their muskets and stepped forward to protect their colonel. Whatever Abel said was drowned in the roar of voices as the crowd reacted to the guards' response. Colonel Winslow, not the least bit intimidated, motioned the guards to step back. He continued with the order. "You may take your money and household effects when you are transported out of this province but your land, buildings and livestock are forfeit to the Crown."

Reine's voice rose above the general chatter. "He means to take away our homes!" She pointed at Lieutenant Simons. "You can tell us what he says! Tell us!"

Lieutenant Simons spoke quickly with his colonel. "Sir, they don't understand what you're saying. They've asked me to translate. May I?"

Colonel Winslow handed a paper to the lieutenant. "Read only the underlined portions, lieutenant."

Simons quickly read down the page ... collect the Inhabitants together in order to transport them in the best manner in your power either by stratagem or force, as circumstances may require .... He began translating aloud into French, substituting the word Acadian for Inhabitant. "The government at Halifax has determined that the Acadians are rebels. Instructions have been issued for the transportation of the rebels out of this province. Acadian lands, homes, livestock are forfeit to the Crown. The transported rebels will be permitted to take their money and some household effects. The Acadians will be held in custody until transport can be arranged."

If there were any more to be read, Lieutenant Simons would not have been heard. Shrieking, Matilde threw herself at the guards who restrained her long enough for the colonel to withdraw to the stockade outside the church. Here, the enraged Acadians were met with a wall of bristling bayonets behind which the withdrawal was continued until all the soldiers were outside the fort. The rear gate was closed and the bars firmly put in place.

Patrols were sent through the village to gather up anyone who had not attended the meeting. The soldiers banked cooking fires and tended to livestock where necessary. Within a few hours, the entire population of Grand Pré was safely locked inside the fort.

Speaking with his officers, Colonel Winslow congratulated them on the success of the operation. He expressed distaste for having misled the Acadians about the nature of the meeting at the church. He said that he had wanted to be more forthright, but then the Acadians wouldn't have been so cooperative. He didn't speak long on this aspect of the operation, but rather stressed that the objectives had been successfully accomplished without casualties. Their long-time foes had been confined as prisoners and would soon be gone. It had been a jolly good show!

\* \* \*

Robert Cameron's hideout was on a pronounced rise in the forest not far from the village. A natural clearing gave a good view of the countryside for several miles. If an unwanted visitor approached, Robert would have ample time to disappear into the deeper forest. He watched a solitary figure climb the last part of the trail to his camp. He could easily discern it was Sylvie.

Cameron was sorely disappointed that it wasn't his wife, but he didn't let Sylvie know that. He greeted her warmly and relieved her of her small burden of supplies. "What's going on in the village, Sylvie?"

"Not much, Robert. There's a meeting in the church this morning. The English chief invited all of the village, elders, men, women and children, to hear some new orders." She pulled a piece of paper from the bosom of her dress. "I have a letter for you from Reine. I know she tells you about it because she made me wait while she had the priest add the news of the meeting."

Cameron took the letter, and offered Sylvie an apple from the bundle. She refused, saying that she didn't want any of his food but she would like a drink of water. "You read your letter, Robert. I know where the brook is."

As soon as he was alone, Cameron opened the letter and read it quickly. He had trouble with some of the French words but he skipped over them; he was able to get the gist of the letter. One thing was certain; Reine loved him and missed him because that was the way the letter started. What disturbed him was the final paragraph: "The English will have a meeting at the church of Saint Charles tomorrow. They say it is very important. They would like to have everyone there. I usually do not go to any meeting where the elders would be. Perhaps the English wish to speak to all of us together because our elders have not yet returned from Halifax. Perhaps there is news of them. Perhaps the governor has listened to our petitions about the guns. Anyway, I will go to the meeting and, afterwards, come straight up to you. See you soon, *chéri*."

\* \* \*

"Did we get them all?" William Gray was sitting astride Shadow, who was impatient to get on the road and just plain antsy. Gray had to hold her in tightly while he talked to Jeremiah Bancroft.

"We did well. One young girl missing, but she showed up three hours later." Bancroft grabbed Shadow's bridle and the horse settled down right away. "Said she had gone for a walk." Bancroft gave Gray an envious look and, with an exaggerated sigh, said, "It must be great to have your own horse."

"My commander expects me to move around the countryside making things easier for the army." Gray winked at his friend, "And he knows how handsome I look on a horse."

"I wish I had a chief like that. My colonel looks at me and thinks of a red-faced rum drinker chasing shadows through the woods."

"He hasn't forgiven that yet?"

"Not a bit. Just this morning he said, 'I hope your company will be able to stand the stress of this duty without resorting to drink.'" Bancroft gave his friend a rueful smile. "I don't think he's forgiven us nor forgotten us."

"What are you going to do about it?"

"We're going to do our job, just the way he tells us to."

Gray leaned forward and patted Shadow's neck. He lowered his voice. "I had a talk with your colonel this afternoon. I suggested that we change the plan about boarding the prisoners at Les Mines. I found a better and much closer place."

"Where?"

"A creek crosses the marsh for a mile or two and goes right up to the village. If the transports moved up the basin and anchored at the mouth of the creek, we wouldn't have to march the prisoners anywhere. Just move 'em out of the fort and into the longboats. At flood tide, the creek is full to the edge of the marshlands. We could work on dry, firm ground right at the village."

"That's great!" Bancroft slapped his thigh, startling the horse.

"Easy, Shadow. Easy, girl."

Shadow seemed to give Bancroft a dirty look for catching her unawares. She snorted and shook her head in annoyance.

"Does she understand English, yet?"

"She's a lovely girl. I'd like to take her to Halifax. A friend of mine is a great lover of horses. He'd like to see her, too."

"Is your friend Bulkeley?"

"Yes."

"You have friends in high places."

Gray nodded his head, and neither man said anything for a moment.

"I think you have a good idea, William," Bancroft said. "Anything is better than a column of prisoners and my men stretched thin along the length of it, wide open to attack."

"Are there still armed parties around?"

"Yes. Lieutenant Crooker just returned from Chignecto. He told us the prisoners are being held in Fort Cumberland while the English garrison lives outside in tents."

"Were they attacked?"

"Wait, William, wait. Let me tell the story! Major Fry had been ordered out to Shepody to burn the villages. An enemy force of French, renegade Inhabitants, and Indians fell upon his party, killing or capturing twenty-three of our men. Lieutenant March was taken."

"Alive?"

"They didn't find his body."

"Do we know who was leading the enemy raiding party?" Gray asked.

"We think it was Boishebert and that miserable bastard, Beau Soleil," Bancroft replied.

"Beau Soleil isn't an Indian, you know. He's one of the Acadians."

"An Acadian gone bad."

"And that's the end of John Marsh."

"Yes. A terrible end."

Gray sat back in his saddle. "You'd better let me go, Jerry. I have to get to Les Mines and convince some transport captains to come further up the basin."

"Sounds great to me, old chum." Bancroft released Shadow's bridle. "Be careful on the road."

"Cheerio, Jerry."

*10 September 1755*
*Grand Pré*
*Inside the Fort*

"Abel!" Young Richard Bourgeois hissed the name again. "Abel! *Ils arrivent!* They're coming!"

Abel Comeau moved quickly to the stockade gate. Once there, he slouched against the wall of the stockade and picked his teeth with a sliver of wood.

Each day the English had allowed twenty men to leave the stockade to look after the farm animals, gather crops, and carry supplies back for the prisoners. The twenty men were selected randomly from those standing near the gate. Comeau and his friends intended to be selected today. They had a plan.

Comeau heard the bar being lifted off the gate. He forced himself to relax. Half of the double doors that made up the gate opened slightly. An officer and two armed guards stood just outside. The officer, Nathan Simons, called, "Men for the working party come through the gate, one at a time."

Comeau sent out three men who had already been on the

working party through the gate first. He listened to the lieutenant refuse them. "You were out yesterday. You can't go again."

Comeau motioned to his friends and went through the gate. *"Quel est votre nom?"*

"Abel Comeau."

Simons wrote down the name. "You give your word you will return before eventide?"

"You want my parole?"

The Acadian's cockiness annoyed Simons. He responded testily, "Give your parole or get back inside."

"I give you my parole."

Something about the way he said it made Simons look him in the eyes. "You will not try to escape but will return here at eventide?"

Comeau stared right back. "I will return at eventide. You have my parole."

"Go see the sergeant. He will show you what must be done. Next!"

"Richard Bourgeois."

"You give your parole?"

As Bourgeois gave his parole, Comeau shivered with excitement. They were going to get away with it! He felt like dancing. He realized that the tall militia officer was watching him. He put his head down and scrunched up his shoulders. He scuffed at the dirt. Take your eyes off me you English bastard, he thought. He didn't look up.

Bancroft watched the men of the work party. He spoke to Sergeant Pollard, "If I had a child acting like that one over there, I'd think he had done something really wicked and didn't want to be caught."

"Which one, Lieutenant? I can send him back inside."

"No." Bancroft stroked his chin. "I think it would be better if we kept him busy. Send out an armed guard with the workers today. Keep a close eye on them."

"Yessir."

A familiar figure was coming down the street. He does look handsome on that horse, Bancroft thought. Aloud he said, "Hello, William. Welcome back. How was your business at Les Mines?"

Gray watched as the working party, under guard, gathered baskets and farm tools and marched toward the orchards. "Some kind of problem?"

"Not really," Bancroft said. "We keep most of the men in the fort, but every day we permit twenty men to do the necessary chores of the village. At the end of the day, they bring produce back for the prisoners."

Gray could see women and children in some of the houses. "What are they doing?"

"The colonel figures they ain't goin' nowhere as long as their men folk are locked up. He lets them out to do woman chores and look after the children."

"What about your favourite bread maker? Have you let her out to do her wifely chores?" Gray knew he was being unfair but he couldn't help himself.

"There are times I would like to thrash you, William!" The naval officer had hit a raw nerve, and Bancroft's face was scarlet. "She's not my bread maker! And of course not! If we let her out she would immediately disappear with her turncoat husband!"

"So, we haven't caught Carrot Top!"

"Not yet. We'll get him. As long as she's locked up, he'll hang around. He'll get careless and then we'll have him!"

Gray slid off his horse. "I have news for your colonel. He can start loading the prisoners tomorrow. The first of the ships will be anchored off the creek by early morning. Longboats will wait for the tidal bore to fill the creek, and then he should be able to load two or three hundred."

"Great. Come along, I'll take you right to the colonel."

Colonel Winslow had been walking his dog, a lop-eared, short-haired black mongrel of which the colonel was very fond. When the colonel saw Lieutenant Gray, he carefully handed the animal's leash to the nearest guard and hurried over to get the news.

There were sly grins all over the village square. When a soldier acquired 'dog duty,' everyone nearby was amused by the antics of the man on the end of the leash. This soldier began by extending the leash as far away as he could so that the animal couldn't get next to him. The dog was intent on getting close to the guard and struggled against the leash. The trick was for the guard to keep the dog away without pulling too hard on the leash; too hard a pull and the dog yelped, which brought on the ire of the dog-loving colonel. Of course, with this advantage the dog could be seen—behind the colonel's back—joyfully humping the guard's leg.

As the colonel approached the two officers, Bancroft said out of the corner of his mouth, "I often wonder why the damned dog doesn't hump the colonel."

"The dog's got taste," Gray managed to say before the colonel was upon them.

"What's the news, William?"

"The boats from the transports will be at the creek in the morning."

"Good! And, Lieutenant Bancroft, how many of the prisoners can we move tomorrow?"

Bancroft was no fool. He knew the colonel wanted to move as many prisoners as possible so he picked the higher number Gray had mentioned. "Probably three hundred, sir."

Colonel Winslow fussed with his grey hair as it blew across his forehead. He was going to say something but thought better of it and only cleared his throat instead. He beckoned to an ensign who was standing at the entrance to the command tent.

Ensign Fasset came on the double.

"Yessir, Colonel." He saluted.

"You and Ensign Gay form a party of fifty men and go to River Canard. Take the names of the people in those villages. We will have room at the Grand Pré fort for three hundred more prisoners by the end of tomorrow. Make a plan of the River Canard villages. When you return, give your suggestions to Captain Phenehas as to the most facile operation for moving those people into the fort."

"Yessir!"

Colonel Winslow beamed at Lieutenant Gray. "That was good work, William!" He continued to smooth his hair back over his ears. "And how was Captain Rous?"

"I don't know, sir. He had left for Chignecto. I worked with the transport captains and hurried back here as soon as I could."

"Well! That was jolly good work. Perhaps my lieutenant will take you along to the mess tent. Get some meat on your bones. The food is good. The prisoners' women do the cooking. We live very well, indeed."

Gray said, "Thank you, sir." But the colonel was already on his way back to his dog.

As they made their way to the mess tent Gray and Bancroft heard the colonel cooing to his dog. "Baby shouldn't do that to nice soldier! Naughty baby!"

Bancroft grunted and said in a very low voice, "The colonel is putting on airs just like a Regular!" He looked over his shoulder. The colonel was walking his dog and watching the two ensigns form up their men for the River Canard expedition.

Wistfully, Gray said, "If the woman is kept prisoner in the fort, her husband comes, and he's hanged. If she's loaded on the transport tomorrow, she never sees him again."

"What woman?" Bancroft saw the look of derision on Gray's face, and was immediately shamefaced. "And if I let her go, she disappears and I get in trouble with the colonel." Bancroft growled, "You make her sound like my problem. Well, she isn't."

### 11 September 1755
### Grand Pré

Abel Comeau had tied a chisel to his belt and let it dangle inside his clothes to his crotch. It was awkward but a good hiding place. Not many of the English would check the prisoners' privates since there had been no wash water for the last week. Comeau pretended to scratch himself and adjusted the chisel so he could easily walk to the end of the stockade to see what was happening. He was dismayed; the English were lining up men in fours. The gates were wide open, and there were guards everywhere. The transport had started. The *maudits Anglais* were actually going to do it!

Frantically Comeau looked around for his friends. Most of

them had been shoved into the lines. It looked like several hundred men had been selected. He tried to spot Richard Bourgeois.

Guards surrounded the column, and not too gently prodded the rearmost of the column to move out the gate.

Comeau thrust his hand deep into his britches and tore the chisel from its thong. Hiding it up his sleeve, he ran forward screaming, "Cousin Richard!"

Bourgeois broke ranks and threw his arms around his seemingly distraught cousin. Comeau thrust the chisel into Bourgeois's blouse. "We must not be separated!"

The nearest guard grabbed Comeau by the collar and threw him to the ground. "Your turn will come soon enough!"

In a moment, the column was gone and the gates were closed.

Comeau went over to his corner where the stockade joined the wall of the church. He sat down against the wall looking very dejected and dispirited. He was careful not to lean back too heavily. He and his friends had cut away the ties for the pickets. With a little effort, he would be able to pull down at least two pickets and disappear into the night. The plan had been to get a tool from one of the farms and arrange the escape of all the young men of the village. What wonderful trouble that would have caused! Maybe enough trouble to delay the sailing of the transports until it was too late in the season. The English weren't stupid. They knew well that the Bay of Fundy in winter was no place for transports. They would delay. He knew they would delay!

Comeau put his head down on his folded arms. Bourgeois might get a chance to use the chisel and release the young men from the transports. It would be more difficult getting away from the transports than getting away from the churchyard, but maybe it could be done. Comeau examined his broken fingernails and hands torn from long hours of digging at the pickets' bindings. They had been so close to getting away with it! Just one more night. He sighed.

Maybe the winter season would be early, and the English would have to cancel. Maybe he could work up another plan. Comeau sighed again. He would have to work out another plan. Soon he was asleep.

*26 September 1755*
*Grand Pré*

"Another hundred were loaded this morning." Reine Cameron was serving soup along with pieces of dark bread to the Acadians who were locked up in the church and stockade. "How did they miss you again, Abel? You must be the last man of our village still in the church. The rest of our men are on the ships."

"Have any of the ships left the basin?"

"No. Aunt Matilde told me the transports won't leave until the women and children are collected."

"How does she know?"

"The tall one told Cousin Marguerite to get her things ready. He said the ships would leave any day now that the transports shouldn't be in the basin when the storms come. His naval friend told him that. Cousin Marguerite told Aunt Matilde."

Reine Cameron looked at her cousin with some concern. He seemed to grow smaller, almost as if he were shrinking inside himself. "Anything wrong, Abel? *Ça va bien?* Are you all right?"

Actually, Comeau felt terrible. His original plan would have worked. If all of the men of Grand Pré had escaped from prison, the English would have been so busy trying to recapture them they wouldn't have had time to get the transports ready. Mother of God! If that tall officer hadn't ordered the soldiers to keep such a close watch on the work party, he could have had the chisel days earlier. If only …

"How did you avoid being loaded earlier, Abel?" Reine Cameron repeated.

"I sit in this corner until the guards have their quota," Comeau said tonelessly. "They haven't come over this far yet." He accepted some soup and a thick piece of fresh dark bread. He brightened up considerably. "That smells really good! Thank you."

"You're hungry, Abel. Everything smells good when you're hungry."

Comeau took a big bite of the bread. He chewed a couple

of times, then pushed the wad off to one side of his mouth. "You're the only woman locked up in the church. Is it because of Robert?"

Reine put down the soup bucket and ladle. She sat beside Comeau on the ground in the corner of the stockade, and brushed a wisp of hair out of her eyes. "The English want to hang Robert. They think he'll try to rescue me."

Comeau nodded his head; that was probably very true. He looked more closely at his cousin. She had circles under her eyes and seemed more hollow-cheeked than was good for her. She looked a great deal thinner, too. "Why don't you have some of your own soup?" Comeau dipped some bread in his soup and held it out to her. "You must be ready to go with Robert when he comes for you." He lifted the bread to her mouth. "Here, eat this."

Reine Cameron brushed her hand against her face again; this time to wipe away tears. "I will never see Robert again."

Comeau pushed the bread at her mouth, and she ate it. He dipped another piece in the soup and fed it to her. He did it for her again and again until there was no bread left.

"You have to take better care of yourself for Robert's sake," Comeau said.

"Robert will be killed if he comes here."

Comeau took her hand and kissed it. "Dear Reine—since Robert can't come here, we will go to him."

Reine looked at him in surprise. "Go to Robert? How?"

Comeau's face wore a devilish young-boy-up-to-no-good look. "When it is dusk, come to me here in the corner. Snuggle down by my side as if we are lovers."

"What?"

"Shhhh! None of these people know us. If they think we're taking a last chance to be together, they'll look away and give us some privacy."

"But you are too young for me to be ..."

"Reine! They don't know that." Comeau handed her his bowl. "Go now and do what you normally do. Don't draw attention to yourself. Come back here at dusk."

Reine Cameron stood and brushed the straw and dirt from her clothing. "I will be here, Abel."

27 September 1755
*Grand Pré*

Lieutenant Bancroft marched into the command tent. "Permission to speak to the colonel."

"Carry on, Lieutenant."

"Two prisoners escaped from the stockade last night."

Colonel Winslow blinked. "How?"

"They pulled down two pickets. The guards found the breach at 0500 hours. The pickets were in the corner of the stockade, up against the church and not easily seen."

"Go on."

"We're attempting to determine who the male escapee was. The second prisoner was Madame Reine LeBlanc, the wife of the suspected deserter and turncoat. I sent a patrol to the LeBlanc house immediately. There was no one there."

"How many should have been there?"

"Two. The old lady and a niece who moved in when we took the traitor's wife to the fort."

The colonel shuffled some papers on the table in front of him. He picked at an insect bite on the back of his hand. Bancroft could tell the colonel was annoyed and thought it better if he continued talking. "From what we saw at the house, they took pots and pans, some food, blankets, and extra clothing. Probably the family strongbox, too, because there were signs they had dug up something."

Both officers knew that every Acadian family had a strongbox. In perilous times, the most precious objects were placed inside. If the family had to run from danger, the box was ready. It could be easily carried or quickly buried so it could be retrieved once the danger had passed.[4]

"The trackers say there was no further sign of digging where they might have attempted to bury it again. Believe me, colonel, my men looked very carefully. The bastards aren't planning to come back."

"Ah!" For the first time, the colonel showed some satisfaction. "Carrying a strong box, pots and pans, food, and blankets, and travelling with an old woman should slow 'em down enough for us to track 'em and catch 'em."

"They stole a horse, sir."

Colonel Winslow's mouth dropped open. "Is Lieutenant Gray back?"

"Yessir, he is. They stole his horse. They ain't going to be slowed down by what they're carrying."

"That's a different kettle of fish!" Colonel Winslow stood, indicating that the meeting was over. "It would have been nice to catch Carrot Top. Not much hope of that now."

"Your pardon, sir," Bancroft continued hastily. "I'd like to keep the trackers on it. I'd like to see us catch the bugger. He's made fools of us comin' in here and takin' his wife right from under our noses!"

"All right, then. Keep the trackers on it, but I don't want to lose any men over it. Send an escort with them. Forty men."

"Yessir." Bancroft threw the colonel a snappy salute and left the tent.

The colonel sat behind the table. His orderly came in with some papers. "Did you hear that, Corporal?"

"Er, yes, sir, I did."

"I know Captain Rous gave the young feller the horse, but it wasn't right! A junior naval officer shouldn't be riding around the countryside while senior army officers are stuck at the garrison!" With a sigh he added, "I get to go nowhere. That young pipsqueak can walk in the dust like the rest of us, now." That comforting thought brought a smile to the colonel's face.

The orderly left the tent without comment.

### 2 October 1755
### *The Hideout near Grand Pré*

Robert Cameron couldn't believe it! Reine was coming up the hillside path! A second look convinced him his eyes weren't deceiving him. Great sobs escaped him as he ran down the path to meet her. They were together again! When he put his arms around her, he realized how thin she was. He held her, gently, rocking her as if she were a babe.

Cameron whispered in her ear, "I went to Grand Pré

every day or two, Reine, looking for you. I never saw you. There were always English guards." He was crying, but he didn't care. There were others around them now, but he couldn't see them through his tears. "One day I tried to creep near the house, but ..."

"Shush, Robert. It doesn't matter now. They locked me in the church with the men. They were waiting for you to try to get me out of there so they could hang you." She kissed him again on the mouth, and then pushed back slightly. "It was Abel who made a hole in the stockade and brought me out."

Abel Comeau extended his hand; Cameron pulled the boy into his arms and gave him a long, heartfelt hug. "I cannot thank you enough, Abel."

Comeau was somewhat embarrassed by the hug but he endured it. When he was finally released, he moved to help Tante Matilde off the horse. Sylvie took one side and Abel the other. Between them, they got her down without any harm to either the large woman or the horse.

"Where did you get the horse?" Cameron asked.

"It was the naval officer's mare," Comeau said. "I took it."

"Wonderful!" Cameron took Matilde's arm and led her up the incline to the camp. "There's not much here, but we can all be comfortable while we wait for the English to leave the valley. Then we can go back down and see what's left."

Reine took Cameron's other hand. "The English are burning everything and taking all the animals. There will be no place left in the Fundy for shelter. They plan for anyone left behind to either die in the winter snows or give themselves up and be transported."

"Transported? Burning everything?" Cameron was shocked, but he could believe it; the English were a dreadful enemy.

Comeau sat on a rock near the camp that permitted him to look out over the path they had just travelled. "We escaped last Saturday. We have been all this time coming here."

"But it's only a few miles," Cameron said. "What delayed you?"

"They have trackers. Twice I thought we had doubled back and lost them, but they're still on our trail."[5]

Tante Matilde was crying. "We had to bury all my things."

Comeau patted her hand. "We had to lighten up or they would have caught us by now."

"*Mon argent.* My silver." Tante Matilde's tears flowed over her cheeks. "I had pieces of silver given to my grandfather by the King of France, you know."

Sylvie sat beside her Aunt and comforted her. "Yes, dear Aunt, I have often seen it. It's safe now. When this is all over, we'll come back and it will still be there, waiting for you safe and sound."

"I buried it deep," Comeau said. Over the head of Tante Matilde he shook his head negatively at Cameron. "The English will never find it." He stood and gazed back down at the valley. "But the trackers will find us here, and soon. They're good."

"We don't have to worry about trackers," Cameron said. "We'll wait for them. A couple of well- placed shots, and they'll be discouraged ... or dead."

"Once when we doubled back we came upon their trail," Comeau said. "There were sure signs that the trackers have a large escort. They're taking no chances."

"How long do you think we have before they're upon us?" Cameron asked.

"They probably stopped for the night. We kept on going in a large half-circle to get here this afternoon. It will take them all day to travel that same distance. I think we can safely rest here tonight. We should be on our way before first light tomorrow."

"*Où irons-nous?* Where will we go?"

"If we can reach Tatamagouche we can find a boat and escape to Isle Saint Jean or Isle Royale."

"They'll expect us to try and slip past Fort Edward and then north," Cameron warned.

"We'll head toward the mountain," Comeau said. "Once on the Fundy side, we can find a boat."

"I heard that the naval officer collected all the boats and sent them to Halifax." Tante Matilde was feeling better and was paying attention to the conversation again.

Comeau frowned. "But maybe he didn't get over the mountain. Maybe he didn't find all the boats."

It was Cameron's turn to frown. "Maybe? Maybe isn't such a good plan!"

Comeau's face turned red, but he kept his voice level. "There's no point staying around here. The English are here and they're burning everything."

Cameron put a hand on the young man's knee and squeezed it reassuringly. "You're right, of course, Abel. We can't stay here."

Reine Cameron took her husband's hand in hers and pulled him to his feet. "It's important we get a good night's sleep." She led him away from the camp toward the lean-to where the camp's firewood was stored. "We can leave the camp to the others. You and I, Robert, will sleep over here."

* * *

Solomon Wyman leaned his musket against the tree. He hunkered down by the small fire with the two other trackers, Willie and Jack. They shared some hardtack and water without speaking.

All around them, the men of the escort went about the business of setting out sentries, defensive positions, and fields of fire. A few set up sleeping tents while two men dug the pit for the latrine.

Lieutenant Bancroft stood with his hands on his hips and surveyed the scene. Satisfied with what he saw, he joined the trackers at the small fire. Bancroft had never been able to sit on his haunches like the trackers so he sat on the ground Indian style, with his legs crossed under him. He looked up at the trackers. "What do you think, Solomon? Can we catch up to them soon? I can't stay out here more than one more day. Then we'll have to give up and go back."

"Well, sir," Wyman said, "me and the boys ain't had no chance to speak on this."

The lieutenant persisted. "I'd like your opinion, Solomon."

"Like I said, Lieutenant, we ain't got to speak on this yet, but I sees it this way. They're makin' as good a time as we are. We found all the stuff they hid, so we know they's travellin' as light as can be. They have that horse, but it will tire soon 'cause it ain't bein' fed right. It'll be finished maybe today, maybe tomorrow. We'll catch them up real quick in a day, maybe two."

"We haven't got two days."

"In that case," Wyman pulled a pipe from his pocket. "Mind if I smoke, sir?"

"Not at all. So, what do you think?"

Solomon Wyman lit his pipe with a twig from the fire. He threw the twig back into the fire and watched it burn. "I think …" He looked at Willie and then at Jack. Both men silently stared at the fire as if transfixed. "They stopped doubling back. They got us goin' in a wide circle. It's just as if they had somewhere to go near Grand Pré and didn't want us in the area when they got there. So I think they're back near Grand Pré."

"They went back to pick up something?"

"Could be." Wyman fiddled with his pipe.

Bancroft waited without showing any impatience. The other two trackers continued to stare into the fire.

"Maybe someone they left behind." Wyman knocked the pipe out and put it back in his pocket. "They know they can't lose us. I think, if they're near Grand Pré, they'll head out in a straight line away from the soldiers and the forts. They'll be lookin' for a boat. They'll be safer travellin' on the water. I bet they'll want to go to Isle Saint Jean or River Saint John."

Willie and Jack nodded their heads in agreement. Bancroft waited for more to be said, but the trackers were silent. The four men sat by the fire for quite some time before the officer asked, "What do you suggest?"

Without hesitation Wyman answered, "Break the boys up into units of five men. Send one of the units to Fort Edward so they can put out patrols. The rest of our boys should head out across the trails between Grand Pré, River Habitant, and River Canard. We just wait for them to come. When we see the horse, we know we got 'em."

"That'll work if they're trying to escape the area." Bancroft smiled at the trackers. "That's a good plan. Thank you." He pulled himself up. "Sergeant Pollard!"

"Yessir!"

"I'll want five-man patrols for independent action in the morning. See to it if you please, Sergeant."

"Yessir!"

### 3 October 1755
### *Near River Habitant*

Abel Comeau and Robert Cameron walked in front of the horse, Comeau leading it by the reins. Tante Matilde, astride the animal, was more or less unconscious. Where the trail permitted, Sylvie and Reine walked on either side of the old woman to steady her. They had been going more slowly with each hour they had travelled. Soon they would have to stop.

"There's a village not far from here. I can smell the cook fires. When we get there, we can rest." It was a cool autumn day, but perspiration ran down Comeau's face. "Maybe they'll give us some food."

The older soldier said, "Maybe the English are there. We'll have to be careful."

Comeau grunted. It had been thrilling to be a young warrior eluding the English, but now that he was back with adults … He grimaced. They keep questioning my decisions, my judgment, he thought. Just like any other adult, Robert has forgotten that it was I, Abel, the so-called boy, who engineered the escape from the English fort. It was I who led the trackers a merry chase around the floor of the valley, and now I'll lead them across the valley to the other side of the mountain to escape and return to the French sphere of power. I'll be a hero! Perhaps I could lead a counter-attack against the English with troops from Louisbourg!

"I see smoke." Cameron interrupted young Comeau's dreams and motioned for the women to come ahead of the horse. When Sylvie and Reine had pushed past the animal, he indicated they should gather in a little circle for a council of war. Comeau joined the circle but stood back slightly.

"I'll go ahead to make sure the village is safe for us to enter." Cameron stood on tiptoe and looked down the path into the village. "I can't see from here."

Comeau said sulkily, "I told you the English were taking everyone into Grand Pré. There won't be anybody there."

"Maybe not. Stay with the women." When Cameron saw the flash of resentment in the boy's eyes he added, "if I should run into trouble, you'll have to look after them." The boy was angry about something, and Cameron gave up trying to please him. He pulled his cap over his red hair and assumed a slouching shamble as he went down the path into the village.

Comeau was boiling mad. He had looked after the women for days all by himself. He didn't need a renegade Englishman to tell him what to do!

At that moment, Tante Matilde groaned and slipped off the horse. She would have fallen to the ground had the three of them not grasped her clothing and eased her descent. Her eyes opened briefly, and she slipped back into unconsciousness.

Sylvie unfastened the water bottle and poured some in her hand. She wiped her wet hand over her Aunt's face and behind her neck. Matilde's lips moved as if she was speaking, but otherwise she did not waken.

Comeau had been watching the path where Cameron had disappeared. He had been gone too long. They had to move off the path. With a great deal of effort, the three of them managed to get Tante Matilde back on the horse. Comeau led the horse into the bushes. The animal protested but Reine smacked her on the rump, and the horse went where she was led. Sylvie walked alongside the horse and helped keep her Aunt in the saddle.

After another half-hour, Cameron came back. "I don't like it. There are no villagers, hot food has been left uneaten, and doors are open as if everyone left in a hurry. No sign of any trouble, though."

"Hot food! We should go in before anyone comes along." Comeau pulled on the reins. The horse didn't want to move, but Reine slapped its rump again. Maybe the horse could smell the food, because she went very willingly into the village.

\* \* \*

"You were right, Sergeant Pollard. They walked right in just like they owned the place." Lieutenant Bancroft and his sergeant were lying in the weeds at the entrance to the village. They had seen the man, possibly the English deserter, enter the village and move from house to house.

The sergeant sucked his teeth. "Now what we gonna do? We need three men to guard the barn where we got the villagers."

"That leaves me, you, and one other," Bancroft said quietly. "Damn! We had to split up to find them, and now we might not have enough men to catch them."

Bancroft thought for a moment. "Go back and bring two men from the barn. I'll move closer to the house."

"That only leaves two men at the barn," the sergeant protested. "Those villagers might have a mind to come out and help these people."

"If that happens, we lose more than just the escapees. Let's not think of that, sergeant."

"Right, sir. I'm to bring two of the boys back with me, and you'll be right over there." Sergeant Pollard crawled backwards until he was out of sight of the street and then ran down the hill to the barn.

\* \* \*

Reine Cameron took a big bite of bread. She chewed and chewed enjoying the taste and texture. "She makes beautiful bread."

"How do you know it's a she?" Cameron thought he heard something from the barnyard. He turned his head but heard nothing again. "It could have been a he."

"I don't know of a man who makes good bread." She chewed some more and swallowed. "Oh, yes, there was a widower at Baie Verte. He did very well for a time but he had to stop."

"Why?"

"Because of the unmarried women of the village." Reine smiled her lovely smile. "He had more fresh bread dropped off at his door than he could eat so he stopped making it."

"Men can't make bread," a voice croaked from the bed.

"Welcome back, Aunt Matilde." Sylvie picked up a bowl and filled it with vegetables. She hurried over to her Aunt and began feeding her. "Sit up, Aunt Matilde. We don't have much time. Eat this." She handed the bowl to the old woman. "I'll get you some water."

Matilde took the bowl from her niece. "I cannot go on, children. I am too old, too heavy to travel like this. When it's time to go, leave without me. I'll lie here and wait for the villagers to come back. They'll look after me."

Comeau had been looking out the windows, first from one at the front of the house and then from one at the side. "Must be the priest's house, to have two windows of glass."

"Aunt Matilde is going to have two glass windows next year. She has ordered the glass already." Sylvie bit her tongue, but continued anyway. "Paul Benoit—you know him, Reine, the big man with the black eye patch—is a cousin. He'll make the windows for Aunt Matilde as soon as the ship arrives with the glass."

"*Oui!*" Tante Matilde cheered at the thought. "It's not just French priests who have the fancy homes. When my windows are done, I'll place my silver on the mantle and the sunshine will come through my windows …"

Comeau held up his hand. "Shhhh! Quiet!"

Everyone was immediately silent. Cameron's face paled. "That's a bayonet scabbard striking the butt of a musket." He stood up quickly. "There are English out there!"

* * *

"For Christ's sake," Bancroft hissed. "Tell them to be quiet!"

Sergeant Pollard signalled the men, who froze in their tracks. "I brought them all, sir," Pollard said quietly. "If those villagers decide to help the escapees, having two guards or five won't mean a thing. So I brought them all!"

"You brought them all?" Lieutenant Bancroft regarded his sergeant as if he were a candidate for the madhouse. "You didn't leave anyone to guard the barn?"

Pollard glanced at his officer, then turned away and sig-nalled his men to move more quietly.

Bancroft chuckled softly. "You're right, of course, Sergeant. As long as the villagers are inside the barn, they don't know if there are five guards or fifty. If they decided to escape, another guard or two wouldn't matter a bit."

The lieutenant examined the situation. There was no back door to an Inhabitant home since the fireplace took up the rear wall. Given enough time, the escapees could cut their way through the clay and straw fireplace and chimney, but he wasn't going to give them any. "Sergeant Pollard, have one of our men ready to shoot anyone who comes through that window.

"Yessir!" Pollard signalled to one of the men, who knelt on one knee and raised his musket, aiming it at the window.

"Tell the boys to spread out from that corner to ..."

"They must have heard us, sir. They're comin' out!"

\* \* \*

Comeau ducked down from the window. "*Je les ai vus!* I saw them! There're a half-dozen coming up to the front from the barnyard."

Cameron picked up their musket. "Reine! Sylvie! Help Matilde to her feet! I'll go out the door ..."

"I can't go, Robert!" Matilde sat flat on the floor in a defi-nite statement of will. "Quick, children, leave me! Remember, *je t'aime!*"

Cameron picked up some fireplace tools and handed them to Reine and Sylvie. "As soon as you hear me on the street, throw the irons through both windows." He glanced at Comeau. "Are they still on that side of the house?"

"Yes, but some of them are moving across the front now."

"No time to waste! We must act now." Cameron took Reine's hand and squeezed it. "Break both windows but only go out the one at the side of the house."

Sylvie knelt down by Matilde. "What about Aunt Matilde?"

"She's right! She has gone as far as she can. You must follow Abel out the window."

Reine held his hand. "Must it end like this?"

Comeau ran to the door. "No, it doesn't have to end! Break the windows!" Then he was gone.

\* \* \*

"Here they come! Shoot anyone with a weapon!"

A quick movement erupted from the shadows in the doorway. Someone had come out and run to the horse. At that moment, the window exploded outward.

The noise distracted the English, and they waited to cut down anyone who came through the window. By that time, the man at the front of the house had pulled the reins from the tie and vaulted onto the horse. He dug in his heels, roughly turning the mare's head toward the road. The Frenchman uttered an oath of anger and humiliation. The horse refused to move.

There was no one coming through the window. The soldiers stood and ran toward the house.

Sergeant Pollard said, "He's just a boy!"

Bancroft recognized the boy. "It's that nephew of Matilde's! Take him alive!"

Comeau was mortified. He struggled with the horse but the mare wouldn't move. He decided to jump down and make a run for it, but the men appearing out of nowhere and closing in on her spooked the horse. She carried Comeau away in a mad gallop down the path. She probably wouldn't have run far—the mare was well spent—but Lieutenant Bancroft couldn't know that.

"Bring him down," he roared to Sergeant Pollard.

Pollard raised his hand. "Fire!"

Comeau kept his seat as the mare took a few more strides. Then he fell in the dust.

\* \* \*

Sylvie had to be torn away from Tante Matilde. She cried, "Aunt Matilde, please come with us!"

Matilde closed her eyes and folded her hands. "Hurry, children. Get away while you can."

Cameron picked up a small rag rug and threw it over the sill of the window. In a second he was outside, extending his hand to help Reine. From the front of the house, they heard Comeau curse the horse.

Reine slid through the window, and looked back for Sylvie. Sylvie was again kneeling by her aunt, pulling at her hands and arms, trying to get her to stand.

"Leave, Sylvie." Matilde gave her niece a severe look. "Do as you're told!"

From the front of the house, they heard, "He's just a boy!"

Sylvie took one last look at her aunt and climbed through the window.

Reine recognized Jeremiah Bancroft's voice when he said, "It's that nephew of Matilde's! Take him alive!" She understood 'take him alive.' The tall one won't hurt us, she thought.

Running past the rear of the house, Cameron saw that they were at least a hundred yards from the limited protection of the branches of alder bushes. The three of them stopped when they saw how far away it was.

"Bring him down!"

"Fire!"

The crash of several muskets drove the trio scrambling toward the shelter of the bushes.

\* \* \*

"Cover the front of the house!" Bancroft ran over to the boy twitching face down in the dirt. He barked another order at the soldiers, "Hold your fire unless they show a weapon!" He knelt down by Comeau. There was a lot of blood. He turned the boy over. If he expected to see the serenity that comes with fast approaching death, there was none. Abel Comeau fixed his eyes on the Englishman and tried to speak.

Bancroft waited, feeling sympathy for this life that was

being rudely snuffed out. He was the enemy, certainly, but it was hard to hate a what, fourteen or fifteen-year-old boy whose blood stained the dirt beneath him. The lieutenant couldn't think of much to say but felt he should say ... something. "You should have gone on the transport, my boy."

Sergeant Pollard came up behind him. "Is he dead yet?"

"No, he's trying to talk. What about the others?"

"They haven't come out yet, sir."

Comeau found the strength to speak. "*Vous ne posséderez jamais cette terre! Il est le nôtre.* You will never own this land! It is ours."

"What did he say, Sergeant?"

"I don't know, sir."

One of the soldiers shouted, "They're getting away at the back of the house!"

Bancroft looked back over his shoulder at the house and, for the first time, noticed the other window. "Shit! There's a second window!"

He glanced down at the boy. Abel Comeau was dead.

The soldiers ran to the back of the house.

Then Bancroft spotted his quarry: a woman, a girl, and the renegade Englishman. There was still a good shot.

"Give me a musket, sergeant!"

"Yes, sir."

Sergeant Pollard handed the officer a weapon. Bancroft sighted on the broad back of the man. He took a deep breath. Steady ... steady ... He exhaled slightly. The redhead turned to help the women over the fence at the end of the property, and their eyes met. The redhead pushed the young girl out of the way, and said something to his wife. She turned and faced the musket as well.

"Jerrie-e-e-e!"

Lieutenant Jeremiah Bancroft, the officer with dreams of honour and righteous causes, shifted his weight slightly and fired.

The three persons climbed the fence and disappeared into the bushes.

"Chase after 'em, sir?" Sergeant Pollard wasn't surprised when his officer said, "No. Burial detail and round up that horse."

"Yessir, Lieutenant."

Bancroft walked to the front of the house. The soldier who had been guarding the front window was still there, his musket at the ready.

"At ease, Jim. Go see if the old woman is still alive."

The soldier gave a casual salute and went inside with his musket at the ready.

Looking down the street, Bancroft could see that the horse seemed to be fine. There would be fodder in the village. At least he could ride back to the fort in style.

The soldier came back outside. "The old woman is still alive, but she can't walk."

Bancroft shook his head; so much for the riding-in-style idea. "When we move out, Jim, put her on the horse. Sergeant Pollard! Get the villagers out of the barn. Have the women prepare food. And find some proper feed for that horse."

"Yessir!"

That night around the campfire the soldiers said they thought the redhead had saluted just before he disappeared into the trees. Sergeant Pollard thought it unlikely. The men also commented on their musketry officer, the best shot in the regiment, missing an easy mark.

"It happens," Sergeant Pollard replied.

* * *

The next morning, the English soldiers herded the villagers along the road to Grand Pré. The Acadians were burdened with blankets, extra clothing, food, and their precious possessions, so progress was slow. Once the column was out of sight of the village, Sergeant Pollard sent two men back to burn the houses, barns, and fences and to slaughter whatever animals the Acadians had left behind.

* * *

Jeremiah Bancroft's men had done a good job of destroying the village of River Habitant. When they were finished, there wasn't a building standing or an animal alive. It was a scene of utter desolation. The only movement was the settling of the timbers or the crash of a wall as the fire burned its way through the once-thriving community until it finally sputtered out.

Hours after the New Englanders had departed, the three fugitives crept out of the woods and carefully approached the village. They saw Abel Comeau's grave dug into one of the gardens near a house where the digging would have been easy. They knew the freshly turned earth was Comeau's last resting place because someone, perhaps Tante Matilde, had made a cross out of two sticks tied together and placed it at one end of the grave.

Sylvie, and Reine and Robert Cameron, stood at the side of the grave and prayed for Abel Comeau. When they were finished praying, Cameron said, "Abel, you were more of a soldier than I ever was. You saved us. *Vous êtes mort un guerrier Acadien.* You died an Acadian warrior."

During the next hour, the three of them wandered through the village searching for salvageable food or clothing. They carried what they found to the centre of the village. Cameron placed each object on the step of the village well. There wasn't much. "Well, it's a start," he said.

Sylvie watched him lift a pole to lower a bucket into the well. "Get a pot, Sylvie. We'll fill it. Then maybe we can cook something. We deserve a hot meal. I'm tired of apples."

The hollow, splashing noise from the bottom of the well was a familiar, comforting sound. Robert pushed down on the pole, and lifted the bucket out of the well so Sylvie could reach it. Without saying anything, she pushed it away in horror and stepped away from the well. "They put manure in the well. We can't use it."

Reine had returned and seen Sylvie shove away the well bucket. "*Qu'est-ce que c'est?* What's wrong?"

Cameron dropped the pole. It sprang into the air as the full bucket crashed to the bottom of the well. "*Maudits Anglais!* They poisoned the well!"

Reine Cameron lifted her face to the heavens. She stood with her feet shoulder-width apart and her hands at her side.

Hands open, palms upturned, she raised her arms to the sky and cried out, "Mother of God! Someday it will be our turn! Someday we will shit in their wells!"

*9 October 1755*
*Near Grand Pré*

Lieutenant Bancroft rode the mare. From this vantage point he was able to see from one end of his column to the other.

The lieutenant was very pleased with himself. Considering all of the difficulties, his little command was in very good shape. They were almost at Grand Pré. He pulled up his horse and let the column pass him. There had been problems, but every problem seemed to have had an advantage. For instance, he told himself, it was aggravating for the column to be moving so slowly, but because it was, he was able to send out patrols and re-form his detachment before they reached Grand Pré. Then, there were so many enemy civilians to look after (they had outnumbered the soldiers until today when the last of his men returned); it was impossible for his men to oversee all aspects of the moving column. Consequently, the men of the village efficiently managed the column for the soldiers. There was the problem of food supply and distribution. His soldiers had difficulty setting up some sort of food ration system for so many people on the move. The problem went away when the village women took over. Now he could safely say that his men hadn't eaten so well since they had left their homes in Massachusetts. Even the Acadian's stubborn pride worked to his advantage. The second day on the trail, Matilde had insisted she get off the horse to walk with the rest of her people. Great stuff, Bancroft thought as he stroked the neck of his horse. He had to rethink that last bit. Actually it was Gray's horse but that didn't mean Bancroft hadn't appreciated her.

His thoughts were interrupted by a shout from the soldier at the point of the column. "Lots of smoke up ahead, lieutenant!"

"Column halt! Detachment to the fore. Form line of skirmish on me!"

Bancroft dismounted and handed the reins to the nearest farmer. He trotted forward about twenty paces, and was joined by Sergeant Pollard. "I suggest flankers, sir, and a rear guard."

The lieutenant nodded his head. "Take a section to the right flank."

"Yessir! Move it, you scallywags!" Pollard was already running off to the right into the trees.

"Corporal Shaw!"

"Yessir!"

"Your section to the left flank!"

Shaw's men disappeared into the thicker bush on the left.

Bancroft decided against setting up a rear guard. The trouble was to the front; he didn't have enough men to do everything. If he was attacked from the rear … He dismissed it from his mind.

"Form skirmish line! Wyman …" Bancroft saw movement on the trail. It was Wyman signalling that he and his trackers were already in position. So the rest of the men could know who was on point, Bancroft completed the order. "Wyman on point." He rapidly surveyed the area and ordered; "Move out!"

The flankers were already advancing through the trees and bushes. The main force followed the point men toward the village of Grand Pré.

Soon there was smoke everywhere. Cinders fell from the sky. The men were quickly coated with grey ash, and it was difficult to see. By the way his men crouched as they walked, Bancroft knew they were apprehensive. The skirmish line slowed as they entered the village. As far as they could see, houses were burning. What if the fort was under attack! Bancroft threw aside all caution. "Rapid advance to the fort!"

The men advanced on the double. Suddenly there was no smoke, no fire. The rest of the village was as they had left it. They could see the sentries, the command tent, the mess tent … there was no danger to the fort, no attack.

Bancroft almost fell over, he had stopped running so quickly. "Detachment hold!"

His men immediately formed a defensive formation around their officer, front row kneeling, and rear row standing.

All of his men were breathing heavily, tears from the smoke making little black rivers through the soot on their cheeks.

Colonel Winslow stepped out of the command tent and looked at the detachment. He applauded. "Fine performance, gentlemen. I suppose we could name this little tableau 'Phenehas to the rescue!'"

Everyone, including the women working around the mess tent, either smiled discreetly or laughed out loud depending upon how safe they felt they were from the ire of the Phenehas men. As far as the men of the detachment were concerned, they felt they had been made the butt of some sort of joke.

Winslow turned on his heel and re-entered the command tent. The men of the detachment could hear the colonel give orders to the duty officer. "Have Lieutenant Bancroft report to me in the morning. First thing."

Bancroft didn't know what to think. "Re-form!" he ordered. "Sergeant Pollard!"

"Yessir!"

"Go back to the column. Make camp on the other side of the fire. I'll find out what this is all about."

Lieutenant Bancroft returned the salute from his sergeant. He strode purposefully to his tent where, after he entered, he pulled the flap down and sat on the edge of his cot. He forced himself to breathe slowly as he tried to contain his anger. It didn't help very much when the flap was raised without any ceremony, and William Gray entered. "Welcome back, old chum! Did you catch the …"

"What the hell is going on here?" Bancroft thundered.

"Nothing too exciting. The colonel lost his temper, and burned a few houses. How did your detachment duties go?"

"Burned a few houses?"

"Yes. Twelve prisoners escaped from the transports last night."[6]

"How the hell did they manage that?"

"They had some sort of tool, a knife or an axe, and did some damage to the ship's hold. They knocked one of our sailors overboard, then swam ashore and disappeared." Gray looked more closely at his friend. "You look a mess! How did your detachment duty go?"

"How do you know they made it to shore? Maybe they didn't escape. Maybe they drowned."

"We found where they scrambled up the mud banks. Must have been hard. There were great slide marks in the mud where they kept slipping back into the water. It was easy to follow their trail from the bank into the village. They picked up fresh clothes and left their wet, muddy clothes on the front step of the houses they went into."

"The colonel must have been angry," Bancroft mused.

"Yes, he was angry. He took it as a personal affront. He went out and burned two of the houses where the wet clothes had been found."

"Only two? It looked like a half dozen!"

"The fire got away from us a little bit, but it's fairly well finished now. Just a lot of smoke and cinders but, fortunately, blowing away from the rest of the village."

"It's not like Winslow to lose his temper like that."

Gray took off his hat and ran his fingers through his hair. "Some of his distemper is my fault. I brought him new orders."

"What kind of orders? Can you tell me?"

"Certainly. There's no secret to them. In fact, I have several copies made by Monckton's staff." He opened the flap of his dispatch case. "I'm supposed to deliver the copies to various sites as far away as Fort Edward." He handed a copy to Jeremiah. "I'm going to be doing a lot of walking. I wish I still had my horse."

Bancroft read the orders.

Governor Lawrence has expressed his concern that transports have not yet sailed out of the bay and off to sea. The season is now so far advanced there is no answering for the consequences of their being detained longer. It is his order that the transports depart as soon as possible.

To that end, you will …

Bancroft looked up and smiled at his friend. "I found your horse. She's at the edge of the village." He went back to reading the orders.

> ... immediately order all the people which you have on board whether all the women be come in or not ...

"You're joshing me. Aren't you?" Gray got up and snatched the paper out of Bancroft's hand to get his attention. "You didn't find my horse, did you?"

With a pained look on his face, Bancroft held his hand out for the return of the order. "She's at the edge of the village. Sergeant Pollard will bring her to you tonight. Now, give me the order so I can finish reading it."

> ... You have previous instructions concerning leaving anything that could afford the least shelter or support to the French or Indians that may attempt to winter in the area. Carry them out now.
> Signed,
> Monckton

Bancroft handed the order back to Gray. "I can see why Winslow was upset. He's supposed to be stuffing prisoners into the transports and not letting them pop back out again."

Gray put the order back in the dispatch case, and closed the flaps. "I wondered about that last part. It has nothing to do with the navy so I didn't get to see the instructions. What does it mean?"

"It means lay waste to the countryside. We're to burn the houses and the barns, kill any livestock we can't bring into the fort, and contaminate any carcass we have to leave behind. I laid waste to River Habitant." Bancroft abruptly stopped talking. He stood up. "I have to get cleaned up and return to my detachment. There's no reason for them to be camped a mile away from the fort. I'll bring them in tonight. We can put the River Habitant prisoners in the fort, and my men can have a rest."

Gray lifted the tent flap. "That was great news about my horse. Thank you, Jerry."

"William!"

Gray stepped back into the tent. "What is it, Jerry?"

"I saw your fellow Scot at River Habitant."

"Carrot Top! Is he dead?"

"No. Got clean away with Reine and that other niece of Matilde's."

"Sylvie."

"Yes, Sylvie. Matilde gave herself up. She just lay down on the floor of a house and waited for my men to pick her up. She's with the detachment right now."

"Poor Matilde!"

"The trackers found her strongbox, of course. At least now we can give her precious possessions back."

Gray looked surprised. "That was nice of them to rescue the stuff for her."

"I don't think that's what Wyman had in mind, but he'll be glad to do it, I'm sure."

Gray smiled in understanding.

## Endnotes

[1] "On Thursday Aug ye 14th we had orders to march with our tents and baggage to Forte Lawrence in order to imbark for Pisquit." Bancroft.

[2] "... arrived at Pisquit Munday morning ye 18tth at 7 o'clock we went ashore Refreshed and Regailed ourselves till eventide then we reimbarkt and sailed for Mines where we arrived the next morning and marcht to there Mass house took possession and hoisted an English Flagg the Colonel Gave Orders to the Soldiers not to take anything from the French not so much as a fowl." Bancroft.

[3] The French knew Les Mines to be an area, Grand Pré being the largest settlement. The English came to think of Les Mines as the beach where their assault forces landed.

[4] From the Bourgeois Family book.

[5] The chase after Cameron is fiction. Bancroft reports that the English went to River Habitant and cleared the people out.

[6] "... about 12 men made their escape from on board the transports which so affronted the Colonel that he went out and burnt two of their Houses. He said if they do not return quic he will burn all their effects. Next day parties was sent out to gather the women and children to put on Board which we accomplished the day following without much difficulty." Bancroft diary.

# Chapter Nine

## 9 October 1755
## *River Habitant*

The time had come to leave River Habitant. Robert Cameron had meant to suggest it to the women at breakfast but he decided to wait until later in the day. He reflected on the past days.

The English had done a fine job of destroying the village but, of course, two soldiers, in the limited time they had, couldn't get to everything. So, with hard work and perseverance, the fugitives had found enough to sustain themselves. Each discovery was a triumph over the despicable English.

In one house, the fireplace, part of the roof, and a wall had survived the destruction, enough to provide shelter for the three fugitives. In another, the mistress had left behind her pots, and the fire had somehow spared them. The soldiers had methodically killed all livestock, leading the doomed animals into the buildings to be butchered so, when the house burned, the flames would have consumed the carcasses. But in one home the fugitives discovered the charred remains of a pig that proved edible. Several hens showed up on the village street; there were eggs. Cameron found the root cellars undisturbed; they had their choice of vegetables and, wonder of all wonders, some *bière d'épinette*. Finally, although the village well had been contaminated, the brook had sparkling water. If it weren't for the sadness of Abel Comeau's shallow grave and the loss of Matilde, Cameron could say their days at River Habitant were the happiest since the French surrender of Fort Beauséjour. He sighed, his mind made up. There wasn't enough here to sustain them through the winter, and the English were too close. It was time to leave.

\* \* \*

They had finished the midday meal, and Robert Cameron belched appreciatively. His wife appeared not to notice, but Sylvie said, "That was a wonderful meal."

"Yes it was," Cameron said, and he burped again.

"Enough of a good thing, Robert." Reine Cameron was usually so even-tempered; it was surprising that her man's burping should easily annoy her.

"It's never enough of a good thing, Reine," Sylvie said, missing the interplay between husband and wife. "It has been wonderful here at River Habitant. If only we had Abel and Aunt Matilde," she added wistfully.

Without looking at her husband, Reine asked, "Will the English come back, Robert?"

Cameron's eyes flashed. "You think because I was a lobster-back I'll know what these madmen will do?"

"That's not what I meant, *chéri*."

"None of the men I knew in my regiment would ever think of uprooting an entire colony and moving them somewhere else. They wouldn't shoot down a boy like Abel! They wouldn't ..." He stopped abruptly. He could see the rows of bodies on the beach the night of the Dartmouth massacre. The English had closed the fort gates and so many settlers had died so horribly. Cameron had deserted; he didn't want to find himself one day in similarly horrifying circumstances on the wrong side of the gate. He didn't want to be one of the bodies on the beach with a stitch through its nose. Abruptly he stood and ran his fingers through his hair. "Damn it all, lass! I don't know *any ... thing ... any ... more.*"

Reine heard his anguish and hastened to his side and put her arms around him. "What I meant to ask, *chéri*," she said softly, "should we be leaving here? It will be winter soon. We must find a place to live."

Taking his wife's hands in his, Cameron nodded his head. "We should gather up as much as we can of what we need. We'll need to make travel packs and put together some warmer clothing. It'll take us a few days to get ready. Then we must find our way to Isle Saint Jean."

*10 October 1755*
*Grand Pré*

Delicious smells emanated from the officer's mess tent. William Gray hadn't planned to have breakfast before leaving for Fort Edward, but bacon and eggs was hard to resist. He tied Shadow to the hitching post and, remembering to take his dispatch case, ducked into the mess tent. The first person he saw was his friend, Jeremiah Bancroft, with his elbows on the table, digging into a healthy serving of bacon and fried dough. "What ho, Lieutenant Church Steeple!" Gray called. "Any left for me?"

"If they ain't got enough, we'll just shoot the cook, Grubby White." Bancroft responded loud enough for the cook to hear.

Gray went to the serving table and received a supply of bacon and four eggs. He sat down opposite his friend.

"I thought you were gone," Bancroft said, "or I'd have come by for you."

Gray was busy chewing so he just nodded his head.

"Got orders today to bring all the women and children into the fort. They're going to be loaded tomorrow," Bancroft continued.

Gray picked up a slice of bread and tore off a piece. "This looks like the bread Aunt Matilde was making for us." He dipped it in the bacon grease and, swirling it around so most of the fat stuck to it, popped it into his mouth. He chewed contentedly and swallowed. He picked up the teacup and took a long drink to wash the fat from his mouth. "Tastes like her bread, too."

"It's Matilde's bread all right. She's happy when she's working at her ovens. I'm gonna keep her here until the very last. I sure love her bread. How long do we have?"

"Well, there are added complications now that the season's so late. The weather's uncertain this time of year, and the transports will have to take on more provisions for the voyage."

"How long will it take to load, William?"

"The ships we have here?" Gray pushed away his plate and sat back. "The captains will have to rearrange their stores since there is to be much more of it."

Bancroft leaned forward and whispered, "I know the meat allowance was planned at six pounds of beef or pork per man, but yesterday I heard a Boston supplier saying there would be merely one pound per week. Could that be true? One pound a week?"

"I hadn't heard that," Gray answered quietly, "but I'm not surprised. I also expect the transport captains will cut back on the amount of personal stuff the prisoners will be allowed to take with them."

"Can they do that?"

"Yes. A captain is the law on his ship. The governor tells captains what has to be done and where, but he can't tell them how to get it done. Besides, I was privy to a letter from the governor to Captain Rous. Although the original instructions said the Inhabitants could carry on their household furniture, more recent orders have changed that as well."

"What is it now? We haven't been told of any changes," Bancroft said.

"The governor now says," Gray explained, "that the Inhabitants are not allowed to take useless rubbish to encumber the vessels."[1]

"Useless rubbish?"

"He says we may permit the Inhabitants to embark their bedding. If afterwards there's room for other articles, 'suffer them to carry on what they conveniently can.'"

"And with the captains worried about loading additional provisions, that will be damned little." Bancroft pushed his plate away. "So how long will it take to load the ships?"

"If the captains are saving space by cutting the ration allowance for the prisoners and reducing the amount of space needed to store their personal possessions—they'll still have to do some load adjustments—about two weeks. The fleet might be able to sail the first of November."

"Maybe me and my men can go home this year. Maybe they'll send some ships for us."

"I hate to disappoint you, Jerry. I told Captain Rous that we needed more transports, but he doesn't think we'll get them."

"What's the problem?"

"The admirals are bickering. Rous said they misled him as to the number of transports. Personally, I think the suppliers in Boston are trying to make more money. They'd rather have fewer ships and bigger loads, and that's dangerous thinking this time of the year."

"They don't care about the risks. It's not their hides."

Gray picked up his dispatch case. "So you're keen to go back to Massachusetts? You're not going to accept the governor's offer to settle here in the Fundy?"

"Nope! And I'm not going to accept the bounty for joining one of the regular regiments, either." Bancroft watched for his friend's reaction and added, "Although it would be an easy way to pay off the money I owe you, William."

"How much is the bounty?"

"I really don't know what they're paying for an officer. For a battalion man, enlistment money is three pounds. A grenadier gets three pounds ten."

Gray put his hand on Bancroft's arm. "Don't you worry about my money, Jerry. You pay me back when you can."

"You're a good friend, William."

\* \* \*

Bancroft's comment gave William Gray a warm feeling that stayed with him for many miles as he travelled to Fort Edward. Late in the afternoon, Shadow sidestepped an object in the path that proved to be some dark brown leaves. Gray lost his balance in the saddle and saved himself from falling only with a great deal of effort. It was time for the two of them to take a break. He stopped at the top of a hill where he could see both directions down the trail for some distance.

He pulled out one of his water bottles and spilled some of its contents into the horse's mouth. Sitting at the base of a tree, he munched on an apple. He was only an hour or so out of Fort Edward. If the river were in flood, he would be forced to wait near Cinq Maisons on this side of the river until the ebb. Of course there wasn't anyone left at the village any more.

Gray sat for a while, at first not thinking about anything much. Then his thoughts drifted over the past summer. Imagine! Getting all of those troops ashore at Fort Lawrence without getting their feet wet. The navy and army had worked together as a team. He smirked. Probably the very first time in the Royal Navy's history, and it was due to that remarkable man, Captain John Rous.

He had been so proud when Captain Rous had selected him to capture and confiscate the French and Acadian ships. Getting crews together to take the vessels to Halifax for prize money had been exciting. He had been so full of hope.

Gray was proud again when Rous chose him as the liaison officer between the army and the navy on a secret enterprise to remove the threat of the French from the isthmus forever. Another amphibious assault at Les Mines, and he had helped make it happen. Being responsible for finding the materials for the fort at Grand Pré and watching it grow .... Gray frowned. But it wasn't a fort he had helped build. It was a prison.

The expulsion of the Inhabitants from the province had been an exciting prospect in the beginning, until he had seen its effects on people like Aunt Matilde. But the Inhabitants were the enemy, and they had been responsible for the horrible Dartmouth massacre. "How could Carrot Top have deserted to such people?" Gray was startled that he had spoken out loud.

Now it was autumn, and the Fundy was full of misery and destruction. Soon Gray could turn his back on the Fundy and go home to Sambro although he and Molly might have to remain in Halifax until he earned enough money for their house, since there wasn't going to be any prize money. The governor had sold the ships and put the money into the colony's treasury. Governor Lawrence had written another order; the governor certainly liked sending out orders.

> "As to the vessels taken, they are not to be looked upon as prizes, nor can the people who took them expect their being shared among them, as there is no war declared but, if war were declared, the vessels must be kept for the use of the Government." [2]

Gray shook his head. The governor was a weasel! There could be no prize money because there was no war, but if there were a war, the government would use the boats and not send them to prize court. He felt despair for the first time in his life. Captain Rous had been so sure of the prize money that he had advanced Gray ten pounds for personal expenses. And Gray had been so sure he had loaned three pounds to Jeremiah Bancroft! The captain expected Gray to pay back the money but Bancroft wouldn't be able to pay Gray back. That money was gone.

Gray didn't feel down for very long. All right, then, he thought. It's a fair exchange. Jerry saved my life and is now my friend. That's better than fair. I'll find the money to pay back old Rous and, as far as Jerry is concerned? Jerry will never find out about the prize money not being shared and I'll not tell him!

Amused that he was talking to himself again, Gray mounted Shadow and rode on to Cinq Maisons. The tide was on the ebb, and he crossed the river without incident. He passed the night safely within the walls of the fort.

\* \* \*

Sergeant Pollard hurried to catch Lieutenant Bancroft before he got too far away from the command tent. He called out as soon as he saw him in the evening twilight. "Lieutenant! Colonel Winslow would see you in the command tent, right away!"

Nathan Simons, who had been walking with Bancroft, laughed. "You'd better let me smell your breath before you go, Jerry. If he wants you out in the woods again chasing unseen Indians …"

Bancroft swung his fist at Simons's shoulder. "You bugger! Why don't you just lay off!"

Simons retaliated with a good-natured shove. "He's coming, Sergeant Pollard!" In a lower voice, Simons continued, "He has to finish his rum!"

Bancroft turned away and started back to the command tent. "I suppose, Nate," he said, "I'll never live that little incident down!"

"Not if I can help it!" Simons called after him, and chuckled loud enough for the lieutenant to hear.

Bancroft was thinking of his options as he hurried along. Their assigned duty for tomorrow was to escort prisoners to the longboats in the creek. There were two flood tides tomorrow, one just after first light and the other just before dark, and that gave them more than the usual amount of time to move prisoners to the transports in the bay, because the creek would be full of water twice during daylight hours. It would be a long day.

Closer now to the command tent, he considered the other two possibilities: his men could be left to guard the fort and do sentry duty, or the colonel could give them some time off to tend their personal gear and write letters home. There were more than enough soldiers at the fort; maybe Phenehas Company would finally get a break. He stepped into the tent hoping for the best. "Lieutenant Bancroft, sir. Reporting as ordered."

He could feel the blush starting. When he had been on the carpet for the 'romp through the woods,' his face had been red from unseen branches slapping it. The colonel had presumed that too much drink had induced the colour. Now, every time Bancroft came face to face with the commanding officer he blushed.

"Oh, yes. Lieutenant, I won't need your men tomorrow."

Colonel Winslow looked up and studied the face of the tall, muscular officer standing before him. I wonder if he's been at it again, he thought. Other than his flushed face, he doesn't look or act like he's drunk. "Come 'round the table. I want to show you this sketch."

"Yessir."

"Early tomorrow I want you to take thirty men and swing west to reach River Habitant by midday. I want you to search for stragglers, and bring any women or children you find into the fort. Destroy anything along the way that might give aid to the French and Indians over the winter." Having satisfied himself that Bancroft had no smell of drink on him, the colonel waved him back to the other side of the table.

"I've sent for the other company lieutenant, Simons. He and his men will sweep toward Fort Edward. I expect both of you back by the end of the second day.

Bancroft silently observed that it would be difficult to accomplish the objectives and return in two days.

"Any questions?"

"No, sir."

*11 October 1755*
*Near River Habitant*

Lieutenant Bancroft's men were tired; they had been on the move the entire day. He would let them rest when they reached the village. Too bad his men had burned it all the last time they were here; it would have been nice to have a stove for a hot meal. However, they would use whatever they could find.

Sergeant Pollard crept up behind his officer. "To the right, sir, about fifty feet. There's movement in them bushes!"

"Section One to the front! Defensive line to the right."

Sergeant Pollard called, "Remainder, stand fast! Fix bayonets!"

\* \* \*

Reine Cameron dropped the pot she was holding. "*Qu'est-ce que c'est?* What's that?"

Robert Cameron came running from the field where he had been searching for potatoes. "The English are preparing to attack! Where's Sylvie?"

"She went to the brook!"

Cameron turned and ran toward the brook. "I must try to reach her!"

"Don't leave me, Robert!"

"*Cache-toi a l'abri!* Hide at the shelter!" Cameron shouted, and kept running.

\* \* \*

"Fix bayonets!" Bayonets clattered as they were affixed to the ends of the muskets.

"Section One, advance!"

Lieutenant Bancroft could see a solitary figure in the bushes, crouched down Indian style.

"Section One, halt!" There was no point in entering the bushes until they could determine what the hazard was.

Solomon Wyman trotted up next to the sergeant and the lieutenant. "It's a dog, sir."

Bancroft didn't argue with the woodsman. Wyman could see in the woods better than anyone. "Stand easy!"

The animal crept silently out of the bushes. It had probably been someone's guard dog; it was far too large for a house pet. It moved cautiously toward the men, low to the ground now, its fangs bared. A growl sounded from deep in its throat.

Wyman laughed. "That beast is going to attack the company!" He raised his musket and shot the dog in the chest as it was preparing to leap.

In the silence that followed, a faint call drifted up the trail. "Sylvie!"

Jeremiah Bancroft smiled. "Ah! They're still here."

\* \* \*

Cameron heard the shot. His heart leaped as he imagined the musket ball tearing into the young girl's body.

"Sylvie," he called, frantic. He was at the brook, but he couldn't see her. The shot had come from the trail. What was she doing there?

"Robert! *Elle est ici,*" Reine cried. "She's here!"

\* \* \*

The detachment re-formed. Another call came from the village, "*Robert! Elle est ici!*" Bancroft recognized that voice.

"First two sections! There are at least three people in the village: two women and one man. The man is an English deserter and may be shot on sight. Skirmish line, Sergeant!"

"First two sections, form skirmish line."

"Advance!"

\* \* \*

When Cameron heard the order to advance, he pushed himself harder to get back to the shelter. His breath became ragged with the effort.

He heard Reine shout, "*Vite,* Robert! I can see the English. They're near Abel."

That meant the English were at the entrance to the village where Comeau was buried. He hoped they were lobsterbacks and not New England Militia. The militia would have trackers with them, and there would be no escape with them this close. If Cameron could keep the standing wall between them and the soldiers, maybe he could gain enough time to get the women into the trees without being seen. Cameron grabbed each woman by the hand and pulled her around the corner of the shelter. Once behind the wall, he felt Sylvie slow down. "Keep running," he cried.

"I'm not going, Robert. You go. I must go back and look after Aunt Matilde."

Cameron yanked her arm. "You won't be able to help Matilde! She's already gone."

"I'm the only one left. I must look after Aunt Matilde. She looked after Abel and me." Sylvie sobbed. She pulled her hand away and stepped back. "*Au revoir,* Reine. *Merci,* Robert. You are a good man ..."

Cameron silently finished Sylvie's unspoken sentence, "... even though you are English."

Sylvie ran back to the wall. She gave a little wave and then stepped around the corner out of sight.

Reine made a move as if to go get her, but Cameron seized her arm and jerked her around. "Come on! We have to make it to the trees."

\* \* \*

Wyman saw her first. He raised his hand to stop the skirmish line. He studied the situation. A young woman, arms at her side, was walking toward them. If she were bait for a trap, she would have stayed near the wall, the only place that could hide the enemy. He gave the signal to move forward.

When they were about fifteen feet apart, Wyman gave the stop signal again.

The woman said something to him.

One of the boys in the skirmish line said, "She says she's alone."

"Ask her where the man is."

The soldier asked, *"Où est l'homme?"*

Sylvie quickly responded with a lie. *"Il n'ya pas d'homme.* There is no man." She held her hands out in supplication. *"Je veux retourner au Grand Pré pour rester avec ma tante Matilde.* I want to go back to Grand Pré to be with my Aunt Matilde."

"She says there is no man. She wants to go back to Grand Pré, but I don't know what a 'tant ma tild' is."

Lieutenant Bancroft came up with the rest of the detachment. "Sylvie!"

Sylvie began to cry and ran to him and threw herself into his arms. *"Ramène-moi! Je veux être avec tante Matilde.* Take me back. I want to be with Aunt Matilde."

"I understand now, sir," the soldier said. "She wants to be with her aunt."

Bancroft gently pulled the girl's arms from around his waist. "Corporal, look after this girl. Take her to the rear."

Sergeant Pollard cast a quick look around. "He's here somewhere."

"Most likely keepin' that wall between us and them and running like hell for the woods." Solomon Wyman sucked his teeth. "You want me and the boys to go get 'em, Lieutenant?"

"How long would it take?"

"As little as ten minutes or maybe as much as five hours. Depends how fresh they are. We're not."

"Go after them, Wyman. Chase them for no more than a mile. We have a lot of work to do here and we have to return to Grand Pré by tomorrow night."

"Yessir!"

"Mind now, soldier. No more than a mile."

\* \* \*

Reine and Robert Cameron sat on a stump just inside the alder bushes. Cameron was badly out of breath, and his wife had several gashes on her shins from the dash across the rough pasture.

"We can't go on any longer, Reine."

"No!" Reine jumped up. "I won't let them have you!"

Cameron insisted. "It's time to give up," he said resignedly. "We have no food, no clothes, and no weapon. The English are everywhere." He held his hand out to his wife. "We can't go on."

There was a commotion near the shelter. Across the pasture, four militiamen rounded the corner of the wall. They were carrying muskets and moving with an easy, animal grace.

Cameron knew that when they caught him, they would truss him and take him back to the village like a hunting trophy. He pictured Sylvie crying, Reine wringing her hands and begging the English to let him go, and the English laughing.

Cameron stood up. He took his wife's hand and led her away from the edge of the pasture. "This is one Scot they're not going to laugh at."

They started running and didn't stop for miles.

*15 October 1755*
*Grand Pré*

"Tell them there will be two or three more transports." Jeremiah Bancroft was speaking to Matilde and Sylvie through Nathan Simons. "Nate, I want her to understand that most of the prisoners will be leaving this week. They can go with these people or they can go later with ..."

"I know, I know. I'll tell her."

While Lieutenant Simons spoke to the two women, Bancroft said good-bye to Sergeant Pollard. "Sergeant, I want you to come back to Phenehas Company in one piece."

"I'd like that too, sir."

"Watch your back at Annapolis. French irregulars have been operating in that area. Remember, we lost Lieutenant March and twenty-two men on the isthmus in September."

"Yessir. I didn't volunteer, sir. You know I'd rather stay here with Phenehas Company."

"I know you don't want to leave, but Hobbs Company is good boys. You'll be the senior sergeant, working with the captain himself. You can teach 'em a lot."

They shook hands.

Sergeant Pollard hoisted his bag and threw it on the back of a wagon. Over his shoulder he said, "At least I don't have to carry my gear all the way to Les Mines. So long."

After the sergeant had disappeared in the dust of the road, Bancroft turned back to see how Simons was getting along with the women. They were walking away, Matilde holding firmly to Sylvie's arm for support. "Well?"

"They want to stay until the last, Jerry," Simons reported.

Bancroft grunted. "They know I won't be able to help them."

"Yes, I told them they'd have to leave."

"And that there'd be no French here."

"I told them that, but the young one ..."

"Sylvie."

"Yes, Sylvie, said this land would always be Acadian."

"Humph!"

They began walking toward the command tent. Bancroft put his hand on Simons's arm for emphasis, "As long as they understand there's no chance of them staying."

"They understand." Simons changed the subject. "But there's something I don't understand. Why did we lose our sergeant to Hobbs Company?"

"Their senior sergeant took the fever and was sent home."

"Why not promote from their own ranks?"

"There are renegades operating on the isthmus," Bancroft explained. "They need an experienced sergeant, and Pollard is the best."

"The renegades are armed and fighting?"

"Yes. The Frenchman Boishebert is leading them, taking in strays and escapees, and causing all sorts of trouble while we have it pretty quiet here."

"It's a good thing there are no French leaders here. The

only choice facing our prisoners is to accept transport, or freeze to death this winter."

"It sure is different at Annapolis. That's why they need experienced men like our Pollard."

"I'm sorry to see him go."

"We'll get him back," Bancroft promised as the officers ducked into the command tent. Inside, they straightened up and saluted. "Lieutenants Simons and Bancroft reporting, sir."

"Ah, the last two." Now that these two had arrived, all the officers at Grand Pré were assembled in the command tent. Colonel Winslow indicated several campaign stools that had been placed around the tent. "Please find a place to sit." Then pointing at Bancroft he added, "You in particular, my tall, florid-faced friend."

Naturally, Bancroft's face turned beet-red.

Speaking to the other officers, Winslow said, "I'm always afraid he's going to lift the tent from its pegs, he's so tall."

There was polite laughter.

When all the officers were seated, Colonel Winslow put his hands on his hips and rocked back and forth, toe to heel. "Starting tomorrow, we begin the cleanup of this expedition, and all the women and their effects will be boarded. The flood tide is at 1100 hours. The longboats will work the creek by 1000 at the latest. I want our men at the creek by 0800 hours. I want all that debris cleaned out of there before the first prisoner is loaded."

"Debris, sir?" Major Prebble had a quizzical look on his face.

"Yes, Major Prebble, debris. The prisoners have been abandoning their personal effects at the water's edge. I want the area cleaned up before we begin again tomorrow."

"What do you want done with the debris, sir?"

"Burn it. No man or officer may take any of it. That would be looting, and we must maintain discipline."

"Yessir."

"Adams Company and the remaining men of Hobbs Company will be on duty at the loading area. The rest of you will dismantle or burn all civilian structures and all produce that is not being utilized by us." Colonel Winslow glanced around at the various faces. "There being no further questions, you are dismissed."

The officers stood and made their way slowly from the tent. Lieutenant Bancroft remained behind.

"Is there something you want, Lieutenant, or were you not familiar with that last order?"

"Your pardon, sir. If I might ask a question?"

"Yes."

"You said all the women and their effects would be boarded, tomorrow."

"How clever of you to remember."

Bancroft felt his face getting warm. "I request that two of the women be allowed to remain at Grand Pré until the last of the transports, sir."

Colonel Winslow regarded the officer with steely eyes. He had suspected this man of having a problem with drink. Now, he dallies with a woman prisoner? Noting the colonel's suspicious look, the lieutenant hurried on with his request. "The old woman, Matilde, wants to stay until the last. She makes the bread for the officers. With your permission, sir, I'd like to tell her she might stay." When the colonel didn't reply, Bancroft added, "Only until the last few transports."

"You said two women."

"The other is her niece, the old woman's only family."

Winslow pulled at his lip. "It's good bread. All right, Lieutenant, but you make sure that when the time comes for them to leave, they go without any fuss."

"Yessir." Bancroft saluted and withdrew.

### 16 October 1755
### Grand Pré[3]

The day began pleasantly enough. The sun rose warm and bright, casting long shadows. A white coating of frost lingered on the roofs and grass in the shady places, and where the sun had reached, water droplets formed on the trees and the grass sparkled. As the sun rose higher, seagulls swirled in the sky over the garbage dump where the soldiers of Phenehas Company were burning the prisoners' debris. Chairs, buckets, benches, and farm tools were the first things to be burned.

Adams and Hobbs companies opened the gates to the fort. The prisoners were led out, and were quickly joined by the captive women and children. Forming a long procession, the Acadians shuffled off, surrounded by over one hundred soldiers with loaded muskets and fixed bayonets, through the village and down the hill toward the marsh. There was no singing. There was no talking.

As soon as the village was cleared of Inhabitants, the Phenehas men grabbed burning brands from the fire. At first, they found it difficult to get the houses to burn properly. Throwing the firebrands into the houses to set them afire didn't work very well. One house caught flames that way, but the brands went out in the others. The men discovered that the secret to setting a house on fire was to pull the bedding loose and pile it on a bed or a table. Touching a firebrand to a blanket or comforter made a very satisfactory fire.

Barns weren't a problem. There was so much combustible material in the barns that the soldiers merely checked the interior for animals and then left the firebrand leaning against something—almost anything—inside, and the flames caught easily.

By the time the first of the longboats arrived at the creek, a pall of smoke hung over the valley so thick it hid the sun. Ash and cinders fell from the sky like dirty snow, leaving black smudges on clothing or skin. Mothers placed blankets or pieces of their fine linen over their babies' faces. Huddled together, they held tightly to their children and possessions.

The boats approached up the narrow, winding creek, and Colonel Winslow ordered the prisoners to line up, six in each row.

"*Qu'est qu'il veut,*" one of the young Acadian men called out. "*Que faut-il faire?*"

There was a general response from the crowd. "*Que s'attendre t'il de nous? Dan quelle bateau est mon mari? J'ai perdu mon enfant! Est-ce que quelqu'un a vu mon Jacques.*"

It seemed as if the crowd was panicking, although none of the soldiers understood what they were saying. Winslow acted quickly. "Captain! Line them up in rows of six!"

Captain Adams gave a series of commands, but the Acadians made no move to obey, not understanding the captain's orders. Instead, the chorus of voices became louder and its tone more demanding. It was a fearful moment, and the actions of both groups were made more difficult by the lack of understanding.

"They won't obey, sir."

"Get that mob into order, Captain, or I'll do it myself!"

Adams Company didn't have to be told a second time. The soldiers entered the crowd, prodding people into position with the butts of their muskets or a thrust of their bayonets. Colonel Winslow breathed a sigh of relief when there was finally a semblance of order. The Inhabitants were lined up in rows of six.

The first boat was ready. Sailors beckoned six Inhabitants forward. When they hesitated, the soldiers again prodded them into action with their weapons. The first six were young boys, each with a load of personal effects. A sailor snatched a box from the hands of the first boy in line and threw it to the ground. "Can't take that with ya, mate! You can keep the blankets! Next!"

The boy resisted and stooped to retrieve his belongings. He was met with the levelled bayonet of the nearest soldier. "Get on board, son."

"*Je dois avoir ma boîte! Je dois l'apporter a mon père!* He made another attempt to reach the box.

The soldier thrust him back roughly with his musket against the boy's chest. "I told you, son," he snarled, "get on the boat." The soldier pushed the boy again, harder.

The boy fell into the boat where a large sailor roughly settled him on a thwart. "Sit there nice and quiet like, boyo. You don't want me to hurt you now, do you?" He held his fist up to the boy's face. There was no mistaking the message.

Resistance quickly faded away. Each person was relieved of their personal effects, usually boarding the boats carrying only some clothing or bedding.

\* \* \*

The longboats weren't returning to the creek. Taking an eyeglass, Colonel Winslow studied the ships in the bay. The boats were being hoisted in. "Get that naval fellow, Lieutenant Gray." Winslow pointed to where William Gray was sitting on his horse looking out over the piles of personal belongings that littered the banks of the creek. He was listening to Captain Adams, who was waving his arms and obviously felt strongly about something.

Winslow watched as the message was delivered to Lieutenant Gray. The lieutenant detached himself with some difficulty from the conversation with Captain Adams. Adams yelled after the naval officer as Gray's horse picked its way carefully across the cluttered creek bank.

Gray dismounted and led his horse behind him. He saluted the colonel and said, "I'm just back from Fort Edward, sir. I see the transports are flying the 'boats return' and 'cease operations' pennants."

"They can't stop now," the colonel protested. "We still have six hundred prisoners here! More were brought from Les Mines this afternoon."

"That's what Captain Adams said. He wants me to order the boats back to the creek."

"That's exactly what you must do! Get them back here!"

"The transport captains have obviously decided they're unable to take any more cargo. That's within their authority. They might be able to take more in a few days when they get everything ready for sea, but right now ..."

"For God's sake, man," Winslow thundered. "As soon as the prisoners realize the situation, they'll riot!"

Lieutenant Gray shrugged his shoulders. "I am sorry, Colonel. The captains have ceased operations, at least for today."

Colonel Winslow motioned for his aide. "Send a runner to Phenehas Company. Tell them to prepare the fort for prisoners."

"I'll go, sir. I can make it faster on the horse." Gray tugged on the reins and mounted swiftly.

"Tell Phenehas to send whatever men are not needed for guard and escort duty. Tell them to come quickly!"

"Aye, aye, sir." Gray urged his horse to a fast trot.

The colonel called after him. "You know the situation. Tell them to hurry!"

\* \* \*

"Well, look who's here!" Jeremiah Bancroft looked tired; he certainly was dirty. "Hello, William!"

"Jerry!" Gray rode right up to his friend and dismounted. Bancroft grabbed the halter to stay the agitated animal. "The colonel wants you to prepare the fort for prisoners!"

Bancroft glanced quickly at the fort. All the gates were open. He had his men cleaning every nook and cranny, removing garbage to be burned, and also ensuring there were no prisoners skulking somewhere to escape transport.

"All right. It won't take long to put the fort back together." Bancroft issued several quick orders, then turned back to his friend. "Why do we have to do this?"

"The transports are full. There are six hundred prisoners left at the creek."

"Where did they all come from?"

"The colonel said they were sent up from Les Mines. I guess the transports at Les Mines are full, too. He expects you to send all the men you can spare to the creek as soon as you can for guard and escort duty."

Bancroft pulled a whistle from his pocket and gave a long blast. Every soldier turned as the lieutenant give the 're-form' signal.

Five minutes later, Phenehas Company was moving through the village to the creek at double time. From a distance, they heard the wailing of the women and children who watched the transports move down the basin to Les Mines. The moving ships meant the ruin of every family that had been assembled on that shore; family members were forever separated.

With the ships gone from sight, the remaining Acadians were silent, numbed by their losses.

Phenehas Company moved to herd the prisoners into the

fort. There was no opposition; the remaining prisoners quietly walked to Grand Pré, where they were locked up.

\* \* \*

On Wednesday 29 October the fleet sailed from Les Mines, leaving six hundred prisoners behind at Grand Pré for want of transports.

On 1 November the Second Battalion of the New England Militia were informed that they would likely winter in Nova Scotia.

During the day on 2 November, Lieutenant Bancroft took a small party of men and began to burn the buildings and farm produce around Grand Pré. The same day, villages on the River Gotreau were also destroyed.

On 3 November Lieutenant Bancroft and a force of ninety men went to River Canard and burned and levelled the villages along that river. Adams Company and what remained of Hobbs Company marched for Annapolis Royal to help gather in the Acadians who lived in that area.

On 14 November Colonel Winslow, after turning over command of Grand Pré to Captain Osgood, departed for Halifax with a force of eighty men. Passing through Fort Edward, thirty of that force were left as garrison.

*14 November 1755*
*Annapolis Royal*
*Nova Scotia*

Sergeant Pollard,[4] newly arrived from Grand Pré and assigned to Hobbs Company of the New England Militia, led a scouting party across the fields of an Acadian farm. They were still within sight of the walls of Annapolis Royal, but as they crested a hill where alder bushes bordered the cultivated fields, the sergeant held up his hand to caution his men. He motioned three of them to spread out and to cross into the next field, while he and nine other men stood watch, prepared to support them in case they ran into trouble.

When the soldiers waved from the next field that all was clear, Pollard motioned three more men to advance. Fairly certain there were no renegade Acadians waiting to pounce on them, the sergeant took a moment to gaze out over the cliffs at the water. It had crossed his mind to take up the colonel's offer of free land. Free land! He could choose a piece right here near the fort. After all, he was a sergeant and could have almost first pick.

The corporal, whose name Pollard hadn't learned yet, asked softly, "We goin' over, Sergeant?"

With a sigh, Pollard's attention was drawn from the beautiful, crisp day to the business at hand. "Yes. What's your name again?"

"Stewart Duncan."

"Well, Duncan, we can move."

More or less together, they walked to the alders. Pollard asked, "Are you goin' to sign on again and take up some land here?"

"Not on your life!" Duncan pushed aside an alder branch with his musket and waited for the sergeant to pass through before releasing it. "'Twas only in September the bastards scalped twenty-two men and one of our officers."

"I heard about it at Grand Pré. I knew Lieutenant March."

"You havin' that kind of trouble at Grand Pré?"

"You mean some of us gettin' ourselves kilt? Nah. We got all the Acadian men locked up in the church. They'll be loaded and gone by now."

"What'cher do with the wimmin," the corporal leered.

"They cooked for the prisoners and looked after their kids. We daren't touch 'em. One man did. He got the lash and went to Halifax."

"Oh."

Both men walked in silence for a few moments thinking about the gibbet, the fate that awaited any soldier who 'went to Halifax.'

The squad was together again on the other side of the alders. The next field was smaller with what appeared to be a sunken wagon track leading out the far side. The corporal advanced toward the track, only to be stopped by Sergeant

Pollard. "I don't want any of us to walk down that track. We'll cross further up, through the alders again."

Corporal Duncan blushed. "I guess that's why you were sent up from Grand Pré."

Pollard nodded. "'Tis my second campaign." He grinned at the other man and patted the top of his head. "Must be doin' somethin' right. Still got my hair."

Duncan moved ahead. "You heard the sergeant! Go through the alders. Don't bunch up!" He signalled for three different men to take the point this time.

Emerging from the bushes the patrol found the field clear. Nestled among some trees were an Inhabitant farmhouse and two small outbuildings.

"Form line of skirmish," Pollard ordered very softly. "If anybody's in there, I'd sorta like to surprise 'em."

The men spread out and, in a crouch, moved quickly to the little fence that kept the livestock away from the main door.

A dog was staked out near a small shed, barking and growling. A younger dog joined the first, creating a chorus of yaps. The first dog strained at his rope to get at the intruders. Someone inside the house shouted something in French.

"So much for surprising them," Corporal Duncan said. Motioning for one of his men to kick in the door, Duncan readied himself to charge into the house.

"Hold it, Corporal." Sergeant Pollard stepped forward. "You three men position yerselves behind me. The rest of you seek cover. Watch the tree line."

Drawing himself up to his full height of five foot eight, Pollard cleared his throat. He raised his chin and spoke loudly. "In the name of the king, come out now. You will not be hurt."

Almost immediately, the door opened and three men, probably farmers, came out into the sunlight. A black-haired man held a clay pitcher in his hands. The other men, one young and the second grey-haired and stooped with age, had obviously been drinking; they still held mugs in their hands.

Pollard motioned the Acadians away from the door. He called to the three men behind him, "Go inside. Look for anyone else. Search for guns."

"No guns, *monsieur*," said the grey-haired man in heavily accented English. He smiled and continued, "Governor take guns to the fort. No guns."

"Why didn't you report to the fort as ordered?"

"We finish *bière*. Then we go." He drew himself up proudly, "Loyal to king. We say oath to king. Make promise."

The New Englanders were aware that a number of the Inhabitants had taken the oath of allegiance to the king. In earlier years in Nova Scotia and even in later years elsewhere in the British Empire, that would have assured them of continued peaceful enjoyment of their homes and possessions. But this was 1755, and the governor in Halifax had declared all Inhabitants rebels, including those who had sworn allegiance to the English Crown. Loyal or not, these men were going to forfeit their lands, homes, and cattle, and it was the patrol's mission to ensure that no one was overlooked.

"Where are your women?"

"Go to fort ce *matin* with 'is son." The older man gestured at the black-haired man. "And we finish *bière*. Go to fort *bientôt*."

Without looking at the farmers Sergeant Pollard said, "You will go to the fort now." He turned his head and looked into the eyes of the older man. He was struck by the old fellow's forthrightness, which reminded him of the hell-and-damnation circuit minister at home. The farmer's hair fell off to one side over his eyes, and as he spoke he stared straight through the errant lock, never breaking his gaze.

"Finish your beer," Pollard said finally. "We must return to the fort."

The grey-haired man offered the sergeant some of his beer, which Pollard politely declined. Quaffing his beer, the old man asked, "What does colonel want?"

Pollard looked away from the penetrating eyes, his gaze falling to the old man's timeworn hands, the same hands as the circuit preacher's. As a boy Pollard had marvelled how reassuring those hands had been when they were raised over the heads of the congregation. He could still hear the minister intoning, "And the peace of the Lord be with you this day and forever more."

"*Pardonnez-moi, monsieur,* what colonel want?"

"No one else in the house, Sergeant!" One of the men of the patrol reported back that they had searched the house. "No guns."

"Check the outbuildings."

"Yes, Sergeant."

Pollard motioned the three men forward. There was some clinking and clanking as one of the soldiers handed Corporal Duncan some manacles. "We only have two sets, Sergeant." He held up the black iron wrist cuffs. "I got some rope for the third guy."

The old man was aghast. He shook his head and resisted as one of the soldiers tried to put the wrist cuffs on him. Two other soldiers raised their muskets and menaced the farmers with their bayonets.

"Mistake! *Je suis* ... I am loyal to *le roi! Pas moi!*" He danced back, pushing aside the bayonets that were attempting to control him so the cuffs could be locked into place.

"I not go! Not in chains!"

The other two men were standing passively, awaiting the outcome of the old man's protests.

"I not French! I ... loyal subject of the king!" There were tears in his eyes, whether of frustration or anger Pollard couldn't tell. "I learn English to be good man for *Le Colonel*." There was a flash of hope in his face, "*Le Colonel* tell you ... *arretêz!* Stop!' In a voice filled with conviction he said, firmly, "Colonel tell you ... no chain for Claude Boutlier!"

Sergeant Pollard nodded to the corporal, "Let them be. They won't cause us any trouble."

Duncan snorted a laugh. "Yes, let the colonel be the one to tell him." He laughed again. "All right, boys. You heard the sergeant. Form escort party for the prisoners."

The old man protested that he wasn't a prisoner and resisted being forced into the formation. Pollard assured the man that everything would be straightened out once they arrived at the fort.

With the corporal and three men at the front, the Inhabitants were in the middle of the column escorted by three soldiers. Four more soldiers, including the sergeant, took up the rear, and the scouting party marched across the field.

Looking back at the buildings, the sergeant thought this little farm might be just the spot for the Pollard family; it was close to the fort, and the land sloped gently. He stopped and studied the landscape. There was a good wood lot that served as protection from the north winds. He should have examined the well. He turned to march on and almost bumped into one of his men. The column had stopped. "What the hell?"

"With your permission, Sergeant, the old man says someone should look after his dogs. He says they'll need water."

"The old man is right. What's your name?"

"Anderson, Sergeant."

"Like I said, the old man is right. It's not the dogs' fault that these Frenchies aren't comin' back."

"Turn 'em loose, Sergeant?"

Giving it some thought, Pollard answered, "Nah. If let loose, they'll pack. Whoever gets to farm here will have a tough time runnin' down a pack of wild dogs." He glanced ahead at the prisoners. "You and ..."

"Tupper, Sergeant."

"You and Tupper go back and do 'em quiet like. We don't want the old man any more upset than he is."

"Yes, Sergeant."

Two of the rear guards left the formation and returned to the farm. The column continued across the field.

Damn! The corporal was leading them up the wagon trail. It was obvious he was going to pass into the next field by using the sunken wagon track. There were bushes close to the track and an elevated slope on either side; just the place for trouble, but Pollard hesitated giving the order to stop. He had already corrected his new corporal once today in front of the men. He wished he knew his men better.

Sergeant Pollard made up his mind. I don't know my men, he thought, and I can't do anything about that right now, but I do know that goddamned wagon track is not safe. He called ahead, "Corporal!"

From the farmyard came the unmistakable sounds of dogs being butchered.

Boutlier gave the sergeant a knowing look and lunged back down the path toward his home. Bowling over his guard, the old man got as far as Pollard before the butt of a musket knocked him to the ground.

Pollard helped Boutlier to his feet. "I can't do nothin' about the dogs. I can't do nothin' about you going to the fort." Sergeant Pollard held on to the old man's arm until he was steady on his feet, then pushed him gently toward the middle of the column. "Corporal, bunch 'em up! Double time outta here!"

The column moved off slowly, as the English prodded the reluctant farmers up the wagon track. Pollard remained behind in the field, waiting for his two men to return from the farmhouse. When he saw them coming, he trotted to the wagon track.

Damn, I must be getting old, he thought as he puffed up the slight incline; head down, musket held 'at the trail.' Sweat was pouring into his eyes, but when he glanced ahead it took him only a moment to realize that his prisoners were standing alone in the middle of the track! There were several muskets lying on the ground. How in Hades did that happen? His men were nowhere in sight!

Pollard set his feet and swung up his musket to check his prime. Anderson joined him, his weapon at the ready. By the sounds of running footsteps crunching on the gravel, Tupper was not far behind. Pollard aimed his musket at the nearest prisoner. "Anderson, advance and get those muskets! I'll shoot the first one that makes a move!"

Behind him a Scottish burr commanded, "Ground your muskets, boys! Do it right now!"

The three New Englanders froze. A man leaped down from the alders and grabbed the musket out of Anderson's hands. The black-haired Acadian grabbed a musket and butted him to the ground.

Meanwhile, Pollard turned to face the threat from the rear. He raised his musket to fire but hesitated; red hair and freckles—

this was the man they had tried to capture at River Habitant! It was Carrot Top Cameron, the deserter from the Fortieth Foot!

"Don't try it, Sergeant!" Carrot Top Cameron smiled coldly.

More men poured out of the alders. Pollard's skin crawled when he saw Indians in the French attack force. He made up his mind; he wasn't going to die without a fight!

"I said don't try it, Sergeant!"

It was then one of the new arrivals shot Pollard in the back.

\* \* \*

Robert Cameron turned the sergeant over. Blood oozed from both front and back of Pollard's blue jacket. He saw the sergeant's eyes flutter. "The ball went right through, Sergeant."

"Where are my men?" The red-haired deserter faded in and out of Pollard's sight, but the sergeant hung on. Maybe he could prevent the scalping. "Are they …"

"They were dragged into the bushes. I don't know …" Cameron stood up. Shielding his eyes from the glaring sun, he glanced up the wagon track and considered the possibilities. The Mi'kmaq warriors were obviously ready to slaughter the prisoners and take their trophies.

"Please, no!" An Englishman called in a pitiful plea for life. "Lord Jesus! Please!"

"There'll be none of that!" Cameron ran to the edge of the bushes and out of Pollard's view.

The Englishman continued his pleading more frantically. Another face loomed over Pollard, Claude Boutlier. He had torn a strip of cloth from his clothing. He balled it up and shoved it into the hole in Pollard's tunic. Pollard almost fainted with the pain.

"They not kill you."

"What about my men?"

"Maybe, maybe not." Boutlier leaned down and filled the space in the sky where Pollard was staring. "My wife? My daughter?"

"They're at the fort. We're waiting for ships to take them away."

Boutlier rocked back as if he had been struck in the face. "But I take the oath. I speak English."

Very tired, Pollard sighed. He interrupted the farmer. "It doesn't matter. You're French. You'll be ..."

"I am *not* French! *Je suis Acadien!*"

Vaguely, Pollard waved his hand. "It doesn't matter." The screaming from up the wagon path had stopped. He heard birds singing and English voices from the main road. Help was coming. He let it all go.

\* \* \*

Robert Cameron glanced at the quiet form on the ground and looked enquiringly at the farmer, who shrugged. "We must go," Cameron said in English. He corrected himself almost immediately and repeated the instructions in French.

"*Je ne vais pas*, I can't go," the old man said. "They have my wife, my daughter."

"You'll do them no good inside that fort. It is better that we strike back. We might be able to rescue them."

When the older man didn't move Cameron pulled on his sleeve. "We must go."

"*Il est facile pour vous dire.* It is easy for you to say. You have your wife with you."

"Reine fights like a man. I could lose her at any time." The approaching troops were closer now. "Please, Monsieur. We must leave now."

"*Où est-ce que nous irons? Qu'est-ce que nous ferons?* Where would we go? What would we do?"

"*Nous suivons les ordres. Peut-être que nous attaquerons le fort. Peut-être que nous irons à Royale d'Ilot.* We follow orders. Perhaps we'll attack the fort. Maybe we'll go to Isle Royale."

Claude Boutlier sat down next to the still form of the wounded sergeant, and lifted his head to his lap. "He lives," Claude said to Robert Cameron, but Cameron, followed by the slight, boyish figure of his wife, had already disappeared into the bushes at the far side of the field.

At the top of the wagon trail, the oncoming troops found

the members of the scouting party trussed like pigs, lying where they had been dragged.

"They're in the bushes!"

"Careful! It might be a trap!"

"Help us," Pollard's men cried plaintively.

"Wonder of wonders! They're alive!"

"You will live, Sergeant," Claude Boutlier said, "but you English will never own this land." Tears sprang to his eyes. "*Je survivrais.* I will survive," he repeated firmly. "We must survive to return to have our revenge."

\* \* \*

On the second of December,[5] five vessels arrived at Les Mines with the rest of the First Battalion. Major Prebble, Parson Phillips, and Captain Speakman travelled further to visit Grand Pré. Lieutenant Bancroft was officer of the guard the afternoon the courier warned them of the proposed visit.

Bancroft arranged to greet his comrades with all the military flourishes that befit a proper fort. He mustered his men at the back entrance to the fort where a flagstaff had been erected and flew the Jack. His men were drawn up in two ranks, bayonets fixed and muskets loaded without ball, ready to give a salute to the visitors to rival any regular army fort in New England. He had asked for volunteers to join his own men so that the honour guard would be larger and the volley more impressive.

At the last moment, five more soldiers appeared at the side of what was now called the parade square. "Hurry on," Bancroft told them. "Our visitors will be here at any moment. I appreciate that you volunteered. You're not loaded with ball, are you?"

"No, sir, we're not."

"Make another two files, at the end." Bancroft craned his neck to see if all was in order. "Parker, move to your left! Make the blank file! Blank file, man! That's right!"

A sentry warned him, "There's a party coming up the main street."

"Guard! Atten-*shun!*"

Major Prebble and Captain Speakman knew what was happening when they saw the honour guard drawn up near the flagstaff. They stopped walking and stood at attention. Parson Phillips, however, completely oblivious, continued walking and talking. "Of course the church is always open to the poor and unfortunate, but one must not be seen to be indulgent to ..."

Phillips was utterly astounded when he was faced with an armed force whose weapons were raised to the firing position. When the order was given to fire, his yelp was drowned in the impressive noise of the salute, but everyone saw his frantic dance as he tried to decide in which direction he should run.

"Guard! Order arms!"

The parson watched as Prebble and Speakman returned the salute and managed, "Thank you, men!" But he couldn't help but see their very broad grins.

Bancroft returned his sword to its scabbard. He ordered an ensign to dismiss the guard with his thanks for a fine show, and joined his friends. They made their way to the command tent, the largest covered area left to the militia in Grand Pré, since all of the structures except for the church had been burned. They sat around the colonel's table enjoying each other's company, some *bière d'épinette*, and good food.

"Beggin' your pardon sirs, but is this a 'no rank' night?" Speakman asked the major and Captain Osgood, Grand Pré's new commanding officer.

Major Prebble quickly agreed. "This is probably the last time we'll be together. Our enlistment is up, and some of us are leaving. Yes, it's a good time to have a no rank evening."

Speakman grinned. "Then, Jerry, I guess you don't miss the old bugger."

"You mean Colonel Winslow?"

"Excuse me, gentlemen. I think I'll retire and gather my thoughts for the morning parade." The parson stood and brushed some crumbs from his black suit. "The food and company were very good, Lieutenant. Thank you." He hesitated. "The bread was exceptionally good. Would you tell the cook ..."

"It wasn't the cook," Bancroft said. "One of the prisoners has been making bread for us. I'm going to miss it when she goes."

"Oh, well, then. Good night, all."

"Good night, Parson."

"The parson's performance lets you off the hook, Jerry," Captain Osgood said as soon as the parson had gone. "Your romp through the woods has been overtaken by Parson Phillips's dance of terror!"

"Yes! Yes!" the other officers agreed.

Prebble shook his head. "It's too bad old Winslow wasn't here to see Parson Phillips's Panic Prance."

Bancroft laughed along with the men. "I never seemed to do anything right for the colonel after that night. He and I were always out of step."

"Not really your fault, Jerry," Captain Speakman said thoughtfully. "Our colonel was trying to act like a regular army colonel. That has its problems when you don't have the background or training."

Bancroft held up his hands to stop the talking. "Well, you boys can say what you like. Sergeant Pollard always told me ..."

Prebble looked up so sharply that Bancroft stopped talking. "What? What did I say?"

"You didn't hear about Pollard?"

"What! Tell me!"

Captain Speakman started to tell the story but Prebble said, "Let me tell it. I was there."

"Sergeant Pollard was on patrol. He came across three Inhabitants. They weren't carrying weapons. He considered they looked like honourable men, so he didn't bind them ..."

"Is he dead?"

"No. Takes more then a musket ball in the shoulder to kill our Sergeant Pollard. He and two soldiers let the men walk down the trail ahead of them. Everything seemed to be just fine for a while."

"What happened? Where did they get the musket to shoot Pollard with?"

"Well, they were walking all in a line: the three Frenchmen in front, then a soldier, Pollard and a second soldier. A man came out of the bushes behind the last soldier. He had a musket and shouted something in French."

Captain Osgood said, "Must have been Boishebert. He's been stirring up trouble."

Speakman said, "I don't think so because his next words were, 'Ground your muskets, boys! Do it right now!'"

Bancroft had a sinking feeling in the pit of his stomach. "Ground your muskets? He must have been an English soldier." He put his head in his hands. "He didn't have red hair, did he?"

"I don't know, but Pollard swears he was the same man who was at River Habitant."

"The deserter," Bancroft said hollowly. "I had him dead in my sights at River Habitant."

Prebble reached across and touched the lieutenant's arm. "It happens, Jeremiah. The lead soldier had his weapon pulled out of his hands. The rear soldier lowered his weapon. Pollard turned to face the threat from the rear and raised his musket to fire."

Speakman couldn't help interrupting Prebble's story. "The stranger said, 'Don't try it, Sergeant!' At almost the same moment, some other bastard shot him down. In the back."

Major Prebble continued, "I was in the area with a patrol of forty men. We heard the shot and weren't more than five minutes getting to our sergeant, but the bastards were gone. We searched for them, but couldn't find them."

"Three more recruits for Charles de Boishebert," Bancroft observed.

"No, only two. One of them stayed with the patrol and was taken into the fort. Seems he had family there."

"What happened to him? Hanged?"

"No, deported, with the rest. Gone."

"The other two escaped to join the renegades?"

"Yes," said Prebble, "but they won't survive the winter because we burned every god-damned thing!" Major Prebble slammed his fist on the table. "There will be no hole for them to crawl into."

"Boishebert is no fool. He'll take his men and their families to Isle Royale or Isle Saint Jean. They'll have a good winter."

The men were silent momentarily, each thinking thoughts of his own.

"Old Pollard is probably back in Boston right now," Prebble laughed. "His winter will be spent in front of a pub's fire with a good, dark ale in his hand."

Speakman hunched his shoulders. "It'll be cold here. We'll soon have snow. I can feel it."

Captain Speakman was right. The first real snow of the season came the next morning as the garrison prepared for morning parade. The visiting party hurried away to Les Mines so they wouldn't be snowbound at Grand Pré. Parson Phillips missed giving his sermon.

*19 December 1755*
*Grand Pré*

"It's time, Matilde." Bancroft didn't know whether or not the woman understood him, but she knew from his pantomime that she had to gather her things and leave.

"Sylvie!"

Her niece came around the edge of the tent wiping her hands on her apron.

"*Il devrait nous faire partir d'ici.* He's here to make us leave."[6]

Sylvie wasn't surprised. Two transports had been loading the six hundred Grand Pré prisoners since the tenth of December. There were forty or fifty prisoners left, and they could hear the soldiers marshalling them at the fort. Sylvie slipped off her apron and folded it carefully before she placed it with the bread pans and utensils. "I'll get the box, Tante Matilde. You please get our clothes."

Matilde picked up the clothes and walked out the door without saying a word. Sylvie carried the box, and they joined the line of prisoners being moved down the hill to the loading area.

The way was clearly marked by the trail of footprints in the well-packed snow. The fallen snow camouflaged the piles of personal effects other prisoners had been forced to abandon at the water's edge. The trail wound through the snowy mounds ending at the red mud of the bank where boats waited to receive them.

The boats were already partially filled by the time it was the women's turn. Matilde was loaded easily, one sailor helping the older woman step into the boat, and another on the boat settling her on her seat. When it was Sylvie's turn to step onto the boat, the sailor wrenched the box out of Sylvie's hands and threw it off to one side. "Can't take a big thing like that, girlie."

"*Je dois prendre notre boîte!* I must take our box!" Sylvie cried. "It has everything important to us!"

The sailor didn't understand French. He lifted the young girl and placed her, none too gently, on the boat. The second sailor reached out to pull her along to sit down by the older woman. Sylvie would have probably gone quietly except Matilde screamed, "*Mes objets d'argent, Je ne peux pas laisser mon argent! Le roi de France les a donnés à ma famille!* My pieces of silver, I can't leave my pieces of silver! The King of France gave them to my family!"

Sylvie struggled against the sailor, who couldn't hold her. She jumped out of the boat. Both sailors moved to get her, and the nearest soldier levelled his musket and threatened her with his bayonet.

Bancroft was standing close by talking with Nathan Simons and William Gray. He heard the commotion and saw it was Sylvie. The two army officers strode to the side of the boat, and Bancroft ordered, "Hold, I say!"

The soldier and the two sailors let Sylvie go, and she ran to the box, turned it right side up, and opened it.

"What is it?" Bancroft asked Simons.

"She seems to want something from the box."

Bancroft told the guard and the sailors to let the girl be for the moment. The soldier turned his back on the girl and began watching the rest of the prisoners in the line. The sailors continued loading.

Sylvie pulled a leather pouch out of the bottom of the box. She hesitated, looking into the box with obvious regret. She selected another bag and slammed the lid shut. When she stood, she became aware that the boat containing her aunt was moving quickly down the creek to the ship named *Union*.

A sailor took her arm and pulled her toward the only other boat left in the creek. The boat Sylvie was being shoved into had a much longer name than the one toward which her aunt was heading. She wasn't going to the same ship as her aunt! "Tante Matilde," she screamed. "Come back! I must be with my aunt!"

Matilde was crying and moaning, "Sylvie. My Sylvie!" One of the sailors had shipped his oar and held the old woman down.

Gray rejoined the army officers. "Having a problem?

Bancroft asked Simons, "What's the matter now?"

"She wants to be with her aunt who's going to *Union*." Simons glanced down at the last longboat. "This boat is going to the other ship."

"Shit!" Bancroft's thoughts raced. Finally he said, "Tell her that both ships are in the same convoy and are going to the same place."

While Simons translated for the girl, Bancroft asked Gray, "Any chance we can recall that boat?"

"Look around, Jerry," Gray said. "This is the last boat. Unless you have more prisoners somewhere, this is the end of the operation. It's over when the transports leave the basin, and they're leaving right away. The convoy sails on this tide."

Lieutenant Simons leaned back and spoke quietly to Bancroft. "She asks if you can bring the other boat back to get her."

"Tell her no. Tell her that both ships are leaving right now and going to the same place." Bancroft smiled at Sylvie. "Tell her to get in the boat. The ships must leave right now."

Simons told the girl, and Sylvie got in the boat. Bancroft reached down and picked up the box and handed it to her. The sailors pushed away from the shore.

All the way out to the basin, Sylvie looked back at the shore, finally giving a little wave just before she went out of sight around the point.

The three officers watched as the boats were hoisted on board the transports and the ships made ready to sail.

Gray extended his hand to Simons. "Nice to have met you, Simons. I'm leaving right now for Les Mines. If I'm lucky I'll catch *Warren* for Halifax. Otherwise, I'll have to sail on another ship all the way to Boston before I can get home."

"Well, I wish you luck with that." Simons shook Gray's hand and left to join his men at the fort.

Gray grasped Bancroft's hand. "I hope I see you again, Jerry."

"I'll probably be among the last to leave. The First Battalion is gone. Tradition says the Second Battalion is always the first into battle and the last to leave."

"I hope you get home soon."

"I'll walk you over to your horse."

"I have an idea," Gray said. "If you like, I can leave the horse at Les Mines with your name on it. That way you could have her."

"No, I'd better not."

"Well, it was a thought." Gray pulled the reins over Shadow's head and mounted. "I'm sorry about that girl, Sylvie."

"Why? It's not so bad really. They won't travel together, but when they get to the other end, they'll be together again."

Gray cast a sharp look at his friend. "One ship's going to Boston, the other to North Carolina."

Bancroft's face turned white. "No! I saw the list. They're both going to Boston. They're in the same convoy!"

"The convoy commander changed that. One to Boston, the other to the Carolinas."

"But ..."

"I thought you were telling her the ships were going to the same place just to get her to leave."

Bancroft didn't answer. He looked out to the basin. Only one ship was in view, and she was moving quickly out of sight.

"I thought you knew, Jerry."

Bancroft remembered the girl's little wave. "No, I didn't know."

\* \* \*

That night, the corporal of the night watch awakened Jeremiah Bancroft.

"What is it, Corporal?"

"The naval officer is back, Lieutenant. Says his horse fell. Says he wants to stay here."

"Is he all right?"

"Yessir. He's a mite cold but we got him wrapped up real good in front of a fire." The corporal grinned. "He's drinkin' tea and eatin' bread covered with maple syrup like there's no tomorrow."

Bancroft ducked his head back under the warm blankets. "Tell him to curl up somewhere. I'll see him in the morning."

"Yessir, Lieutenant."

\* \* \*

In the cook tent Bancroft regarded his friend with some concern. "Looks to me like you got a touch of frostbite on your nose and ears."

Gray put his hand up to his nose.

"Don't rub it! You'll be sorry if you do. Just leave it be. If it's going to drop off, it'll drop off."

"God! You're a cheerful sort of person."

Bancroft laughed. He enjoyed teasing his friend. "Tell me what happened."

"Shadow slipped on the ice. She couldn't get up. I had to shoot her."

"It was closer to come here?"

"Yes. I had a choice, either come here or go all the way to Les Mines. There is absolutely nothing in between. Somebody went around and burned it all down."

"Yes, we did a good job."

"There was nowhere for me to seek shelter. Just here or Les Mines." Gray shivered. "It was cold!"

Bancroft took a sip of his hot tea. "Let's hope that the escaped prisoners have as hard a time out there."

Gray hunched his shoulders and cradled his teacup for warmth. "After last night, I pity the poor bastards."

"What are you going to do now? You missed your ship."

"Yes. *Warren* is gone, and the fleet has sailed. I'll have to make my own way to Halifax."

"That's not easy," Bancroft warned. "You'd better wait until the next draft of the Second Battalion to leave here."

"Will that be soon?"

"Probably. We burned so many houses to the ground, there isn't enough winter lodging for the number of men garrisoned here. That church is as cold as a whore's heart, and after a night in a tent it takes hours for the chill to leave a man's body."

"I felt that last night." Gray had a blanket over his shoulders. He pulled it tighter around his chest and tucked it under his arms. "When do you think the first party will leave for Halifax?"

"Not until after Christmas now."

"We can pass the time with a little bit of hunting."

"Hunting? It's too hard to move around in the woods. Too much snow."

"We could try those hoop things on our feet like the Micmac."

"Not me. Good food, a good fire, and lots and lots of sleep should keep me busy until spring, William." Bancroft closed his eyes. "When I'm asleep, I think of home and Elisabeth. Maybe I'll be on the first draft out of here."

"You never know," said a shivering Gray. "I know I will."

## *Endnotes*

[1] Governor's letters. NS Archives.

[2] Governor's letters. NS Archives

[3] Description of the day and events are from the Bourgeois Family book.

[4] The story of Sergeant Pollard is based on a tale that is told by the Brewsters in the Annapolis Valley.

[5] The visit is fact according to Bancroft's diary but much of the detail is fiction.

[6] One of the last ships, on the last day, was diverted from its original destination, according to the Governor's letters.

## Chapter Ten

*1 January 1756*
*Pisiquid River*

They had begun the trek to Halifax full of resolve, but that had been days ago. The snow, the cold, the endless hiking uphill and down had stripped them of every thought or concern except seeking shelter.[1]

"See that smoke over there?" Solomon Wyman pointed with a snow-encrusted mitten. "That's Fort Edward." Wyman had a scarf wound over his hat and under his chin. His breath came in long streams of white vapour in the still, cold air. His feet were wrapped in portions of a blanket which was tied around his ankles with pieces of rope. He had slung his musket over his back with another rope when they were leaving Grand Pré, advising the eleven other men in the party, "Don't touch no metal with your bare skin. If you do, you'll stick to it." Since that time, Wyman hadn't touched the weapon again.

The men had taken on strange shapes. Blanket rolls and muskets were slung over their backs. Their chests and legs were twice their normal size with bits of cloth and blankets stuffed into their clothes to help conserve warmth, and they had all followed Wyman's example of footwear. They were festooned like Christmas trees with the various bits and pieces of military accoutrements that no longer fit their current external body sizes. Bayonets and scabbards were tied to bedrolls, cartridge pouches dangled from rope belts on one side, water flasks filled with rum on the other, and personal effects hung on one arm while ration pouches and mess kits were on the other.

The men stopped to gaze at smoke in the distance that promised rest and warmth. "How far do you think it is, Solomon?"

William Gray recognized the top of the hill. He had rested here one fine autumn day and ate an apple. "A couple of miles. It's downhill from here to the river. I've been here before."

Jeremiah Bancroft wiped the drip from his nose on his sleeve. "No problems from here to the fort?"

"The river is tidal at Fort Edward, so most of it won't be frozen. If the tide's in, we'll have to wait until ebb tide to cross."

"Christ!" Wyman said. "We have to wait in this cold for the damn water to go down?"

"There's the village. We could seek shelter there," one of the other men said.

Remembering the desolation on the trail from Grand Pré to Les Mines, Gray wasn't so sure they would find shelter, but he kept his mouth shut. It was bad enough he had mentioned the tide.

Without another word, the men rushed down the hill and headed for the comfort promised at Fort Edward. The going was easy; the snow was not deep and what there was had been packed by the winds and coated with a firm crust. They were soon at the river, which was flooding. The muddy red water swirled upstream carrying slush and chunks of ice past the men.

There was no discussion as to what the group had to do next. "We need some shelter," Wyman observed. "Where's the village, sir?"

Gray looked where he had last seen the village of Cinq Maisons. "There were five houses just over there." He didn't bother to say that they were gone; the men could see that.

"Let's go see if there is anything left."

"If the Fort Edward boys did their jobs properly there won't be."

Bancroft waved his men forward. "They weren't Phenehas Company. We'll find something!"

It was getting colder. Darkness had brought with it a numbing wind. The men investigated every mound, scuffing the snow with their feet in an effort to find something, anything. The cold settled deeper into their bodies. Karl Schuppel, the one they called the 'little German' fell down in a tangle of his own feet. He groaned. "It sounds … hollow."

"Look under Karl! Move him over and look under him!" Bancroft grabbed Karl's bayonet and began to dig.

"There's nothing down there," Wyman complained. Nevertheless, he grabbed his bayonet and began to scratch the ground. "The French didn't have cellars!" "Aha!" Bancroft giggled. He had dug out a black space. He stuck his hand in and then his whole arm. "We got ourselves a cellar!" With help from two of the half-frozen men, Bancroft tore out a couple of boards. Using one of the boards as a prod he felt around in the hole. Thump! Thump! "Feels like a table down there." Before anyone could stop him, he lowered himself into the hole. "It's big!" he hollered up to the waiting men. "Come down, one at a time. There's a table and a dirt floor. Come down! Come down!"

Wyman was the next man down. He opened his flint and tinder and struck a light. By the feeble flare, he found some fancy candles and lit some.

It was a big cellar. All of the men fitted in with some space to spare. The combined heat from several candles and their bodies was welcome relief from the cold. Bedrolls were broken out, and soon the men were asleep.

The next day was bright and colder, if that was possible. Bancroft had wakened every time the candles had gone out, so there was only one left. He lit it. The shaft of light through the hole and the light from the candle allowed him to inspect the cellar. There were stairs, but there was no way to open the trap; it was frozen over and covered with debris.

Little Schuppel held up a badly stained green jacket. "Looks like part of a Ranger's uniform."

It was Bancroft who found the red coat. "Fortieth Regiment of Foot," he said. "They were with us at Fort Beauséjour." He opened it. "Initials are H. M. We'll make a note of it and report our find to the regiment. Any initials on the other jacket?"

Schuppel gingerly inspected the inside of the Ranger's coat. "It could be C. R. Or maybe G. R."

Bancroft pointed up the hole. "Let's go have a nice warm meal at Fort Edward, gentlemen. That is, if the tide's right."

The tide was just right.

\* \* \*

The eleven men rested a day at the fort. William Gray nursed his tender ears. They had been touched by frost at Grand Pré and had been very sensitive to the cold of the march.

At Fort Edward, all of the men adjusted their gear according to where the cold had sapped heat from their bodies. They used a double layer of blankets for their feet. The fort had plenty of Inhabitants' blankets left, so each man doubled his blanket roll even though it made them very bulky.

On 3 January, the men resumed their march early in the morning. They walked all day, and had a warm meal around the campfire that night. The men slept spoon-style wrapped in their clothes and all of their blankets. In spite of this, Karl Schuppel was found frozen to death in the morning.[2]

The next day was a long tedious march full of recriminations as to who let the fire go out. The men were short-tempered with each other, suffering as they were from the cold, fatigue, and guilt at having lost one of their own to carelessness. By the time they reached Fort Sackville at the end of the fourth day of the march, the comradeship of Phenehas Company was gone. They were strangers to each other. Lieutenant Bancroft and Lieutenant Gray were not spared.

### 15 January 1756
### *Halifax, Nova Scotia*

"Will it hurt much?" Molly Gray held tightly to her husband's arm as they walked down George Street. It was a cold, miserable day. The wind off the harbour attacked exposed flesh as if it meant to flail the skin. Tears ran down Molly's face as her eyes protested the wind's assault.

William Gray, huddled into his coat as much as possible, glanced up long enough to get his bearings. He tucked his chin into his collar, turned his wife around and, with the wind at their backs, they made easy progress to the door of a naval supply store where Gray often did business for the Crown.

Through the store window the proprietor saw them coming. He forced open the door against the wind to allow the lieutenant and his wife to enter. He slammed the door against the cold.

"Ah! The lieutenant and his good wife," the proprietor said in jolly tones.[3]

"Yes, Mr. Stairs." Gray unwound the scarf that he had wrapped around his throat and chin. "This is my wife, Mrs. Gray. Molly, I'd like you to meet Mr. Stairs who, I hope, will allow us a few moments of warmth in his establishment before we go down the hill on our errand."

"How very nice to meet you, Madame, and, of course, Lieutenant, I am pleased that you thought to seek shelter in my place of business." With a bow, Stairs swept his arm somewhat theatrically in the direction of a little alcove. "Please! Warm yourselves by the fire." He raised his voice, "Phillip! Another chair for the lieutenant." Stairs pulled a wooden chair closer to the stove. A moment later, a young man came from the rear of the shop and placed another chair next to it.

"You are so very kind, Mr. Stairs," Molly said as she loosened her outer clothing and sat down. "I was near to perishing."

"Couldn't have that, now could we," Stairs said with a laugh. "Oh dear! Here comes another refugee from the cold! Please excuse me!" He hurried to the front of the shop to help the man in.

With a blast of cold air, the customer came into the shop, stamping his feet to rid his boots of snow. The door closed behind him, he asked about chains and link sizes. Soon, Stairs and the man were talking business. William and Molly Gray had the little corner to themselves.

Gray gave his wife a kiss on the cheek. "You asked me if it would hurt. No, it really won't hurt, but it's very dangerous."

"Then why do it?"

"Because it's more dangerous not to have it done, Molly."

Molly Gray didn't say anything.

"Molly," William continued, "you saw Mr. Stair's face and neck, didn't you?"

"Yes."

"Well, he's one of the lucky ones. He just has the scars. He could have died or ... "

"He could have gone blind. I know, dear."

"Surgeon Thomas treated me and a lot of the men at Fort Lawrence. I was sick for a day or two."

"How sick, William? You didn't mention it in your letters."

"I had fever and nausea, but I didn't die."

"Did all of the men have it done?"

"No. There were several men I knew well, close friends, who wouldn't have it done."

There was another gust of air. The customer had left. Molly squeezed her husband's hand. "Smallpox! It is so frightening!"

Mr. Stairs came across the shop. "Smallpox! It's started again?" He put his hand to his face, unconsciously rubbing the deep scars. "Last year my wife caught the pox. The doctor bled her so much there was nothing left to her when they carried her out. By that time, my son was sick. The doctor bled him, too. I was supposed to give the dear boy washings and apply plasters to raise fever blisters, but he died the second day of my fever. I was too sick with smallpox to help him."

"You lived. You were lucky." Gray avoided studying the marks on the other man's face, but Molly couldn't take her eyes off him.

"What did the doctor do to save you?" Molly Gray asked as she finally took her eyes off the man's face. She turned her attention to the pattern of the wood on the arm of the chair.

Mr. Stairs gave an embarrassed laugh. "Your pardon, Madame, but there wasn't very much left of me either. The doctor gave me six consecutive enemas. It must have worked because here I am! But has it started again? The smallpox, I mean!"

Gray shook his head. "As far as I know, there isn't any sickness in the city."

"You don't get it twice, you know. The doctor told me once you've had it, you don't get it again."

Stairs was agitated with thoughts of a smallpox epidemic so Gray was quick to reassure him. "I believe that. I want my wife to have some smallpox given to her so she only gets it a little."

"Oh, no! Don't do that! Smallpox is terrible! Stay away from anyone with the pox! Burn everything. Don't let your wife have any sort of contact with it!"

"I had it done."

Stairs, despite his belief that he couldn't get the pox again, stepped away from Gray. "You have the pox!"

Gray gave the man a lazy smile. "Of course not. I had a little fever months ago. I was a bit sick for a couple of days but otherwise quite all right, and I won't get it again."

Stairs leaned closer, examining Gray's face. "No scars!"

"No scars." Gray pushed his chair back and extended his hand to his wife to help her up. "I think we had better go along, dear."

"Yes, of course, William." Molly Gray stood and adjusted her clothing for the cold air. "I am truly sorry about your family, Mr. Stairs."

"Thank you, Madame." He helped Gray push the door open. "God be with you, Mrs. Gray."

When the door had closed behind them, Molly put her arm through her husband's.

"Shall we go back home, Molly?"

"You want me to have the treatment, don't you, William?"

"Yes, I do, Molly. You might get full-blown smallpox by taking the treatment and," he hesitated, "you might die, but Surgeon Thomas convinced me it is the best thing to do. He said the risk of taking the treatment is less than the risks we take being in a city with the pox on the loose. I'd ask Thomas to do it for us, but he has no more treatment materials."

Molly pulled on his arm and led him downhill to the appointment.

\* \* \*

The room, a small space in the back of the Duke Street Apothecary, was clean. The midwife was so old it was almost impossible to see her face for wrinkles. Her hands were young though, and it was her hands on which Molly Gray concentrated.

The old woman took three needles and laid them side-by-side. "There's no one else in the city who has the knowledge and materials to do this for you."

"Yes," Gray answered. "I asked everywhere. You were recommended to us, Mrs. Forbes."

"I like to be called Midwife Forbes, please."

Molly Gray blinked her eyes a couple of times. "Midwife Forbes, what are you going to do?"

The midwife patted the younger woman's arm. "Don't you worry at all. I'll explain as we go along." She glanced over at Gray and then back to her patient. "You're not shy with your man, are you? Do you want him to leave?"

"Oh, no! I want William here!" Molly reached for her husband's hand. He got up from where he had been sitting and stood by his wife, taking her hand in his.

"You'll have to let go of him, dearie, but he can stand close. Open the front of your habit, please. What I am going to do is prick your skin in several places." Midwife Forbes waited while Molly loosened her clothing. Then the midwife reached down and opened Molly's clothes so that her breast was exposed. "First I'll take a small amount of blood from your right breast. "

Molly flinched but didn't say anything as the midwife drew the blood.

"Then from the hollow of your stomach." The midwife probed the flesh until she had some blood on the needle. She placed the specimen on a plate near the sample from the breast. "Then from your belly button," she said as she worked, "your right wrist ... and your left ankle."

By this time Molly's face shone with perspiration. She became more frightened as the procedure got closer to the awful moment when smallpox would be put intentionally into her body.

Midwife Forbes reached under the table and with a sense of drama brought forth a sealed jar. She held the jar at eye level. "This contains liquid matter taken from the heads of ripe smallpox pustules."

Molly Gray gasped.

"I assure you," Forbes said, "it is the very best kind, removed from a person who eventually recovered. The others I threw away." She broke the seal. Taking some liquid she mixed it with each of the blood samples on the plate. When she was through, she said, "Now, dearie, if you are ready?"

Molly didn't answer, so Forbes cautioned, "Once I start I

can't stop, because the mixture must be presented to the body in the order the samples were taken."

When the young woman remained silent, Midwife Forbes took Molly's chin in her hands and lifted her face. "You'd rather not have the pox. You don't want that face scarred, do you, my pretty?"

### 21 January 1756
### Customs House, Halifax

"My dear William! How very nice to see you again."

Gray heard Richard Bulkeley's voice before he saw him, and made a wager with himself. I bet he's dressed in his dragoon greens and sword, he thought. His man is also dressed in green and standing about four feet aft. Gray turned. Whoops! He lost. Bulkeley's man was at the counter retrieving some papers. "Hello, Richard. You're looking well."

"I believe I'm looking a sight better than you are, my hearty! Why you would ever walk out of the Fundy in the dead of winter, I will never know. You almost died!"

"There weren't enough winter quarters for all the soldiers garrisoned at Grand Pré. I had to come back anyway, so I joined the first draft leaving the Fundy. You're right, though. Damn near died. When our army burned everything, they were thinking about the French who might want to move about the countryside in winter; they weren't thinking about themselves! The winter damn near got us!"

"One of the soldiers died, didn't he?"

"Unfortunately, yes. The campfire went out, and he froze."

"Yes. Well." Bulkeley glanced around the customs house as if looking for a change of subject. "What are you doing here, William?"

"Molly wants me to order some windows from Boston. I came to find out what the tariff would be."

"Don't ask your questions here, my friend. Come see me at Government House. I'll put you in touch with people who can be of service, like my good friend, Mauger."

Gray's face registered his surprise. "Christ, Richard, Mauger?

He was the smuggler I was trying to catch back in 1750! Governor Cornwallis wouldn't give that crook the time of day!"

"Times are different, William." Seeing the disapproval on his friend's face Bulkeley asked, "And where is Molly? I haven't seen her since …"

"She's been sick. Nothing really serious, but I stayed by her side."

"So your rundown condition can't all be laid at the door of Old Man Winter." Bulkeley put his hand on Gray's arm. "Dear friend, I'm having an evening to wish the officers of the New England Militia a safe trip home. Would you and your lady like to come?"

Gray thought fleetingly of the rift between Jeremiah Bancroft and himself. "I don't think so. Thank you, Richard."

"Isn't Molly well enough?"

"Actually, she's feeling much better, but …"

"Amy will be hostess, and she'll be very disappointed if you don't bring Molly." When he saw Gray's hesitation, Bulkeley beckoned to his man, who responded immediately. "Ensure that Lieutenant and Mrs. Gray have an invitation to the militia soirée." Not waiting for an acknowledgment, Bulkeley put an arm over Gray's shoulder. "Now, William. You come see me at your leisure, and we'll find out what Mr. Mauger can do about your windows."

Bulkeley gently steered Gray to the door of the customs house and out into the cold air. "It was good to see you again, William. You look after Molly. Bring her to the soirée now, mind." Bulkeley held the door open for a thickset man who stepped around Gray to get in the building.

"Jolly good of you to hold the door for me, Mr. Bulkeley."

"Not at all, Captain. I want to stay in the good graces of customs agents."

*3 February 1756*
*Halifax, Nova Scotia*

William and Molly Gray descended from the cab-for-hire and stood in the driveway of Richard Bulkeley's house. The afternoon had been very spring-like, and they inhaled deeply the warm sea air that was melting the snow and causing water to drip and run everywhere.

"I was here several times with Penelope Hay last year. You know, William, you can't see them now for the snow, but Richard has large gardens on either side of the verandas. He has the best vegetables and flowers in Halifax. Over there, behind the house are the stables."

Gray raised his arm and pointed. "Look, Molly! Isn't that a pretty sight?"

"Yes, considering it is probably the largest private building in the city."

"I didn't mean the house. Look! Dartmouth is still in bright sunlight while here, on the side of the citadel, we're in evening shadows." Gray lapsed into silence as the ships in the harbour, one after another, were swept up in the darkening folds. Dusk overtook Dartmouth Cove, which was in the lee of the town, and then, like a lamp being blown out, the brightness disappeared from the faces of the houses. Here and there, already, lights winked at the young couple.

Molly Gray, quick to sense her husband's moods, waited while he took in the scene of the most wonderful harbour in the world.

"We could probably fit the whole of the Royal Navy in this harbour and still have room to run races with every longboat in the fleet." Gray sighed. "I love it here. I wish my mother could have seen it." He took his wife into his arms. "I wish she could have met you, Molly."

The music from inside Bulkeley's house got suddenly louder as a door opened. "I see you two."

"That's Amy," Molly said.

Gray gave his wife a quizzical look.

Molly whispered, "Amy Rous, your hostess." She pushed at her husband's arm. "You men! If it isn't a ship, you don't pay any mind."

"I want you to come in here, right this minute," Amy called. "I heard you arrive ten minutes ago. What in the world have you two been doing?"

"Admiring the view, Miss Rous." Gray addressed the daughter of Captain Rous formally. "It's magnificent from here."

They stepped inside. Perhaps fifty people were gathered in the foyer and the drawing room. Two hearths burned brightly with lively fires. A small group of musicians played softly at the end of a reception room on the opposite side of the foyer from the drawing room.

A manservant took their coats. Amy, meanwhile, pushed Molly along with other ladies who were heading to the 'ladies' room.'

Gray hadn't quite finished getting rid of the coats when Amy took his arm. "William, I'm a friend of Molly's, and I want to be a friend of yours."

"Thank you." Gray felt his face going crimson.

"And I can't be a good friend if you go around calling me Miss Rous." She didn't let him answer. "I was speaking to Lieutenant Simons. He told me about another friend of yours." Without letting go of Gray's arm, Amy Rous reached into a circle of militia officers and pulled one of the men out of the gathering. "Excuse me, gentlemen. I have need of Lieutenant Bancroft." She led both officers into the dining room, and from the doorway motioned for someone to join her. "Wimper, these men have an important meeting. They are not to be disturbed until I say so."

Jeremiah Bancroft and William Gray watched Amy and Wimper pull the large doors closed.

Both men spoke at once. "I meant to see you ..."

"Sorry, I didn't get in touch ..."

They tried again. "We weren't well when we had the disagreement ..."

"We shouldn't have argued ..."

Bancroft stuck out his hand. "I've missed you, William."

Gray took Bancroft's hand. "Me too."

"Did you bring Molly?"

"Yes."

"Let's see if we can get out of here." Bancroft put his hand on the door latch.

"I dunno, Jerry. Wimper's on the other side of the door. Maybe not."

The door slid open. "Maybe Wimper listens on the other side of doors, gentlemen." Captain Rous's man grinned and walked away.

Amy Rous spotted them and smiled. She indicated with a movement of her head that they should go to the end of the foyer, where Gray saw his wife at the centre of attention, surrounded as she was by members of the militia. Major Prebble was complimenting her on her beautiful blue dress.

"Why thank you, Major," Molly responded as space was made for Gray and Bancroft. "I like to wear blue because it complements my husband's uniform."

Gray laughed and took his wife's arm. "That's not so! She wears navy blue because it's the perfect setting for her pearly shoulders."

Bancroft took Molly's hand and raised it to his lips. "You, Molly Gray, are the most beautiful woman I have ever seen. You must be from New England."

Molly blushed prettily. "And you, sir, are ..."

"William's friend, Lieutenant Jeremiah Bancroft, Phenehas Company of the New England Militia, soon to be a Massachusetts civilian again."

"Oh! William has written so much about you. You saved his life!" Molly put her arms around the tall officer and would have kissed him if she could have reached his face. "I know about your wife and daughter. I know that ..."

"Enough! Enough, dear lady." It was Bancroft's turn to be embarrassed. "Don't tell these jaded personages any more. They'll take advantage of me."

The men laughed, protesting they would never take advantage of a fellow officer.

A soft bell sounded, and the guests slowly made their way into the dining room. Just inside the door was a large diagram showing the seating arrangements for the meal.

Gray squeezed Molly's arm. "My God! Look over there! That's Penelope Hay!"

"Yes, my dear." Molly bowed slightly to Penelope and her

escort, a regular army major. "She's Major Baxter's wife now."

"How could she?" Gray stared, his mouth open.

"Smile and acknowledge her, William."

Gray did as he was told. The major gave a friendly smile and bow to the Grays before he and his wife entered the dining room.

"But, Molly! How could she? William Hay died just a few ..."

"What else could she do? She has no family here. If she doesn't have a protector, she'll end up on Water Street."

Gray had more to say about Penelope, but it was his turn to read the seating plan. He smiled. "I see your friend is up to her old tricks."

"What has Amy done?"

"You're seated between Simons and Bancroft."

"Where will you be, my love?"

"I'm seated as a host officer between Parson Phillips and Colonel Winslow."

"Charming." Molly waved at her dinner partners. "I will carefully remember everything they say," she said with a mock seriousness, "so we can discuss it at length before we go to sleep tonight."

Gray groaned in mock despair.

*9 February 1756*
*Halifax, Nova Scotia*

"Where will you be today, William?" Molly called from the bedroom.

"Captain Rous has asked me to meet him at Government Wharf. I don't know what he wants me for, but I expect I will return by eventide."

"Will you see Jeremiah again before he leaves?"

"No. He boarded his ship. The sloop of war *H.M.S. Vulture* was assigned the convoy duty. I saw her topping up her water casks yesterday. They'll be gone on the flood tide."

"That's too bad. He's such a good friend."

"We'll see him again, darling." Gray adjusted his uniform

and made sure his sword belt was set properly. He picked his hat off the clothes peg. "I must run along, Molly. If you don't come to the door, you'll miss your kiss." Gray rattled the doorknob and shuffled his feet at the same time.

With a squeal, Molly ran out of the bedroom in her nightdress, her hair rumpled by sleep. She threw herself into her husband's arms. "You silly man! You think I fall for your rattling-doorknob trick every time!"

"You do." He gave her a hug.

"Ouch!" Molly pushed against his chest. "You have so many buttons and they're so hard!"

Gray gave her a kiss at the end of which he found himself a little breathless. He held her close. "I love you, Molly. If it wasn't for that old sea dog wanting to see me this morning ..."

"Then hurry back to me this evening." Molly gave him another kiss.

"Yes, I will." Gray let go and backed away, his hand on the doorknob.

Molly grabbed one of his tunic buttons. "Wait a minute. What did you mean when you said we'll see Jerry again?"

"We really don't have time to talk about it right now." Gray tried to pry her hand from the button, but she wouldn't let go. "Oh, all right. Through his regiment, Jeremiah has spoken for some land at Fundy."

"And?"

"Colonel Winslow had promised the governor that New England officers and men would take up grants in the Fundy. So Winslow put a lot of pressure on his men to take up the offer. Winslow wouldn't let up on the matter with Jerry until he promised to speak of it with his wife."

"Where is the land?"

"Jeremiah said the land grant stretches from King's Road to the waters of the basin at Annapolis Royal. Now, really Molly, I have to meet with Captain Rous."

Molly didn't let go. "Why didn't you tell me about this last night?"

"You fed me and then bedded me," Gray leered, "and afterwards I ..."

"… Fell asleep. You're forgiven for now. You'll have to really be attentive tonight to make up for it."

Gray tried to kiss Molly again, but she pushed him away. "Run along to your precious Captain Rous."

\* \* \*

Wimper stood slightly behind the two naval officers as they watched *Vulture* lead the New England convoy down the harbour. Tucked under his arm were sheaves of papers and maps; Wimper had brought with him everything he thought the old captain might want to use in his chat with the lieutenant. He had made arrangements for them with one of the vendors, Carmichael, who had a stall on the pier. Carmichael had reserved a table at the back of his stall. "Nice and quiet," he had said, "so your gentlemen won't be disturbed."

Despite the cold, they were still talking. Rous pointed now and again at various points at the south end of the harbour. Wimper regarded the younger man fondly. Gray was good for the captain, he thought. He's bright and willing to carry out the captain's wishes. Shame the boy is already married. He would have made a fine son-in-law. There's something wrong with that Richard Bulkeley. Supposed to be a fine family and all that, but the Bulkeley family crest carries a bull's head. What kind of family would want any part of a bull on its crest? The Grays obviously aren't a prominent family, but William must have had some connections to obtain his post with Governor Cornwallis. I wonder where the Grays hail from? Scots, yes, but from where?

The captain shifted his feet; he was ready to move on. Wimper stepped forward and said, "Captain, I made arrangements with Mr. Carmichael for a quiet little nook in his establishment. That way you'll be out of the cold while you continue your chat."

"Thank you, Wimper. Show us the way."

Carmichael saw them coming and ushered the officers to a table, and then showed Wimper a vacant chair at a table where a number of customers were already seated.

"You are indeed an understanding man, Mr. Carmichael," Wimper said as he gratefully sat down with his feet pointed at the fire. "A truly understanding man," he repeated when Carmichael placed a glass of ale on the table in front of him.

"Your captain said you could have several if you like. There will be no further duty this day, he said."

"That's very fine, Mr. Carmichael, but one is always enough." Wimper smiled up at the man. "Although you can put a second ale on the captain's tab in appreciation of your service."

"Thank you. I hope your officers have a pleasant chat."

"They will, Mr. Carmichael."

* * *

Captain Rous chaffed his hands to get a bit of warmth into them. "Look at Wimper. He's like a cat, always lands right side up, feet up to the fire. Look! The barmaid just took him some pork crackles."

"We could sit over there, Captain."

"No. Got some things to discuss. Then we can get pork crackles. You think I should choose land around Halifax and not down the shore?"

"Aye, Captain. If you're getting a land grant, you should speak for one at Halifax. I like the site at the end of Eastern Passage with the wooded island just offshore."

Captain Rous spread a chart on the table, and ran his finger along the coastline. "The approaches are good."

"Yes. Even on the island, boats can easily approach. Build an ell right here." Gray pointed at the chart. "Or here, and you could shelter a dozen boats. Fishermen will pay for landing rights. Oh, yes! I think you should take the grant with the island."

Rous folded the chart. "The other thing I mean to talk about ..."

"Your pardon, sir. There's one more thing about the island. There are Indians at Eastern Passage." Gray dragged the chart out again. "They have cleared the forest on a point of land just opposite Cornwallis Island. They're not friendly."

"How much not friendly?"

"They probably did some scalping during the Dartmouth

massacre. Now, a man can't tell one from another, but the local Indians helped the Acadians kill off all those settlers. You can bet on it."

"What you're saying is?"

"If you choose land at Eastern Passage, you'll have to get rid of the Indians sooner or later."

"I'll speak to Richard about it. He's the government and can make it happen."

"Don't tell anyone about your choice until …"

"I have to tell Richard! He's going to be my son-in-law."

Gray held his tongue. After a moment he asked, "You have something else, sir, you wanted to discuss?"

"Lord Loudon will be conducting next year's campaign against the French. The fleet will arrive earlier in the season than ever before."

"That's good news! Where will the campaign be? Louisbourg and Quebec? Up the Hudson Valley?"

"Wait a minute, young feller. I know the fleet's coming, but I have no idea what Loudon's plans will be or what the king's orders will contain."

Gray thought about what he had just heard. How did an old Royal Navy captain acquire information like that? "How do you know Lord Loudon will be assigned? It hasn't been announced, has it?"

"I have my information from an impeccable source—Joshua Mauger."

Gray shook his head in disbelief. "When I was on Governor Cornwallis's staff, we tried to shut that smuggler down. He's a crook!"

"Cornwallis should have known better than to interfere with the business of Joshua Mauger with all his contacts in England. When Cornwallis took on Mauger, he took on some very important people at court. No, that was a big mistake."

Gray remembered how enthusiastic Governor Cornwallis had been when he had first arrived at Chebucto, building a bulwark of the empire on the east coast of North America. But he was worn down and eventually worn out by the fiddling details of unexplained overruns in the costs of governing, unexpected resistance from the Inhabitants and the Indians, and undercutting in England by friends of a murderous, thieving smuggler. Somewhat dazed, Gray asked, "Your information comes from Joshua Mauger?"[4]

"Yes." Rous leaned forward so that only Gray could hear him. "Mauger wrote to his Boston supplier that Lord Loudon had told him there would soon be a large fleet of ships of war at Halifax. He's been buying up all the molasses he can. His distillery has been running overtime."

"Rum and beer for the fleet!"

"Of course."

"How did you find out?"

"I was once a privateer. The Boston supplier was once a privateer with me, too." Rous grinned and squeezed Gray's arm. "My friend would like to have a better cut of the profits than the eighth Mauger is giving."

"Mauger's greedy?"

"There's plenty of money for all of us."

Gray looked dubious.

"There's nothing illegal," Rous said. "We buy molasses, we ship molasses, and we sell molasses. We never get involved with rum."

"What do you want me to do, Captain?"

"I need you to go to Boston and make the arrangements. You'll have to leave at the end of the week. You'll be back in six weeks or a month."

"What about my naval duties?"

"You'll be detached on my authority. The navy won't pay you, but you'll still hold your commission. When you return, I'll expect you to resume your duties unless, of course, we've made too much money in molasses." Captain Rous stuck out his hand.

Gray took the outstretched hand and sealed the agreement.

*28 March 1756*
*Halifax, Nova Scotia*

Molly Gray watched the look of surprise steal over her husband's face when he realized that she was on the pier waiting for him. William Gray raced down the gangway and picked up his wife, twirling her around and around as his lips sought hers.

Molly had been aware of the stares from the hangers-on around the waterfront while she had waited for the ship to be warped, so as soon as she could, she pushed her husband away and rearranged her dress and jacket. "La, sir! You must not take liberties with such an innocent young girl, at least not in broad daylight."

Gray knew she was teasing but he also realized that Halifax was no longer a frontier town. Upright citizens had a role to play in setting the proper social tone for the city. Halifax was, after all, a garrison, and army wives were perhaps the most prudish women in Christendom.

He gave her a mock bow. "How did you know I would be on this ship?"

"I watched the harbourmaster signals. When it showed 'traffic up-harbour,' I came down to the pier. I've met every ship during the last ten days. This was the first from Boston. I truly prayed you were on it."

A sailor brought Gray his bag and a trunk. Gray handed him a coin, thanked him for his help, and asked him to fetch a cab-for-hire.

"I'll have to wait until a cab comes," the sailor said. "There should be one shortly."

Molly slipped her hand in her husband's. "Did you see Jeremiah in Boston?"

"No, his ship hadn't arrived. All the other ships of the convoy came in, but Jerry's was unaccounted for. I'm worried about him."

"Did you see his wife?"

"No, he told me before he left that she was in Harwich, and I didn't have time to go there. I finished my business and came home on the first ship. Have you seen Captain Rous?"

"I've seen Amy at least once a week. She says her father is fine."

The sailor came back. "There's a cab for you at the end of the pier, sir." He hoisted the trunk to his shoulder with ease and carried it to the luggage rack of the cab. Gray tossed him another coin, then put his arm around Molly and hugged her tight. "We have some serious business to get into."

She could tell when her husband was being funny. "And what kind of business is that, kind sir?"

"I can't understand why we don't have any family, my sweet. It's time we started. We aren't getting any younger, you know."

"Yes, my love."

### 2 April 1756
### Halifax, Nova Scotia

"I'm to captain *H.M.S. Success* for Lord Loudon's expedition. I want you with me, William." Captain Rous and William Gray were seated in Carmichael's nook enjoying a beer. This time, Wimper was seated at the table with them, and he had chosen dark ale.

What should I say, Gray wondered. The fleet wasn't staying at Halifax. Lord Loudon was going to campaign near Fort William Henry. "What do we do with all that molasses, Captain?"

"Joshua Mauger will buy it from us."

"All of it?"

"Yes. If we promise not to try to compete with him again."

"At a profit?"

"At a profit."

"I'll make enough to pay you your ten pounds?"

"And then some."

Gray chewed on his lip. He looked to Wimper for some sort of comment, but the man was busy with his ale. "I need to stay home for a while. Molly and I want to start a family. I want sons. Everyone else just rubs up against each other and there are kids!"

Wimper, without looking up, commented, "Perhaps you're trying too hard. Just enjoy yourselves. The children will come naturally."

Blushing to the roots of his hair, Gray retorted, "I don't see you with any children, Wimper!"

"I am his only child, William," Rous interjected, "and, as I get older, I become more childlike. He has enough of kids with just me to look after." He didn't wait for a response but waved his hand as if to make the subject go away. "If you're not coming with us, there are things you'll have to do while I'm away."

"Of course, sir."

"Don't say yes until I tell you what it is I want you to do and how much you'll get paid for it."

"Aye."

"The Indians at Eastern Passage became very defiant, and the government was compelled to expel them. While you were away, they were deported to Cornwallis Island, where the government believed they would cease to be a threat."

"That's good news! Has your grant been approved and announced yet?"

"Not yet. I have absolutely no doubt that it will have royal assent and be announced shortly. That's not the problem. The Indians are still the problem."

Wimper set down his ale. "The Indians are building a fleet of birch-bark canoes. They mean to have revenge."

"And it's too late for me to change my land grant." To Gray, Rous sounded very much like a spoiled child as he said, "That land, my island, will be of no use to me until the Indians are deported or wiped out!"

Gray glanced at Wimper, but the other man was carefully examining the bottom of his mug and had apparently failed to notice the captain's petulance.

The captain continued, "Richard says the government doesn't see the Indians as much of a threat to the citizens of Halifax. The most the government will do is build some earthworks at Cogel's Point and put a few soldiers in there."

"That's not much," Gray agreed, "but it is something."

"It won't get rid of the problem. My island won't be worth anything until the Indians are dealt with!" Rous spoke in a commanding voice. "So I made some plans of my own."

Wimper touched Gray's arm to get his attention. "That's where you come in, sir. The captain has purchased two cannon."

"On naval carriages." Rous added.

"From Joshua Mauger," Wimper continued. "The government has given permission for such cannon to be mounted in the Eastern Passage fort. A naval officer will be assigned to train the soldiers to handle the cannon."

Gray slapped his knee with his hand. "It sounds to me like I'll be training soldiers!"

"And here's the best part, William." Rous delayed speaking to add to the suspense. "When you're finished teaching the redcoats to handle their new cannon, you'll be assigned to the navy planning staff. The Royal Navy will be building a dockyard at Halifax."[5]

"Oh, I know just where they'll put it. Governor Cornwallis planned it years ago. Based on soundings we made all along that shore ..."

Rous held his hand up to stop Gray. "It will all have to be checked again." Rous smiled at Wimper. "This boy is too honest for his own good." He squeezed Gray's arm again. "You're a good naval officer, William, but, I must tell you, Halifax isn't just the navy. It's politics. Dirty politics, reaching all the way back to people in England who don't even know or care that we exist."

Gray didn't respond.

"These are different times, William. You want to make a place here for your sons?"

Gray remained quiet, and the three men sipped their drinks.

"All right. I'll teach the redcoats how to shoot the cannon," Gray said. "And I can help plan the location of a Royal Navy dockyard."

"That's my boy."

* * *

"Molly! Molly! I have great news!"

Molly Gray came to the front of the house with a letter in her hand. "I have good news, too!"

Gray continued as if he hadn't heard her. "I'm to remain here for this campaign season. I have to teach some soldiers how to handle naval cannons, and then I'll stay right here in Halifax on the naval planning staff!"

"That's truly wonderful, sweetheart!"

In the midst of their hug and kiss, Molly dropped a letter. Gray picked it up.

"Is this a letter from Jeremiah? Is he all right?"

"He's fine. They were almost wrecked. Read the letter."

Dear William.

After leaving you at the pier, we remained on Halifax Harbour for two days. On February 9, 1756, being favoured with a wind, our battalion being on board the transports, we sailed from Halifax under convoy of the man o' war sloop Vulture. We put into Mallagash for fear of a storm where we lay till the fourteenth. The whole fleet intended to stop at Port la Tour, but we becalmed and anchored in La Have, but came to sail before morning.

Leaving the fleet, we had good wind on the seventeenth. We were in hope of arriving at Boston on the eighteenth, but a storm arose and we were cast on Nantucket Shoals. We all expected to be lost not knowing where we was, and at daybreak we found to our sorrow that we had lost our way. We were forced to go forward and it was very foggy, but before night we got to Nantucket to our great joy.

We lay wind bound till the twenty-fifth, and then we set sail having got a good pilot, but we were obliged to put into Cape Cod where we were again wind bound till the end of the month. Then, being favoured with a good wind, we arrived at Boston, our desired port, having lost four men on our passage. Full of sorrow I am that I must tell you that Nathan Simons was lost to us at sea.[6]

I made my way home where it is I am writing this letter at my first opportunity. I found my family well, thanks in good part to you, my good friend.

I remain your humble and obedient servant,

Jeremiah Bancroft

Gray read the letter a second time before commenting, "Poor Nathan. He was always intent upon doing the right thing. He was the officer on your left at Bulkeley's soirée."

"Yes, I remember. He was the sweet man who was going to be a teacher."

They remained silent and thought of Nathan Simons—she remembering the man she had conversed with at the dinner, he remembering the man who had conversed with the Acadian girl at the creek.

"Well, at least Jeremiah isn't going to soldier any more. As soon as he packs up his family, he'll be on a ship coming back here. I'll arrange for him to have good passage to Annapolis Royal...."

"He didn't say in his letter that he was coming to Nova Scotia."

"No, he didn't. But he told me he was coming."

"Things change. He didn't mention it at all."

"We'll see." Annoyed at Molly, Gray turned away and sat down in a chair. He put the letter down. "As soon as I finish at Eastern Passage, I'll write him and I'll ask him."

*22 April 1756*
*Eastern Passage, Nova Scotia*

There had been little difficulty using the dockside crane to lift the cannons from the pier onto the lighter. After that, William Gray had nothing but trouble. The soldiers had no idea how to tie down the cannons to keep them from shifting as the lighter was moved to the cove just off Cogel's Point. Gray wished he had a few sailors instead of a dozen soldiers, but eventually the cannon were tied down well enough for the barge to make the journey across the harbour.[7]

Moving the cannons from the lighter to the shore was a frightening experience. Gray had given no thought to the displacement of the lighter as the weight of a single cannon was transferred to the makeshift crane on shore. The tie-downs for the remaining cannon failed, the cannon slid to the opposite bulkhead, and the lighter, despite its ample width, began to capsize.

Gray frantically ordered the release of the cannon being lifted to stabilize the lighter before seawater could spill over the bulwark. Before that was accomplished, one side of the lighter rose enough to pick up the lifted cannon's weight and the problem was momentarily solved. He ordered the soldiers to stop trying to drop the cannon.

"Belay that order!" Gray's shout had no effect on the soldiers' actions. They were still intent on releasing the lifted cannon to the deck of the lighter. "Belay, I said!"

The corporal had found the rope for the pawl on the large gear of the crane. With one pull, the pawl would jump out of the restraining gear and send the cannon crashing onto the lighter, undoubtedly putting a hole in her, and sending the lighter, cannon, and Gray's reputation as a competent naval officer to the bottom of the cove.

"Belay! Belay!" The corporal continued to pull on the rope. "For Christ's sake, stop!" Gray finally shouted.

The corporal looked up. "Yessir."

Gray took his hat off and wiped the sweat from his forehead and hatband. He put his hat back on and ordered the soldiers to stand down from unloading.

"You want us to stop unloading, sir?"

"Aye. Yes, I do. Take a few minutes while I think about this."

"May we smoke, sir?"

"Yes."

The soldiers enjoyed a quiet smoke while the naval officer pondered what to do next. Since there were no other naval personnel around, Gray decided the most direct route would be the best, despite how unprofessional it looked. He ordered the little crane dismantled and two winches set up. Then the cannon was pulled over the bow—or stern, Gray really didn't know which on the double-ended craft—onto the beach. The cannons were then winched from the beach to the fort, and the cannon carriages were carried with slings made of ropes. The crane was reassembled at the fort and the cannons were lifted onto their carriages. Munitions were carried on the backs of the soldiers and stacked temporarily, until a magazine could be built for ammunition storage.

When it was all done, Gray breathed a sigh of relief. There was no evidence that they had manhandled the cannons into place in a most unseaman-like manner. Let any naval officers come now, he thought, and they'd never know how we did it. He was very smug about his accomplishment until he saw the furrows that dragging the cannons had made in the side of the hill. There was just enough time before sunset, he decided, for the men to fill in the furrows. Or, he reconsidered, they could use the remaining daylight to prepare the weapons for use—sight in the cannons and lay out the swabs, fuses, and plungers.

"Have the men gather round, Corporal. We'll have our first lesson tonight."

"Yes, sir!"

\* \* \*

Someone was tapping the tag on the flap of his tent. It wasn't even light yet. William Gray thought the army had some really bad habits. If waking a man before dawn was one of them, he wasn't impressed. He responded with restraint. "Yes! What do you want?"

"Sir, Corporal Evans here. There's some noise at the end of the cove. The sentry woke me. We might need your cannon."

When Gray didn't answer right away, the corporal spoke louder. "Did you hear me sir?"

"Yes, I did. Wait a moment. I'll get dressed."

"Sir, I do believe there are Injuns, and I wish you'd come, sir."

"I'll be but a moment, Corporal."

When Gray left his tent, the first signs of dawn were touching the sky. Corporal Evans and his men were in their shirts and trousers, but they had neither hats nor weapons.

"Corporal," Gray ordered, "get your men into uniform, and take me to where you heard the noises."

They walked to the edge of the earthworks where, if it were daylight, they could look out over the whole cove. The first thing Gray noted was there were no bird sounds. Birds were usually very active just before the dawn. He heard the unmistakable sounds of wavelets hitting the side of a vessel—many vessels. Suddenly a flock of ducks, disturbed at the entrance to the cove, spluttered and squawked as they rose into the morning air. Those Indian canoes Captain Rous was talking about were coming right into the cove.

It was getting considerably lighter. The soldiers appeared, dressed and armed.

"Grapeshot," Gray cried. "Get me bags of grape! We'll load with grape."

Indian war cries echoed across the cove; they had decided to attack!

Gray pointed to the second cannon. "Corporal Evans, do exactly as I do. We're going to load these cannon. Remove the covers and plugs." Gray grabbed the sleeve of one of the nearest soldiers. "You, help me!"

"Yessir." He put down his musket and pulled the cover off the cannon that Gray was serving. Gray continued with the routine while giving orders to the remaining soldiers. "You two, guard our rear. If you hear musket fire from the fore and you see no sign of the enemy at the rear, come help us repel the bastards. Do you understand?"

"Yessir." The two soldiers ran off to do picket duty at the rear of the fort where there were no earthworks.

"Take the powder charge, push it in as far as you can with your arm. Then take the plunger like this, Corporal. No! Like this!"

The war cries were much closer. Gray glanced over the earthworks. Maybe a dozen canoes were filled with warriors all paddling like hell! For a fleeting moment he thought of Bancroft coming to his rescue the last time he was in real trouble.

"The rest of you! Assume a firing position along the earthworks. Space yourselves out as best you can. Do not shoot until I order it."

The redcoats moved quickly. Some of them affixed their bayonets. Gray thought that was a good idea. "Fix bayonets!" Over the noise of the approaching Indians, he heard clicks from the pickets at the rear of the fort as they affixed their bayonets.

"Wedges! I need wedges! Lever that gun! No, the other way!" Gray sighted over the barrel of the first gun. It would have to do. He ran to the second gun. He was sighting that weapon when he remembered he had no lit fuses! Shit! "Flints," he hollered. It would soon be too late. The Indians were almost too close!

Corporal Evans came running with two lit fuses. "I seen it done before. Got 'em ready!"

"Good man! Cut the end of another fuse short! Light it, now! Now!"

Bam! Kablam! The two cannons fired almost simultaneously, spewing shrapnel in a wide arc over the cove.

Gray waited for the smoke to clear. He didn't think to reload. Either the grapeshot had done its work or ... he felt for his sword. He hadn't put it on! There were no spare muskets. He felt helpless and vulnerable.

The clearing smoke revealed the cove littered with bodies and wreckage. What Indians were able, were paddling out of the cove. Several in the water were feebly moving, but as he watched they slid under the water. It was over.

Gray was exhilarated and felt like dancing. They had won. "Well done, lads! Boys, that was your first lesson. Later on this afternoon we will have another one, but hopefully without such lively targets!"

The redcoats cheered.

### 2 May 1756
### Halifax, Nova Scotia

Gray was working with some new, updated maps and charts of Halifax and its approaches. He noted that the little fort at Cogel's Point had been entered as a visual landmark for seafarers. The clearing on the point of land where the Indians used to live before being deported to Cornwallis Island was marked too. The cartographers hadn't missed a thing. The charts were getting better, and that was good news for one William Gray, Esquire, who was going to be a harbour pilot. Yes, sir! The better the charts were, the easier it made the pilots' job.

Gray had been working at the naval staff office re-recording soundings of the harbour for the latest charts. His work would establish the location for His Majesty's Dockyard Halifax.

Sounds impressive, he thought, Dockyard Halifax. It would bring a lot of employment for civilians if the Halifax dockyard were run like all of the other Royal Navy yards. And for men like Joshua Mauger, who would make more money than anyone else would.

Closing the chart file he remembered something. He thought he had seen a new name for the little island Captain Rous was interested in. He reopened the file and ran his finger along the coast to Wood Island. He pictured the little spot in his mind. The island was covered with trees and had been aptly named. He liked the practical way the English named places. If they weren't named after the sovereign or members of the royal family, they were named after the minister or general involved with the expedition or operation: Ives Point because the first King's Harbourmaster was a well-respected man; Black Rock because the damn rock was black. Bulkeley's Point? He looked more closely. Bulkeley's Point, where the Indians had cleared the land, and the point from which they had been deported because they were interfering with Captain Rous's land grant. Why would Richard Bulkeley put his name on a piece of land that was going to belong to another man? Aloud, he said, "Make no mistake, William Gray. That name appears there because Richard wants it there."

"Did you say something, Lieutenant?"

Gray was startled. He thought he had been alone. Lieutenant Commander Brown had come into the chart room.

"Not really, sir."

"Have you heard? The Indians killed five men early this morning. Scalped 'em."

Gray knew it couldn't have been very far away or they wouldn't have heard about it this quickly. "Where, sir?"

"The fort at Eastern Passage. The Micmac crept 'round the rear where there were no cannons. They sneaked in before dawn, took out the sentry, and murdered four others in their tents before the alarm was sounded. The garrison fought them off. There couldn't have been very many attackers since the remainder of the garrison ..."

"Five redcoats."

The commander regarded Gray thoughtfully before continuing. "… easily fought them off."

Gray remembered the keen faces of the men he had taught to serve the cannon. How proud they had been when they had driven off the Indians the first time. The Indians weren't stupid. The second time, they came from behind.

The commander had been speaking to him.

"I'm sorry, sir. What did you say?"

"Can't imagine why they'd want to attack the fort."

"I can, sir. Revenge. Not too long ago we killed a dozen or so Micmac with grape."

"They must have asked for it."

"They had been forced from their homes and deported to Cornwallis Island."

"Doesn't mean they can go around killing people. Anyhow, now they'll have to clear out of the area entirely. The Rangers will hunt 'em down until they get them all."

"I guess that's the end of the Micmac at Eastern Passage."

Rising from his desk, Gray excused himself. He went down the hall looking neither left nor right into the little rooms where members of the naval staff were working. He was upset. It was partly my fault, he thought. Another part of him argued that he had merely been sent to the fort to teach the soldiers to handle the guns. He couldn't teach them anything about soldiering. Why was he so concerned?

He stepped out into Nova Scotia's beautiful May sunshine, and paused to let his eyes adjust after the dark hall. Questions plagued him. Why were the soldiers sent on detachment without an officer? He felt the hairs rise on the back of his neck. The soldiers were supposed to be sent there without cannon! It must have been Rous who bought the cannons and arranged for a naval officer to train them. Rous must have known the soldiers were to be used as bait! At least Rous gave them a fighting chance. Richard Bulkeley, on the other hand, had meant the redcoats to be murdered to give the Rangers an excuse to hunt down and exterminate the Indians. Bulkeley knew the land at Eastern Passage would be more valuable with the Indians gone.

Jamming his hat on his head, Gray made his way home slowly. The city bustled around him. Halifax had grown so much since the day he had first come ashore. He should be proud at what had been accomplished. But it had been accomplished at the expense of so many lives.

His dark thoughts were interrupted by a cheerful voice. "Good afternoon, Lieutenant Gray. How's the missus?"

"Fine, thank you, George." George was the stable boy where Gray occasionally rented a cab. George's brother, David, had disappeared one night when there were a large number of Royal Navy ships in port. Most likely the boy was taken up by a press gang, even though the governing council had ordered there should be no press gangs in Halifax. But a ship's captain, short-handed and due to sail, would do what he must. If they ever heard from David again, it would be a miracle.

Tonight I must write Jeremiah and find out what he's doing, Gray thought. I think I'll tell him I'm through with this town. Molly and I will go to Sambro. We'll get away from Halifax with its dirty politics and money grubbing.

\* \* \*

Home at last! Gray pushed open the door. Molly was standing in the front room trying to catch her reflection in the window glass. Putting his arms around his wife Gray whispered in her ear, "I came home early today."

"I'm so glad you did, darling!" Molly's voice bubbled with happiness. "I'm with child!" She spun around in his arms, then placed his hands on her flat belly. "Right here! I want to introduce you, William, to the next generation of Grays!"

"Are you sure?"

"All the signs are positive." She spun again in the circle of his arms and planted a big kiss on his lips. "What do you want to call him? I'd like to name him Charles after my father."

"And after his grand-uncle Charles Gray. Little Charlie Gray."

Molly gazed into her husband's eyes. "You came home early today. What did you have in mind, sweetheart?"

"You, Molly." He swept her up and kissed her. "Just to be with you." He carried her into the bedroom, kicked the door closed, and tossed Molly onto the bed.

*27 October 1756*
*Halifax, Nova Scotia*

"Amy Rous was here today, William," Molly Gray said. "She picked the date for the wedding."

Gray was pouring himself rum after a long day at the naval offices. It had been a hot, gruelling summer, a miserable September, a rainy October, and he had no better hopes for November. "That's nice. Who's she marrying?"

"Arghhh! You've been so difficult lately, husband dear! They'll be married at Saint Paul's the first week of May next year. I've forgotten the exact date. We'll get an invitation."

Gray replaced the bottle, carried his drink into the front room, and sat down.

"What," Molly continued, "will we get them for the wedding? Since you and Richard are such friends, it should be something really nice."

Gray grimaced at the taste of the rum. Next time he would buy Barbados rum and not the stuff that Mauger made. "We're not friends," he said. "I've merely known the man for a long time."

"What's the matter with you?" Molly came into the room. She placed her hands on her hips—or where her hips would have been if she weren't so heavily pregnant—and asked, "What's chewing at you, William? You haven't had a good word to say about Richard for months."

After another sip of his drink, Gray decided to tell her. "Sit down, Molly. Let me explain what's bothering me. Captain Rous is getting a land grant."

"Oh, that's good! The successes that man has had for the Crown ..."

"Molly, please. Just listen. Captain Rous had the choice of several land grants, and he picked Wood Island and the land ashore from it. Rous was worried that the Indians would be a threat to fishermen who could lease landing rights on the island. Richard managed to get rid of the Indians. There's been a delay in promulgating the title for Rous, but Richard had arranged to name some of the land after himself. When I mentioned it to Richard, lo and behold, Rous's name immediately appeared on the charts. Wood Island became Rous's Island, but Bulkeley's Point is still there."

"You're just imagining things, William. It sounds like a prospective son-in-law is simply looking out for the interests of his fiancée's father."

"Like I said, I've known Richard a long time. He doesn't do anything without putting his own interests first."

Molly shook her head and made as if to leave.

"Wait, Molly. Consider this. Richard built that big house, then he organized the volunteer fire brigade, and Halifax bought all those leather buckets to carry water from the harbour to fires. He likes to run horses so he organized the horse-racing club. He needed labour to fix the racetrack so he reorganized the militia, gave himself a highfalutin' title and rank, and paraded his soldiers at the racetrack. Our dear Richard has something going for him on this land grant thing. I can smell it."

"I think if he's that powerful, you should forget about it."

"I can't! I owe Captain Rous too much. I'll have to speak to him about it as soon as he comes back, which will be any time now."

"I think you should forget about it."

*7 November 1756*
*Halifax, Nova Scotia*

William Gray held the letter loosely in his hand. If he had been alone, he would probably have cried.

"What's the matter, William? Bad news?"

Gray passed the letter to John Rous. "I thought it was from my friend, Jeremiah Bancroft. You know, the tall New Englander who saved my life on *Yorke*." He sighed. "Well, it isn't."

Rous handed the letter back. "I can't read much any more,

even with spectacles, and I hate to use the magnifying glass. You'll have to read it to me."

Gray read the letter aloud:

> Dear Lieutenant Gray,
>     Enclosed please find a draft for three pounds, the amount you loaned Jeremiah when we were in need. I thank you for your kindness.
>     I had asked my husband what we should do concerning my obligation to you, since I had no resources of my own. He kindly told me to send the draft on behalf of Jeremiah.
>     My first husband, Jeremiah Bancroft, died with the smallpox March 3, 1756, in the thirty-second year of his age. Our daughter, Catherine, died March 11, aged four years eighteen days.[8]
>     You were a good friend to Jeremiah. He spoke of you fondly.
>
> Respectfully,<br>Elisabeth Emerson

"I'm sorry, William."

"He was a good man. A real good friend." Gray signalled Carmichael to bring two more beer. "I thought ..." William swallowed hard and stopped.

"Go ahead, William."

"I thought he would come to Nova Scotia and ..." William snorted and wiped his nose with the back of his hand.

"Come to Nova Scotia," Rous prompted.

"I thought we'd always be the good friends we were. I mean ..."

"I know, son. I've lost my friends." Carmichael placed two beer on the table. Rous pushed one of them toward William. "You just hold 'em close as you can for as long as you can."

They drank their beer in silence. William sighed. "I want to be a friend to you, too, sir."

"You are, son."

"Then I might be free to talk about your land grant."

"Thank you, William, but I found out what's going on."

"Then tell me, sir."

"The man we know as the Honourable Richard Bulkeley procured title to the lands associated with Wood Island and to the island itself. Title passed to the honourable gentleman while I was absent this campaign season. When I returned to Halifax, I found the notice waiting for me that the fishermen who had leases from me for this season would, henceforth, take their leases from Bulkeley."[9]

Gray's jaw had dropped open. The captain smiled and said, "It came as a surprise to me, too."

"But ..."

"The honourable gentleman knows I will do nothing to jeopardize my daughter's marriage. In my last, and I sincerely hope, my very last dealings ever with the honourable gentleman, he said it meant very little whose name appeared on title. At my age, and having only my daughter to inherit my estate, he would have title to the land eventually. This way it cuts down on legal costs and procedures."

"I can't believe he would ..."

"He claims he already has an interest in the grant. He claims to have added considerable worth to the grant by virtue of ridding the area of Indians. Had he not done so, the island would have little use." Rous sat straighter in his chair. "I suppose it's advisable, planning ahead that far, but I hope he's just as quick to lay claim to my grave."

"And be quick to jump in, sir!"

"Aye." Rous brightened at the thought. "You wanted to speak to me. Was it about that?"

"Yes, it was, sir."

"I thank you, William, for your concern. I have no idea what prompts Richard to do what he does, but he's a man of considerable power and he enjoys wielding it."

Gray made up his mind at that moment. "And sir, I wanted to tell you I'll relinquish my commission at the end of next month."

"What will you do? Do you have enough money to establish yourself at Sambro?"

"I think we'll get along, sir. I want to thank you for all of your kindness."

Captain Rous's face turned red. He struggled to maintain an even voice but the petulance of a child being denied a treat could be heard. "If you must go, you must."

Wimper had heard the tone and came to the table right away. He placed his hand on the captain's shoulder, and spoke over the captain's head as if he wasn't there. "Our captain isn't always able to express himself as well as he used to." Picking up on what he had overheard, Wimper said. "He will regret your leaving, Lieutenant. We will both miss your service very much."

*10 May 1757*
*Sambro Harbour, Nova Scotia*

The shallop took a starboard tack to make the entrance to Sambro Harbour.

Molly and William Gray were standing among the boxes of possessions and supplies they were taking to start their new lives. Molly was slim again, and in her arms, wrapped snugly against the nip of the sea air, lay Charles Gray, their first son and the first of a long line of Grays who would live and die on the edge of the Atlantic.

The shallop caught the swell once, twice, throwing salt spray high in the air before she settled on the new tack. She passed the headlands and entered the harbour where the water was much calmer. The captain called out to the couple, "Which arm of the harbour do we take? Do you have a pier, lad?"

"To the head of the harbour, Captain, if you please," Gray replied. "You'll see the seawall dead ahead. The pier is to starboard."

Now that the noise of the sea working the ship and the clamour of the wind passing through the rigging had abated, Molly spoke. "It was a fine wedding, wasn't it? Amy was beautiful." She sneaked a quick glance at Gray's face as she asked, "Is there something wrong with old Captain Rous? He didn't seem well."

"Wimper explained that the old man is having problems. When he's upset, he becomes very irritated. He said if the old man doesn't stay calm, something inside his head might burst."

"It's a wonder they still give him command of a ship."

"Only Wimper knows."

"You know!"

"Yes, that's true, but none of his staff would ever say anything. We're known as Rous's boys. He can trust us to the death."

They were well inside the harbour now.

"Look," Gray said. "There's the little church." A small building with a spire was tucked against the shore at the base of the point that formed the arms of the harbour. "That's Cemetery Point, where as many Grays as God will allow can be laid to rest, Molly."

The captain turned the shallop into the wind to slow her down, giving the Grays a good view of the village known as Sambro. Molly pulled the shawl away from her son's face and held him up. "Look Charles! We're home." She grasped William's hand. "And we're here to stay."

## *Endnotes*

[1] "... I set out for Halifax with a party of 10 men and coming to Pisquit River the tide be in flood we were forst to camp on this side opposet to Forte Edward ye 1 night at a village calld the Five Houses." From Bancroft's diary.

[2] Ye 3 (miles) in the woods north at Forte Sackville after a tedious days march one of our men being froze.

[3] Molly's visit to the midwife is fiction. The source of the procedure is general reading at the Archives.

[4] The details of the molasses venture in the novel are fiction. One of my Gray ancestors is reputed to have tried it so I included it.

[5] Family tales tell of a Gray who helped create HM Dockyard at Halifax. I could find no trace of such participation in the Archives but liked the concept.

[6] Only the reference to Nathan is fiction. With slight modifications to make it more readable, the rest is from Bancroft's diary.

[7] There was an incident near Cogel's Point where five red coats were scalped, related by HW Hewitt in one of his articles. The details are mine.

[8] A memorandum from Elizabeth Bancroft was attached to Bancroft's diary. It told of the death of her first husband and their daughter and her remarriage to James Emerson. NS Archives. The mention of Gray or debts is fiction.

[9] From an article by HW Hewitt.

## Epilogue

Grays live at Sambro to this very day.

Amy Rous, the only child of Captain John Rous, married the Honourable Richard Bulkeley in 1757. At the death of her father, she inherited from his estate three hundred pounds a year. Amy Rous Bulkeley died of consumption on June 7, 1775, in her thirty-seventh year.

Richard Bulkeley, at various times Grand Master of Freemasons for Nova Scotia, Judge of Vice-Admiralty, President of the Society for the Promotion of Agriculture, Brigadier General of Militia, and Provincial Secretary, married again. When he died in 1800 his second wife went home to England leaving the title of Rous's Island, by this time called Devil's Island, in doubt. The Horne and the Henneberry families argued the title before the courts for years.

Thomas Pichon, alias Tyrell, was the chief stores clerk at Fort Beauséjour. It is said avarice and ambition in everything he did drove Pichon. Certainly he acted as a spy for the British, supplying information to the competing British Fort Lawrence, leading eventually to the capture of Fort Beauséjour in 1755. After that he lived in Halifax and London, acquiring a reputation for moral dissipation.

Lieutenant Horatio Gates married at Halifax and was later successful in obtaining a transfer to New York. He was a general during the American Revolution, fighting on the side of the colonials. At the battle of Camden, General Gates faced an army commanded by General Charles Cornwallis, a nephew of Governor Cornwallis. Gates made an error in judgment, causing the Virginia and North Carolina regiments to panic and abandon the field without a fight. For a time, the Maryland Brigade of General William Smallwood held the line, but at a terrible cost. The British won the day. General Gates was last seen that day at Charlotte, some sixty miles away, astride his horse and heading away from the battlefield. Although he denied it, he was widely believed to be guilty of deserting his army in the face of the enemy and disgraced.

MEMBER OF SCABRINI GROUP

Québec, Canada
2006